THE COMPLETE BOOK OF
GOLF
TECHNIQUES · GREAT GOLF COURSES · HISTORY

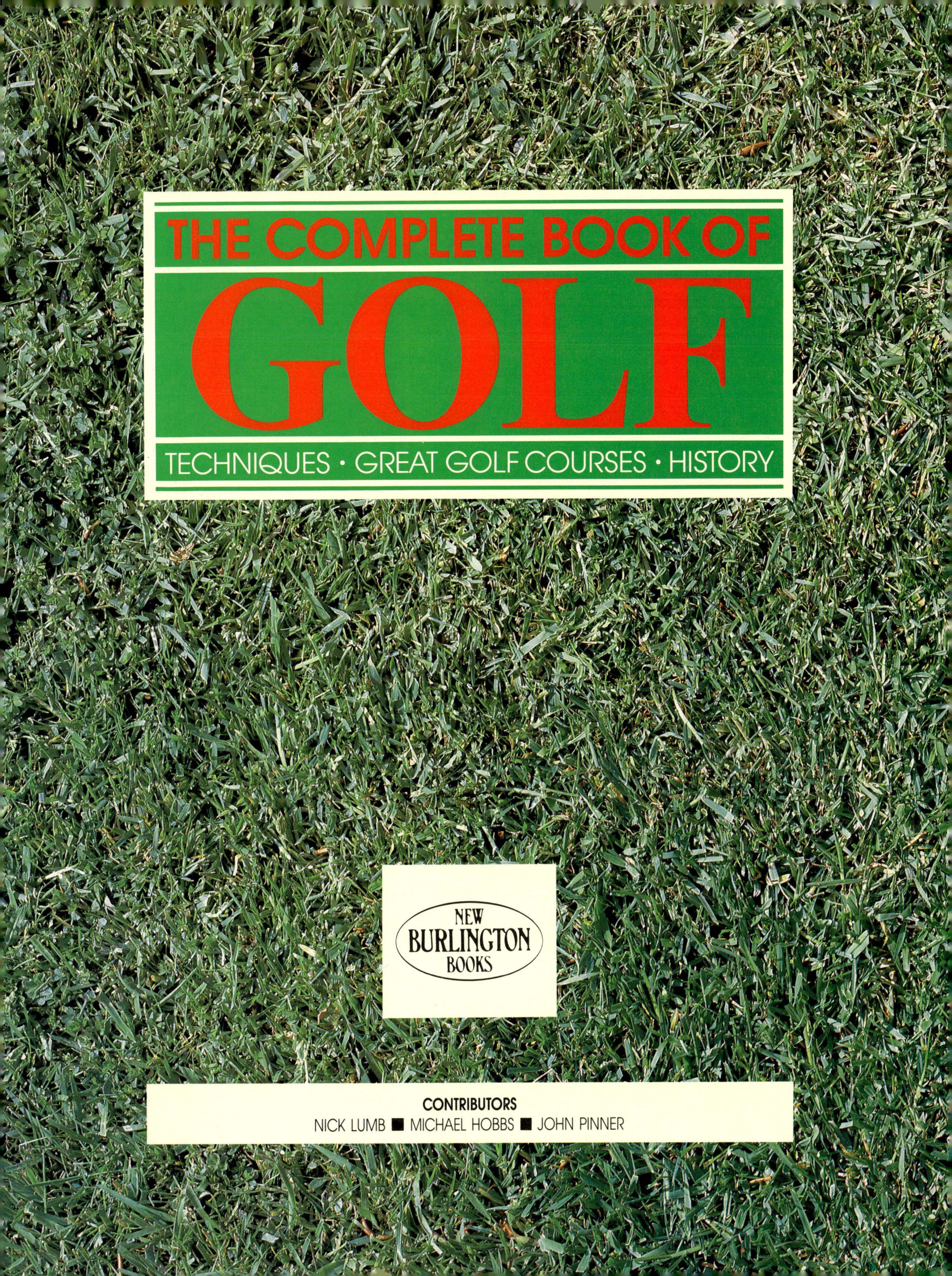

THE COMPLETE BOOK OF GOLF

TECHNIQUES · GREAT GOLF COURSES · HISTORY

NEW BURLINGTON BOOKS

CONTRIBUTORS
NICK LUMB ■ MICHAEL HOBBS ■ JOHN PINNER

A QUINTET BOOK

Published by New Burlington Books
6 Blundell Street
London N7 9BH

ISBN 1 85348 038 X

This book was designed and produced by
Quintet Publishing Limited
6 Blundell Street
London N7 9BH

Art Director: Peter Bridgewater
Designer: Linda Henley
Editors: Peter Arnold, Paul Barnett, Shaun Barrington, Judith Simons

Typeset in Great Britain by
Central Southern Typesetters, Eastbourne
Manufactured in Hong Kong by Regent
Publishing Services Limited
Printed in Hong Kong by South Sea Int'l
Press Ltd.

CONTENTS

INTRODUCTION

Golf is one of the world's fastest growing sports. Television, with its knowledgeable commentators and probing cameras, has brought international championships into the home. The tournament players themselves are marvellous ambassadors for the sport; they behave impeccably and bring excitement to every event. By its very nature, golf is a game which breeds good manners and courtesy.

This is one sport which the whole family can play together. It is a game that you can play on your own, or as a member of a group. Beginners everywhere are queuing up to learn the skills needed to take up the challenge of the golf course. The working week is getting shorter: which means more players. The retirement age is getting lower: which means more players. People are now more than ever aware of the need for exercise: which means more players. Everywhere, people are taking up this fabulous game.

The system of handicapping in golf enables players of varying abilities to compete on level terms: one of golf's particular advantages. Another asset is the great variety of courses across the world, each posing different problems to the golfer; but even if you were to stick to your local course for a lifetime, no two rounds would be identical. The shot permutations needed to master 18 holes are never quite the same twice; and the variety of skills, the ingenuity and judgement employed each time you take up the challenge, can be endlessly honed and improved.

LEFT One of golf's particular attractions is the beauty and tranquility of the courses themselves; but those seemingly innocuous greens and fairways pose a tremendous challenge to your physical coordination, your skill and nerve.

ABOVE It is possible to buy just one secondhand club with which to begin learning the game – a 5-iron is fine – along with a putter. By hiring or borrowing clubs at the outset, you will not find yourself stuck with expensive equipment ill-suited to your game at a later date.

The Equipment

When you are choosing equipment to play golf, the points to bear in mind are the same as for any other pastime: do not buy more than you need to start off with, make sure that what you do buy will have enough use to justify the initial outlay, and above all, ensure that the equipment suits your physique and style of play.

RIGHT A set of irons consists of nine clubs. A half set is either the four even, or the five odd numbers. A wood and a putter make up the half-set.

Golf, and the equipment used to play it, have changed out of all recognition since the birth of the game. The days of playing with little more than wooden sticks have given way to current demands for equipment built to complex technical specifications. The development of equipment has matched the changes in the game and in the courses.

In the early days, when golfers used clubs with hickory shafts, their swings had to suit the characteristics of the shaft. The hickory shaft had torque, or twist, giving a natural turning in the shaft. Yesterday's golfer did not work against this, but turned it to his advantage. His swing plane was flatter, with a lot more hand and arm action. Opening up the club-face on the way back, he then brought it square to the ball and closed it on the way through. This meant the player had to aim to the right to allow for the draw that this swing had fashioned. This gave the shot over-spin, or top-spin, and so the run factor was very important. Neither fairways nor greens were watered, so golf courses suited the type of game where the object was to make the ball run after pitching. The ball used to run and run on the courses of the day.

With the introduction of steel shafts without torque, the golf swing had to change to suit the clubs and the modern square-to-square method came into favour. It eliminated the opening and closing of the club-face

This coincided with the change in golf course practice. Watered greens came first, soon to be followed by watered fairways. Golf balls do not run as far on lush grass, so the swing concept changed, to provide height and flight.

When choosing equipment, you may start to play golf with a single club, a half-set or a full set, with new or used clubs. Many beginners buy a single used iron to begin swinging into the game to see if they enjoy it.

If you begin with just one new club, buy it from a source – a professional or sports shop – which can supply matching clubs singly. You can build up your set as your needs gradually grow.

If you decide on a half-set, bear in mind that you may not be able to add matching clubs at a later date. Often manufacturers change models.

The third option is to buy a full set, new or used, straight away. A full set contains a maximum of 14 clubs. It usually consists of nine irons, four woods and a putter. Make sure, when choosing a full set, that the irons all match. Mixed irons do not constitute a set.

THE PUTTER

Many golfers think that a putter has no loft, but it actually has between two and four degrees. When struck with a putter, the ball skids for the first 20 per cent of its journey and then rolls, with over-spin, the remaining 80 per cent.

Putters come in many shapes and sizes. Whatever the design of the putter you must strike the ball consistently out of the 'sweet spot'. Many putters have lines or spots to help with the lining up, and players assume that this must be the sweet spot, but this is not always correct. To find the sweet spot, most professionals hold the putter loosely between the forefinger and thumb, allowing it to hang. Then, using one of those pencils with an eraser on the end, they tap the club-face with the eraser until they find the place which feels the most solid. This place is the sweet spot.

A ball not struck with the sweet spot of the putter will lose distance. That happens to any ball struck with either the toe or heel of the putter. The longer the putt the greater the error will be.

When putting, the putter should be grounded with the sweet spot directly behind the ball.

The lengths of putter shafts vary between 33 and 36 in (84 and 91 cm). The shafts are usually stiff. The weights vary between 15 and 18 oz (425 and 510 g).

Your choice of putter should be influenced by the speed of the greens at the course where you intend to play most of your golf. If they are fast, choose a lightweight putter: the slower the surface, the heavier the putter should be.

THE SWEET SPOT

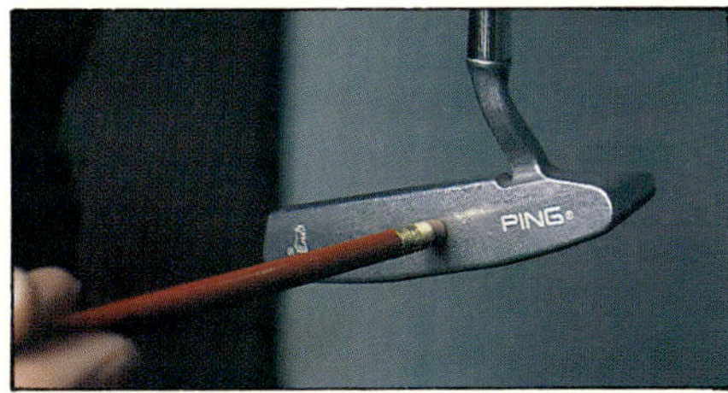

To find the sweet spot of a putter, hold the putter loosely between the forefinger and thumb, allowing it to hang vertically. Using a pencil with an eraser on the end, tap the club-face with the eraser until you find the place which feels most solid. This is the sweet spot.

BELOW LEFT When you buy a full set, make sure that all the irons are by the same manufacturer and of the same model.

RIGHT The loft on the clubs decreases as their numbers decrease.

IRONS

There are two different ways of manufacturing iron heads for golf clubs: casting and forging.

The method for cast heads allows mass production of even complicated designs and ensures consistency of weight in each clubhead. It also means that the lofts of each set will be perfectly matched. The materials used are of hard steel, and the production methods therefore make it difficult to manufacture heads to suit players who are not of standard height and build.

Forged heads are made from softer metals. Their softness means that they can be custom-ground and shaped to suit individuals. For this reason, most touring professionals choose to play with this type of club.

CLUBHEAD

The long irons used for distance have the smallest numbers of the clubs in the set. The chipping, pitching and sand irons have the highest numbers. All share built-in design factors allowing the golfer to meet his individual needs. Golf clubheads come in different shapes to do different things. You must decide what you want your golf club to do. The centre of gravity and the lie of the clubhead are the important features to examine when choosing clubs to suit your physique.

The centre of gravity relates to the distribution of the weight in the clubhead. If you have trouble getting the ball into the air, you must select a club with the weight at the bottom of the clubhead. When striking the ball, the centre of gravity will be below the centre of the ball, helping to lift it in the air, and resulting in a soaring flight.

On the other hand, many golfers feel that they

DEFINITION OF LIE ANGLE

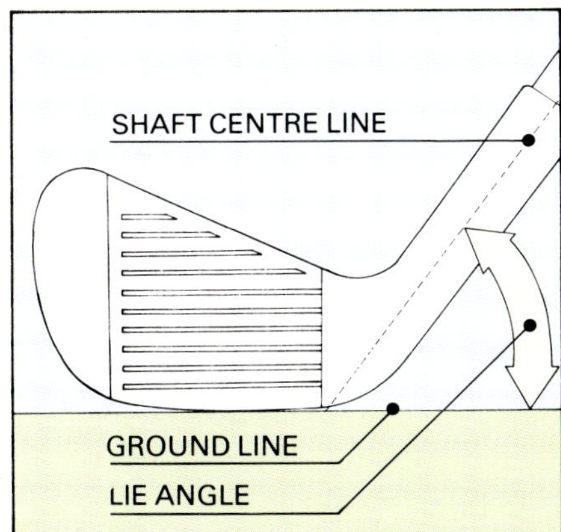

The lie angle of the clubhead is extremely important and is dependent upon the angle of swing.

hit the ball too high, and they must therefore select a club design where the weight has been positioned higher in the clubhead. When striking the ball, the centre of gravity will be above the centre of the ball. This will help to keep the ball lower in flight. If the centre of gravity lies in the middle of the blade – behind the ball – then mid-flight will be achieved.

The lie of the clubhead is the angle formed by a line through the centre of the shaft and the ground, when the clubhead is placed flat in the address position.

An upright lie is favoured by taller golfers because their hands are farther from the ground. The flatter lies put you slightly farther from the ball in the address position and are therefore more suited to the shorter golfer. If you take a club with too upright a lie for you, the heel of the clubhead will be on the ground but the toe raised off it a little. When swinging into the ball with too upright a lie, the heel will hit the ground

The rules of golf are codified and approved by the Royal and Ancient Golf Club of St Andrews and the United States Golf Association. The rules were last overhauled (and simplified) in 1984. You should find little difficulty in learning the basics very quickly, and should carry the rule-book out on the course for reference.

If you consider for a moment the *potential* complexity of rule-making for the game of golf – what may be fair, for example, when you are faced with an impossible lie, or what happens if your ball goes out of bounds – then you will realise that the rule-book is really a surprisingly short and succinct document.

CLUB DESIGN AND NUMBERS (RULE 4)

All clubs you are likely to come across will of course comply with the rules; any manufacturer who is unsure about the legality of a new design must submit a prototype to St Andrews for a ruling. The ruling on the *number* of clubs allowed is more important for the beginner; you can play with a maximum of 14 clubs, and cannot replace a damaged club or add to your set, once you start to play, by borrowing from another player who is playing out on the course.

OPPOSITE A set of woods can consist of three or four clubs. Most modern sets have only three: the driver and the three and five woods. The driver has the biggest head and the deepest face. The clubheads become smaller as their loft increases, which gives the five wood clubhead a lower centre of gravity.

IRONS

Iron NUMBER	Strong loft DEGREES	Standard loft DEGREES	Weak loft DEGREES
3	22	24	26
4	26	28	30
5	30	32	34
6	34	36	38
7	38	40	42
8	42	44	46
9	46	48	50
Pitching wedge	50	52	54
Sand wedge	54	56	58

before the ball is sent away and the 'free' toe will come round, closing the club-face and sending the ball, for a right-hander, to the left. If the lie is too flat, the opposite will happen. At the address the toe will be on the ground but the heel will be clear of it. When striking into the shot, the toe will hit the ground, spinning the heel past the toe and opening the club-face, shooting the ball to the right.

Spend some time and seek professional advice over obtaining clubs. They should suit you for length, lie, swing weight and centre of gravity. Between each number in a set of irons, there are four degrees of loft, representing 10–12 yd (9–11 m) of flight.

The weight of each iron club increases throughout the set. In an average set, the lightest is the 3-iron at 15 oz (425 g) and each succeeding iron gets heavier, with the 9-iron weighing 16 oz (454 g). The sand wedge and pitching wedge are designed to be even heavier for their particular roles.

WOODS

There is no end to the selection of drivers and fairway clubs coming onto the golfers' market, with new designs of heads, and variations in weight displacement and shaft tensions. They are all still generally referred to as 'woods', although many clubs now attracting increasing support are metal-headed. These are hollow and the design places the weight around the perimeter of the head. This helps the golfer to achieve consistency in his shots, even when he fails to strike the ball in the middle of the club-face. He also finds help from the lower centre of gravity of the clubhead, as opposed to the wooden clubhead. This sends the ball higher and makes the club easier to use. Many professional golfers are switching to metal. A wider selection of lofts is now available for metal-headed clubs.

The heads of wooden clubs are still either persimmon or laminated maple. Persimmon is thought, quite wrongly, to be the harder of the two. Laminated maple has an advantage over persimmon, in that a matched set of laminated woods – a driver, a 3-wood and a 5-wood – have a greater consistency of weight. Irons should, as was emphasized, be bought in a set, but this is not a must for the woods. It is acceptable to find three unmatched clubs to do the jobs required: a driver to hit off the tee, a fairway wood to play long shots and a more lofted club for the intermediate shots.

A good quality set of headcovers should always be placed on these clubs to protect them from being marked by the heads of the irons when they are taken out of the bag and replaced. When the headcovers get wet, take them off after the round of golf and dry them. Leaving them wet on your clubs will cause gradual but severe deterioration in the clubhead. It can cause rust on metal heads. On persimmon, it can cause the wood to swell and with the laminated clubs the polyurethane coating is attacked, ultimately causing the thinning paint to chip.

WOODS

Wood NUMBER	Strong lofts DEGREES	Standard lofts DEGREES	Weak lofts DEGREES
1	10	11	12
2	12	13	14
3	15	16	17
4	18	19	20
5	21	22	23

SHAFTS

A golf shaft starts as a tube about one inch (25 mm) in diameter which is drawn through a die until it is the diameter required. Shafts come in many different types, weights and flexes. The most flexible shafts are distinguished by the letter 'L' and these are put in most ladies' golf clubs. After these come the 'A' flex, suitable for the stronger lady and the slow-swinging man. The most popular flex is the 'R' flex, suitable for the majority of men. The stronger player and the player with a faster tempo to his swing will find the 'S' flex most suitable for his game, and the very strong player should use an 'X' flex. A shaft acquires its flex from the thickness of its walls. The thicker the walls, the stiffer the flex and the greater the weight. A standard men's shaft weighs between 4 and 4¼ oz (113 and 120 g).

GRIPS

Grip lengths vary between 10 and 11 in (254 to 280 mm). Weights vary between 1.5 oz (43 g) for ladies and 1.65 oz (47 g) for men. Thicknesses also vary and should be chosen to suit the length of your fingers. Grip thickness is very important. If the grip is too thick, it will restrict the movement in your wrist and, if you are right-handed could cause many shots to go to the right. Similarly, a grip that is too thin will cause excessive use of the hands, forcing many bad shots to go to the left.

CLUB SUMMARY

When choosing golf clubs, consider these very important points: the loft; the shape of the head; the centre of gravity (these determine the flight of the ball); the lie (to suit your posture); the weight; the flex of the shaft; the thickness of the grip (to suit your hands). If any of these aspects of the clubs is not to your liking, then you might need to have the clubs altered slightly, or, as it is known in the trade, custom-made.

Who might need custom-made clubs? The answer is every golfer, but some will benefit much more than others. People who need custom-made clubs, or clubs which can be altered, are those with longer or shorter fingers than normal, tall players with short arms and *vice versa,* those with a tendency to hook, slice, push or pull the ball.

A waterproof suit, such as the one worn here by Sandy Lyle, should not be too tight-fitting, particularly across the shoulders and under the arms.

ABOVE The golf umbrella is effective in heavy showers but cannot give protection in high winds. You may prefer a hat or cap which can protect your eyes against the rain and can even be an aid to concentration, particularly on the putting green, focusing attention on the ball.

WATERPROOFS

The fun of playing golf tends to drain away when you have to play in the rain. Whether you choose to begin a round in the rain or get caught on the course when the rains arrive, you will need waterproofs as part of your golfing equipment. Some people are willing to withstand a little wetness, provided they are warm. You may prefer a suit which is windproof rather than waterproof. There is a wide choice of both waterproofs and windproofs.

When buying a suit for those windy or wet days it should not be figure-hugging. Give yourself plenty of room inside it so that your swing is not impeded and you can bend with ease. If you do not keep supple and free-moving in rainy conditions, any hopes of good golf will, literally, be a 'wash-out'. Manufacturers of wet weather clothing offer varying guarantees concerning the 'dry time' you might expect inside rainproofs. New materials developed recently are very efficient in keeping the golfer comfortable and dry. Enquire about these new light-weight suits if you plan to go 'Swinging in the Rain'. Until these new developments, waterproofs did not breathe, and perspiration trapped inside was uncomfortable. Now you can keep dry, swing your clubs with ease, and any perspiration you are generating can flow out, keeping the body temperature even.

GLOVES

A glove is worn on the left hand to help the foundation of a good, firm grip at the top of the shaft. It can be of pure leather or synthetic material and the price varies accordingly. Both materials assist a non-slip left hand which is essential when you bring your right hand into the anchored left to make the grip.

Do not choose gloves which fit too sleekly. If they leave pressure marks they will be impeding circulation. Some gloves carry instructions and advice on fitting. Follow them.

RIGHT The only important choice in footwear is between spiked or non-spiked shoes.

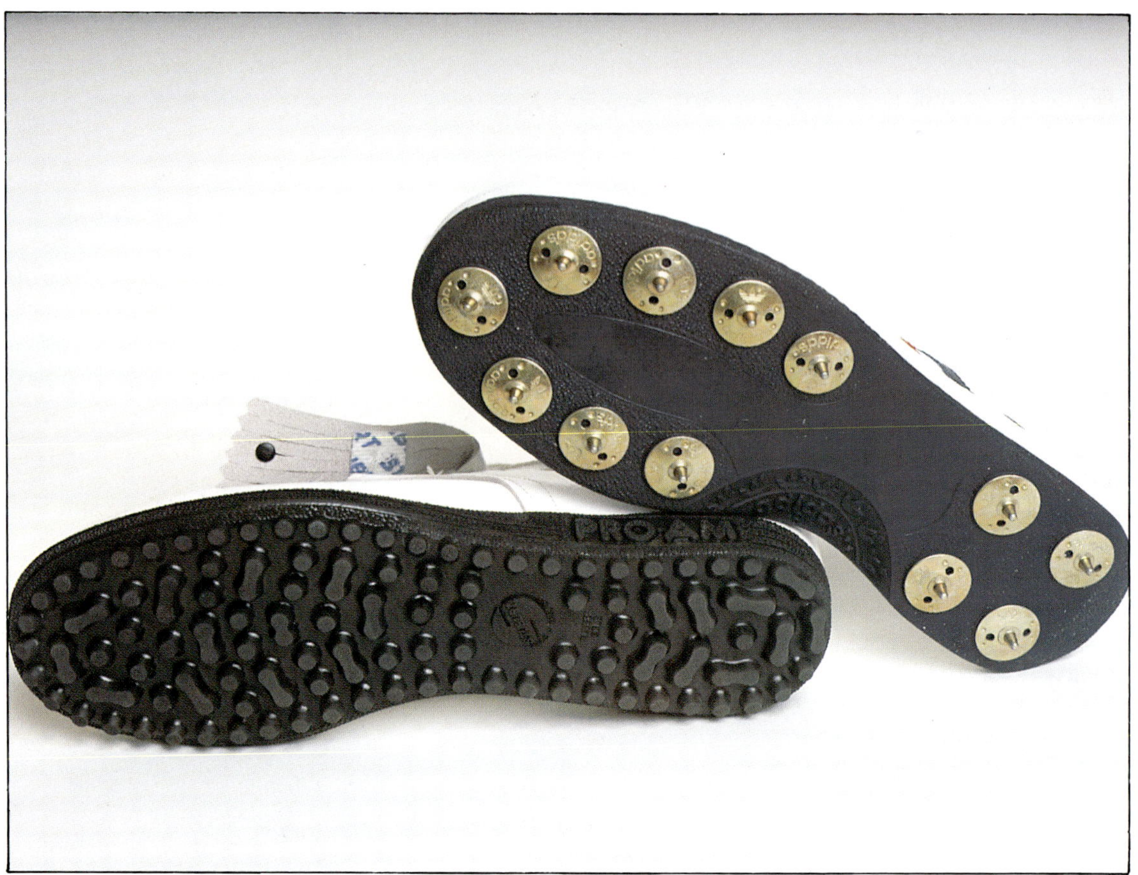

SHOES

Golf professionals' shops are usually stocked with a wide choice of golf shoes in various colours. This market is highly competitive, with Far Eastern countries claiming a share. Your priority is to seek comfort. You walk a long way on a golf course (especially if you do not keep to the fairway), you climb and you descend, you stride out and you wait about. A comfortable pair of golf shoes are two good companions you should choose to take with you.

Should you buy spiked or non-spiked golf shoes? The weight of spikes makes these shoes heavier to wear. Spikes give a slightly better grip to the ground and are helpful when walking on hilly courses, but on hard fairways where they do not fully bite, they lose their advantage over the non-spiked and lighter shoe. Take care not to damage the green when wearing spikes.

The choice of shoes now available to golfers dazzles the customer. Should you buy leather or non-leather uppers, with leather or non-leather soles? Comfort is the deciding factor, plus, of course, how much you can afford to pay for it.

ABOVE Golf shoe spikes are not of course as sharp as those of an athlete's shoe. They are made of stainless steel and should not deteriorate.

GOLF BALLS

The game of golf has evolved around the little white ball. This book is about hitting it correctly. Take away some of the golf clubs and you still have a game. Take away the ball and you are left with practice swings. The pursuit of this ball on courses across the world has provided pleasure and despair, has led to new industries manufacturing clubs and equipment, has created thousands of jobs, has made millionaires of top players and has led to improvements in its own manufacture.

Briefly, there are three separate types of golf ball: solid, three-piece and two-piece. The solid ball is at the bottom end of the market and is favoured by many beginners, mainly because of its low price. Older golfers may remember taking golf balls to pieces, peeling off the outer covers so that they could unravel miles of rubber bands wound round the soft centre of the ball. This type of ball is still manufactured today, although its components and Balata cover have been improved by modern technology. It is known as the three-piece ball.

New technology has also given birth to the two-piece ball, which has a harder feel in its blended Surlyn cover, and is a lot less likely to be damaged by mis-hit shots. Inside the two-piece is a resilient core of blended resins.

There are two sizes of golf balls, the 1.62 and the 1.68. The numbers refer to the diameter in inches. The traditional golf ball is the 1.62 as approved by the Royal and Ancient Golf Club of St Andrews, the ruling body of golf. From America came the slightly larger 1.68. This size has now won international approval and is the only one permitted in national and international competitions. Golf ball manufacturers still produce the 1.62, but in decreasing numbers.

THE TWO-PIECE BALL

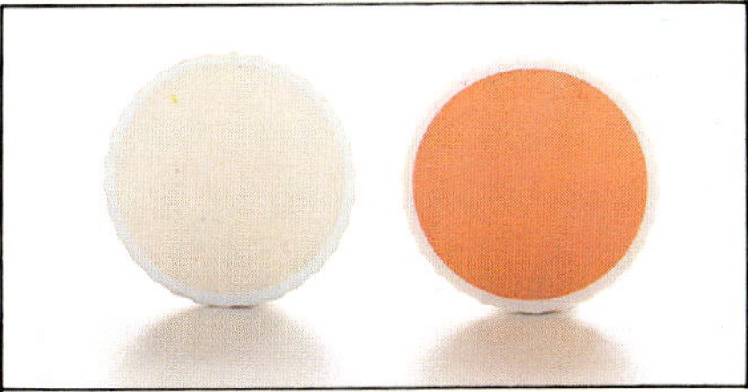

This ball has a solid centre core made of moulded rubber, covered with a pigmented Surlyn cover.

THE BALATA BALL

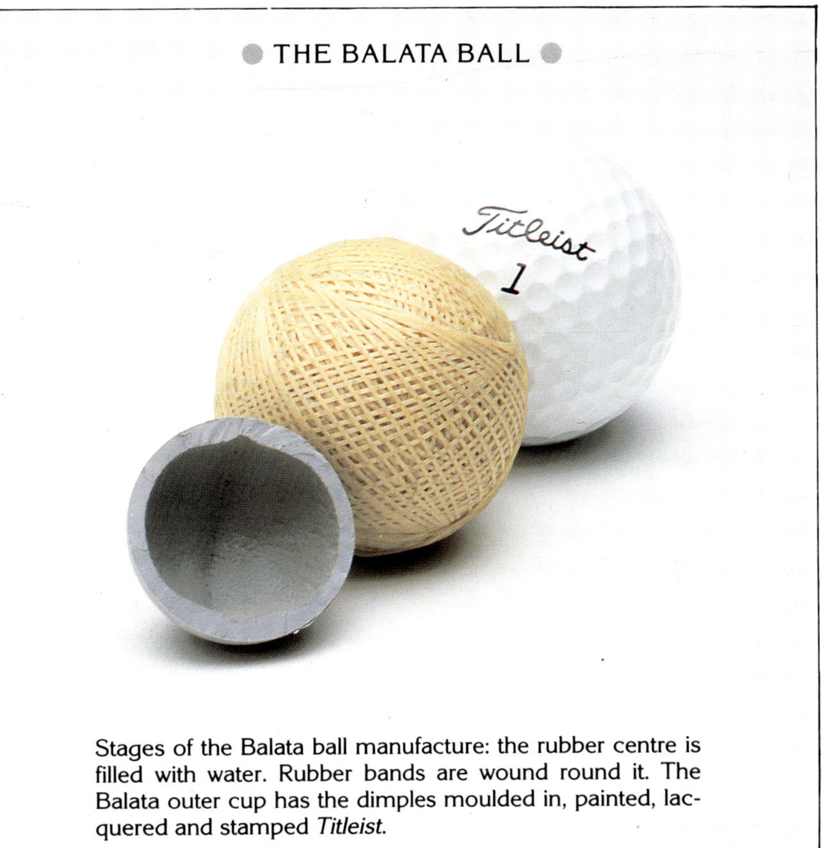

Stages of the Balata ball manufacture: the rubber centre is filled with water. Rubber bands are wound round it. The Balata outer cup has the dimples moulded in, painted, lacquered and stamped *Titleist*.

THE SURLYN COVERED BALL

Manufacture of the Surlyn covered ball: in the US this ball is called the *Titleist DT* and in the UK, the *Titleist 384 pts.* The solid rubber centre has rubber bands wound around it. It is then given the Surlyn cup, which is not painted but pigmented.

Always place your marker behind the ball in direct line with the hole.

Clearly, a pitch mark like this spoils the putting surface for everyone else.

Lift up the impacted turf and tap the area flat with the sole of your putter.

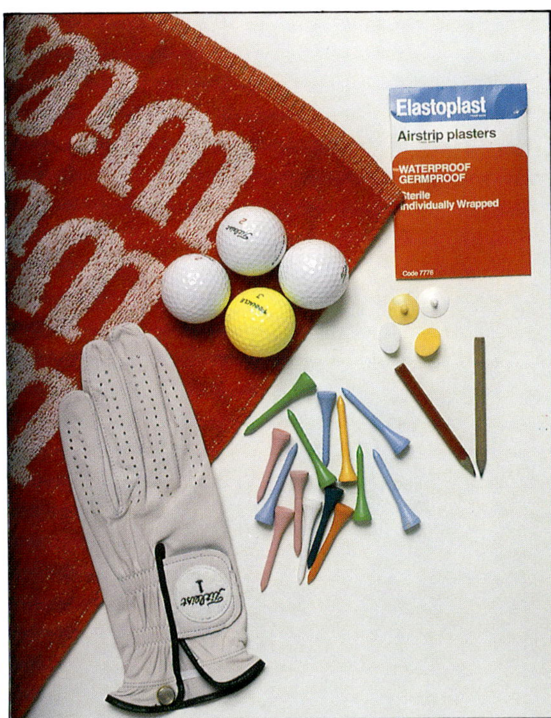

LEFT Important items needed when you go onto the course: a left hand glove to help give you added strength and adhesion in your grip; tee-pegs, marker, pencils, golf balls, and adhesive tape.

OPPOSITE Equipment you will need before you begin to play a round of golf. All are necessary and of equal importance to your success.

GOLF BAGS

To carry or to trolley – that is the question. The best carry bags are collapsible and therefore have no supports, but a trolley bag needs some side supports to keep it firm on the trolley. When buying a carry bag lightness is the important factor. It is a long way round a golf course and, when full of the other accessories as well as the clubs, the bag is carrying quite a heavy load. A trolley bag on the other hand can be a little larger. The small amount of extra weight when placed on a trolley will not be noticed.

Many players judge a bag by how big or wide the top is. That is only half the story. The bottom is as important, if not more so. If it is too small, then the grips get jammed together and rub against each other when they are pulled out. When watching the touring professionals, week-end golfers look at the size of their golf bags and think how uncomfortable it must be for their caddies to carry them around. In fact they are well designed so that the weight is distributed evenly over the whole bag.

Whether you carry or trolley depends ultimately on your fitness and your pocket.

TROLLEYS

It is a false economy to choose a trolley from the cheap range. The difference in design is usually considerable, while the difference in price is much less. Choose a trolley which you can pull standing upright.

MISCELLANEOUS ITEMS

Other useful items you will require on your round include the following:

Umbrella: Be prepared for that shower which hits you on the hole furthest from the clubhouse. Remember, you may not seek shelter when playing in a competition.

Tee pegs: Both wooden and plastic pegs are available. The wooden pegs are favoured by those golfers who dislike the plastic pegs sometimes marking the faces of their woods. However they break more easily than the plastic pegs, which are cheaper and more popular.

Ball markers: Markers are small discs which are used to mark the position of the ball on the green when you have picked it up for cleaning, or because it is impeding the shots of others. They are a must for the golf bag, or better still, a handy pocket. Some ranges of golf gloves have detachable markers.

There is only one correct way to use a marker. Stand behind the ball facing the hole. Place the marker behind and underneath the ball, making sure that you do not touch the ball. Never place a marker in front of the ball, or at the side of it, because there is a risk that, with loss of concentration when studying the next putt, you could place the ball back in front of the marker. Although you may have made the error inadvertently, it could look suspiciously like an illegal trick to gain ground.

Pitchfork: A pocket pitchfork is carried by all golfers who extend courtesy to other players. A constant complaint in the locker room is aimed at golfers who have not repaired their pitch marks on the green. The ball dropping down into a soft green from its high arc makes an indentation on the putting surface. It is every golfer's duty to repair his own pitch mark.

Pencil: You must not forget a pencil for scoring.

Scorecard: Similarly, you need a scorecard bearing all the local rules, including information on those holes of the course at which shots may be claimed when playing a match.

Towel: You should carry a towel to wipe clean your golf balls and clubs.

Stretch fabric plasters: Plasters are not carried for any expected personal injuries, although sometimes sore fingers and heels may need attention. Temporary repairs to equipment can be made with this useful adhesive tape.

Book of rules: A book of rules is a must.

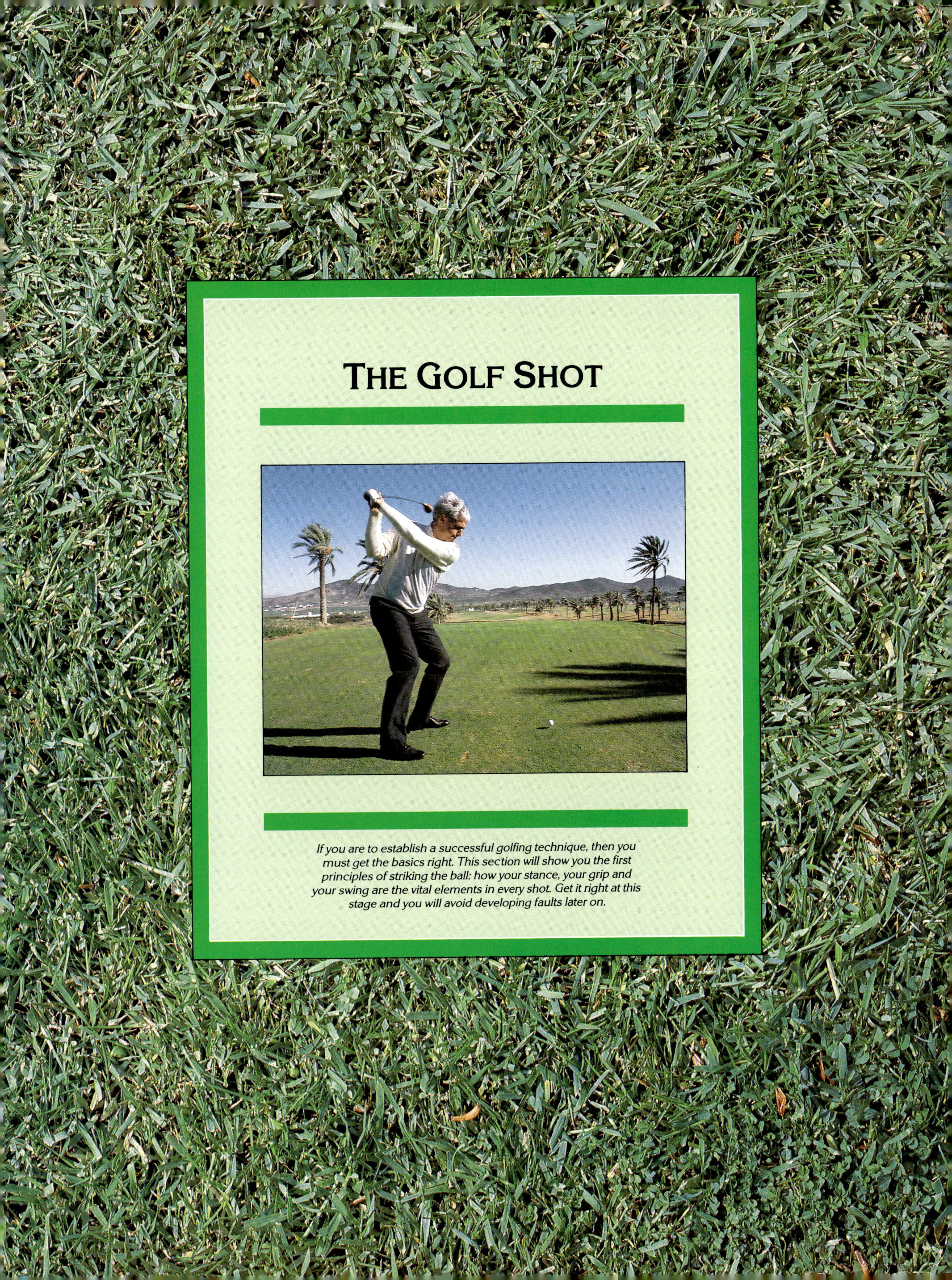

THE GOLF SHOT

If you are to establish a successful golfing technique, then you must get the basics right. This section will show you the first principles of striking the ball: how your stance, your grip and your swing are the vital elements in every shot. Get it right at this stage and you will avoid developing faults later on.

Golf is a world-wide game played by millions of people with many different standards, but they all have one thing in common – they can improve. Whatever your standard, it is hoped that this chapter will teach you through simple, easy to follow instructions, how to make your shots more consistent.

Later in the chapter, the shots themselves are analyzed, starting with the short shots on the green where all holes end, and working back from flag to tee to take in the long shots. This follows the way a child is helped to gain confidence in catching a ball. The ball is not hurled at first from long distances but gently lobbed into eager but unsure hands from only a few feet. In that way, confidence is increased until the high catches are easily taken.

Unfortunately the golf shot is not as simple as catching a ball. It consists of four separate components:

Aim: This ensures that the ball will be sent in the desired direction.

Grip: This controls the clubhead.

Stance: This ensures correct positioning and posture when making the shot.

Swing: This controls the plane of attack, and ensures that the ball is hit correctly.

All four components are important and each is dependent for effectiveness upon the other three. None can be neglected if the shot is to be effective. All deserve equal thought and practice, and are dealt with separately in the following pages.

THE TARGET LINE

Place two clubs on the floor parallel to each other, like railway lines, to help you to picture the target line and position your feet correctly.

The start of the address position, with the feet on one line and the club pointing square down the target line.

THE AIM

'It's all in the mind' is a phrase used in many sports, particularly those like golf, where a stationary ball is to be hit. It leads to positive action. The idea is that you must imagine the shot to be played before addressing the ball, and you must be confident that you can make it. You picture the shot you are about to make – then go ahead and make it.

Stand directly behind the ball looking towards the flag and imagine two clubs lying on the ground going away from you like railway tracks running from the ball towards the target. One line will be the target line for the ball, the other line will be for the correct positioning of the feet. Look for this target line. If you cannot see it, a simple exercise might help. Clench the fist of the right hand, and still standing behind the ball, gently swing the arm backwards and forwards as though you were going to throw a ball underhand along a line to the target. This action helps many beginners to see the imaginary line of flight.

Stand opposite the ball at right angles to the target. Place the clubhead square behind the ball. You are now *addressing* the ball. The sole, or bottom of the club, will be sitting flat on the ground with the face square to the target, and you will be aiming correctly.

THE CLUB-FACE ANGLE

The sole of the club must be flat on the floor, with the blade square to the target line.

The shorter the shot, the closer together the feet.

Swing the club to the top of the backswing; the club shaft will point towards the target, keeping the club-face square to the plane.

THE GRIP

All the world's top golfers have one thing in common: a correct grip. Only through the correct grip can you control the clubhead. The following descriptions assume a right-handed player, and obviously should be reversed for left-handers.

Many newcomers may find adopting the correct grip uncomfortable at first, but they should persevere. It will become a natural asset.

On forming the grip, it should be firm but not white-knuckle tight. The back of the left hand and the palm of the right hand point to the target and are square with it. Both hands must work together as one unit. The swing generates the power and passes it onto the clubhead through the hands. Your clubhead fires the ball to the target.

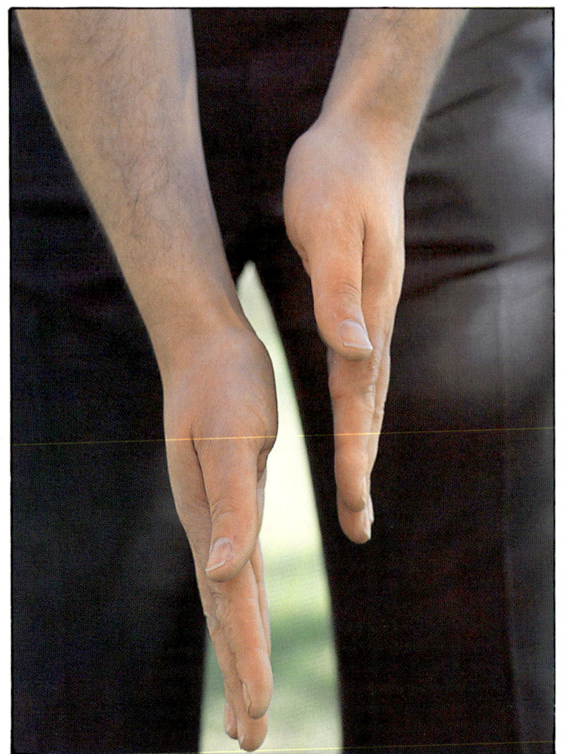

RIGHT When gripping the club, the back of the left hand and the palm of the right hand must point towards the target.

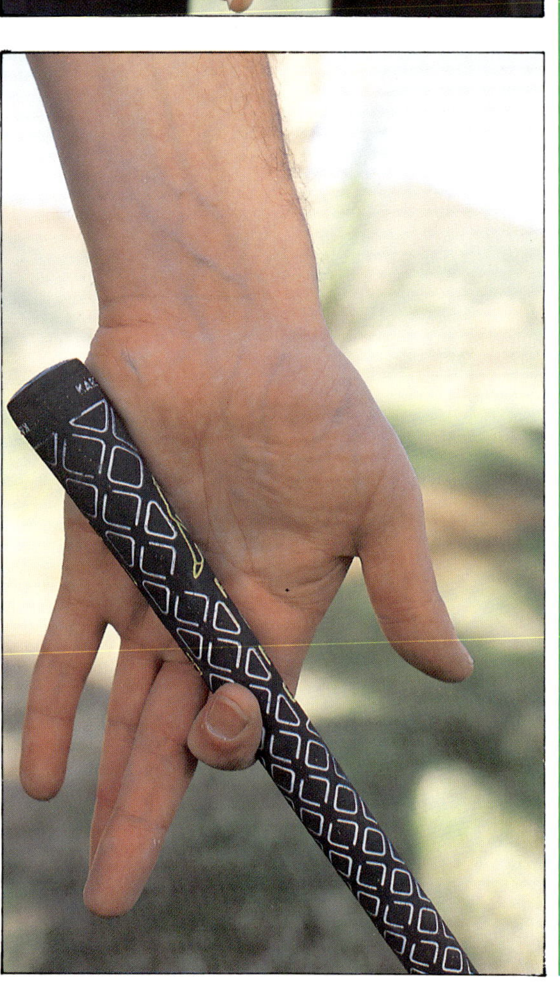

RIGHT The club grip lies across the left hand. The heel of the hand is on the top of the grip and the forefinger underneath, as though you were pulling a trigger.

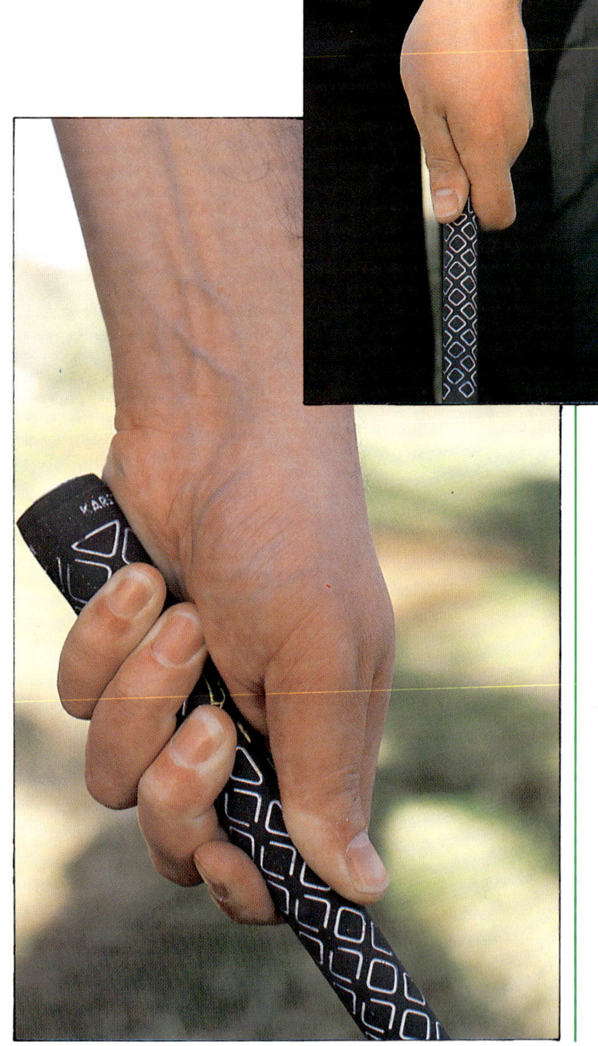

FAR RIGHT AND INSET When the left hand is closed, the thumb and first finger should be level and the 'V' from the thumb and forefinger should point to the right shoulder.

THE LEFT HAND

Place your feet together at right angles to the target, with the toes pointing towards the ball, so that the ball is on a line which would pass between your feet. Drop the left arm, keeping it firm, with the back of the left hand square to the hole.

With the clubhead grounded behind the ball, place the club grip across the left hand. The butt (or the top of the club grip) will be lying snug along the palm. It is essential that the club is gripped by the fingers against the palms of the hands so that the wrist stays in a relaxed position, enabling a natural wrist-break to take place in the swing. You will see that the forefinger is underneath the grip as though about to pull a trigger. Now place the thumb on the top of the club grip and close the hand. The thumb and forefinger should be nearly level. The V created by the thumb and forefinger should be pointing between your head and right shoulder. You are now ready to bring in the right hand.

THE RIGHT HAND

With the right hand, the palm points towards the target. The two middle fingers must have the control of the club. Let these two fingers grip the club and slide them up to meet the left hand, with the little finger overlapping the forefinger of the left hand. Now close the hand, with the thumb lying across the left hand side of the club grip. The V formed by the right thumb and the right forefinger should follow the same direction as the V on the left hand, i.e. it should be pointing between your head and right shoulder.

This grip is internationally known as the Vardon Grip, after its pioneer Harry Vardon, who between 1896 and 1914 won the British Open six times and in 1900 the American Open. Some beginners may discover that this grip is uncomfortable even after they have practised it for some time, so an alternative grip must be tried. Two commonly used ones follow.

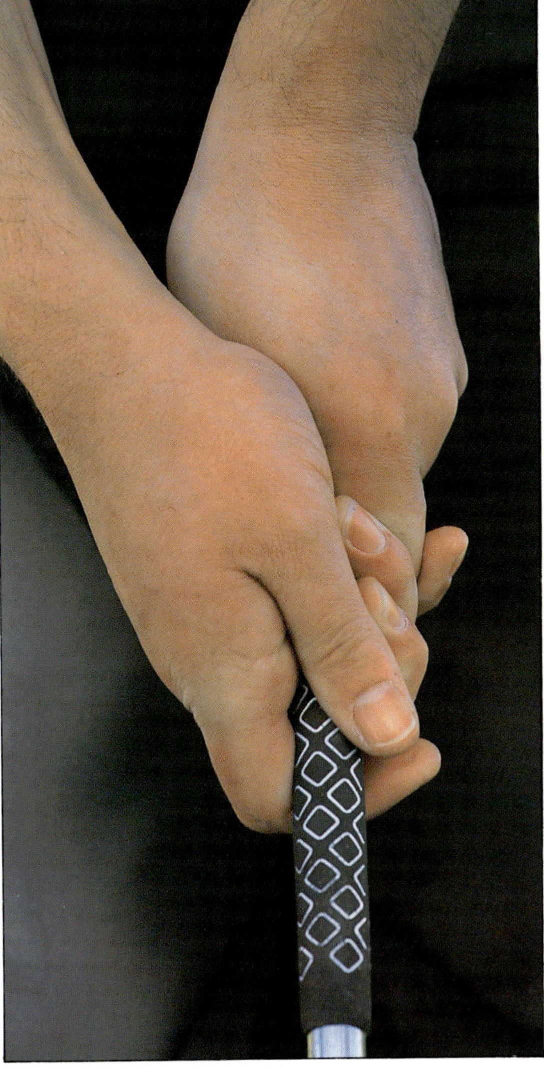

TOP LEFT The grip should be laid across the middle two fingers, as these need to have control of the shot.

ABOVE AND LEFT When closing the right hand, the left thumb is hidden. Both hands should grip the club with an even amount of pressure.

THE VARDON GRIP

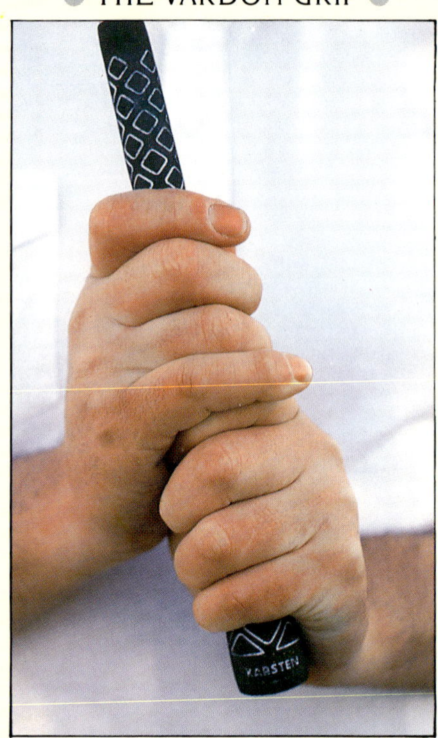

The little finger of the right hand rests on the forefinger of the left hand.

THE INTERLOCK GRIP

The left hand takes the same role as before, but when the right hand closes over the club grip the little finger of the right hand interlocks with the forefinger of the left hand. Instead of merely overlapping it, it comes between the first two fingers of the left hand, thus locking the hands together.

There is one other acceptable grip if you find you cannot feel comfortable with the first two.

THE DOUBLE-HANDED GRIP

Once again, the left hand takes the position on the club grip described before. To complete the grip, you bring in your right hand on to the club so that all four fingers of the right hand grip the club equally. The right thumb lies to the left of the club grip, completing a V pointing between the right-hand side of the head and the right shoulder. The palm of the right hand smothers the left thumb. It must be stressed that this grip encourages excessive use of the hands, and unless the hands are kept as close together as possible, shots will start to go astray.

The Vardon, or overlapping grip is recommended, but you must use the grip with which you are comfortable.

COMMON FAULTS

Two faults are common when gripping the club. The first is called a 'strong grip' and occurs when one of the hands (usually the right) slips round to the right hand side of the grip. This takes the palm off its square line to the target, and the V of the hand is now running up the right arm.

The club-face, in addressing the ball, may appear square to the target, but the hands are not. When the ball is struck, the tension created in the arms will bring the hands square to the target line but the club-face will be twisted. In effect, the club-face will have been closed, sending the ball to the left.

The other common fault is the 'weak grip', which occurs when one of the hands (usually the left) slips round the left hand side of the grip. The back of the left hand is now off the target line, although the clubhead appears to be square. The V of the left hand will be running up the left arm. When the ball is struck, tension created in the arms will bring the hands square to the target line but, again, the club-face will be twisted. This time it will have been opened, and the result will be a wayward shot to the right.

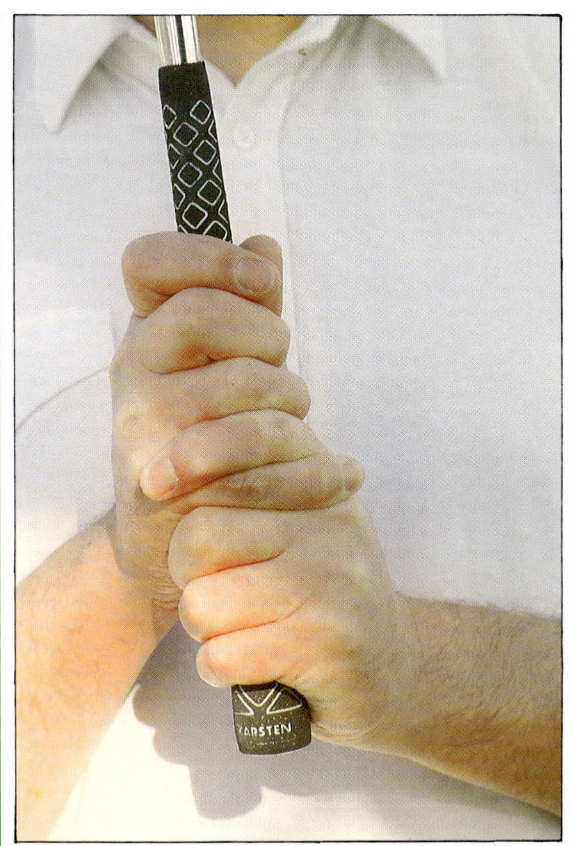

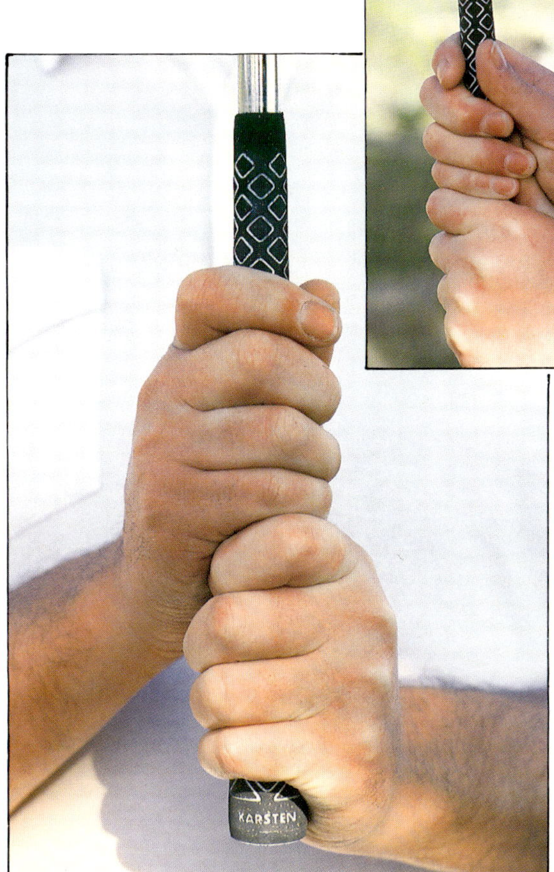

FAR LEFT *The interlocking grip:* the index finger of the left hand interlocks with the little finger of the right hand.

LEFT AND INSET ABOVE *The double-handed grip:* all eight fingers are on the club. When this grip is used, great care should be taken to keep the hands as close together as possible.

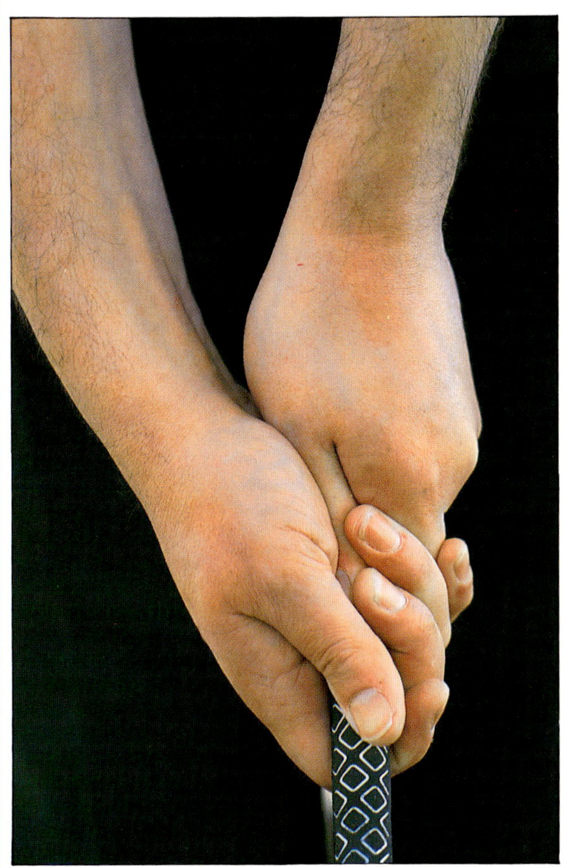

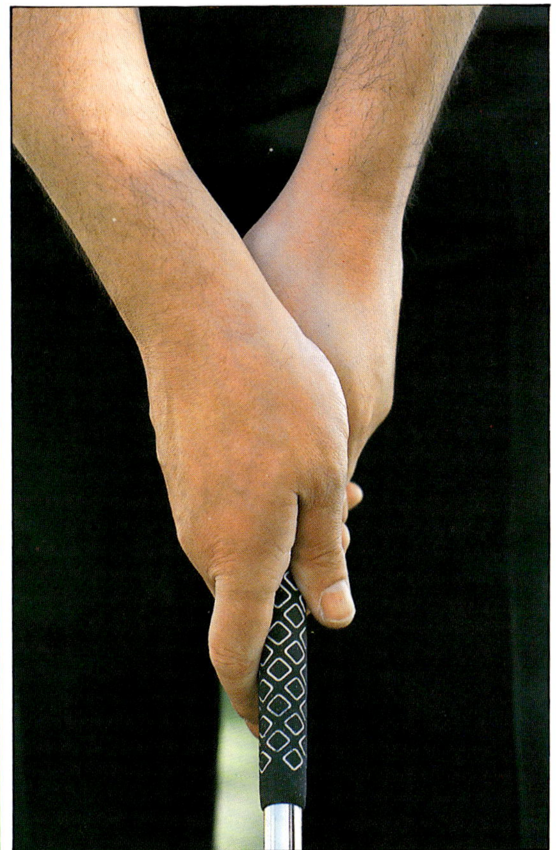

FAR LEFT *The strong grip:* the 'V' of either hand (usually the right), points to the right shoulder. When the ball is struck, the hand becomes square, which closes the club-face.

LEFT *The weak grip:* the 'V' formed by the thumb and forefinger points towards the left shoulder. When the ball is struck the hand becomes square and opens the club-face.

THE STANCE

The width between the feet at the stance is determined by the club chosen, which in turn depends on the type of shot to be played. The feet are closest together for the putting stroke, and they get farther apart as the shot gets longer, being at their widest for the drive.

Except for special awkward shots, the shoulders and hips should be square with the toes, which should be on a parallel line to the target line – or the 'railway track' as imagined when taking aim. The body weight will be evenly distributed between the feet.

The position of the stance in relation to the ball is also determined by the choice of club. There are two acceptable positions, the first favoured by beginners and the second by players with greater experience and confidence.

For beginners the address position varies through the range of shots from driver to wedge. Because the ball needs to be struck on the upward swing path, the drive should be addressed in line with the left heel.

The address position then moves forward about an inch (25 mm) for every club needed until, when you use the wedge, because you need to strike the ball at the bottom of the down swing, the address is made with the ball in line with the mid-point of the space between the feet.

The second address position is for the more confident golfer and is the one favoured by most golf professionals. All the shots are played with the ball lying opposite the inside of the left heel. With this method the feet are close together for the wedge shot, and the stance widens gradually for shots using clubs going up the range. So the driver would be taken with the ball still lying opposite the left, heel, but the stance would have widened to shoulder width.

BALL POSITION

When you take up the address position, the ball should be about an inch further forward for every club used, from the short-irons to the driver. The less loft on the club-face, the further forward the ball needs to be.

THE ADDRESS POSITION

1 Stand up straight with the shoulders back, the head up and arms at your sides.

2 Keeping your back and legs straight, push your bottom out, bringing your head over towards the ball.

3 Keeping your back straight, relax the tension in your knees.

4 Now let your arms hang straight down, enabling you to swing your arms freely.

5 Grip the club; you are now in the address position.

POSTURE

Your posture is your general bearing in the stance. Begin by imagining you are in the services and stand to attention. Stand straight, shoulders back and head up. Now bend over from the waist, keeping the back and legs straight. Push your bottom out and bend over one more notch. To release any tension, let your knees flex a little. Let your arms and hands hang down towards your left thigh, and grip the club. You are now in the address position.

SHOT SAVER

When you are in the address position your hands should block your view of the shoelaces of the left shoe. If they do not, step back and take up your position again.

ON THE GREEN
(RULES 8-2B, 16-1A)

You are not allowed to put any guide mark down on the green to help you find the target line. You can remove sand or loose soil between your ball and the hole by brushing it aside with your hand or club, but you must not press it down.

LINING UP THE PUTT

1 Stand behind the ball and try to imagine the target line running from the ball to the hole.

2 After assuming a comfortable posture, your eyes should be positioned over the ball.

THE SWING

Many novices embrace the full game of golf from pitch and putt courses where their appetite for golfing enjoyment has outpaced their ability. They wish to graduate to 18-hole courses to meet new challenges on manicured greens and trim fairways, which means learning the full swing.

Before you start the patient build-up of the swing, it will help if you understand its different components. Familiarity with the aim, grip, stance, the position of the ball and posture have already given you a basic technique on which you can build as you seek to swing the club. New ingredients will be added as you progress.

The golf swing is a circle designed by the hands, and described by the clubhead. The hands swing the club in an arc on the backswing, downswing and follow-through. These all form part of the same circle which is centred on the upper region of the chest. A putt is a small sector of a circle, with the clubhead making a small arc, but as the shots build up, your hands go further back until the arc increases to a circle – and you have formed your swing. Shots in the golf game which you are now about to play as you read begin with a winner – the short putt. This is a shot you need never leave home to practise. The short putt is as important a part of your game as a 250-yard (230-m) drive. Remember the old adage of the professionals: 'you drive for show but you putt for dough'.

THE SHORT PUTT

No matter how you play on the fairway, it is your putt which wins the hole. There is no shot in golf where individuality is expressed as much as in the putt. But as in all golf shots, you need golfing disciplines. You have to follow the 'Golden Rules' of aim, grip, stance, position of ball and posture before you swing the club.

Start with a two-foot (60-cm) putt. This putt introduces you to the feel in your hands when the clubhead strikes the ball. The club needed is, of course, the putter, one of the most 'personal' clubs in the set. The putting stroke is a backwards and forwards movement, like a pendulum. For this two-foot (60-cm) putt, it will be three to four inches (75 to 100 mm) back and three to four inches (75 to 100 mm) through.

Let me introduce another maxim here: it is recognized that good golf, reduced to its simplest elements, means doing the same thing over and over again . . .

Stand behind the ball and try to imagine the target line running from the ball to the hole. Once that line is in your mind, walk to the side of the ball, taking aim, and place the head of the putter behind the ball, square to the target line. Assume your grip. Then settle into the stance, with the ball opposite the middle of the feet, which should be four to five inches (100 to 125 mm) apart. Now check the posture, get comfortable, position your head over the ball so that your eyes are directly above it. Your head has to remain steady over the ball throughout.

With such a short putt you will not need to look for the hole. Now start the pendulum, keeping your wrists firm but your arms relaxed, taking the clubhead back about three to four inches (75 to 100 mm). Make sure that the clubhead is not straying from the target line, then let the pendulum swing through gently, striking the ball in the middle of the clubhead on its forward movement, rolling the ball along the target line.

Repeat this shot until you can judge the pace and distance of the ball consistently. This is a part of golf you can practise on your carpet, rolling the ball up to an imaginary hole. It will give you confidence in the feel of the putter. Keep practising this two-foot (60-cm) putt until you are confident you can make it every time.

SHOT SAVER

To sharpen your concentration, place two clubs parallel to the hole, one above the target line, the other below it. Putt through this corridor of confidence.

LIFTING THE BALL (RULES 16–1B, 20–1)

If you want to clean the ball when you are on the green, you can; but remember to mark the position of your ball, or you will lose a stroke.

TESTING THE SURFACE (RULE 16–1D)

All of the rules of golf are simply a matter of common sense; when putting, it would of course be a great advantage to roll or tap a ball toward the hole before your putt, to test the borrow of the green and the quality of the surface, but doing so would negate so much of the challenge to your judgement and skill. Not surprisingly, it is against the rules.

THE LONG PUTT

When you can putt out the two-footer (60 cm) regularly, start moving away from the hole until you reach the longer putt. Any putt from about 12 feet (3.5 m) to the edge of the green, can be called a long putt. With the longer putt, the striking power, which dictates the speed of the ball and therefore the distance it will travel, has to be practised to increase your confidence on the green. For the longer putts it does not matter if you do not hole out. The exercise is to try always to leave the ball 'dead' – so close that you can hole it next time. Do not forget: it is recognized that good golf, reduced to its simplest elements, means doing the same thing over and over again . . .

With the long putts, always look for the target line, then take your aim, grip and stance and make sure you keep your head still over the ball. Bring your clubhead back, keeping it square to the target line. Let the putter head strike the ball on its through swing, so that it rolls towards your target. The backswing and the follow-through will be about the same length. Both will become longer as the distance from the hole increases. Balance plays a very important part in the game of golf, and the general rule is that as the distance from the ball to the target increases, then your stance will have to widen. General tips about putting will be discussed later.

The long putt begins to involve a longer swing and is giving you more of the feel of the club as it strikes the ball. Fortunately, you need not play a full round or even one hole to refresh your putting confidence, as this can be practised indoors on a carpet. When you can rely on the putting stroke and your confidence has built up, move away from the green to get the feeling of the next shot in the build-up to the full swing.

This is going to be 40 yards (36 m) away from the target and you will use a club which for the first time will lift the ball off the ground, before it pitches and rolls on towards the target. This is a valuable shot made from just off the green, and is known as the 'chip and run'.

THE CHIP AND RUN

The chip and run is, as its name suggests, two shots in one. The chip part of the shot forces the ball into the air. The run part is when the ball runs along the ground towards the hole, where you will be in a position to use one of your 'home-grown' putts that has been shaped and styled on your carpet.

For the chip and run you will need a 7-iron or an 8-iron. The loft on the club-face will chip the ball off the ground for the first part of its journey towards the target. Loft leads to lift. It is the clubhead striking the ball which lifts it into the air. You do not scoop the ball into the air with the clubhead; you let the loft on the club-face do the work. The swing action is the same as in putting, a pendulum, with the clubhead striking the ball as it swings through towards the target.

There is a 'new ingredient' to consider with this shot: head position. Your head has a heavy responsibility during the swing. It contributes one-eighth of your total body weight. It must not move until the ball has been struck and the clubhead is following through. Any slight movement of the head in any direction before this could have disastrous effects on your shot. After the clubhead has struck the ball your head will come up naturally, your eyes seeking the flight.

Stand behind the ball to picture the shot. Imagine you are going to throw the ball underarm towards the target. Picture its flight, and judge where it should land for the perfect result.

Do not attempt to hit the ball until you have had a few practice swings. This will help you visualize the shot. Take your address position, keeping your hands and wrists firm. For this practice exercise you are going to swing the club like a pendulum, as in the putting stroke. Keep your wrists firm (because you are going to make a wider arc), to take the clubhead back about two feet (60 cm) from the ball and two feet (60 cm) through it. Try to make this a crisp, positive action. Imagine that you can feel the clubhead sending the ball up and away towards the target. Let the turning of the left shoulder – to the right and away from the target – start the pendulum moving, keeping the left arm, hands, and golf club shaft all in a straight line. Your hands and wrists stay firm to ensure the clubface is square with the target line when it strikes the ball.

When you are happy with the method and confident with your practice shot, then you are ready to play the ball. Remember: it is recog-

FAIRWAY CHIP AND RUN

Swing the club two feet back and two feet through, keeping your wrists firm and your head still, the ball should be in the middle of the feet. The outside edges of your feet should be a shoulder-width apart. The body weight should be evenly distributed and your hands in line with your left thigh, square to the target.

nized that good golf, reduced to its simplest elements, means doing the same thing over and over again . . .

Now take aim. Stand with the feet at right angles to the target line and ground the club-head behind the ball, square to the target line. Take your grip two inches (50 mm) from the top of the club grip. As you take up your stance the ball should be equidistant from your feet, with the outside of your shoes being a shoulder-width apart, and the body weight evenly distributed. Your posture should be comfortable, with your legs slightly flexed. Your hands should be opposite the left thigh and blocking your vision of the left shoe laces.

The right knee should be kept in the flexed address position throughout the shot. This is very important. Now swing the club – remembering the pendulum – two feet (60 cm) back and two feet (60 cm) through, letting the momentum of the clubhead strike the ball and lift it off the ground on its way to the target.

The chip and run to the green played correctly and cleanly must be one of the most rewarding shots in golf. Just as you did not rely entirely on being on a green to gain confidence in the putting action, you may now develop your rhythm for the chip and run shot by just swinging the club without hitting a bail.

You have discovered how loft on the club-face can lift the ball through the air with the chip and run shot. You are now beginning to build up the golf swing. The next stage is the half-swing, before you take the final instructions for the full swing. The half-swing will help to give you feel and rhythm. By varying the distance in practice, you will gain control over the flight of the ball.

THE HALF-SWING

With the chip and run shot, your hands only went back a few inches. Now, with the half-swing, the hands are going to swing to waist height. The arc described by the hands in the back-swing, downswing and follow-through, form part of the same circle, centred in the upper region of the chest. The arc gradually gets fuller as the distance of the shot increases. With the short putt, the hands only move back a few inches so the arc is very small. As you progress through the range of clubs to the full drive, the arc will increase to its maximum.

From the chip and run position, walk back up the fairway towards the tee. When you are about 90 yards (83 m) from the green you are in a position for a half-swing. The club required is a 6- or 7-iron. Imagine the ball is lying on the fairway.

There is another new ingredient for this shot: weight transference. An exercise to help you to understand the concept of weight transference is the simple one of throwing a ball underarm. Hold a ball in your right hand and face the target. Stand with your feet slightly apart, the weight even. Now take your arm back and let the weight move onto the right foot. Take a step forward with the left foot and gently swing your arm forward to release the ball. The weight is now on the left foot. Repeat this exercise a few times, then swing the club and be conscious of feeling your weight transferring from your right leg at the top of the half-swing, moving onto the left leg as you swing your arms through.

You are about 90 yards (83 m) from your target, so stand behind the ball to picture its flight. Work out your aim. Ground your clubhead behind the ball square to the target line. Form your grip, then assume your stance with the outer edges of your feet at shoulder-width. The hands should be four to five inches (100 to 125 mm) from the left thigh.

The right knee must stay in the flexed address position throughout the backswing. The left shoulder, arm, hand, club, as well as the left knee, all turn together, with the left arm pushing the golf club back and away from the target, to a position where the hands are at waist-height. The right hip moves backwards away from the ball. Your head stays steady, looking at the ball. Your posture will have remained at the same angle as at the address position. Your shoulders will have turned about 45°. At the top of the backswing, your hands will be waist-high, and

TRANSFER OF BODY WEIGHT

1 Throwing the ball underarm: a pointer to weight distribution. The weight transfers from the right leg to the left leg. This must be repeated in the golf swing, but without the head movement. Stand with your feet close together, facing the target with the ball in the right hand and body weight evenly distributed on both feet.

2 As the arm comes back, the weight transfers to the right leg.

3 The left leg steps forward, transferring the weight from the right to the left leg.

4 The ball has been released and the weight is on the right foot with the right heel off the ground.

THE HALF-SWING

1 Stand behind the ball and picture the target line.

2 Take up the address position, with the club-head behind the ball, square to the target line.

3 The hands are waist-high, with the weight just on the inside of the right foot and the shoulders turned through 45°.

4 The hands have come through to waist height, the weight has transferred to the left leg and the head has not moved.

your weight will be just on the inside of your right foot.

The downswing starts with a lateral movement of the hips, the hands beginning to move at the same time. The force of the clubhead striking downwards transfers the body weight onto the left foot. The clubhead strikes through the ball on its path towards the target. The hands will finish waist-high. The half-swing has become a half circle. Let your right heel ease off the ground as your weight transfers.

Practise the half-swing until you can control the shot, before moving on to the full swing.

Remember my motto: it is recongized that good golf, reduced to its simplest elements, means doing the same thing over and over again . . .

No two players in the world have exactly the same full swing because of differences in height, build, age and fitness. Like the carpet putt which builds up confidence on the green, the half-swing can be practised anywhere, and without a ball, to build up confidence for tackling the full swing.

THE SWING
(RULE 13–2)

You cannot remove obstructions to your swing, such as grass or branches, or anything marking the area which is out of bounds such as a fence post or wire. It is alright to touch these obstructions in the backswing, so that you can, for example, push the club back through long grass.

THE FULL SWING

There is a whole recipe of ingredients needed for the full swing: aim, grip, stance, posture, swing, weight transference, wrist cock, body turn and swing plane.

Wrist cock is a new ingredient. It is an integral part of the back-swing and should not be cultivated as an independent action. The weight of the clubhead, provided the grip is correct, allows the wrists to cock naturally throughout the back swing. Here is an exercise to give you the feel of the wrist cock, an action which will accelerate the clubhead in the shot. Stand straight, feet slightly apart for balance. Grip the club correctly. Lift up the club, pointing it away from you at shoulder height, with your arms fully outstretched and the shaft of the club parallel to the ground. Keeping your arms straight, 'break' the wrists so that the club shaft points vertically upwards. Turn the shoulders 90° to the right. This is the feel of a wrist cock.

Body turn is another new ingredient – and note it is body turn and *not* body sway. An exercise to give you the feel of the body turning also doubles as a second exercise to give you the feeling of wrist cock. The movement is similar in style to that of a baseball player when striking a ball. Select any golf club, form the grip with your hands, and stand up straight, with your arms stretched out in front of you parallel to the ground. The head remains in the central position. Let your knees bend slightly. The right knee must stay in the bent address position throughout the first part of the turn.

Now let your left shoulder lead the turn of your left side to the right, keeping your left arm firm and turning the shoulders through a full 90°. Your hips will have turned 45° if your right knee has stayed in the bent position as at the address. Your arms will have rotated like the hands of a clock. The back of the left hand will be facing upwards, as will the palm of the right. The right arm will have bent, with the elbow pointing down to the ground. The left knee will have bent in and pushed forward slightly, pointing to a spot about twelve inches (30 cm) behind the ball. This will have helped the weight to transfer onto the right leg and your right side.

Keeping your gripped hands parallel to the ground, you start the turn in the opposite direction to the left, drawn by a slight lateral movement of the hips. Your arms move anti-clockwise, unwinding the movement. When your body is facing the left, your hands will have naturally

WRIST BREAK IN THE BACKSWING

1 Stand straight. Grip the club correctly with your arms fully outstretched at shoulder height and the shaft of the club parallel to the ground.

2 Keeping your arms straight, break the wrists so that the club shaft points vertically upwards.

3 Turn the shoulders through 90° to the right. This gives the feel of the wrist-cock at the top of the backswing.

BODY TURNING EXERCISE

1 Stand straight, with your arms outstretched and the club parallel to the ground.

2 Turn the left shoulder to the right through 90°, which will automatically turn the hips through 45°. The back of the left hand points upwards, the back of the right points downwards.

3 Turn the shoulders in the opposite direction so that the right shoulder turns to the left. The back of the right hand now points upwards and the back of the left points downwards.

rotated in an anti-clockwise direction, so that the back of the right hand and palm of the left hand face the sky. The right arm will be straight, the left arm bent, with the elbow pointing straight down.

Repeat this body turning movement several times, feeling your weight transferring from one leg to the other. You will discover that the transfer is governed by the position of your hands. Your weight transfers as your hands move from the backswing to the follow-through. You will achieve a natural wrist cock, or break, at each end of this lateral arm movement, which will be used in the full swing exercises.

The third new ingredient in the full swing is the plane. The plane is the angle of the circle of the swing shaped by the hands as they move the club around the body. The posture which creates this is determined by the club needed to play the shot. The wedge and the driver mark the two opposite ends of the spectrum, which give an upright and a flat plane respectively. The shaft of the wedge is shorter and the lie angle more upright. This forces the player to stand nearer the ball and take a more upright stance. And because of this, the swing will follow a more upright plane. The driver, with the longest shaft in the bag and the flattest lie, forces the player into a flatter swing plane.

Many mechanical devices have been produced down the years to perfect a personalized swing for the learner golfer. Some eccentric home-grown ideas are now prize relics in golfing museums. Golf is one sport where new technology is always waiting to help. A warm welcome is now being given to the golf 'Swing Simulator', which personalizes swings for golfers of all heights and physiques. It gives a constant plane and operates on muscle memory.

With or without the help of a swing simulator, you are now ready to practise the full swing.

You have learnt that the golf swing is a circle defined by the hands, with the chest being the centre of the circle. It is important that the distance between the hands and the chest remain as near constant as possible throughout the swing. This is popularly known as 'keeping the left arm firm'. A swing must travel full circle, taking the ball with it along its perfect path.

Select a middle iron for this shot, a 5-iron or 6-iron. After lining up your shot and taking aim, form your grip and assume your stance. Your feet are a little wider apart than for the half-swing on which this full swing is built. The middle of

MOVABLE OBSTRUCTIONS (RULE 24–1)

What happens in the rare event that your ball comes to rest against someone's golf bag or rolls under a golf cart? An obstruction is defined as anything artificial (except objects marking out of bounds). If the obstruction can be moved without disturbing the ball, go ahead. If not, and you are not on the tee or the green, you will have to drop the ball: hold the ball at shoulder height and arm's length to do this.

LEFT Most of the time you will be aiming to strike the ball squarely with the club-face and therefore the stance you adopt should be square to the line of the shot, as shown. If the clubhead remains on line to the flag from the top of the backswing, through the ball and to the top of the follow-through, just before the wrist break, then you will have achieved a *direct swing path*. You should be able to feel through the grip that the clubhead is working on a straight line.

THE GOLF SWING SIMULATOR

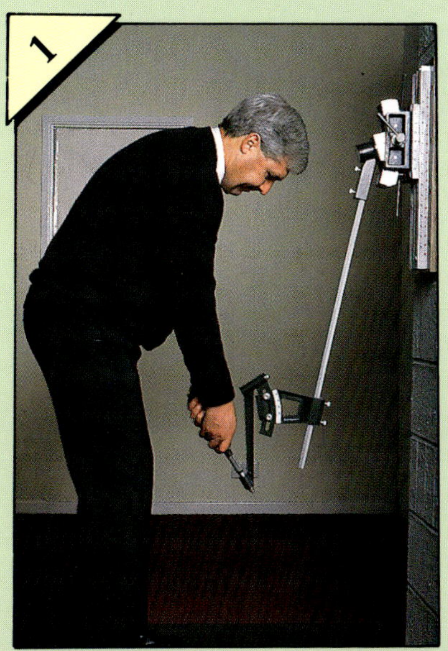

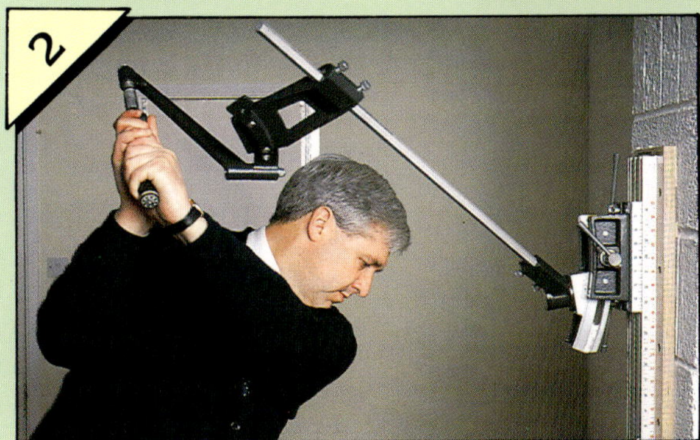

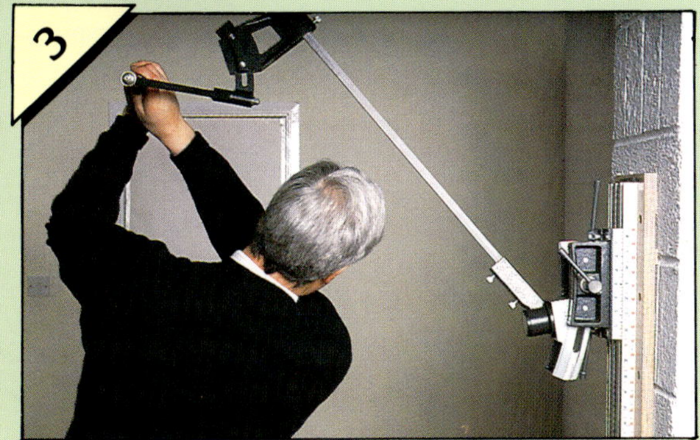

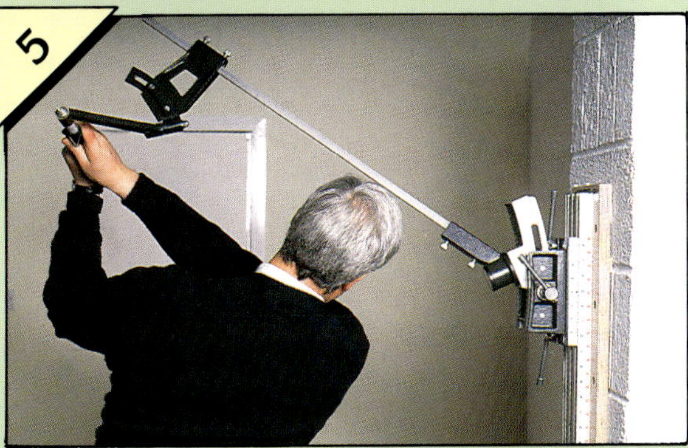

The golf Swing Simulator can be adjusted for the full range of planes, from flat to upright. 1, 2 and 3 show a setting for a more upright plane than 4 and 5.

THE FULL SWING

1 The posture must remain the same until the ball is struck.

2 Select a five-iron and take up your address position.

each foot should now line up with your shoulders. Your club is square to the ball. Recall the importance of the target-line. Remember to keep the posture the same throughout the swing. The right knee remains flexed. Allow the left knee to bend naturally, as with the half-swing, when the left shoulder turns and the left arm pushes the hands, shaft and clubhead back away from the ball.

From about waist-high the arms will start moving clockwise – as in the baseball exercise – and the wrists will start cocking. The backswing follows a constant plane. The hands reach the height of the right shoulder. The shoulders are turned through 90°. The hips have now turned 45°. The weight has transferred to the instep of the right foot. It is acceptable for the left heel to have lifted slightly off the ground. As the wrists break during the backswing, the club shaft is pointing towards the target and the club-face is square to the plane. The right thumb is under the shaft. The right elbow is pointing straight down behind the line of the heel. The left knee points to a spot 12 inches (30 cm) behind the ball. The downswing and follow-through complete the full swing, as the clubhead goes

3 Push the club back to waist height before beginning the wrist cocking procedure.

4 At the top of the backswing, the club shaft is in line with the target. The left arm is firm and the right elbow points to the ground, behind the heel line.

through the ball, sweeping it towards its target.

The enemy of accuracy in this part of the full swing is body sway, which can be generated too easily by the momentum of the arms and hands coming through as the body weight transfers. If you keep your body posture the same throughout the swing, it will prevent the temptation to sway. The hands and the lateral movement of the hips initiate the downswing, and the force of the clubhead striking downwards unlocks the wrists, as the hands and arms sweep on smoothly through the ball to the high finish of the swing. Keep your eye behind the ball as you strike it. The hips have turned, to bring the front of the body to face the target. Your right shoulder will have pushed your chin up.

The body weight follows your hands. It moves from the right foot and left instep at the top of the backswing, through to the left foot at the finish of the swing. The sole of the right shoe will be off the ground and pointing away from the target, and your knees will be close together. This follow-through gives power and flight to your shot. Finish high and let it fly! Remember that when you throw a ball underhand, you get no height or flight unless you follow through.

CLUB POSITION AT THE TOP OF THE BACKSWING

1 The club-face is square, with the club shaft pointing towards the target. From this position, there is a good chance the ball will be on target.

2 The club is pointing across the target, resulting in an out-to-in swing which lends slice-spin to the ball, making it go left in a straight line or on a slice trajectory.

3 From this position, an in-to-out swing will result in the ball going either right in a straight line, or hooking around to the left.

POSITIONING THE RIGHT HAND

1 Positioning the right hand at the top of the backswing. Swing the club to the top of the backswing, with the shaft pointing towards the target.

2 The right elbow must point straight down behind the right heel. The shaft is parallel with the ground.

3 Swing the right arm through until your arm is level with your shoulder. You must keep your head still throughout and keep looking at the ball.

Applying Your Skills

Once you have established the basic principles of striking the ball with reasonable control and accuracy, you must adapt your technique to the demands of the golf course. You must review and refine your shots to meet the different challenges you will meet from tee to green.

You are now familiar with the rudiments of the golf swing. You know the importance of the disciplines of taking aim and lining up your clubhead square, after establishing a target line for each shot. You should follow them as naturally as you look both ways before crossing a busy road.

Now is the time to analyze all stages of your game from tee to green. As before, the best way to start is to sharpen your skills in the short game around the greens. Then you can move back down the fairway towards the tee. As you go, you can take a second look at the structure of every important shot. You will learn to take more than one look before every shot. You will appreciate again my motif: it is recognized that good golf, reduced to its simplest elements, means doing the same thing over and over again . . .

FOUR-FOOT PUTT

1 When lining-up a putt to help you judge the distance, stand behind the ball and imagine rolling the ball towards the hole. This will help to get the strength right when making the putt.

2 You must take great care in lining up the face of the putter with the hole.

3 Make sure your eyes are over the ball when assuming the address position.

4 A smooth putting stroke must be in your mind when you take the clubhead back.

5 Keep your wrists firm as your putter head goes through to roll the ball towards the hole.

PUTTING

Putting is a pressure shot in golf. It can be the most exciting. In the televised international golf tournaments which make heroes for the more modest golfer to emulate, it is the greens which are the arenas of drama, and the shot which excites both the armchair spectators and the crowd on the course, is the putt which drops.

When you are facing any putt, short or long, do not trust to luck. Watch the care the top players take with even the simpler looking putts. See how they go through the routine of seeking the target line, taking aim, assuming stance – and how they achieve steadiness. You too can become a master of the green.

To putt well, it will help if you understand a little about the construction of a green. Flat greens are optical illusions. Golf course architects cannot build them. The necessary drainage requires greens to have a high and low point. So there must be a slope, which in golf is called a borrow. Often you have to aim off-line to compensate for the slope or borrow. When on the green, look for these high and low spots which will affect your putt. Because of the way greens are cut, the amount of slope on a green can be disguised.

Your putter can be a useful plumb line in assessing the borrow and in finding the target line. Stand behind the ball, lining it up with the hole. Hold the putter out in front of you, thumb and first finger on the grip, shaft pointing vertically downwards and blade pointing out towards the hole for balance. From behind the ball, with one eye closed, line up the straight side of the shaft with the side of the ball and the hole in your vision. You are using the hanging shaft as a plumb line. It will give you an idea of the borrow between the ball and the hole, and how much you need to allow in your putt for the ball to swing in towards the hole.

From anywhere on the putting green – and greens come in a wide range of sizes – your hope is to hole out with one putt. But to take the pressure off the long putts, modify your objective a little. Try to roll the ball close to the hole. Your primary objective is to lay your putt dead, just a tap away from the hole. Your putting standard will improve if you weigh up the length of the grass on the green. If it has been cut that day, the pace will be faster. The way the nap lies will affect speed and borrow.

RIGHT AND BELOW RIGHT To find the amount of borrow on the green, use your putter as a plumb line. The putter should be gripped between the thumb and forefinger and allowed to hang vertically. The side of the shaft can be used to find your line.

OPPOSITE The most common alternative putting grip, known as the reverse-overlap.

Every shot calls for concentration and smooth movement. Remember that each hole on the course is precisely 4¼ inches (107.95 mm) in diameter. Putting is no pushover. It breeds in some players unbelievable reliance upon a particular design or weight of putter and leads to extraordinary idiosyncracies in style, stance and grip. But you should try to putt accurately with the orthodox methods, although your grip may change slightly as you progress.

One rule in putting is never to let the clubhead pass your hands. This common fault arises when you try to anticipate the strike, causing the wrists to flick or break just before the ball is struck. To stop this happening, many players use an alternative grip known as the 'reverse overlap'. With this method the left hand is on the putter grip, with the thumb going straight down the grip. When the right hand is placed in position, the forefinger of the left hand covers the two smallest fingers of the right. The thumb of the right hand also points straight down the shaft. The overlapping forefinger helps keep the arm, wrist, hand and finger all in one line, firming up the wrist. It also keeps the two hands close together, making them work as one unit.

The putt is the only stroke in which you should move away from the orthodox grip. Another, used to great effect by the German champion, Bernard Langer, is the 'cackhanded' grip. For this you place the left hand in a line below the right. This keeps the arms, wrist and hands moving as one unit. It is in some ways a left-handed golfer's grip, used by a right-hander.

Some players favour their trusted putter for short shots from off the green in preference to chipping. This shot has been dubbed the 'Texas Wedge'.

Putting's golden rules are that your eyes must be over the ball and your head must be still throughout the putting stroke. Your whole body should resemble a statue, except for a smooth movement from your arms and shoulders.

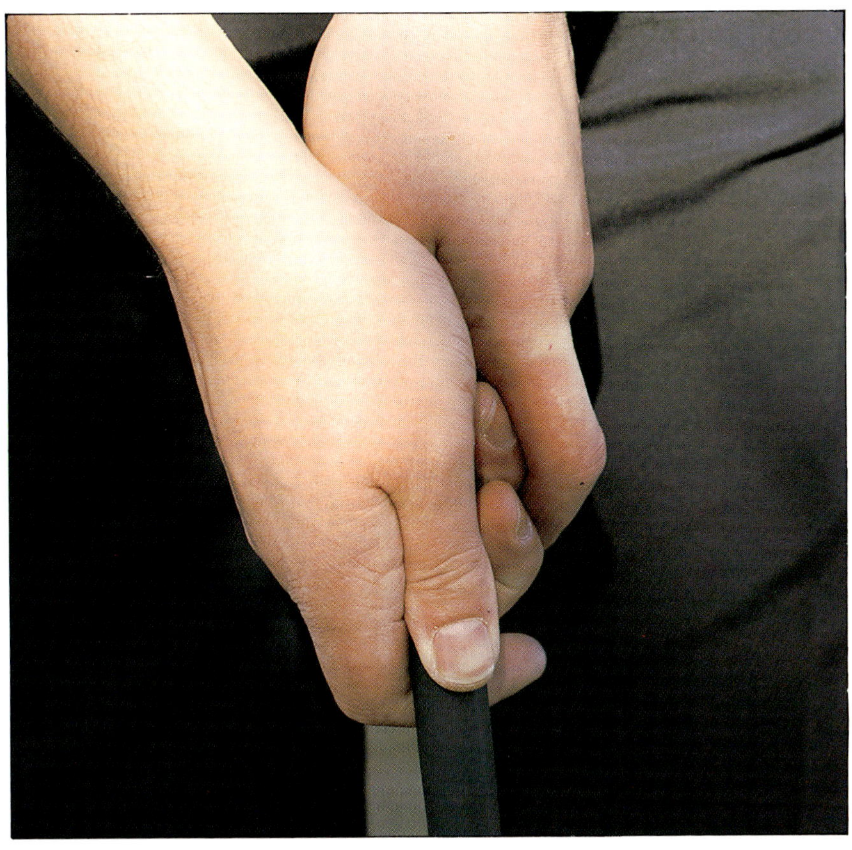

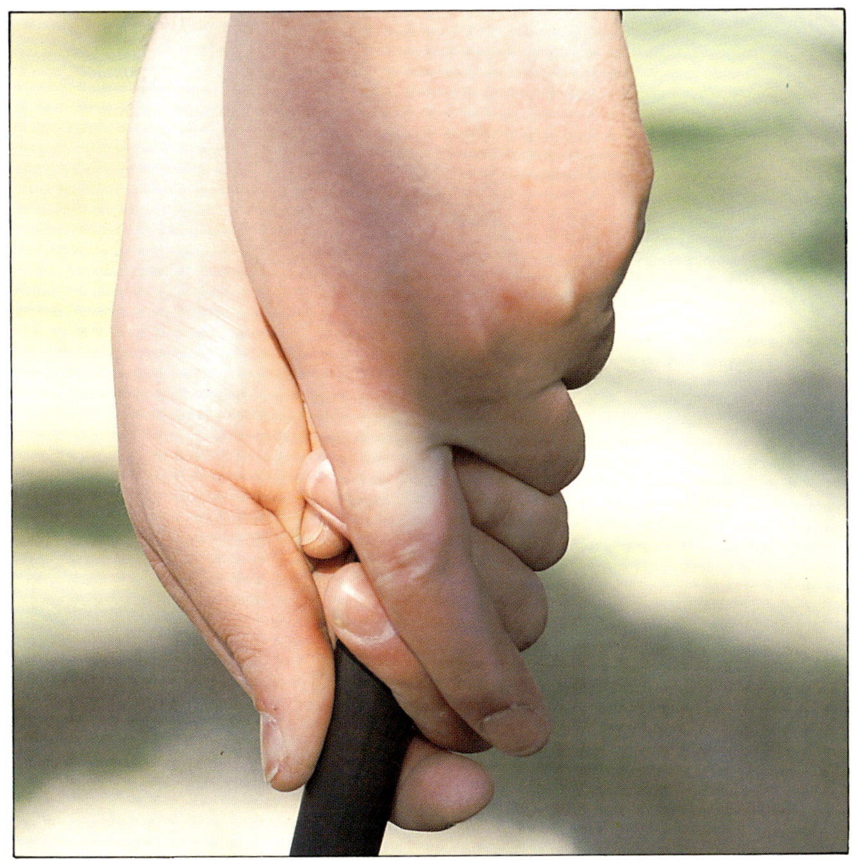

SHOT SAVER

Before playing a round, check whether your eyes are directly over the ball in your putting stance with a novel test you can carry out on the practice green. Line up for a putt, then hold a spare ball to the bridge of your nose, between your eyes. Let the ball drop. If it hits the one you have lined up, you know your eyes are not going to let you down. If it misses, reposition your head until you get it right. This will boost your confidence for the putts out on the course.

ABOVE The golden rules of putting are that your eyes must be over the ball at the address position and that your head must be kept still throughout the stroke.

ABOVE To see the result of your putt, *turn* your head to follow the ball's path to the hole. Do not lift your head to watch the ball.

Pitching and Chipping

Around the green you will be faced with a variety of shots which demand either short, high flights to leap hazards, or low flighted runs to the hole. The first shot is a pitch, the second a chip. Where you cannot use a putter, a chip is safer than a pitch. As a famous player once said: 'With all greenside shots, always try to make the ball land as near as possible to you.' The point is that, as a general rule, it is easier to judge run than flight; although the speed of the greens is an important factor in deciding which route to take to the hole.

The pitch and chip shots are the foundations of an accurate short game. The loft of the club does the work for both. The pitch will be played with the more lofted club, the chip played with the straighter face.

LEFT To pitch a shot, use a lofted club to help give more lift to the ball.

BELOW LEFT To chip a shot, use a straighter faced club. The ball will stay closer to the ground and will have more run.

THE PITCH

A typical pitch shot is the one needed to clear a bunker which guards a green. Stand behind the ball and visualize just where you wish the ball to land, and its flight. Face the hole and swing your arm backwards and forwards, giving you the feel of the shot. Imagine for a moment that you were going to throw the ball. The follow-through would be longer than the backswing. This is also true of your pitch shot. Remembering this will help ensure that you don't stop on the shot: think of it as one-third back and two-thirds through.

In the early stages, it is advisable to play to the widest part of the green for safety. This will make for an easier shot. One thing you do not wish to do is to take your next shot from deep in the bunker. Even tournament professionals do not always aim for the pin, but play 'percentage shots', those which offer the greater percentage chance of success in the end.

Now you have the flight in your mind, select your club and study the lie. You may be tempted to loft the ball with the sand wedge, because that has the greatest loft of all the clubs in the bag. The danger is that if the ball is not cushioned by the grass, the heavy flange of the sand wedge will work against you. The ideal club for a pitch must therefore be the pitching wedge.

For the high pitch shot, assume a stance that positions the ball nearer to the left, or front, foot, forward of the centre line between your feet. Your feet should be fairly close together, the outsides of your feet no wider than your shoulders. Your weight will be slightly more on your left side, with your knees relaxed. This cuts down the transference of weight when you swing the club and helps to keep the body still. This in turn helps you to hit down and through the ball.

With this shot, a slight amount of wrist break is necessary to steepen the clubhead on the downswing, and give a little extra clubhead speed into the ball. When striking the ball, the blade of the club, coming down under the ball, will lift it up and over the bunker to the green. Remember to follow through to ensure you don't 'quit' through the ball. Let the loft of the club do the work. Do not try to scoop. If you do, you are likely to find yourself in the bunker.

The length of your follow-through will be determined by the distance you wish the ball to pitch on the green – and remember you are not relying on much run.

DIFFERENT ABILITIES

Beginner A 6- or 7-iron should provide him with enough club strength and enough loft to pitch safely on the green.

Intermediate player Now well within striking distance of the flag, he can use a club with plenty of loft (a 7- or 8-iron) to carry the step of the green.

Beginner The moment of truth: he can either take a 3- or 4-iron, hoping to carry the water and avoid the bunkers, or (more likely for a novice) take a 5-iron and play to the left of the danger area, allowing for any excess power in the stroke by seeking a lie some way short of the bunkers.

Playing a Par Five

Different Solutions for Players of

The very fact that a system of handicapping (first officially introduced in 1926) is used in golf will tell you that the approach to each of the challenges posed by any hole is – and should be – different for players of different standards. The illustration shows the routes taken to the green by three golfers of varying abilities and experience. All three, in effect, play an ideal game from tee to green, according to their own capabilities.

FADE

The clubhead is swung on an out-to-in path, with the club-face open from that path; the ball is faded from left to right.

THE PITCH SHOT

1 A pitch shot is often necessary to clear a bunker. Stand behind the ball and visualise the flight you would like the ball to take.

2 The ball must be closer to the left foot than the right. Keep your feet fairly close together.

SHOT SAVER

If you decide to putt from off the green imagine the hole not as a drainpipe but as big as a manhole cover. It would be a huge stroke of luck to hole from such a distance. But by using your imagination like this you could be encouraged to put the ball close enough to hole out next time.

If you take a mid-iron for chipping, the ball does not need to be struck so forcefully because of the lesser loft of the club.

Imagine the shot, face the hole and swing the arm – one third back and two-thirds through. You must not fluff this shot by hitting the ground before the ball. So whereas the width of your stance should be the same as for the pitch, inside a shoulder-width, the ball should be positioned opposite the middle of the space between your feet. Your hands should be opposite your left thigh, with your weight over your left foot. The weight stays there throughout the shot and the only movement is from the arms and shoulders. Your head stays still over the ball.

Because there is no wrist break needed for this shot, the position of your hands assumes even more importance. As you play through the shot, keep the same angle of hands to clubhead; do not let the clubhead fly through because of floppy wrists. There is no place for wrist flicks in golf.

3 A slight amount of wrist break is necessary in the back-swing, to steepen the arc on the down-swing.

4 The length of the follow-through is determined by how far ahead you wish the ball to pitch onto the green. Let the loft of the club do the work. Do not try to scoop the ball.

THE CHIP

The chip gives run to the ball and is used for equally short approaches to the green as the pitch, being preferred where there are no trouble spots to fly over. It is played with a straighter-faced club, like a mid-iron.

Before considering your chip, ask yourself if your putter, used as a 'Texas Wedge', might be more successful. If you were, say, 12 feet (4 m) off the green with 45 feet (14 m) of green to the hole and, using the putter, swept the ball towards the hole so that it stopped 6 feet (2 m) from it, you might feel disappointed. But if you got to the same spot by chipping, you could feel pleased. Your expectations are greater with a putter.

SHORT IRON PLAY

The short iron is played for accuracy and not length. With the 7-iron, 8-iron and 9-iron the ball should be struck from just forward of the middle of your feet, with your hands opposite the left thigh covering your view of the left shoelace. Your body weight should be evenly distributed and your knees slightly flexed. Your feet should be slightly closer together than a shoulder-width. Take a three-quarter backswing. Because of the position of the ball, the clubhead will strike down slightly into the ground, taking a shallow divot, as the hands complete the arc through the ball to the top of the follow-through.

You will find greater consistency if you take a stronger club than you think you need. Do not force your shot. You will be more consistent with

SHOT ONE

• Professional or scratch golfer •
In order to reach the green in two shots, the professional uses the driver and closes his shoulders to impart a degree of hook spin, drawing the ball around the trees from right to left. (See illustration A.)

• Intermediate player •
Without the control necessary to draw the ball around the trees, he uses the driver to gain maximum distance straight down the fairway, allowing himself plenty of room at the turn to avoid the copse with his second shot.

• Beginner •
From the front tee position (which can be as much as 50 yards in front of the professional's competition tee) he might take a 2 or 3 wood instead of the driver, for greater control and confidence, happy to clear the stream and delighted to reach the turn of the dogleg.

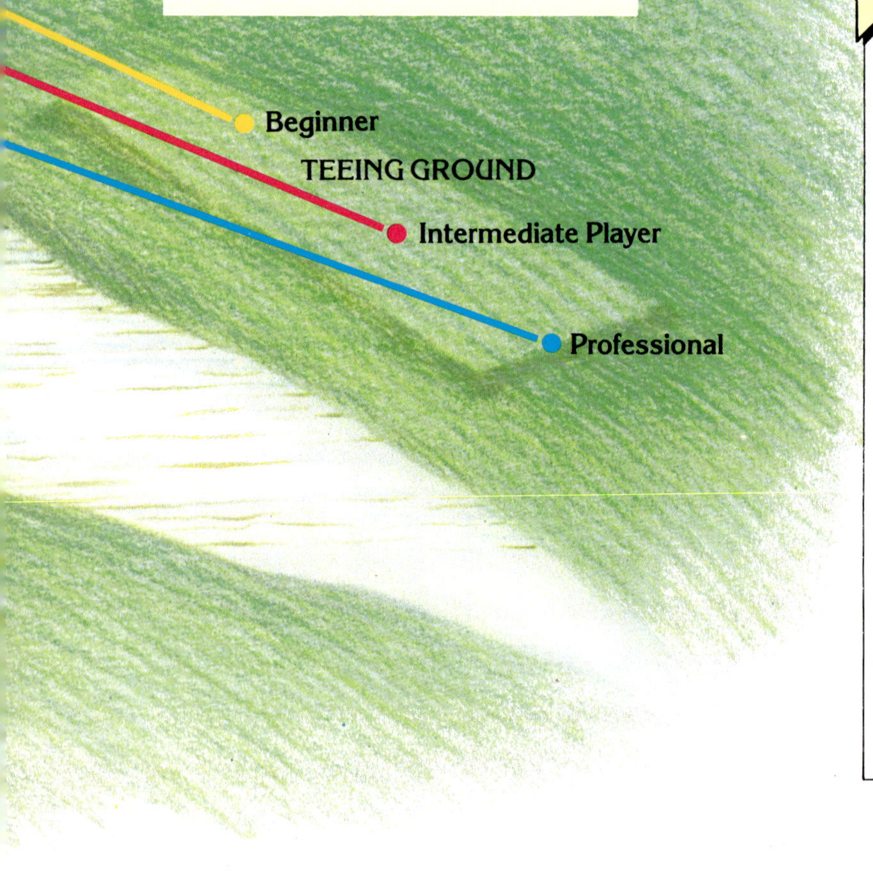

Beginner
TEEING GROUND
Intermediate Player
Professional

• Club Selection •

Distance (yardage) and probable club used for each shot from tee to green.

Professional

250-300 yd/driver
250-300 yd/2 or 3 wood or 1-iron.

Intermediate Player

180-200 yd/driver
180-200 yd/3 or 4 wood
120-140 yd/7-iron.

Beginner

125-175 yd/2 or 3 wood
125-175 yd/2 or 3 wood or 3-iron
125-150 yd/3-iron or
80-100 yd/5-iron and 60-80 yd/6- or 7-iron

• DRAW •
The clubhead is swung on an in-to-out path and the club-face closes from that path; the ball is drawn from right to left.

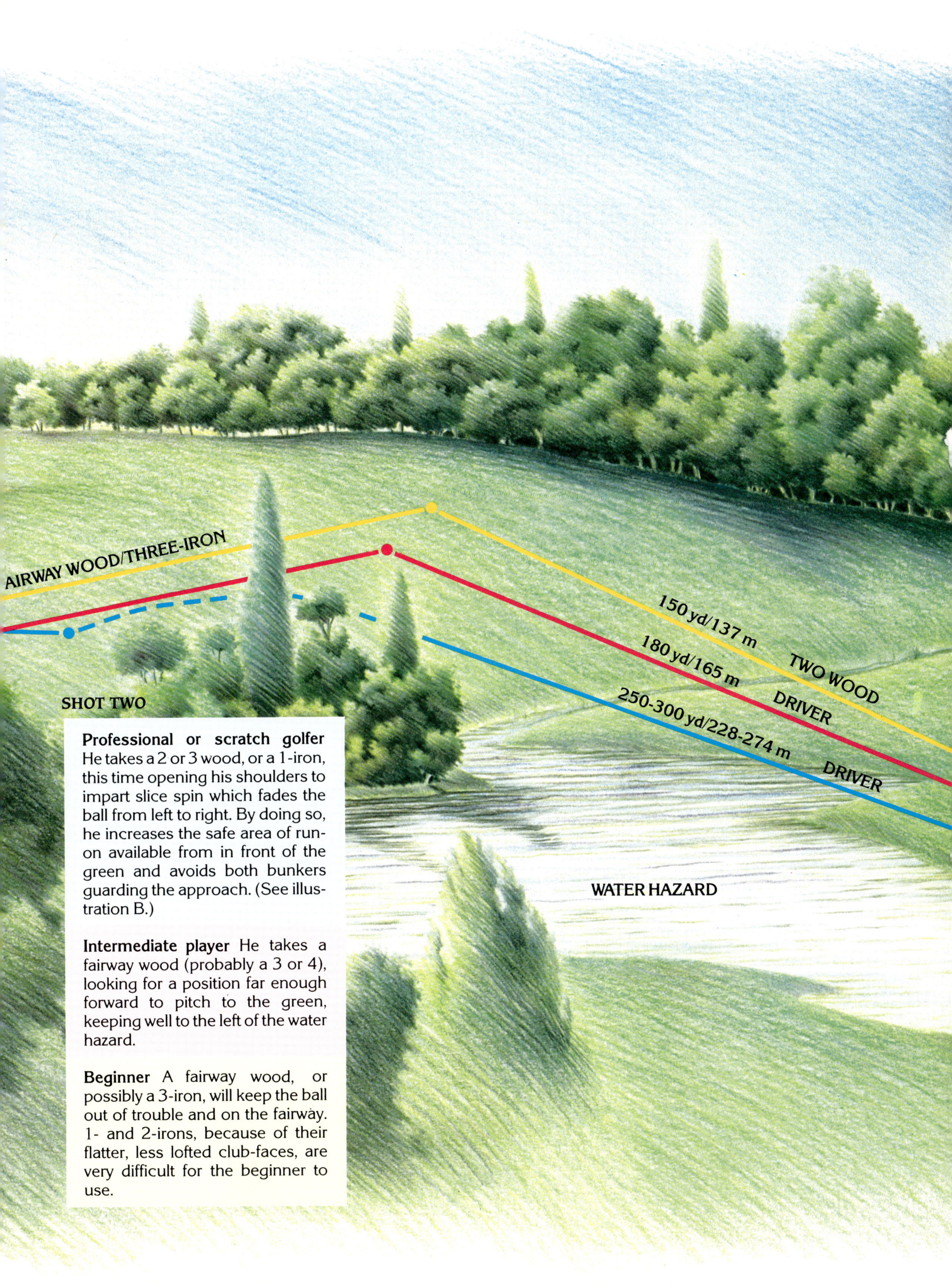

Professional or scratch golfer He takes a 2 or 3 wood, or a 1-iron, this time opening his shoulders to impart slice spin which fades the ball from left to right. By doing so, he increases the safe area of run-on available from in front of the green and avoids both bunkers guarding the approach. (See illustration B.)

Intermediate player He takes a fairway wood (probably a 3 or 4), looking for a position far enough forward to pitch to the green, keeping well to the left of the water hazard.

Beginner A fairway wood, or possibly a 3-iron, will keep the ball out of trouble and on the fairway. 1- and 2-irons, because of their flatter, less lofted club-faces, are very difficult for the beginner to use.

LEFT The ball position for the seven-, eight- and nine-irons should be opposite the middle of your feet with the hands in line with the left thigh.

BELOW LEFT The short-irons are used for accuracy. The length of the backswing is not as important as with the longer shots. Make sure that your backswing is compact. The most important objective is to ensure that your clubhead is on-line.

a stronger club and a shorter, but firmer swing. Let the clubhead do the work, and fight the temptation to scoop the ball.

The shorter irons give height to the flight of the ball, due to the shape of the club and the steeper arc and plane from which the ball is struck. These impart back spin to the ball; when it pitches on the green, very little run will occur.

MID IRON PLAY

The 5-iron and 6-iron have shafts which are a little longer than the short distance irons and are therefore slightly more difficult to use.

To use them, your feet should be a little wider than for the short irons. Strike the ball from opposite a point between your left heel and the middle of your feet. When you stand behind the ball looking down towards the target and seeking the target line, imagine a corridor the width of the green you are playing towards. Try to flight the ball down that corridor. The length is not as important at this stage of the game as accuracy. The ball can always run on. The backswing need be only three-quarters of the full swing. When coming down and through the ball, take very little divot.

LEFT For the mid-iron shot, the stance should be a little wider than for the short-irons. The ball should be between the left heel and the middle of the feet.

ABOVE When playing a mid-iron, keep the swing under control and do not over-swing. The club-face should be square to the plane and the shaft of the club pointing on-line to the target.

THE FAIRWAY WOOD

1 Stand behind the ball to picture the shot.

2 The ball should be towards the left heel as you take up your stance.

3 Push the club back, keeping the arc wide.

4 At the top of the backswing, the shoulders should be turned through 90° and the club on-line with the target.

5 Strike through the ball with the correct weight transference. A good finish is essential.

LONG IRON PLAY

The shafts of the 3-iron and 4-iron are even longer than those of the mid irons and the concept of swing plane discussed in the previous chapter comes into play. The lie angle of these irons is a little flatter than that of the others, and you will need to stand slightly farther away from the ball. This will flatten your plane and help you to sweep the ball forwards. Beginners should not be too ambitious in trying to carry this shot all the way to the green from the fairway. Look for the corridor towards the green as for the mid-irons.

The feet should be wider apart with these irons than with the others, and the ball position should be further forward, towards the left heel than when using the mid irons. You should not take a divot, and the positioning of the ball towards the left foot will help. Swing and sweep it away off the turf down the 'corridor of confidence' you have set for yourself.

Be careful not to snatch this shot. Build confidence in your backswing to let your body turn and take your body weight through the shot, as it follows your hands.

PROVISIONAL BALL
(RULE 27–2)

If one of your long iron shots were to go astray and there was a possibility of the ball being lost or out of bounds, it would be tedious to trudge down the course looking for it, only to have to return to the original lie to play a second ball. The rules allow you to play a provisional ball from as close as possible to the original position *before* you go forward to search. When you reach the area where the first ball came to rest, if you find it, then no penalty is incurred and the provisional ball doesn't count. If the first ball is lost, then carry on with the second, losing a stroke as normal.

RIGHT Note the differences between the driver and the fairway wood; the latter has a shorter shaft, a lighter clubhead, and greater loft. The shallowness of the head means its centre of gravity is below the ball, which assists in lifting the ball into the air.

LEFT The straighter face of the driver clubhead makes the shot more difficult to control than the shallower and more lofted face of the three wood.

RIGHT The height of the tee-peg plays a very important part in driving. The ball should be positioned opposite the left heel, with half the ball above the centre of the face and the other half below. The ball is swept away as the club starts its upward climb from the bottom of the arc towards the top of the follow-through.

DRIVING

The drive, taken from the tee, is the most powerful shot in golf, and can be the biggest trouble finder. It is usually played with the No. 1 wood, but if confidence in your swing is lacking there is no disgrace in taking a 3-wood. Although you are setting up your stance and swing to get the maximum distance with the ball, your main objective is to find the fairway with the shot. The penalty of missing the fairway and finishing up in the rough – in Indian country – or out of bounds, can be disappointingly harsh. So don't gamble with the driver. Play the percentage shot from the tee: try to place your ball down the fairway in a spot where your lie for the next shot is clean, even if you are sacrificing some distance.

The height of the tee peg for the drive is important. Whichever wood you take to drive, you will find the height of the tee peg must rule the position of the ball as you set up your shot. You know that the golf swing is a circle and that the middle of the feet is the bottom of the arc. Therefore the higher you peg up, the further forward the ball should be positioned from the centre of your feet. If you tee up the ball on a high peg in the centre of the feet, the driver would sweep under the ball, making it fly off the top of the clubhead.

To use the driver your feet should be at their widest in the stance, the insides of your feet being as wide as your shoulders. As the numbers of the woods increase, so the stance on the tee narrows slightly.

The ideal spot to position the ball for the drive is to tee it up just inside the left foot. This will mean your head is slightly behind the ball. Half the ball should be above the club-face as it sits square on the ground behind it. As you swing into the ball this position allows your body weight to come through, achieving maximum power through your hands, arms and turning shoulders. The ball should then be smack in the middle of the club-face. Keep your head still. Do not let it drift in front of the ball, or that circle swing will loop you into trouble.

Once you have decided to take your driver, you should be totally committed to that shot. Take care to take a full body-turn away from the ball so that you may come back into the ball with a confident, smooth swing and the power to send it out on its way towards the target. And so watch that head. Keep it behind the ball.

LEFT The driver should be positioned just inside the left foot. The feet are a shoulder-width apart.

BELOW The ball is opposite the inside of the left foot and the clubhead is square to the target line.

THE DRIVE

1 The correct alignment of head, feet, club-face and hands during the drive: look for the target line.

2 The address: note that the hands should be just opposite the ball. CENTRE 3 You will find that the tee itself is a confidence booster. You do not have to worry about the lie of the ball or about your clubhead digging into the ground.

TEMPO

For a full-blooded shot like the drive, the tempo of the shot is important. For the backswing you should take the clubhead back slowly, brushing the ground, until it naturally lifts. The arc builds up and the wrists break at waist-height. Then you make the downward sweep into, and through, the ball.

No high-tech meter can measure and programme your individual tempo. Mature club golfers carry their own built-in ideas to regulate the tempo of their swing in the full shots. Until practice boosts your confidence a mental trick or two might be useful. Some players seeking self confidence softly hum the opening bars of the main musical theme of the Blue Danube waltz to themselves as they form the swing arc and follow through. It seems to have the right tempo. If it works for you: keep humming. A good drive, after all, is music to your ears.

4 Your left side becomes firm while your right leg and right side bend as you come up onto the toes of your right foot.

5 The club comes to rest almost diagonally across your shoulders.

SHOT SAVER

A tip I learned years ago came from a veteran Scottish professional golfer, who was asked how to improve the tempo of those big hits off the tee. His dour reply was 'Alexander Cadogan'. I've forgotten who that professional was, but I pass on his tip. Just think of that name as you take the clubhead back slowly ... 'Alexander' ... and down the clubhead swoops through the circle of the arc and out again ... 'Cadogan' ..., the ball being struck on the middle syllable. The rhythm of the syllables is so similar to the different pace of the backswing and follow-through.

Off The Fairway

You won't be on the fairway for all of your golfing life: this section will help you to understand the causes of wayward shots and what to do when faced with an awkward lie.

Golf shots fly off-line for many reasons. The fault may be in your own hands, your stance, your head position, swing, aim or balance. To identify typical faults you must first understand the concepts of target line and swing line. The target line runs from the ball to the target. That is the line which you take when lining up your shot. The swing line is the actual line taken by the clubhead as it goes from the backswing down into the ball and through to your finish.

If the clubhead goes back and then through on the same line, then it is in plane. If, however, from the top of the backswing you are in an upright position and at the finish of the shot you are in a flat position then you will have swung out of plane, on an out-to-in swing line. The opposite occurs when your hands at the top of the backswing are in a flat position and at the finish of the follow-through have moved into an upright position – then you have swung from in-to-out.

CAUSES OF BAD SHOTS

The causes of bad shots are easiest explained in terms of table tennis. In this game slices and spins are exaggerated and intentional, and the effects easier to see than in golf.

THE SLICE

The slice is a shot where the ball sets off to the left of the target line (still in terms of right-handed players) and swerves in the air to finish right off the target line. The ball has the same flight as the back-spin shot in table tennis. To play this shot the table tennis bat is held open to the target line and the swing line is from out-to-in and the bat cuts across the target line under the ball. The ball swerves from left to right.

THE SWING PATH

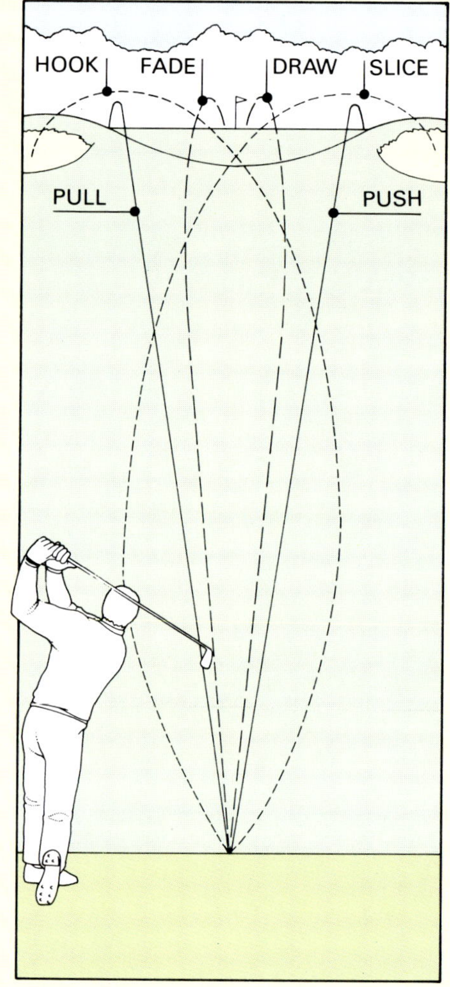

The golfing terms for the direction of shot.

THE SLICE

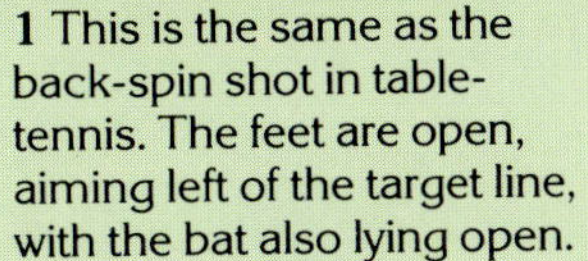
1 This is the same as the back-spin shot in table-tennis. The feet are open, aiming left of the target line, with the bat also lying open.

2 The hands are in an open position at the top of the backswing.

3 To reach the top of the follow-through, the table-tennis bat cuts across the target line, putting back-spin on the ball.

THE PULL

The pull shot goes straight to the left of your intended target line without any swerve. In table-tennis the bat takes an out-to-in swing, coming across the target line, but with the face of the bat square to the actual swing line. The ball would miss the table on the left.

THE PUSH

The push shot sends the golf ball straight to the right of the target line. Its equivalent table tennis shot also flies straight and misses the table on the right. It is effected by an in-to-out swing path with the bat face square to the swing line.

THE HOOK

The flight of a hooked ball starts to the right of the target line and swings in the air to finish left of the target line. In table tennis, its nearest equivalent is the smash, which has an in-to-out swing with the bat face closed to the target line, putting top spin on the ball.

1 The hook is closest to the table-tennis smash. The feet are closed to the target line (pointing to the right).

THE HOOK

2 At the top of the backswing, the bat is on the inside of the target line.

3 To reach the top of the follow-through, the bat travels from the inside, at the top of the backswing, to the outside at the top of the follow-through. The table tennis bat turns over, closing the face as it strikes the ball, putting top-spin or over-spin on the ball. The flight of the ball is from right to left.

COMMON FAULTS

You must analyze your own game to find any faults with your aim, grip, stance, the position of the ball or your swing to discover the cause of any of your own wayward shots. Listed below are some ideas to help diagnose the possible cause of the trouble.

You might ***slice*** shots because:

- In your aim the club blade is open to the target.
- Your grip is too weak.
- Your feet or body are lined up left of the target in the stance.
- In your swing, you open the club-face at the start of the backswing.
- Your wrists cup at the top of the backswing, which also causes an open face.
- You are starting the downswing with the right shoulder coming out towards the ball, causing an out-to-in swing.

TOP At the top of the backswing, the back of the left hand and wrist must be level. This ensures that the clubhead is square to the plane.

FAR LEFT If your grip is too weak, the club-face will open on impact, causing the ball to slice.

ABOVE AND LEFT If the wrists are cupped at the top of the backswing, the club-face will be open.

You might ***pull*** shots because:

- In your aim, the club-face is pointing left of the target.
- In your stance and position in relation to the ball, your body alignment is forcing you to the left and the ball is too far forward.
- In the swing you are not transferring your weight properly in the follow-through, but continuing to support your body weight on your right foot.

You might ***push*** shots because:

- In your aim, the club-face is pointing right of the target.
- In your stance and ball position, the body alignment is forcing you to the right, with the ball too far back from the centre line between your feet.
- In your swing, your body weight is being transferred too early onto your left leg.

You might ***hook*** shots because:

- In your aim, the blade of the club is closed to the target.
- Your grip is too strong.
- In the stance and ball position your feet and body are facing to the right of the target.
- In your swing you are closing the club-face at the start of the backswing.
- Your wrists are bowed at the top of the backswing, which closes the club-face

TOP If you pull your shots consistently to the left, it could be that your clubhead is pointing to the left of the target at the address position.

CENTRE LEFT Make sure that your wrists are not bowed at the top of the backswing, which will tend to make you hook.

CENTRE If you push your shots consistently to the right, your club-face may be pointing to the right of the target.

FAR LEFT Make sure that your grip is not too strong: this will also make you hook the ball.

LEFT If you close the club-face at the start of the swing, you will hook.

AWKWARD LIES

You will be straying soon enough off the straight and narrow fairways of golf. Do not be too disheartened to find yourself with awkward lies. You may have graduated from pitch and putt courses on which the crisp shots and the soaring golf ball gave you an enhanced view of your ability. You may have come from the driving ranges where you found life and power in your hands, which must now be applied in a wholly different situation. Some of the world's top golf courses are designed in undulating countryside which the course architect wished to preserve, as a challenge to your skills and a pleasant sight to your eyes. He aimed to bring out the best in you. It is up to you now to bring out the best aim for him.

When in an awkward lie, do not be too bold, and watch where you position your weight. These cautions should come into your mind when you find your ball in two of the most awkward of lies: an uphill or a downhill lie.

ADJUSTMENT FOR THE DOWNHILL LIE

1 The loft of a club is decreased from an eight to a seven or six, depending on the steepness of the slope.

2 The ball should be towards the back foot. Your weight is is in front of the ball. From this position it is easier to ensure that you strike the ball first and not hit the ground behind the ball.

1

2

3

3 Restrict body movement by taking only a short backswing, keeping the weight in front of the ball.

4 Don't try for too much length. Ensure that you keep your balance.

DOWNHILL

You look at the target line with the ground flowing away from you in the downhill lie and you feel that on a flat fairway you might need an 8-iron, say, to pitch the ball onto the green. But you are striking down into the ball because of the slope. Depending on the degree of slope, that position is going to tighten up the loft of the club, giving it the action of a 7-iron or perhaps a 6-iron. It is the same as hooding the club-face over the ball, closing the face, and thus reducing the loft.

Assume a stance where the ball is well back towards the right foot so that you swing directly into it. Take care not to hit the ground first. If you hit the ball first and it goes up and away you will put slice spin on it, like the back spin chopshot in table tennis. The ball will go left and come back to the right. If the lie of the ball allows you to reach for a straighter-faced, less lofted, club, because the target is more than a long pitch away, aim further left. The slice spin should bring it round, if your swing matches your chosen club.

When taking aim, grip the club a little lower than normal – it's called going down the shaft. It will give you more control for this awkward shot. Keep your hands forward of the ball.

You must feel comfortable for this shot, confident that you will not lose your balance as you swing the clubhead through the ball. Flex your knees – the right one will be bent inwards a little to balance your weight on the slope. Begin with a short backswing. Take the club back with your arms, not your shoulders, on a line suggested by the slope of the ground. Keeping your head still will bring confidence that you will not lose your balance as you strike downwards and through the ball.

ADJUSTMENT FOR THE UPHILL LIE

1 The angle of the clubhead is increased. A seven-iron will become an eight- or even a nine-iron, depending on the steepness of the slope.

2 The ball should be in front of the centre line, enabling you to swing through, with the slope, to achieve maximum lift.

The length of the backswing should be determined by the angle of the slope. You must not swing so far back as to lose your balance.

UPHILL

The slope increases the loft of the club so that a 7-iron played on an upward slope will carry the ball the shorter distance of an 8-iron or, on a steeper slope, a 9-iron.

You are swinging into a ball on an uphill slope. This will have the effect of increasing the loft on the club-face. This makes you think twice about club selection. It is not enough to choose a club which will suit the distance. It has to carry enough loft to lift the ball clear of the slope.

Boldness is not your friend when you are facing a ball with your left leg and foot higher than the right. The ball must be struck on the upswing. This will cause it to have a hook spin, so allow for this built-in movement in the flight by aiming off a little to the right.

Facing a steep slope, you will need height to clear it. You will be tempted towards a stronger club to achieve distance. Do not be too greedy: you may catch the slope and lose distance. Watch out, too, for that natural tendency to move your body weight into the slope on the downswing. This troublemaker means your downswing will lose its arc and will come in too steeply, 'de-lofting' the clubface to lower the trajectory of the ball, which will fly into the slope.

Here is how to play the shot. Stand behind the ball and picture the flight. Seek the target line. Remember the ball will move slightly to the left. Do not be tempted to be too bold. Take aim. Grip the club lower down than normal to give you a little more control. Take your stance with the ball positioned more towards the left foot than the right. Your posture will depend on the steepness of the slope, your left knee bending more than your right, so that your body angle is as near as possible to 90° to the slope. Keep your weight on your right leg so you may sweep through the ball when making the strike. Keep the backswing short to a maximum of a three-quarter swing. Swing through the ball, with a follow-through high enough to ensure that you do not lose your balance.

ABOVE THE FEET – FLAT SWING

1 Take a more upright stance at an angle of 90° to the slope. From this position the swing plane will be flatter than normal.

2 The swing should be within your balance limits. The longer the swing, the greater the likelihood of loss of balance.

3 In the follow-through, keep your head still a little longer than usual.

ABOVE THE FEET

Another tricky situation is playing the ball when it is above your feet, on a slope going upwards from left to right. Balance is always the keystone when building a stance for awkward lies.

Flex your knees so that you have your weight solidly over your feet and can feel that it is not going to slip onto your heels. Once again, go down the shaft a little with your grip to gain more control and allow you to stand closer to the ball. Assume a more than normally upright stance at an angle of 90° to the slope. Take the ball from a spot nearer to the left foot than the right, to help a smooth action through it, when you strike.

The swing must be within your balance limits: the longer the swing, the more likely it is that you will sway away from the ball. The stance will give you a flatter swing plane and, coupled with the fact that the toe of the club will be slightly off the ground, the club-face will close slightly. This gives the bail draw – moving right to left in flight.

Your stance allows you to take a confident swing because there is no restriction on the body turn. With a maximum three-quarter back-swing, concentrate on sweeping the club through the ball to a good high finish.

BELOW THE FEET – UPRIGHT SWING

1 To anchor your balance at the address, your weight should be on your heels. Stick your bottom out more than usual as you flex your knees. From this position the swing plane will be more upright than normal.

2 From this position, the hips will not be able to move, so concentrate on generating power from the shoulder turn.

3 As with shots from all awkward lies, the head should be kept still a little longer than usual to prevent loss of balance.

BELOW THE FEET

When the ball is below the feet, that is on a slope rising from right to left, it presents the most awkward of the four lies discussed here. The amount of slope will determine the distance that you stand from the ball.

To anchor your balance, keep your weight back on your heels as you address the ball. Stick your bottom out a little more than usual as you flex your knees. You can feel immediately that this position will restrict the amount of shoulder and body turn in the swing and will encourage a steeper than normal swing plane.

Your balance is threatened in this shot. You have no shoulder turn to help your swing. You must leave that to your arms and hands. Spread your feet to provide the best chance of balancing confidently.

Aim down to the left of the target. This will help you to keep the clubhead square. Take your stance so that the ball lies in the middle of your feet, and grip the club at the top end of the grip, as you need to use as much of the shaft as you can.

Let your arms and hands control the swing without affecting your balance.

Bunker Shots

Although the word bunker is said to be a Scottish term for receptacle, do not look upon it as being the trash can of your game. While average golfers curse their luck when the little white ball kicks off-line down the fairway and pops into a bunker, most tournament professionals shrug their shoulders. To them, the ball is in a position for an attacking shot.

Bunkers *can* be fearsome, like the infamous 'Hell Bunker' guarding the 14th green on St Andrews Old Course, or 'Hell's Half-acre' the biggest bunker in the world, at the 7th at Pine Valley, New Jersey; or they can be shallow traps laid well down the fairway to catch the wayward tiger-line drivers. Not only are they all shapes and sizes, but the sand within them sometimes differs even around the same course.

To discover what you have to beat, you need to be in the bunker getting the feel through your feet. But before you ever go into a sand bunker at all, there are two rules that you must always remember. The first is that you may only ground the club in striking the shot. If you touch the sand while in the address position or in the course of the backswing you will be penalized. When addressing the ball therefore, make sure that your clubhead is clear of the sand. It is better to hold it three inches (75 mm) above the ball at the address position than 1⁄16 inch (1.5 mm) too low.

The second thing to remember is that when you have played your shot out of the bunker, always rake the sand flat, both where you have played the shot and where you have made foot marks walking in to play the shot. However, this carries no penalty, unless a golf club committee has made a local rule.

One other thing worth mentioning is that when you are taking your stance in a bunker to address the ball, you are allowed to twist your feet into the sand. This will give you a good solid base from which to start your swing, and it will give you an idea of the depth and texture of the sand in the bunker.

The club for bunker play is, not unnaturally, the sand wedge, which is designed with three outstanding features: it is the heaviest club, which helps when striking down and into the sand; it has the greatest loft of all golf clubs to help lift the sand and ball up and away; and it has a flange which will level off the clubhead as it travels under the ball.

TOP AND ABOVE Imagine there is a circle around the ball which is the white of a fried egg; the ball itself is the yolk. When taking the shot, strike the sand behind the ball, sending the sand and the ball onto the green.

Bunker Shot Stance

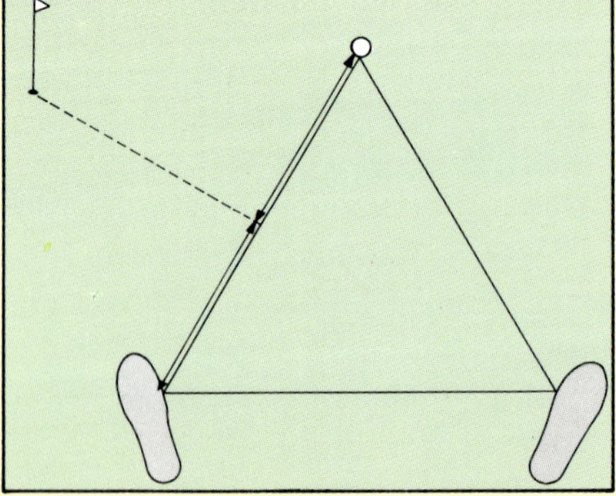

For the standard bunker shot, visualize a line from the flag bisecting the triangle of feet and ball.

LEFT When addressing the ball for a sand shot, make sure the club is well clear of the sand.

LEFT It is a penalty for the clubhead to touch the sand, except when it actually strikes at the ball.

LEFT You are allowed to twist your feet into the sand to give you a solid base from which to start your swing. It also gives you an idea of the depth and texture of the sand.

1

2

3

5

6

7

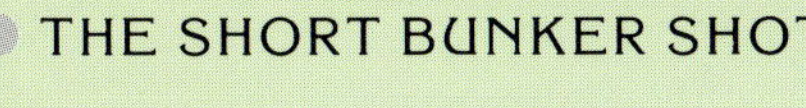

THE SHORT BUNKER SHOT

1 Remember that a trap shot can be an attacking shot.

2 Even in a bunker, stand behind the ball and always look for the target line.

3 Always point to the left of the target with both feet and shoulders.

4 The wrist must break early in the swing.

5 The length of backswing will be determined by the length of the shot.

6 Strike the sand behind the ball.

7 Make sure you follow through to control the flight of the ball.

THE SUNNY-SIDE UP SHOT

When you see your ball roll or pitch into a sand trap, do not let your hopes fade. For you could be facing a 'sunny-side up' shot. Look at the ball lying in the bunker and imagine it is a fried egg lying there sunny-side up. The ball is the yolk and the sand circle around it the white. Take your sand wedge and note the big flange on it. You have to use this to take that fried egg out of the sand, white and yolk together.

Line up your feet and your shoulders, pointing slightly left of the target – an out-to-in plane. When you come through the shot, as you must, the flanged clubhead will cut nicely under the fried egg, exploding it onto the green. The strength of the shot and the amount of sand you take will determine its length.

THE SHORT BUNKER SHOT: FRONT VIEW

1 The ball is not too badly plugged and has not landed on a slope, two of the worst things that can happen in the bunker.

2 The swing is upright to ensure lift.

STRIKING THE BALL (RULE 14)

If you are caught in the bunker, you cannot use your club like a spoon: remember that the ball must be 'fairly struck at'. (For the truly devious among you, note that rule 13–3 forbids the building of a neat sand platform for your feet, which could help when you play from a slope!)

3 Because you want to get maximum lift, you should hit slightly across the ball, rather than straight through it. The ball is forward and the line of the feet and shoulders aims off to the left.

4 Try to keep the swing at an even pace throughout, to avoid misdirecting the ball.

THE EXPLOSION SHOT

To explode out of the sand, lay your clubhead open with the bottom of the blade square to the target. This will force your hands to be forward of the ball. Aim your feet left of the target and open to the target line, with your shoulders pointing in the same direction. Shuffle your feet into the sand. This will put them slightly below the ball and help you in taking some sand with the shot. This stance should allow the ball to be well forward. Take the hands down the club grip just a little. The swing should be long and slow, rather than a short, quick swing. Swing the club back smoothly, breaking the wrists almost straight away to the top of the backswing. Then bring the clubhead down and across the line striking the sand two inches (50 mm) behind the ball to send the sand and the ball onto the green. *The clubhead does not hit the ball.* It is the force of it striking down into the sand behind the ball which propels the ball upward onto the green.

TOP RIGHT When playing up the slope from a bunker you cannot use the sunny-side up shot without adjustment, because there is no cushion of sand behind the ball. Try to compensate for this by leaning with the slope as far as possible so that, in effect, you are playing from flat sand.

TOP FAR RIGHT You are permitted to settle your feet into the sand; this will give you a firmer base and some feel for the sand's consistency.

RIGHT When the ball is plugged, take up a square stance and hit through the sand with the clubhead square to the ball.

FAR RIGHT If you are in a fairway bunker and therefore want to gain distance with the shot, it is better to stand on the surface of the sand to avoid giving the ball excessive loft.

THE LONG BUNKER SHOT

Bunkers are placed as hazards around the course, not only to guard the green, but to make approach shots more challenging. You will need to know how to play the long shot out of one of these bunkers, where the object is to get the greatest distance.

The club you need must be able to achieve the maximum distance but must also be able to lift the ball clear of the bunker wall. Long bunkers, sometimes laid to trap the long hitter, have low walls so you may be safe playing a mid iron or even a longer iron. Do not gamble by taking a club which has to be perfectly struck to be safe. Play the percentage game. Remember that with this shot, if you hit the sand before the ball, you will lose many yards. Think of a clean hit.

In taking up your stance do not shuffle the feet deep into the sand to make a deep base. This will set you too low and lessen your chance of clearing the lip of the bunker cleanly. Just twist the soles of your shoes into the sand to get a firm base from which to swing. Take a stance so that the ball is positioned towards the front foot, your knees bent only slightly to keep the swing above the ground. Look at the top of the ball rather than behind it. This will further help you to achieve a clean hit. Employ a full follow-through.

GAINING DISTANCE FROM THE BUNKER

1 The disciplines involved in this shot are no different from any other shot you play. Stand behind the ball looking towards the target. Find the target line.

2 Address the ball, making sure that the clubhead does not touch the sand.

3 and **4** Stand more upright than usual, looking at the top of the ball.

5 and **6** Don't over-swing, as this will cause a swaying movement.

7 For the long sand shot, a high follow-through will help ensure a good, clean hit and achieve maximum distance.

ABOVE The rough at La Manga golf club is not severe; courses in a dry climate do not have the long summer grass found off many European fairways.

OPPOSITE If you are unlucky enough to land in a divot, use a club with more loft and take up a stance with the ball well back toward the inside of the right shoe. This will help you to achieve a more effective chopping action, driving the clubhead down and through the ball.

FROM THE ROUGH

When you find yourself in the rough, the only plan you should have in your mind is to get out. Be satisfied to find a line which will get you back on the fairway. Do not be too ambitious.

Your normal, smooth, free swing can spell danger. The clubhead arc will shave the ground at the start of the backswing, at the bottom of the downswing and at the beginning of the follow-through. If the rough is thick, it will tangle the clubhead causing problems with the shot. You must visualize an action which will strike into the back of the ball, without getting the clubhead caught up in the grass. You must strike down into the ball on a steeper arc than normal. Select a lofted club. This will help to get more flight.

If the rough is slight, take the ball in the middle of a slightly open stance. The thicker the rough gets, the further back from the ball your stance should be.

Grip the club down the shaft a little for more control, but do not attempt a full swing. A three-quarter swing will be sufficient – even a half swing might be best for the job. And don't worry about the follow-through – just let it happen. Indeed sometimes you might not be able to follow through at all because of the lie.

The important thing is to concentrate on bringing the clubhead into the ball at an angle. The angle will be determined by the lie and the thickness of the grass around the ball.

ESCAPING FROM THE ROUGH

1 (INSET) Line up the shot, looking for the all-important target line.

2 When addressing the ball, make sure you do not press your club down behind the ball as this could improve the lie and thus incur penalty shots.

3 Stand with your weight slightly in front of the ball, enabling you to strike downward, which ensures that the ball is struck before the ground.

4 Take a backswing which will not unbalance you.

5 Strike through the ball, keeping your head still to ensure a solid contact.

LOW SHOT – STRONGER CLUB

1 You will often be faced with hitting a low shot, either under the wind or under some trees.

2 Look towards the pin, find the target line.

3 Select a club to achieve the required distance without using your full swing. The harder you hit the ball the higher it will fly. A stronger club than necessary, with an easier swing, will result in a lower trajectory.

4 Do not unbend at the waist as you go through the ball and don't follow through too far.

LOW SHOTS

Many times in your rounds of golf you will want to play a low shot. Perhaps overhanging branches of a tree are impeding your path to the green.

Remember that the harder you hit the ball, the higher it will fly. With this in mind, when you have pictured the shot and worked out your club selection, take at least one club stronger, or better still two clubs stronger, than you need. The more club you have to spare, the easier your swing can be, while still achieving the required distance. You will therefore keep the ball lower.

You will need to keep your weight slightly in front of the ball throughout the shot. Gripping down the club will help to give you a shorter, more compact swing. The tendency when playing from this forward position is to close the club-face, so aim a little to the right of target. Position yourself further back from the ball in your stance than you normally would for the club selected. Then swing nice and slow, keeping the swing short and easy, not letting your weight move behind the ball.

HIGH SHOTS

If you can play high shots confidently, you can make nonsense of the planned hazards of bunkers and the natural hazards of trees which suddenly get in your way. You soar over them.

The rough guide lines for this shot are naturally the opposite of those for the low shot. The harder you hit the ball, the higher it flies. You throttled back the fullness of your swing for the low shot, now you open it up again for the high shot. The swing is full and firm, and the club is one which is going to make the ball clear the hazard. Fix it into your mind that you are going to do just that: clear the hazard.

Stand behind the ball and line up where you intend to fly and land the ball. Forget eating up extra distance. You are seeking take-off, flight and happy landings in this short-haul shot. With the shot picture in your mind select the club with sufficient loft for the planned flight. Take aim. Position the ball nearer to your front foot than you normally would with that particular club. When making your swing, make sure that the full loft of the club is square to the ball and your body weight, although moving onto your left foot, stays behind the ball.

The common error in making this shot is over-enthusiasm. Too much strength is put into the swing in an attempt to smash the ball out and over trouble, causing the body to lunge forward. This sway de-lofts the club, cancels out the specially designed asset, the angle of its club-face, and causes loss of height, resulting in too early a touchdown.

AVOIDING TROUBLE WITH THE HIGH SHOT

1 You will need to hit the ball high on occasion, to clear trees or overhanging branches.

2 When standing behind the ball and looking for the target line, think height! Select a club to clear the trees easily and don't gamble.

3 Address the ball in a forward stance, keeping your weight behind the ball.

4 Don't take too big a backswing; as with all shots, balance is the important factor.

5 When hitting through the ball, make sure your weight is behind the ball to guarantee a positive strike.

TOP Always smooth over the sand after playing out of a bunker; a rake is sometimes provided for the more 'popular' bunkers!

ABOVE If you are playing alone out on the course, remember that you must give way to matches of any kind coming through.

RIGHT Take care not to remove divots when taking practice swings, even in the rough. Do not take practice swings on the tee.

The enjoyment of golf depends on the conduct of players and the courtesies they extend to each other. One of the most voiced criticisms you will hear in the locker room concerns slow play. The time it takes to play a round seems to be increasing. Another criticism is aimed at golfers who do not replace divots or rake bunkers after use. At all times you must show consideration for other players.

PRIORITY ON THE COURSE

In the interests of all, players should play without delay. On the other hand, no player should play until the players in front are out of range.

Players searching for a ball should signal the players behind them to come through, as soon as it becomes apparent that the ball will not easily be found. They should not search for five minutes before doing so. Having signalled others through, they should not continue to play until the players following them have passed and are out of range.

When a hole has been completed, players should immediately leave the putting green.

BEHAVIOUR DURING PLAY

No one should move or talk, or stand close to or directly behind the ball or the hole, when a player is addressing the ball or making a stroke.

On the tee, the player who is first off should be allowed to play before his opponent or fellow competitor tees his ball.

In the absence of special rules, two-ball matches should have precedence over, and be entitled to pass, any three-ball or four-ball match. A single player has no standing and should give way to a match of any kind.

Any match playing a whole round is entitled to pass a match playing a shorter round.

If a match fails to keep its place on the course and loses more than one clear hole on the players in front, it should allow the match following to come through.

Before leaving a bunker, a player should carefully fill up and smooth over all the holes and footprints made by him.

Through the green, a player should ensure that any turf cut or displaced by him is replaced at once and pressed down, and that any damage to the putting green made by the ball is carefully repaired.

Damage to the putting green caused by golf shoe spikes should be repaired on the completion of the hole.

Players should ensure that, when putting down bags, or the flagstick, no damage is done to the putting green, and neither they nor their caddies damage the hole by standing close to it in handling the flagstick or in removing the ball from the hole. The flagstick should be properly replaced in the hole before the players leave the putting green.

In taking practice swings, players should avoid causing damage to the course, particularly the tees, by removing divots.

Local notices regulating the movement of golf carts should be strictly observed.

TOP Never stand in front of, or directly behind, the player taking the shot. It is not just the responsibility of the player to avoid accident, but of the onlookers as well.

CENTRE RIGHT At most golf clubs you will not often be so lucky as to have the course to yourself. Do not dawdle on the tee.

RIGHT The green is the most vulnerable part of the course. Leave all clubs, bags and trolleys off the edge of the putting surface.

The Golf Courses

AUGUSTA

When the course at Killarney, Ireland, became the passion of Viscount Castlerosse towards the end of his life, he hired a skilled horticulturist to design him the perfect plant scheme so that the course would be in bloom every day of the year. The plans were produced but never put into practice, owing to Castlerosse's death early in World War II. What Castlerosse had in mind was Augusta – the world's best known golf course – in the spring at Masters time.

Castlerosse was an early admirer of the course. It was to be many more years before Augusta, particularly the last nine holes, became familiar worldwide. This came with the arrival of television in the mid-1950s, only a short time after the Masters had become recognized as a major title (it is not a championship of anywhere or anything). Some say that this recognition came immediately after World War II; others that the 1954 play-off between the two greatest players of the day, Sam Snead and Ben Hogan, was what brought it about. Whatever the truth of the matter, the players had long regarded the tournament as well above all the rest on the US Tour except for the two championships. With the passing of the years, the Masters title has become as desirable as those of the British and US Opens.

The Augusta course was originally Fruitland Nurseries, founded in 1857 by Baron Louis Berckmans. Bobby Jones, after he had won the Open and Amateur Championships of both the United States and Great Britain in 1930, wanted to be involved in creating a championship course in the American South. In 1929, over on the West Coast to play the US Amateur at Pebble Beach, he had also played Cypress Point and been highly impressed. The architect there had been Dr Alister Mackenzie. A couple of years later, a civic leader in Augusta, Georgia, wanted to promote the town to encourage visitors, and he is said to have suggested that the nursery might make a golf course. Clifford Roberts, later to mastermind the Masters for over 40 years, saw the property and later took Jones along. Both felt it had superb possibilities, and the combination of Mackenzie and Jones was at work by 1931. Jones did not think of himself as the designer in any sense but he did hit hundreds

AUGUSTA NATIONAL GOLF CLUB
AUGUSTA, GEORGIA
UNITED STATES

RIGHT Augusta's magnificent clubhouse is of comparable age to the Royal and Ancient Golf Club's home at St Andrews, Scotland. It dates from before the Civil War.

ABOVE FAR RIGHT A practice day scene at the Masters. These competitors are on the 18th tee.

of shots to help decide where tees, greens and bunkers should be sited to test the best players, and no doubt he also expressed many opinions to Mackenzie.

The course they arrived at is still close to unique in being a frightener for very good players yet a course where handicap players who know their limitations may well score better than on their home course. Bunkering, for example, is not severe. There were not many more than 20 on the original course, and that number has only doubled over the 50 years since then. Those flanking fairways were a threat only to long hitters out beyond 200 yards (180 m). Water hazards, too, were more in play for those trying to reach par 5s in two than modest players expecting to pitch on – except, many may say, the par-3 16th, much less menacing to handicap players in the original design of the hole than it is now. Then there is the rough – or, more accurately, the lack of it: if you cannot find your ball at Augusta you just didn't see where it went!

In short, although the course allows – even helps – moderate players to enjoy themselves, it is one of the great tests of the best players. Why? In part it is due to the extreme pace and contouring of the greens. The shot in to the green must be well placed to give a birdie chance, and it is usually desperately difficult to get a long approach putt close to the hole. The course also favours long hitters who can carry the rises of

ABOVE Tom Watson waits to play as Gary Player stoops to retrieve the ball.

RIGHT Although Jack Nicklaus will never rank as one of the great bunker players, he certainly learned to be good enough. He has now been the Masters champion on a record six occasions.

ground at some holes, who fly the ball high, and who draw the ball. Trevino hates the course, yet Nicklaus, who has almost always tried to play moving the ball left to right, just like Trevino, has performed brilliantly here, winning a record six Masters. To play Augusta superbly, you need to drive long and high, have perfect touch for long putts and chips, and be very resolute in holing the short but missable putts.

The first hole Jones and Mackenzie 'found' at Augusta was, apparently, what is now the 13th. Most course designers see a few holes they think would be superb and then try to make the rest fit in. The 13th is a very short par 5 indeed, at just 465 yards (425 m) (under British regulations it would be a par 4). Ideally, you draw the ball from the tee around the angle, menaced by an innocent-seeming creek, and with your second carry that same creek as it curls in front of the green. If that really was the first hole 'discovered' then the discovery was a great one, a hole that rewards two well played shots with a certain birdie but is an easy par for a competent handicap player – or a disaster if you find the creek with your tee shot or close to the green.

Originally, this hole was the 4th, because what is now the testing championship stretch to the finish constituted the first nine holes. Then it was realized how much drama was included in the first nine, mainly as a result of the fact that four shots to the green have to be played over water.

Nevertheless there is nothing too wrong with what are today Augusta's first nine. Here Seve Ballesteros made one of the great bursts of major golf on 19 April 1983 – with a start of birdie, eagle, par, birdie – which thrust him to the front of the field in the final round. Generally speaking, the first half of the course yields fewer clear-cut birdie opportunities, but fewer titles are lost here.

The second nine begins with one of the sternest holes at Augusta. If the 13th is a very short par 5, the 10th makes up for this by being possibly the longest par 4 in the world – 485 yards (443 m). However, there is plenty of run for the tee shot if the player keeps left along the fairway, which is also the shortest line to the green. Although Jones and Mackenzie are rightly credited with the design of the course, this hole was much improved before World War II when architect Perry Maxwell moved the green from low ground to its present elevated position. The 11th was improved at the same time, and at some 450 yards (410 m) needs a long second shot – perilous as the flag is set well left with water hard by that side of the green.

The 12th, a par 3 of 155 yards (142 m), provokes perhaps more doubt in the player's mind than any other hole of the course. Rae's Creek runs across the front of the green, which has little depth to it. If you play safe with a long shot you risk landing in the bunkers at the rear of the green, with a dangerous shot back in the direction of the creek. The water's threat is greatest to the tee shot when the flag is set well right, which lengthens the carry so that the player has little more than a 10-yard (9-m) margin between success and disaster. Tom Kite lost the 1984 Masters when he took 6 on this hole while Ben Crenshaw went on to win after a 2. Kite later commented that choice of club is a matter of total guesswork on this hole, because of the winds that swirl above the trees behind the green.

The par 5s are often the key to a low round at Augusta. As we have seen, if the tee shot is drawn around the angle at the 13th, prospects of being on in two are excellent, but Rae's Creek is still a threat, both in front of the green and then swerving around the right-hand side. Jones called it 'one of the finest holes for competitive play I have seen'.

The next par 5, the 15th, is some 50 yards (46 m) longer, but the tee shot looks very inviting. Even so, line is important, the right-centre giving more run and a better line to the green. A really big drive may leave you with something like a 4-iron shot in to the green. If you overclub, or if you shut the face a little (as Larry Mize did in the 1987 Masters), it is easy to run through the green and on to the pond on the 16th. Best of all, then, is to hole your second shot, as Gene Sarazen did in the 1935 Masters – which enabled him to tie with Craig Wood and then go on to win the play-off the next day.

The dramas are not over! The 16th, a medium length par 3, has water all the way from in front of the tee to the green and even then along the green's left-hand side. Nevertheless, the hole has certainly been kind to Jack Nicklaus. It was the key to his winning the 1975 Masters, when he holed a vast putt for a 2, and in 1986 he played a spectacular tee shot that might easily have been a hole in one.

The finish is not quite up to the standard of what has gone before – yet it should not be underestimated. A Masters player who is a stroke in the lead at this point thinks he needs merely to par both the closing par 4s to wrap up the title. Yet neither is by any means easy, the 17th being the hole most open to criticism on the course because the second shot is semi-blind even after a good tee shot. The 18th has seen many dramas over the years, and a shot towards the rear of the long green when the pin is set more to the front very often leads to three putts; Ben Hogan lost the 1946 Masters this way. By contrast, Gary Player holed a very good down-hiller in 1978 and later emerged the champion.

Augusta may be neither the most beautiful nor the best course in the world, but there is no obvious candidate that one could prefer to it. Its condition may be unparalleled in part because it is so little played. There are few members, most of whom live far away, and even a Masters champion cannot invite a friend or two along for a game. With even tickets to watch the Masters virtually unobtainable, you can imagine how difficult it is for a golfer to have a chance to play the course!

ABOVE Although many fairways are tree-lined at Augusta, amazing recoveries are possible since players can often find a way through the trees instead of having to chip out sideways.

THE AUSTRALIAN GOLF CLUB
KENSINGTON, SYDNEY
NEW SOUTH WALES
AUSTRALIA

RIGHT A fish-eye lens captures some of the feeling of tournament play at The Australian, Sydney. Note the vast bunkers and the threat of water.

THE AUSTRALIAN

As with the United States, England and numerous other countries, it was Scots or people of Scottish descent who brought golf to Australia. Credit is sometimes given to James Graham from Fife, Scotland. He began organizing a little golf in Melbourne in the late 1840s, while John Dunsmore played in Sydney a few years later. However, Alex Reid introduced the game down south in Tasmania during the 1830s, and was in at the foundation of Australia's oldest club, Bothwell, which claims 1830 as its birth date.

The Australian can certainly claim to have been there at the beginning of the explosion of golf popularity in the country. As in England and the United States – and even, for that matter, Scotland – this was at the end of the 1880s. The club was founded in 1882, but lost its course a few years later. The present course dates from 1902, but has been much altered over the years. Dr Alister Mackenzie did some work in the late 1920s, while Jack Nicklaus designed new holes in 1977. Besides setting bunkers in the drive area at most holes, Nicklaus greatly increased the influence of water hazards on the course. Nicklaus has the distinction of having won the Australian Open on the previous lay-out in 1975 and 1976 and again in 1978 after the changes had been made. This was the last of his six

Australian Open victories.

The course was first used for the Australian Open in 1920 and, as the best tournament course in the Sydney area, has been the venue for it many times since. It is an excellent choice because there are many vantage points from which spectators can look down on the action, while for the performers themselves the course is one of the most testing in the country. The hazards are well placed to take account of the modern ball and equipment. At over 7,100 yards (6,490 m) it is certainly long enough!

The first few holes do not demand great length for the shot to the green, but thereafter the long par 4s dominate the course, some being unreachable if you are playing into anything more than a breeze. The finish is as it should be, the most demanding and challenging section of the Australian.

Many people find the three holes immediately prior to the last the most challenging. The 15th is just over 200 yards (183 m), with the green almost an island surrounded by sand. The 16th causes considerable irritation: many shots which find the green at this 400-yard (365-m) hole bound through – only a superbly struck shot will hold.

The 17th, measuring about 430 yards (390 m), may be the most difficult on the course. The long second shot has to carry water – often into the wind. However, the last hole, a par 5, offers a do-or-die chance of being up in two but has an expanse of water in wait to the right of the green for those who fail.

ABOVE A view of the 4th hole. When Jack Nicklaus made his design changes in 1977, he brought water much more into play.

LEFT Norman von Nida was the best Australian golfer for several years following World War II. A very straight hitter, he was also superb from sand – and much more variable on the greens. Von Nida was always ready to help and advise a succession of talented young Australians, including Greg Norman.

BALLYBUNION OLD

BALLYBUNION GOLF CLUB
COUNTY KERRY
IRELAND

That a course is used for major championships does not necessarily mean that it is one of the great ones. Ballybunion, on the Shannon Estuary in the west of Ireland, is remote from large population centres. As a result, no great championship is ever likely to come here, but the two courses are still among the world's greatest. Between them they provide perhaps the best 36 holes of true links golf in the world. If you could play a game on the best 18 holes of the 36, there is no doubt at all that you would be playing the best links course anywhere – every hole demanding, yet all of them fair.

Today, Ballybunion Old ranks, at worst, among the world's top 20 courses. Little more than 20 years ago it was known to only the locals and the well informed. Herbert Warren Wind was perhaps the man initially responsible for changing all this. He came to Ballybunion in the 1960s and went away saying: 'Very simply, Ballybunion revealed itself to be nothing less than the finest seaside course I have ever seen.' He wrote at length about it in the United States, and the news slowly spread. Since then, Tom Watson has preached the Ballybunion gospel: 'A man would think the game of golf began here.' Watson, at times a severe critic of present-day architects, also wrote: 'Ballybunion is a course on which many golf architects should live and play before they build golf courses.' Watson liked the wild contours and the relative absence of blind shots on such a primeval course. He appreciated the way that at Ballybunion iron shots must find not only the green but the *right area* of the green if they are not to squirt away sideways. Also he liked the fact that short or slightly long shots are less severely punished than those that miss to right or left.

The start of the Old is not severe, a par 4 of less than 400 yards (365 m) partly alongside a road and a graveyard. The first few holes are fairly flat and uninteresting except the 2nd, which is just about the most testing of the entire course. The drive is uphill, and then the second shot must fly between two humps and carry to a green on the top of a ridge. The 4th and 5th, when they were the 17th and 18th, used to make people shake their heads. They are flat and uninspiring and, before the new clubhouse was built in the 1970s so that the order of playing the holes changed, made for a dull finish to the course. They are much more acceptable holes now they are positioned early on.

After the 5th, the real Ballybunion begins. The 6th, with its narrow green right by the sea, demands a very precise iron shot in and, into the wind, plays far longer than its 360 yards (330 m). The 7th, well over 400 yards (365 m), plays all along the sea cliff, with no hope for the slicer. There follows one of Ballybunion's strengths, a really great par 3. From a tee that backs onto the ocean the flag is only 150 yards (135 m) or so away, but it has been claimed that even Tom Watson could find no shot in his armoury which would hold the green. The ground falls away rapidly to either side, and so you might do better to finish in sand.

RIGHT Nearing home at the end of the day, the 17th green is a superb golf hole and the real climax of the round.

FAR RIGHT Many shots to the short 8th find sand and the recovery shot can easily overrun the green into yet more trouble.

BELOW RIGHT The 5th green used to end a round at Ballybunion before the routing of the course was changed. The village is a popular holiday destination.

The 11th is one of the most inspiring holes. In the tee shot, a mound on the left is very much in play, and a slice will put the ball onto the beach. The 12th is a very difficult par 3. It may have only one little bunker at the back-right of the green, and thus seldom in play, but that green is up in the sandhills with severe slopes at either side, and the shot is usually into the prevailing wind. The 13th, a kindly par 5, comes next. The tee shot is downhill and, as the hole is only a little over 480 yards (440 m) in length, there should be no difficulty getting home in three. A long second to the green, however, faces a small target, a stream if you drop short, and a sandhill that prevents an approach from the left. The par 5s are sometimes said to be the weakness of the course – there are four of them, and only one is more than 500 yards (457 m) – but in fact this used to be thought just about the right length for such a hole.

A short par 3, uphill, follows and then another – an unorthodox sequence of three par 3s in four holes. The last of them, the 15th, is a great hole. About 200 yards (180 m) in length, with humps and bunkers crowding the putting area and a large mound in front of the two-tiered green to the left, you can be supremely satisfied if you find the green. The 16th and 17th both have sharp doglegs to the left, played between the dunes with the drive at the 17th being played from a high tee. The last hole is not so fine. Good players have to drive short of a vast bunker some 250 yards (230 m) away and then play a blind pitch to the narrow green.

After the 18 holes of the Old the golfer can retreat to the clubhouse or embark on a journey among the even wilder dunes of Robert Trent Jones's New course. This one can be just too difficult for moderate players a little off their game, the shots to the green sometimes leaving little margin between success and catastrophe.

BALTUSROL GOLF CLUB
SPRINGFIELD
NEW JERSEY
UNITED STATES

ABOVE The present courses at Baltusrol were constructed after World War I. Ed Furgol plays the winning putt for the US Open title in 1954 – the first time the championship was held on the Lower course.

Baltusrol Lower Course

Baltusrol has two splendid courses lying at the bottom of one of the Watchung Mountains. It takes its name from a certain Dutch farmer, Baltus Roll, who was bludgeoned to death by two thieves who believed that he kept all his cash in the house.

That was in 1831. In 1895, a nine-hole course was created and, by the time the United States entered World War I, two US Opens had been played here, won by Willie Anderson (1903) and Jerry Travers (1915). After that war, A.W. Tillinghast was called in to construct 36 holes. The Open returned in 1936 and was played on the Upper course. It was won in that year by a surprise champion, Tony Manero, who produced a final round of 67; his total of 282 broke the record aggregate which had stood since 1916. The same year saw the first Open appearance of Ben Hogan: he made no headlines, missing the 36-hole cut.

The US Open was first played on the Lower course in 1954. It was won by Ed Furgol, who had a withered left arm and gave the appearance of hitting with just his right side. In the trees on the final hole, Furgol managed to play out onto the Upper course; as this was not out of bounds, he was able to come through with a par 5. Another player, Dick Mayer, took 8 on the hole: a par would have made him the champion.

In 1967, it was at Baltusrol that Jack Nicklaus won his second US Open. His finish on the 543-yard (497-m) 18th was unusual. He hit off fairly poorly with an iron, played a pitching club short of the creek, and then hammered a magnificent 1-iron to within 6-7 yards (5.5-6.5 m) and holed the putt for an unconventional birdie and a course record 65. He had begun the day level with Arnold Palmer, who had faltered not one bit but whose 69 nevertheless left him four strokes behind Nicklaus.

The 1980 championship was another famous occasion. By this time, Jack Nicklaus's career was very much on the wane. Since 1975 he had won only a single major championship – the 1978 British Open – and in 1979 he had slumped to 71st on the US prize-money list.

TOP Looking back towards Baltusrol's clubhouse from the 4th green. (© TONY ROBERTS 1979)

LEFT The 1st at Baltusrol Lower is a 478-yard (437-m) par 5. (© TONY ROBERTS 1979)

ABOVE Jerry Travers won the second US Open held on the original 9-hole course at Baltusrol in 1915.

1980, despite many lessons on the short game from Phil Rodgers, had likewise not gone well for him. However, in good conditions for scoring and with fast but very holding greens, Nicklaus began with a round of 63, which equalled the lowest round ever shot in the US Open (by Johnny Miller in 1973). Amazingly, it did not give him the outright lead! Tom Weiskopf was already in with the same score. Weiskopf quickly faded away and Nicklaus certainly faltered, being caught by Isao Aoki after the third round, but he carried on both to win the Open and to beat the US Open scoring record with his 272.

Although Jack Nicklaus has twice set US Open scoring records over Baltusrol Lower, this does not mean that the course is easy; rather that it is fair. The greens are neither vast nor small and the contours are gentle. Fairways are relatively wide and bend only gently.

One of the most famous Baltusrol holes is the 4th, a par 3 of nearly 200 yards (180 m), almost all of which is carry over a lake to the green. The green is faced by a stone wall, so there is no chance of a shot that is 'nearly good enough' clambering onto the green. The hole was redesigned by Robert Trent Jones before the 1954 Open and was initially disliked by some of the club's members, who thought it too difficult. Jones went out for a round of golf and holed it in one. No further comment was really necessary!

The course has a great deal of variety; for example, the par 4s are anywhere up to near-maximum length, yet there are five under 400 yards (365 m). The last two holes, however, may between them set a distance record. Two par 5s, they total well over 1,100 yards (1,000 m), a long way to walk if you start off tiredly thinking there are just two holes left to play! The 17th is a monster, at 630 yards (576 m), and is said to be the longest hole ever used in the US Open. It is heavily bunkered, with a patchwork of sandtraps (nicknamed the 'Sahara Desert') at 375 yards (343 m) forming a barrier for some second shots. There is more of the same just short of the green. Nicklaus was ecstatic when he birdied the hole in his 1980 victory: he knew the championship was as good as in his pocket. The last hole is a much shorter par 5, but that statement is relative: it is still over 540 yards (495 m).

Banff

BANFF SPRINGS HOTEL
BANFF, ALBERTA
CANADA

This may not be a great championship test, but it is one of the great places to be, some 4,000 feet (1,220 m) up in the Rockies. The fact that it is too remote for tournament play is one of its strongest attractions.

The course was originally owned by the Canadian Pacific Railway. Nine holes were built before World War I, and more added during that war, German PoWs providing the labour. Several years later, when improvements in equipment made dramatic changes to the landscape more possible, Stanley Thompson redesigned Banff. There was much quarrying, blasting and removal of tree stumps; he also increased the bunkering. Today, there are about 150 bunkers, at least 25 of these being on the 18th!

There is no doubt at all which is the most famous hole on the course. This is the 8th, also known as 'The Devil's Cauldron'; it is one of the most scenic in the world. It is a par 3 of 175

RIGHT The vast Banff Springs Hotel, itself dominated by its spectacular setting in the Rocky Mountains, looms above the 9th green. (© TONY ROBERTS 1979)

BELOW Another view of the hotel, with the clubhouse and 1st tee in the foreground.

BELOW FAR RIGHT An aerial view of the 1st (left), 18th (right) and the 2nd (left foreground). The 17th green can also be seen (right foreground).

yards (160 m), played from a high tee to a green set close up to the fringe of a pine forest, with the Rockies rearing up behind. But those are not all of the spectacular features of the hole. Between the tee and the dropping shot to the green lies an expanse of water. The hole plays relatively short and so it looks more testing than it actually is; even so, poorer golfers can find themselves running out of golf balls.

The start of the course requires a tee shot over the Spray River; no great carry is needed. It is the Bow River which is the main feature of the course. It provides a threat to the right of holes 12 to 18, with Thompson's bunkering being often heavy along the left. The 14th is a very demanding par 3 of more than 200 yards (180 m). The tee shot is over water, with the ground in the landing area sloping towards this pond. Perhaps the most interesting hole, however, is the 7th, a par 5 of just over 500 yards (460 m) which can in the thin mountain air be reached in two – but it is a perilous task, with the precipitous slopes of Mount Rundle to the right, bunkers along the left, and a sharp dogleg leading to the green.

The Country Club

THE COUNTRY CLUB
BROOKLINE, BOSTON
MASSACHUSETTS
UNITED STATES

The very name sounds arrogant, but this was the first club of the type in the United States (1860), so the choice was natural. Golf did not arrive until about 1890, however, when the club's committee made provision in the annual budget for $50 to be spent on the preparation of a nine-hole course. Four years later, The Country Club was one of the five founder members of the United States Golf Association. By 1909, golf had caught on in the Boston area to the extent that a further nine holes were added. By then the annual match against Royal Montreal Golf Club had become almost a part of The Country Club's traditions; this match, first held in 1898, was the earliest international golf match.

The Country Club's greatest fame dates, however, from 1913. Only two US Opens have been held on the course, but the 1913 Open was one of the greatest and was also, in its way, an international match. It almost saw the emergence of Walter Hagen, who came in fourth. Ahead of him, tied for first place were Henry Vardon and Ted Ray, of England, and Francis de Sales Ouimet of the United States. Vardon had won the 1900 US Open and the British Open five times (he was to win it a sixth time in 1914). Ted Ray had won the 1912 British Open. Ouimet, by contrast, was a 20-year-old US amateur who in four attempts had only once qualified to play the US Amateur event and who was having great difficulty at the time in breaking the 90 barrier. He entered the competition solely because the Open was being played at his home town!

After three rounds, Ouimet was level with Vardon and Ray, but then apparently threw his chances away with 43 to the turn quickly followed by a 5 on the 10th (then a par 3). Yet he managed to play the last six holes in two under par to tie. No one thought it mattered much. He had had a very good day and deserved full credit.

BELOW Vast bunkers threaten the narrow entrance to this Brookline green. (© LEONARD KAMSLER 1987)

LEFT One of the most elegant clubhouses in the United States, the old mansion house has been much extended since the Country Club was founded in 1860. (© LEONARD KAMSLER 1987)

BELOW The protagonists in the greatest upset in the history of golf – Harry Vardon (left), Francis Ouimet (middle) and Ted Ray. Here they are pictured on the morning of the 18-hole play-off for the 1913 US Open.

But the general attitude was: who would win the 18-hole play-off, Vardon or Ray?

Each of the three took 38 strokes for the first nine, but at the 10th Ouimet took the lead. He finally made the championship his with a birdie 3 on the 17th, where Vardon took 5. The final scores make it look even easier for Ouimet: he was round in 72, to Vardon's 77 and Ray's 78. Although Ouimet was not the first US-born winner (that was Johnny McDermott in 1911), he was the first to beat Vardon and his is still the outstanding rags-to-riches story in terms of a major golfing championship. His victory greatly increased interest in golf in the United States, especially on the sports pages, where golf had tended to be treated as a pastime of the rich rather than as a popular sport.

The US Open returned to The Country Club in 1963 to commemorate the 50th anniversary of Ouimet's feat. During Ouimet's victory, the course had been waterlogged, and for Julius Boros's second Open win (he had previously won in 1952) the weather was just as bad – perhaps not as wet, but colder. His 293 is by 3 strokes the highest winning score in the US Open since World War II, mostly because of the conditions rather than any innate difficulty of the course.

Brookline, at first view, looks like a mere parkland walk, the 18 holes used for the Open being made up of a selection from the club's 27. The start, however, is stiff: between a couple of long par 4s is a 190-yard (175-m) par 3. The other six of the first nine present less of a challenge, although the 500-yard (460-m) 9th offers the chance of playing short of a stony rise or going for the carry.

Thereafter, the course retains its parkland character, but it is much narrower. The 10th, 11th and 12th are all long 4s; the 12th is especially so, almost par-5 distance, with the long second shot inevitably finding a greenside bunker unless it is perfectly judged in terms of both strength and direction. The last three holes are strangely short for a championship course, a par 3 needing no more than a medium iron followed by two drive-and-pitch holes to complete the round. However, as we saw, Vardon foundered on the 17th in 1913, and he has been far from alone. In the 1963 Open Jackie Cupit would have won outright had he been able to complete the last two holes two over par: he took 6 and Arnold Palmer 5, to tie with Julius Boros. (Tony Lema, who had been in contention, like Palmer took 5.) Boros, who had single-putted the 17th, went on to win the play-off the following day. Clearly any hole which can so dramatically affect the result of major championships is not as innocuous as it looks!

Cypress Point

Although undeniably one of the world's very greatest courses, Cypress Point is under 6,500 yards (5,950 m) long. With Merion, which is of a similar length, it constitutes one of the best arguments in golf that a course does not have to be 7,000 yards (6,400 m) long to be fit to host a championship. In fact, Cypress Point is much more of a test than most of the 'monsters'.

It does have two weaknesses. Everyone agrees that the last hole is little more than a shortcut back to the clubhouse, a drive-and-pitch hole with usually only the top of the flag in view for the second shot. The 16th is more controversial, and is probably the most photographed hole in golf. It is 233 yards (213 m) long and requires a drive with a carry of about 210 yards (190 m) to cross a Pacific inlet to the green, which is set on a headland. The irony is that Dr Alister Mackenzie, who designed the course in the 1920s, is thought to have planned the hole quite differently: he made it as a par 4, with the tee set further back and needing a drive of only moderate carry. The second shot was to be from the area of fairway that modern players who cannot hope to make the 210-yard (190-m) carry play for. As it is today, however, the 16th demands just about the most heroic shot in the game – but is it golf? Even so, there have been holes in one here – Bing Crosby was the second to do it.

The holes either side of the 16th are more strategic. The 15th does need a direct carry over a rocky inlet to the green but, since the distance is only 130 yards (120 m) or so, the bunkers that follow the inlet are more of a threat. The 17th, at 375 yards (343 m), is a magnificent par 4. The drive is from a high tee up in the cliffs, with the Pacific on the right. The golfer has to decide exactly which angle to attempt as the cliffs bite in.

These are the holes providing the highest drama, set at the very tip of the Monterey Peninsula, but all of Cypress Point gives the player very good golf. The 1st is played down to a valley curving to the right, and at 420 yards (384 m) is a severe enough start. The 2nd, nearly 550 yards (500 m) in length, is the longest hole on the course and has a demanding tee shot requiring a diagonal carry. There are trees along the right and dunes to the left, and the green is

CYPRESS POINT
GOLF CLUB
PEBBLE BEACH
CALIFORNIA
UNITED STATES

RIGHT AND FAR RIGHT The most photographed hole in golf is the 16th (far right) at Cypress Point with its frightening carry over the sea. There is less to fear at the 15th (right), which is also a par 3 and scenically every bit as spectacular.

heavily bunkered.

After the 2nd the course heads for a wooded hillside, the setting of the 5th through to the 11th. The 7th is a par 3 of 160 yards (146 m) played from one hill to another over a valley, and the 9th shows that even a downhill par 4 of just 290 yards (265 m) can be difficult; its small hard green can be very tricky to hold.

The 5th and 10th greens are at the farthest points of the course. At the 11th tee the golfer heads back towards the rocky peninsula, with the 13th and 14th being seaside holes before the clifftops are reached.

Cypress Point is manifestly a course of championship standard: it is one of the best in the world. However, no championships have been held on it, although Bing Crosby moved his tournament to the peninsula from Rancho Santa Fe after World War II. Since then Pebble Beach and Cypress Point have been used for the tournament each year – as, since 1966, has Spyglass Hill.

Ironically for such a highly respected course, Cypress Hill breaks a few of the 'rules' of golf-course design. It has two par 5s in a row (the 5th and 6th), and indeed all four of the par 5s come between the 2nd and 10th. Similarly, two par 3s (the 15th and 16th) are back to back. No one, however, complains of anything at Cypress Point – except the 18th, and that may partly be simply a product of the contrast with the glories just experienced.

Many superlatives have been used about the course. One reverential comment was that Cypress Point is the Sistine Chapel of golf; while a newspaperman once said that it was the dream of 'an artist who had been drinking gin and sobering up on absinthe'. It is unlikely that there is a better-looking course in the world.

Durban

Carved out of bush and through sand dunes in the early 1920s, this is South Africa's finest course and plays host to most major events held in Natal. The original architect was Laurie Waters, in 1920. His course has remained basically little changed although many later architects, including S. V. Hotchkin from Woodhall Spa, England, and Bob Grimsdell, late in the 1950s, have had a hand in it. By that time, the main aim was to cope with the modern ball and increase the course's length to nearly 6,600 yards (6,035 m). Even so, this distance is still a little short by modern standards, mainly because the par 3s are reasonable in length and there are a number of drive-and-pitch par 4s.

Durban is a popular venue for the South African Open. Indeed, it was thanks to this event that the course was created in the first place: the Royal Durban course became hopelessly waterlogged during the 1919 national championship, and it was felt that the city needed a more reliable alternative. Since that time, many Open Championships have been held here. Among the Durban champions have been Bobby Locke, Gary Player, Bob Charles and Bobby Cole (in 1980 doing something to justify his earlier promise). Gary Player won his first Open here in 1956 and over 20 years later overhauled Bobby Locke's record when he won his 10th championship.

Another famous achievement on the course belongs to the Duke of Windsor (Edward VIII). When, as Prince of Wales, this keen golfer played the 12th, a shortish par 3 of under 150 yards (137 m), he needed no fewer than 17 strokes to hole out; the green is raised and the future king went down a bank to the right, returning only after some little while! Among the course's four par 3s, however, the 180-yard (165 m) 2nd normally gives more trouble. It is played from a high tee to a raised green, surrounded by bunkers and scrub, with a valley in between.

The 3rd is the most famous hole on the course. This again has an elevated tee shot down into a valley. The ground then rises to the green, humpy all the way with scrub and trees on either side. Only just over 500 yards (460 m) long, the 3rd offers the prospect of getting home in two – but both shots must be long and placed with absolute precision.

The majority of the middle holes of the course are played on flat land, but the finish is among dunes and close to the Indian Ocean. The 16th, a little under 400 yards (365 m) in length, plays long because there is a climb to the green which is set up among the dunes. The 17th has as tumbling a fairway as you could find. The 18th, only 276 yards (252 m) long, seems superficially hardly a testing finishing hole. It is indeed drivable, but the ground falls away steeply to the right and there are bushes along the left. The temptation of going for the green with a big drive causes many golfers to come unstuck. However, the 1928 South African champion, Jock Brews, finished in style: he drove the green, holed the putt, and won by a stroke.

DURBAN COUNTRY CLUB
DURBAN, NATAL
SOUTH AFRICA

ABOVE Bobby Locke won nine South African Open Championships, a record surpassed by only Gary Player.

LEFT The approach to the 18th green with the clubhouse in the background.

FAR LEFT TOP An aerial view of the Durban Country Club complex with the 18th green to the right of the clubhouse.

FAR LEFT BOTTOM This panoramic view reveals the humps and hollows of the course which was carved out of sand dunes and bush. The 1st, 2nd, 17th and 18th holes and the 16th green, surrounded by three bunkers, are on view.

GLENEAGLES KING'S COURSE

GLENEAGLES HOTEL
AUCHTERARDER
PERTHSHIRE
SCOTLAND

When James Braid was asked before World War I to design two courses for Gleneagles, his brief was a testing one. Building courses of stunning difficulty presents its fair share of construction problems, but Braid was required to produce golf courses that holiday-makers would find enjoyable. He designed the King's Course (18 holes) and the Queen's (only nine holes at first). In the years since then Gleneagles has grown to become a golf complex with four courses, the King's, Queen's, Prince's and Glendevon. Of these, the King's supplies the sternest test, mainly because it is easily the longest. The Queen's is the most beautiful of the four. All, however, benefit from their exquisite natural surroundings: the Ochil Hills, the Grampian Mountains and the Trossachs, all seen from a moorland setting some 500 feet (150 m) above sea-level.

The 1st hole of the King's offers an inviting start, a par 4 of 360 yards (330 m) with a wide fairway, the ground rising to the green, which is on the skyline. Although the line in to the green is barred by a cross bunker, this should cause little difficulty as most golfers will have only a pitch to play from the fairway. However, the green itself causes problems with its back-to-front slope. This presents more difficulties to players of professional standard than to ordinary club players: the professionals find their shots can spin back and off the green. At over 400 yards (335 m), the 2nd might seem more of a challenge, but it is played downhill and the only real difficulty is that the fairway is narrow with, as is usual at Gleneagles, gorse, bracken and heather on both flanks. The 3rd, uphill, needs an iron shot carrying all the way to the correct level of the two-tier green. Most people agree that the

BELOW The famous hotel at Gleneagles, completed in the early 1920s.

LEFT On a clear day the views from the Gleneagles courses can be superb. Are they bettered anywhere in the world?

ABOVE Of the Great Triumvirate – Vardon, Braid and Taylor – only Braid went on to become a leading figure in golf course design. Here he is pictured near the beginning of this century after winning the first of his five British Opens in 1901.

5th is the best of the par 3s. It has a little of the appearance of an Iron Age fort, with the ground falling away all around; it is set with large deep bunkers.

The finish, however, betrays the fact that the course was never intended as a championship test. The 14th, although a par 4, is played as a par 3 by strong hitters, the main problem arising if the flag is set to the front of the green – the shot in can readily run to the back. The 15th is more formidable in length, at 460 yards (421m), but the second shot is downhill and so the hole does not play long. The 16th is quite a short par 3; but the 17th has the tightest tee shot on the course and is followed by an approach to a plateau green which you have to judge carefully. A par 5 at the finish of any course should always be relatively easy, and the 18th on the King's is welcoming indeed. 525 yards (480 m) in length, it is played from a high tee and the green is one of the biggest targets in golf. Tom Watson once had a measured drive of 486 yards (444 m) here, helped by the run of the ground and a following wind. Average club players will find an intervening rise more difficult to carry, but rich rewards follow.

Although the Gleneagles Hotel did not open until the mid-1920s, the King's Course was ready to play in 1919, and two years later the first match between the United States and a combined British and Irish team was played here, the US team being trounced. A professional tournament was played here in the 1930s, as well as the 1936 Curtis Cup, but the courses were mainly reserved for holiday golf, a facility of the vast luxury hotel.

In 1987, however, the Scottish Open was played at Gleneagles. There was some remarkable scoring. The Spanish golfer Jose-Maria Olazabal set a new course record over the 6,800 yards (6,218 m) of the King's Course, with a 62, and Ian Woosnam, in a dominating performance, opened up with a pair of 65s and was 20 under par when he won by 7 strokes. The weather created no problems and the greens were both holding and superbly true for putting, a recipe for low scoring, but even so the lengthened course proved that it would yield only to very good play. Many felt that Woosnam might well go on to win the British Open Championship the following week, so well was he striking the ball and putting. Instead, it went to another British player, Nick Faldo, who won from a likely future star, Paul Azinger.

HARBOUR TOWN
GOLF LINKS
HILTON HEAD ISLAND
SOUTH CAROLINA
UNITED STATES

HARBOUR TOWN

Pete Dye already had a reputation as a golf architect before he created Harbour Town, but this course made him a celebrity. There was almost instant exposure of his work, with Arnold Palmer winning the Heritage Classic here only a few weeks after the course opened, in 1969. The name of this US Tour event pays tribute to the United States' golfing past, which goes back at least as far as 1779 (and possibly over a century earlier). The South Carolina Golf Club, the first in the United States, was founded in Charleston in 1786. This great antiquity of the game in South Carolina is paralleled by Dye's interest in traditional golf achitecture, which manifests itself in a liking for undulations in the ground, liberal bunkering and the use of heavy timber shoring for bunkers and greens. At Harbour Town, however, Dye was hardly able to indulge his liking for undulations: the highest point of the course is no more than a few feet above the lowest. The main hazards are water features, which have a profound effect on most of the holes. Although there are no great unavoidable carries to be made on the longer holes, the par 3s tend to be frighteners. The first of these is the 4th, about 180 yards (165 m) long, where the green pushes out into the water on one side and is shorn up by timbers. The 7th is a little shorter, under 170 yards (155 m); although there is again a water carry, the main hazard comes immediately afterward: a large sandy area. The 14th, at 150 yards (137 m), is carry all the way, and also has a creek circling the green to the right. And the last of the par 3s, the 190-yard (174-m) 17th, is highly unusual. Although a creek runs all along the left of the green, it is separated from the green itself by a long bunker, with a retaining wall of timber. The position of the tee was changed here early on because tournament professionals protested that they could not hold the green.

The 17th is followed by the most severe hole on the course, a par 4 of near maximum length. Two big shots are needed to clear the encroaching tidal salt marsh of Calibogue Sound, the drive being to what is in effect an island fairway. Played this way, the hole is virtually dead straight, but the power of shot needed is beyond the capacity of most golfers. The alternative is to play right of the marshes. This approach puts

the green out of reach in 2, but renders the hole a relatively easy 5.

As well as the water, trees provide a major hazard on a course which is generally pleasant rather than frightening to play. Aside from those carries to the par 3s, water is used mostly as a feature to the sides of greens and fairways. Trees serve to define and narrow the landing area for tee shots. The course, at less than 6,700 yards (6,125 m), is short for a modern tournament course. Although the professionals have produced some very low scores during the Heritage, it is recognized that only the very best are ever likely to win here. Yet there are several par 4s of only drive-and-pitch distance. The 9th, at only just over 320 yards (295 m), is the shortest of these and is indeed drivable for some – the only snag being the large bunker that blocks the line into the green. The 13th proves that a par 4 does not need to be long to be good: it is just over 350 yards (320 m), but the narrow fairway must be hit precisely, because the encroaching trees make the line in to the green – which is slightly elevated and surrounded by sand, except to the rear – extremely tight.

Although bunkers of often extravagant shapes are a notable sight at Harbour Town, there are only about 50 of them in all, and not a few are placed to define the target areas rather than to trap balls. This represents an intelligent approach to golf architecture, especially on flat land.

ABOVE A typically extravagant design feature of Harbour Town are the vast swathes of sand encircling the green. This is the 165-yard (150-m) 7th hole.

LEFT With the 9th green in the foreground, this scene epitomizes the period charm of South Carolina.

RIGHT There is more than golf at Harbour Town as can be seen in this view of the yacht basin and the 18th green.

INVERNESS

INVERNESS CLUB
TOLEDO, OHIO
UNITED STATES

RIGHT The clubhouse and 18th green during the 1986 PGA Championship.

FAR RIGHT The scoreboard tells the full story of Greg Norman's slump during the final round of the 1986 PGA Championship.

One reason for the fame of Inverness is the way that two of its holes have been played 'the wrong way' to great effect.

First came Ted Ray in the 1920 US Open, playing the 7th, which was then a doglegged par 4 of 334 yards (305 m) with trees and a deep pit at the angle. A prodigious hitter, perhaps, could carry the lot and finish on the green. Ted Ray, one of the most violent of men in his dealings with a golf ball, threw everything into the shot in all four rounds. Each time he was successful in making the carry of some 270 yards (250 m); each time he came out with a birdie 3. As he won the Open by just one stroke from a cluster of players – Harry Vardon, Jock Hutchison, Jack Burke and Leo Diegel – it could be claimed that his scoring on the 7th won the last US Open to go to a UK player until Tony Jacklin did it exactly 50 years later, in 1970.

The other hole to have been played 'the wrong way' is the 8th. Before the 1979 US Open at Inverness, architect George Fazio made four new holes. One that disappeared was the historic 7th, which was used as part of one of the new holes, the 8th, a par 5 of 528 yards (483 m). But Fazio slipped up: he failed to realize that players could drive through a gap in the trees onto the 17th fairway and so make the hole easier. After a few players had done this in the first round, the USGA planted a 25-foot (7.6-m) spruce tree overnight to close the gap. However, the tree was not tall enough, and some players continued to play up the 17th. Today the gap is filled by a generous clump of trees!

The Inverness Club was founded in 1903 and named for the castle in Scotland where in 1040 Macbeth had King Duncan murdered. Nine holes were planned for a start, but the first architect to work at Inverness had a problem with his arithmetic. As he stood back to admire his handiwork it was suddenly realized that there were in fact only eight holes. Very embarrassing! However, Bernard Nicholls hurriedly tacked on a par 3, which in the event proved to be a very good hole.

Other architects have been involved in the development of the course. A year before Ted Ray's Open triumph, Donald Ross designed a second nine; A W Tillinghast made revisions a few years later for the 1931 Open; and Dick Wilson did likewise for the 1957 Open. And then, as we have seen, came Fazio.

All Inverness's four US Opens to date have been remarkable in some way, sometimes with elements of the absurd. Take 1931, the first after the retirement of Bobby Jones. Billy Burke and George Von Elm tied. The play-off in those days was over 36 holes – but not that year. After the day's play they were still tied, so out they had to go the following morning to do it all again. Burke came through, but only by a single stroke after the 144 holes of golf, making the 1931 US Open the longest major championship of all time.

In 1957, Jimmy Demaret thought he had the championship in the bag, but then Dick Mayer

holed a birdie putt of nearly 20 feet (6 m) to edge ahead, in due course tying with Cary Middlecoff, who was able to birdie the same hole during his second 68 of the day, a remarkable finish. Middlecoff was one of the first of modern golf's really slow players, taking an age to align and set himself up for a shot. Mayer thought there was a point to be made. He took out a camping stool for the 18-hole play-off. Perhaps the success of the psychological ploy was more important than Mayer's comfort while he waited for Middlecoff to play his shots. The result was: Mayer 72, Middlecoff 79.

Hale Irwin, neither a very long hitter nor an outstanding putter, has often performed best on the more difficult courses. Difficult Inverness most certainly is. The greens are much smaller than average, and they are as subtly contoured and frighteningly fast as any. It is vital to place the tee shot perfectly to give a good line in and to land the shot to the green below the hole (with a downhill putt, the player has to think mainly about how he or she can stop the ball running well past the hole).

In the 1979 US Open Irwin managed this very well so that, with nine holes to play, he was a full 6 strokes ahead of anyone else in the field. Then he began to come apart. The problem was his tee shots: he hit a succession of them into the rough to the left or right, behind trees and into bunkers. He finished his round with a double bogey and a bogey. However, he had still managed to preserve enough of his lead to win by a couple of strokes.

ABOVE In the 1986 PGA Norman and Bob Tway went into the last hole level. Tway holed out for a 3 from a greenside bunker and was suddenly champion.

JAGORAWI

JAGORAWI GOLF AND COUNTRY CLUB
CIBINONG
INDONESIA

Approached by a 35-mile (56-km) dirt road from Jakarta, Jagorawi is a course that was cut through jungle; as a result, it has the 'feel' of being entirely divorced from the outside world. Each hole is almost a tropical garden in its own right, and great attention has been paid to detail: witness the stonework and timber revetment on some of the bunkers. Water comes strongly into play on half of the holes, sometimes as a barrier for the tee shots and elsewhere for shots to the greens.

Architect Ronald Fream had the aims of beauty and tranquillity, as well as the provision of a good test of golf. He learned his trade with Robert Trent Jones before working with the Thomson and Woolveridge partnership and then becoming independent.

There are five par 5s which challenge a brave line of shot. The 1st is a memorable hole, with a tee set high above the fairway and a carry to be made over the Cisadene River; as the hole is set in a U-bend of the river, water continues in play up either side of the narrowing fairway. The 9th, doglegging right, tempts longer hitters to cut across the angle, although a well placed bunker catches many.

The choice is much the same on the 15th, a banana-shaped hole where the golfer has the option of playing either for safety or for the glory of being home in two; because the paddy fields along the right were owned in penny packets, there were continuous delays in negotiating the sales to the club, and the architect eventually settled on the extreme left-to-right shape of the final design.

Besides the Cisadene River, there is a tributary stream that forms a hazard running through the middle of the course. Often the stream has to be carried for a shot through the green, while at other times it is in play for shots that stray to the left or right.

Jagorawi was opened towards the end of the 1970s and the tropical climate means that it already has a mature appearance. A second course, intended to be public, is at the planning stage. The great tournaments may never come to Jagorawi but, when dusk comes suddenly, this is one of the most beautiful places in the world for a golfer to be.

LEFT The course at Jagorawi was cut through the tropical jungle. Here is the 10th with the 11th green in the background.

MEDINAH NUMBER 3

MEDINAH COUNTRY CLUB, MEDINAH
ILLINOIS
UNITED STATES

One man more than any other has come to be reviled in the history of golf architecture – Tom Bendelow. He was a Scot who came to the United States to work as a printer for a New York newspaper and, by the mid-1890s, found himself working for Spaldings as a golf-course architect. How did this happen? We can only speculate, but it was probably because of Scotland's reputation as the home of golf: anyone from that country should be able to design a course in an afternoon! Which is precisely what Tom Bendelow often did. Arming himself with a bundle of stakes, he knocked one in for a tee. Then he walked forward a hundred yards or two and banged in the next stake to indicate that a cross bunker should be dug. After choosing the site for his green, he put in his fourth stake to mark it (the third stake was already in to show where a bunker should be dug or some humps built up short of the green). Tom then left instructions as to how the course should be built and maintained, took the cheque – usually $25 – and was on his way.

Actually, Tom was no worse than anyone else: that was the way golf architecture was in the United States in the 1890s – and it was little better in the UK. He improved with time, gave the subject far more thought, and in due course even lectured about it at the University of Illinois. He is still given credit for Medinah Number 3, which is absurd as he set it out as a course specifically designed for women and it has been totally transformed over the years since then.

Today, Medinah is a formidable course indeed. The whole complex was originally built for members of the Ancient Arabic Order of Nobles of the Mystic Shrine. Appropriately, the clubhouse is Moslem in inspiration, little expense being spared in its construction during the free-spending 1920s, when the club included also provision for skiing and polo.

The Medinah Number 3 course has been used for two US Opens, those of 1949 and 1975. They were won, respectively, by Cary Middlecoff, a qualified dentist turned golfer, and Lou Graham. Both matches turned on the last holes.

In 1949 the central characters in the drama were Middlecoff, the late great Clayton Heafner – the angriest man ever to play golf! – and Sam

RIGHT A view of the 17th (to the left) and 18th greens. The par-3 17th requires a carry over Lake Kadijah. (© TONY ROBERTS 1986)

Snead. Heafner dropped a shot on the 17th and missed a shortish putt on the last. Snead tried to run a putt through the fringe around the 17th instead of lofting his ball over, and failed. Both finished a stroke behind Middlecoff. With Ben Hogan not in the field, following his famous car smash, these were just about the best players in the field.

It was all rather different the next time the US Open came to Medinah, in 1975. This time, the two contenders at the end had somewhat less charisma. They were John Mahaffey and Lou Graham. They tied, with Mahaffey, unable to hole a putt, losing the 18-hole play-off – the last (to end 1987) required in the US Open. The 1975 championship, however, is probably more notable for the collapse of a future great player. After two rounds, Tom Watson was three strokes in the lead and his start of 67 and 68 had tied the

ABOVE The trees crowd around the 2nd green at Medinah No 3. A par-3 hole of 190 yards (175 m), it must be played over the main feature of the course, Lake Kadijah. (© TONY ROBERTS 1986)

US Open record. His finish of 78, 77 was dismal, to put it mildly, and gave rise to much talk about his lack of nerve. The following month, as an unknown in Great Britain, he confounded his critics by winning the Open Championship.

Medinah Number 3 can often feel a claustrophobic course, trees seeming to cramp you on almost all of the holes. Lake Kadijah is the main feature, although it is in play on at most three holes. The first occasion is at the 2nd, a par 3 of around 190 yards (175 m) played over the lake; the next tee shot is played over a finger of water but no carry from the tee is needed. By this time, golfers are well into heavily wooded country. Soon they come to the first of the three par 5s. This one, the 5th, is no 'monster' – at about 530 yards (485 m) – and provides a birdie opportunity for tournament players. The 7th, however, is brutal: close to 600 yards (550 m), and with a dogleg, it has a very heavily bunkered green.

The 13th, however, is the most difficult hole on the course. Over 450 yards (410 m) long, it doglegs sharply left around the woods. Only a precisely placed drive gives any real chance of getting home in two with anything other than a wood or a long iron.

But the hole that has decided championships is the 17th, a par 3 of around 220 yards (200 m) which starts off requiring a carry over Lake Kadijah, followed by one over a bank set with a deep bunker. The shot to the green requires absolute precision: there are no alternative routes. Here, in 1975, the young Ben Crenshaw, then heir-apparent to Jack Nicklaus, hit a 2-iron a little towards the toe of the club and took 5: he may never win the US Open which, because of Medinah's 17th, so narrowly slipped from his grasp way back at the beginning of his career.

MERION EAST

MERION GOLF CLUB
ARDMORE
PHILADELPHIA
PENNSYLVANIA
UNITED STATES

ABOVE Hugh Wilson was a complete amateur in golf architecture, but produced one of the United States' greatest courses at Merion.

The Merion club dates back to Civil War times, but one should not think that golf arrived here particularly early. Cricket was more the thing for Philadelphians at that time. They even sent touring sides to England during the 19th century: these proved to have some very fine players and gave promise that the United States could well become a leading cricketing nation; despite Philadelphia's John King topping the English first-class bowling averages in 1908, this dream was never to be realized.

Anyhow, Merion Cricket Club it was for many years, the adjective not being changed in favour of 'Golf' until 1942. By then, however, golf had long been established, and had been the main activity of the club since about 1900.

The first course, with nine holes, was opened in the mid-1890s, and a farther nine were added a few years later. In 1904 and 1909, the US Women's Championship was played over it. For men, however, the arrival of the rubber-core ball around the turn of the century was making virtually all courses too short. The members of Merion wanted a championship lay-out. They formed a committee to consider the matter and one member of it, Hugh Wilson, showed such a grasp of golf architecture that he was asked to do the job. Like Charles Blair Macdonald in the matter of the National Golf Links, he decided to make a pilgrimage to Britain. Beforehand, he asked Macdonald which courses were the best for him to inspect. He was away from the United States seven months, and he returned with many notes and drawings of what had impressed him.

The 127 acres (51 ha) he had to work with is near the minimum for a championship lay-out, and the land itself was hardly promising: thin layers of clay soil over rock. The ground was undulating (some might say bumpy) but it did have some natural features that he could put to good use – two brooks and a disused stone quarry. In fact, he put them to such good use that some people consider Merion East the finest course in the United States. Two of its holes, the 1st and the 11th, are listed in Dan Jenkins' book *The Best Eighteen Golf Holes in America*: no other course has more than one hole honoured.

In 1914, the US Amateur Championship came to Merion and saw the first major appearance of a man who was to have associations with the course throughout his career. That man was Robert Tyre Jones Jr, who arrived in 1914 as a 14-year-old who already had a local reputation down in his native Atlanta. Bobby Jones, playing on the West Course, also designed by Hugh Wilson, started off with a 74 – phenomenal scoring in those days. The spotlights were concentrated on him for the second qualifying round and he subsided to an 89, but this was still good enough for him to qualify and go on to beat a former amateur champion in the first round before going out to the defending champion, Bob Gardner, later.

In 1924, Jones won the first of his five US Amateur Championships at Merion and it was here that, six years later, he won his last: with this victory, he completed the almost impossible feat of winning the British and US Open and Amateur Championships in the same year (1930). That Merion win was his last: Jones felt he had done it all and retired, 13 major championships to his credit. No one has equalled his five US Amateur titles while, of current players, it took Jack Nicklaus until 1980 to match Jones's four US Open titles, a feat earlier accomplished only by Willie Anderson and Ben Hogan.

The US Open first came to Merion in 1934. Coming from eight strokes behind after 36 holes, there was a new champion, Olin Dutra. His total of 293 says something for the difficulty of the course. Sixteen years later, Ben Hogan tied for the championship with 287, one of the highest scores since World War II, and won the play-off. This was one of his most impressive victories because he had been left for dead in a car smash early in 1949 and had been out of golf for nearly a year. Even by the time of the 1950 Open in June, although most conceded that Hogan was the best man in the field, just as many doubted that his legs would carry him for the 36 holes of play on the final day. Hogan managed, although he nearly withdrew with cramp on the second nine of his last round; he then had to go another 18 holes the following day in the play-off.

By 1971, there was a new generation of

RIGHT, Walter Hagen, here pictured late in his career, was an ardent admirer of the course.

BELOW LEFT Bobby Jones retired shortly after winning his last major championship at Merion. This was the 1930 US Amateur which gave him the Grand Slam of the then four major titles – the US and British Amateur and Open Championships.

BELOW RIGHT In February 1949 Ben Hogan was terribly injured when his car was in collision with a bus. Surely he would never play golf again? Here he is winning the 1950 US Open at Merion.

golfers, and no one doubted that the two outstanding players were Lee Trevino and Jack Nicklaus. It was entirely fitting that they should tie for the title, which Trevino won in the play-off over 18 holes. Their 280 for 72 holes was even par.

In 1981, however, par was beaten, this time by five players, David Graham's total being 273. His last round 67, in which he hit nearly every fairway and all the greens in regulation figures, is reckoned the equal of any round of golf ever played.

The scores given here say something of the difficulties of Merion (Masters champion George Archer once declared that 95 per cent of the US Open field of 1971 were just not good enough to play it!). Yet it is no monster. Its length, 6,544 yards (5,984 m), is a good 300 yards (275 m) shorter than is otherwise used for any major championship, and almost the same comment applies to any tournament played on either the US or European Tours. Surely a winner ought to come home with an average of 66, but this has never seemed likely at Merion. Trevino, when he first saw the course, went out and played a few holes and thought that the key was to hit the tee shot into the fairway after which everything would be straightforward enough. A very short while later he was calling Merion the hardest course he had ever seen!

Trevino's judgement – that the best ploy was to make sure to hit the fairway – was right as far as it went: the rough is certainly punishing. But the real key is to find the right part of the fairway so that the shot to the green can be eased. For the same event, Jack Nicklaus planned to use his driver on only three holes; the rest of the time he felt position was far more important than length. The greens must be attacked from the right quarter. They are often small and well defended and, for championship play, they are hard and very, very fast.

Most architects make their 1st hole a gentle introduction. To the unwary this can at first seem to be the case at Merion. Only 355 yards (325 m) long, it is on the face of it certainly just a drive-and-pitch hole, although very well bunkered to either side of the fairway and with a green that slopes both from right to left and, more of a problem, front to rear. Later, there is a spell of four more short par 4s in the space of five holes.

One of these — the 10th — is only 312 yards (285 m) long, and so obviously the big hitters look to drive it. Twice in the 1971 Open Jack Nicklaus was not on in two. The 11th has seen much history. When Jones parred it in 1930 in the final he had won the US Amateur by 8 and 7 and completed his slam. Four years later, Gene Sarazen, leading the US Open, took 7 for

LEFT Although the 10th hole at Merion measures only 312 yards (285 m) it can be fatal to miss the small green as you could find an impossible lie in this bunker.

the hole and went on to lose the championship by a stroke. In the same event, Bobby Cruickshank hit a poor second shot which pitched into Cobb's Creek before the green. His ball struck a rock and bounded up into the air and onto the green. 'Thank you, Lord!' cried Bobby, tossing his club on high. A second or two later, it felled him. Cruickshank lost his championship lead – and his playing partner's concentration disappeared too as he collapsed in laughter.

At the finish, strong hitting is needed. At each of the last three holes the disused quarry is a feature. The 16th, about 430 yards (395 m), needs a second shot that carries all the way to the green; and the 17th, over 220 yards (200 m), easily the longest of Merion's four par 3s, is over the quarry to a green flanked by bunkers, with a swale reminiscent of the Valley of Sin at St Andrews' 18th. Merion's 18th, about 460 yards (420 m), needs 220 yards (200 m) of carry to reach the fairway, and the second shot is always a long iron. Needing a 4 to tie in 1951, Hogan hit a 1-iron to the green: that historic club was promptly stolen from his golf bag.

Perhaps Walter Hagen made the best summation of Merion. He thought it a fair course where you always believed you would break 70 . . . next time. Playing past his prime in 1934 Hagen started with a 76, then got a 69. Had he discovered the secret? Apparently not. He finished with 83 and 80.

ABOVE The clubhouse at Merion has seen the climaxes of many great championships.

MUIRFIELD

THE HONOURABLE
COMPANY OF
EDINBURGH GOLFERS
GULLANE
EAST LOTHIAN
SCOTLAND

Founded by 1774 and responsible in that same year for the first known code of golf rules, the Honourable Company of Edinburgh Golfers is the oldest golfing club or society with a continuous history. These men of Edinburgh first played over Leith Links, but in 1836 they moved to Musselburgh. Use of the course by other clubs led to the move to Muirfield in 1891, the Open Championship going with the club – much to the anger of the men of Musselburgh. Ironically, when the first Muirfield Open was held, in 1892, the course came in for much criticism. One St Andrews competitor called it 'a damned water meadow'. The great golf writer Bernard Darwin thought that it gave 'the impression of an inland park'. And five-times Open Champion J.H. Taylor later wrote that the course was not fit to be the home of such a great club.

Perhaps the main problem was that it was new. Who would think in modern times of playing a championship on a course laid out only a year before, as Muirfield had been (by old Tom Morris)? It was also, even for the days of the guttie ball, rather short: 5,500 yards (5,030 m). One aspect of the design was revolutionary. Almost all courses before Morris's scheme for Muirfield had had an out-and-back layout, but he produced what amounts to two loops of nine holes, an outer one and an inner one. Little remains of his original design today except that principle. It means that you do not find yourself playing half the course with the wind behind you and then have to force your way back through it. As you play Muirfield, the wind is never from the same direction for long.

Despite its shortcomings, Muirfield was firmly on the Open Championship rota – perhaps, in

BELOW A great par 3, the green at the 13th has some perilously deep bunkers guarding it. Just getting out of one bunker can be a triumph and the player can still find himself in yet another.

the beginning, mostly because it is a mere 15 miles (24 km) or so from Edinburgh. Harold Hilton won in 1892, the second amateur to do so after John Ball, two years before; Bobby Jones is the only other amateur to have won the championship (1930). Four years later saw the arrival of Harry Vardon as a champion, the course by this time considerably lengthened and three or four strokes harder. In 1901, James Braid won his first Open here, and as a memento named a son after the course – Harry Muirfield Braid.

There was a gap in Muirfield Open Championships after 1912, perhaps because the R & A felt the course was a little substandard. However, during the 1920s Muirfield was substantially redesigned to take its present form; the only changes since have concerned bunkering and a very few new tees.

In 1929, Walter Hagen won the last of his four Open titles at Muirfield, and in 1935 the little favoured Alf Perry triumphed. Next, in 1948, came the last of Henry Cotton's three championships, followed by the first of Gary Player's, in 1959. Player thought he had thrown it all away with a double-bogey 6 on the last hole, but he was in luck that day.

The Muirfield Open of 1966 has gone into legend. The rough was so high that Doug Sanders remarked that he would rather have the hay concession than the prize money! General comment was that the course had been set up to reduce the dominance of the power players. Even so, it was the most powerful of them all at that time, Jack Nicklaus, who came through to win his first Open Championship, leaving his driver in the bag most of the time.

In 1972 there came one of the most remarkable British Opens of modern times. Nicklaus, far behind, threw his normal caution to the winds and stormed in with a 65, a round which with a little good fortune might have been even better. Even so, with a couple of holes to play, it seemed that Tony Jacklin would be the winner. With Lee Trevino onto the rear fringe of the 17th in four strokes, Jacklin took four to hole out from only a little pitch short of the flag while Trevino holed his chip shot – one of several outrageous strokes he played during the event. Jacklin then bogeyed the last as well. Trevino won, with Nicklaus finishing second.

Eight years later, in 1980, there was a new world number one, Tom Watson, who gave perhaps the most dominant of his major-

ABOVE The clubhouse, the 18th green and the famous bunker with its island of turf. In the 1987 Open, Paul Azinger took 5 and Nick Faldo a par 4 at this hole. The championship title rested on this one stroke.

LEFT William Inglis, captain of the club between 1782 and 1784.

championship-winning performances. With a third round 64 he spreadeagled the field, and in his final round he gave nothing at all back, winning the event by 4 strokes – and, some thought, humiliating Muirfield in the process with his total of 271.

In the most recent Open Championship, 1987, the weather came to the aid of the course. Though Rodger Davis shot a 64 in the first round to lead by 3, neither Davis nor anyone else repeated that kind of scoring as the winds rose and the rains lashed down. Only seven finished under par for the championship this time, and the champion, Nick Faldo, was the only man not to be above par in any single round.

Although the US entry for the Open Championship has been at a high level since the mid-1960s, often a few of the year's best players do not come. They do, however, inevitably turn out at St Andrews, because of its aura of history, and at Muirfield. In the latter case, they have heard that it is by no means just some joke links course with a lot of bunkers in the 'wrong' places, and sometimes impossible stances when you have rasped a drive down the middle. This is perhaps the reason why Muirfield is now rated so highly: there is very little to dislike. From the tee the troubles ahead are usually plain to the eye. The fairways are not wildly undulating, and neither are the greens. The rough, though it may well look severe, is only really dense after wet, warm weather. Furthermore, to US eyes, it matches modern concepts of golf-course design by having scarcely a blind shot.

Only the depth of the bunkers is controversial. Some think that it should be possible to play a wooden club from a fairway bunker, if a golfer can strike with enough precision. At Muirfield, a sand iron sideways can be the only sensible choice. This, some say, reduces those capable of playing daring long shots from sand to the level of those content to wedge the ball out. The same argument can be put forward regarding the greenside bunkers. These are deep. At Muirfield, although the greens are usually holding enough, you do not see players walking into the sand and looking as if it is going to be a

RIGHT Old Tom Morris designed the original Muirfield layout at the beginning of the 1890s. It has been much changed since.

FAR RIGHT In 1896 Harry Vardon, kneeling, lines up a putt while J H Taylor waits during the play-off for the Open Championship. Two caddies and a marker stand by – but not one spectator!

RIGHT A painting by Harry Rountree shows the 4th and 14th greens as they were at the beginning of this century.

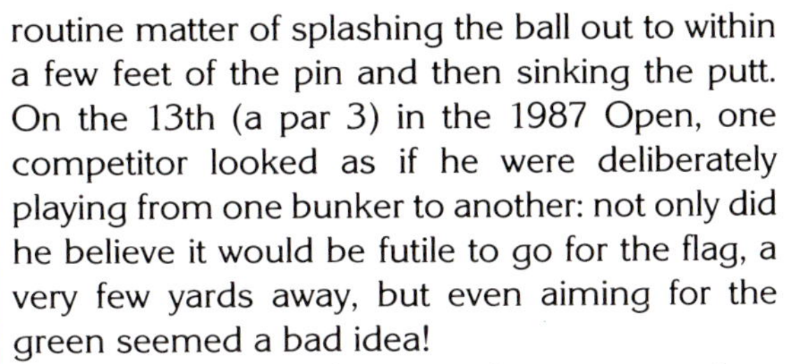

routine matter of splashing the ball out to within a few feet of the pin and then sinking the putt. On the 13th (a par 3) in the 1987 Open, one competitor looked as if he were deliberately playing from one bunker to another: not only did he believe it would be futile to go for the flag, a very few yards away, but even aiming for the green seemed a bad idea!

Muirfield is one of the very few courses, given modern sand irons and professional skills, where players in an Open Championship wonder not how close they can get to the hole but simply if they can get their ball back into play. In 1987, Bernhard Langer, a 3-1 bookmakers' chance after 36 holes, put his second shot into a cross bunker some 30 yards (27 m) short of the green on the 8th; by the time he reached the green he had played 5. His hopes were gone. The day before, Arnold Palmer had seemed to be making the 36-hole cut until he bunkered his second to the 14th and took an interminable 5 to get out.

Difficult holes are not necessarily great ones. Par is hard to get on the 1st, for example, at least partly because targets are not well defined and the hole is more than 440 yards (400 m) long. The par 3s, however, none of them long, are uniformly excellent, and the last six holes supply a test fit for a championship. Good straight shots are needed for the par-3 13th and 16th; the 14th is out of range in two when the wind is against; the 17th is reachable in two as a par 5 only with wind assistance. The 18th, about 450 yards (410 m) from the championship tees, is a hole that sets two challenges: keep out of the fairway bunkers or you will not find the green with your second shot; hit the green with your second or your recovery is not likely to be close to the flag.

MUIRFIELD VILLAGE
COUNTRY CLUB
DUBLIN, OHIO
UNITED STATES

BELOW The 9th green and fairway showing the stream so often in play on this splendid hole.

MUIRFIELD VILLAGE

Jack Nicklaus was very impressed with Scotland's Muirfield when he first played it during the 1959 Walker Cup. He liked its fairness and the fastidious revetment of the bunkers. He was hardly likely to alter his opinions when in 1966 he won the British Open on the same course! For these reasons he decided to name his home-town course for Muirfield. However, the design inspiration in fact came much more from the rolling terrain of Augusta National. Nicklaus wanted to produce an equivalent to Augusta, and this he did in woodlands a few miles outside Columbus.

Although Nicklaus's course was not ready for play until 1974, he was prepared for the next stage of his master plan. This was the Memorial Tournament, which began in 1976. There can be little doubt that Nicklaus aimed for his event to become a fifth major. This has yet to come about but, backed as it is by his immense prestige, the Memorial, which celebrates the achievements of great players of the past, is currently the most likely event to achieve the status of a major championship.

Constructed with no regard to expense, Muirfield Village has specially prepared vantage points for spectators. As at Augusta, water hazards are a great feature, as are the rewards for bold shot-making on the par 5s. Greens are small and tightly bunkered – one reason why it was not until 1983 that any player managed to break par in every round of the Memorial. Indeed, there had been protests early on from Tour players about the course's difficulty, and Nicklaus had shown himself willing to respond. He swapped the lake in front of the 530-yard

(485-m) 11th for a stream and modified the bunkering to reduce the number of downhill bunker shots with water beyond.

Although such a formidable tournament test, Muirfield Village is designed so that it can be much shortened for everyday play, using different teeing grounds; these are actually separate tees rather than the more common single, long tee. Whatever the length of individual holes, however, the course calls for the use of every club in the bag.

In September 1987 Muirfield Village hosted the Ryder Cup, which was won by Europe. Having built up a commanding lead in the foursomes and fourballs during the first two days, Europe's eventual margin of victory was narrow as the United States fought back superbly in the singles on the last day.

ABOVE The course that Jack built, with Nicklaus himself in play.

RIGHT The treacherously shallow 12th green. This par 3 has some of the features of both the 12th and the 16th at Augusta.

THE NATIONAL

THE NATIONAL GOLF
LINKS OF AMERICA
SOUTHAMPTON
LONG ISLAND
NEW YORK
UNITED STATES

Charles Blair Macdonald was certainly fully convinced of his own importance as a great golf architect. It is no surprise, then, that the name he selected for his masterwork is about as imposing as it could be. However, he had an excuse for his grandiosity. Macdonald from the very start set about designing this course with the highest ambitions – to produce the United States's first great golf course – and he achieved exactly what he set out to do. In some ways it proved superior to any other course in the world at the time.

His preparations were perhaps the most thorough ever. Beginning in 1902, Macdonald paid annual visits across the Atlantic to study UK golf courses. Many have said that he copied what he found and merely reproduced the results at The National, but this was neither his aim nor indeed the truth. Macdonald noted important features of good golf holes and later used what he had learned. At no stage did he ever intend to 'borrow' the 18 best holes in the British Isles and replicate them on Long Island; he did want to have 18 good holes, and he felt that courses like North Berwick West and St Andrews Old were by no means without weak or dull holes. He was, therefore, as eager to find out why bad holes were bad as to analyze why good ones were good.

The names Macdonald gave to his holes at The National show clearly the occasions on which he felt he had imitated a British hole. The 2nd, for example, he called 'Sahara': it was based on the 3rd at Royal St George's. The 3rd, called the 'Alps', was 'borrowed' from the 17th at Prestwick; it too has a blind second shot and a bunker right across the front of the green. The 4th, 'Redan', shares with North Berwick, another Scottish course, the feature of a long green set at an angle to the line of shot and similar bunkering. Two more – the 7th and 13th – borrow Old Course features. The 7th, which he actually called 'St Andrews', uses features of the Road Hole which include a bold carry over bunkers (instead of the old railway sheds), a pot bunker towards the front left of the green, and severe bunkering on the right of the green (substituting for the road at St Andrews). The 13th owes some debt to the 11th at St Andrews, the Eden hole, with some similarity in the front bunkering and the nearness of water.

Macdonald also took a long time over another part of his painstaking research – finding the right piece of land. He settled for 250 acres (100 ha) or so by the Sebonac and Peconic bays and close by Shinnecock Hills. Work began in 1907, and the course was opened a couple of years later. Originally it was short (by modern standards), at around 6,100 yards (5,580 m). By the mid-1920s, however, it was over 6,500 yards (5,945 m), and today it is over 6,700 yards (6,125 m) – perhaps not quite long enough for PGA Tour events or the US Open. The most important event so far to be held at The National, in fact, has been the 1922 Walker Cup. It was highly praised by both teams then – as, indeed, it had been from the beginning.

Although much has been made of Macdonald's 'borrowings' from overseas, he introduced original features of his own. His little 6th hole, only 130 yards (119 m), may have been the first hole ever to have a green wholly ringed by bunkers, and he also made use of water

carries from the tee (although not close to the greens) at several holes. The classic hole on The National is the 14th, about 360 yards (330 m) in length. The tee shot is played over an arm of the bay to a fairway which doglegs sharply, following the line of the water to a tightly bunkered green which is set quite close to both a road and water. The water carry, however, is not severe, for Macdonald recognized that few club players can hit the ball a distance approaching 200 yards (185 m). Normally in the courses he designed he liked to give short hitters an alternative route; here he simply allowed for their limitations.

Probably Macdonald would have liked, really, to design a links course, but was unable to find suitable land. If he was frustrated in this, he certainly made up for it by the sheer quantity of bunkers he incorporated – there are said to be about 500 of them.

Similarly, since he could not have all his holes close to the sea, he compromised by producing a grand finale, with the last seven holes close to water.

ABOVE LEFT The plain, even severe, clubhouse at the National perhaps reflects Charles Blair Macdonald's love of Scottish simplicity. (© LEONARD KAMSLER 1985)

ABOVE A view over the course from the clubhouse. (© LEONARD KAMSLER 1985)

LEFT The course was used for the 1922 Walker Cup. Here is Macdonald with Chick Evans (left) and Jess Sweetser (right).

OAK HILL COUNTRY CLUB
ROCHESTER, NEW YORK
UNITED STATES

OAK HILL EAST

Before the 1956 US Open, the first that Oak Hill hosted, Ben Hogan had said that the course was not difficult enough for the championship. Perhaps he was right. Cary Middlecoff's 281, the winning total, was the lowest ever up to that time except for Hogan's 276 at Riviera several years before, in 1948. Even so, the cream came to the top, for Middlecoff was followed home by Hogan himself, Julius Boros, Ed Furgol, Peter Thomson and Ted Kroll. In 1968 the championship returned and the scoring was even better, Lee Trevino equalling the record set the year before by Jack Nicklaus at Baltusrol with 275 and scoring every round below 70. After this, the USGA decided that there would have to be changes if the Open was to come again to Oak Hill.

The course was originally designed by Donald Ross in 1926, and it features his much-loved raised greens; also he had thousands of trees planted. After Trevino's win, however, the members agreed with the USGA that there would have to be some alterations, and George and Tom Fazio were called in. They certainly produced one great hole, the 5th, a par 4 of 419 yards (383 m) with a creek all down the right. The creek comes closer as it nears the green before swinging around the green's front and winding down the left side.

The next major championship to come to Oak Hill East was the 1980 US PGA. The course had by now also been 'tricked up' through encouraging rough to grow at the approaches to greens in order to catch a straight shot pitching short. Nicklaus had one of his greatest victories. With the US Open already under his belt that year, when many thought his great days over, he had a 66 in the third round to lead by 3, and then went on to a 7-stroke victory. It was his fifth PGA title and his 19th major championship. Nicklaus was 6 under par but the people at Oak Hill were probably satisfied with the new difficulty of their course: the next best score was Andy Bean's one over.

For the members, Oak Hill is now a very difficult test. If you can cope with the length Oak Hill plays, most other courses will seem shorter. There is very little roll on the fairways, and the rough is very dense. The greens are very fast, but they will always hold a well struck shot.

The start is intimidating, with a couple of long par 4s followed by a 200-yard (183-m) par 3; this means that, for good players, a long iron at least will be needed for all the shots to the greens. Next comes a par 5 of 570 yards (521 m) that even professionals do not expect to reach in two. (There is another par 5 later, the 596-yard [545-m] 13th, that no one has ever reached in two.) In all, there are 10 par 4s that are over 400 yards (365 m), three of them in a row constituting one of the toughest finishes in championship golf. Each of these final three is around the 450-yard (410-m) mark.

ABOVE AND ABOVE RIGHT Two views of Oak Hill taken before the 1980 PGA Championship which was won so convincingly by Jack Nicklaus. Note the dense texture of the semi-rough, one of the most difficult features of the course. (© TONY ROBERTS 1979)

RIGHT Cary Middlecoff, shown here in practice, won the 1956 US Open at Oak Hill ahead of Ben Hogan and Julius Boros.

OAKLAND HILLS
COUNTRY CLUB
BIRMINGHAM
MICHIGAN
UNITED STATES

OAKLAND HILLS

Tournament players expect to be able to get up in two at par-5 holes. Their great length helps make a steady round seem spectacular. They also used to expect to look out from the tee and feel able to ignore the fairway bunkers – those only trapped club members who strayed to one side or the other. Professionals could fly most of them with ease, which made long driving much less hazardous.

All this changed before the 1951 US Open. Robert Trent Jones was called in to revise Donald Ross's 1917 design of the Oakland Hills course. He threw at the Open competitors bunkers galore, the majority being sited so as to narrow the fairways and positioned so that most competitors could not carry them from the tee. Obsolete fairway bunkers were filled in. The players did not like it and the course was nicknamed 'The Monster' after Ben Hogan, having won his third US Open, commented that he was glad he had 'brought this monster to its knees'.

Although Hogan was a very controlled driver by this time in his career, the task had not been easy. His chances seemed to have vanished early on when he bogeyed five of his first nine holes, finishing the round in 76. But he improved on that in every succeeding round – 73, 71, 67. When golfers start chatting about the greatest round of golf ever, that Hogan 67 al-

ABOVE Ralph Guldahl at the peak of his career. He won the 1937 US Open over the course, one that Sam Snead, then at the outset of his career, had seemed bound to win.

LEFT The 18th with the clubhouse behind during the climax of the 1985 US Open. (© TONY ROBERTS 1985)

FAR LEFT Ben Crenshaw acknowledges applause for his hole in one during the 1985 US Open at Oakland Hills, but Andy North was the surprise champion.

ways has to come into the reckoning. He played the first nine that day in par, and then came home in 32. The climax came at the 18th, a dogleg of about 460 yards (420 m). Hogan carried the bunkers Jones had set into the angle, fired a mid-iron to about a yard, and won by 2 strokes. In the whole championship only one other competitor broke 70, the late Clayton Heafner: he had a 69 and finished second.

Afterwards, Jones was defensive about his changes. He considered he had achieved what he had set out to do: provide a severe test of professional golf. Perhaps he did indeed start the trend followed ever since by the USGA, that of 'taking the driver out of the game'.

In fact, by the time Jones came along, Oakland Hills had already hosted two Opens. In 1924, the little known English-born Cyril Walker won by 3 strokes from Bobby Jones. But 1937 was a far more significant year in US Open history. Sam Snead seemed to have won – it was the first time he had played in the championship – but Ralph Guldahl came through on the post to win. Snead, despite his plethora of other titles, was never to be US Open champion. How improbable that would have seemed back in 1937!

Since Hogan's year, 1951, there have been two further US Opens at Oakland Hills. The first of these was won by Gene Littler, his only major championship as a professional. The next came in 1985, Andy North winning his second US Open. This too was an oddity: North has won only three tournaments in his career, but two of them have been the US Open.

As Jones intended, the finish from the 14th to the 18th is what most tests players of all levels. Each of the holes (four par 4s and a 200-yard [183-m] par 3) usually demands a long shot to the green. However, Gary Player broke this 'rule' when playing the 400-yard (366-m) 16th in the final round of the 1972 US PGA. He was far to the right in the rough with his tee shot, but on a line which shortened the dogleg. He took out a 9-iron and gave the ball a smash which sent it soaring over the trees and the lake beyond. It came to rest a little more than a yard from the hole.

The 18th, played so well by Ben Hogan in 1951, is a daunting finishing hole. It doglegs gently right, with bunkers in the landing area for the tee shot. The green itself is heavily bunkered, both short and close-up, with a very narrow entrance, and throws off many shots that are good but just not quite good enough.

OAKMONT

OAKMONT COUNTRY CLUB, OAKMONT
PENNSYLVANIA
UNITED STATES

RIGHT Oakmont photographed during the 1973 US Open which was won by Johnny Miller. (© TONY ROBERTS 1973)

BELOW RIGHT The famous Church Pews bunkers.

FAR RIGHT William C Fownes Junior, the son of Oakmont's founder, repeatedly redesigned the course, adding features to make it harder and harder to play. Though still a challenging course, Oakmont is less difficult now than when Fownes was the supremo.

This course is the product of the labours of Henry C Fownes, followed by a lifetime's work from his son William, a US Amateur Champion. Both were consumed with the idea that a golf course should be punishing. As the land chosen by the village of Oakmont, 10 miles (16 km) or so outside Pittsburgh, had none of the natural threats of a Pine Valley or Pebble Beach, the father-and-son architects had to do it through bunkering and the speed of the greens. Oakmont's bunkers are indeed legendary. Today there are still nearly 200, and there used to be more than 300.

But the Fowneses were not satisfied with sand alone as a hazard. They did not like the idea of players finding a fairway bunker and then being able to fire their next onto the green from long range. Just after World War I, a special rake was introduced at Oakmont. The idea was not to leave the sand unblemished but rather to make lies more difficult. After the green-staff had departed satisfied, the sand was deliberately well furrowed: almost all shots rolled into the troughs so that the hapless golfer had very near the same thing as a buried lie.

Some professionals complained. They made the valid point that such practices took the skill out of recovery shots: all anyone could do was blast out. After World War II, however, the furrows became less severe and today they are a thing of the past. The river sand too has departed – players found that more difficult as well. It has now been replaced by the brilliant white sand demanded by most US golfers.

It is no wonder that there were such a vast number of bunkers on the course. If William Fownes noticed that players could carry one from the tee or, nearer to the green, were escaping their just deserts after inferior shots, he would simply order another bunker to be constructed!

There have been fewer changes to the greens: these were designed to be terrifyingly fast, and they remain so. In the early days, barrels of sand were used as well as a 1500 lb (680 kg) roller, a practice probably unprecedented. In one way or another problems of soil compaction were avoided, or at least overcome, and Oakmont had greens receptive only to very well struck

shots. The greens were also, aided by cutters set to about 3⁄32 inch (2·4 mm), terrifyingly fast to putt. A player once claimed that he had marked his ball with a dime, but that the coin had slid off the green . . .

Bobby Jones was surely the likely man to cope with fast greens, yet in Oakmont's first US Open, played in 1927 just after the first Ryder Cup match, the course beat him. His best round was a 76 and, for once, he finished down the field. (Tommy Armour won after a play-off with a total of 301.) The next Open at Oakmont came in 1935. The winner, Sam Parks, was the only man to break 300 – he did it by just 1. The runner-up, long-hitting Jimmy Thomson, was destroyed by the 17th. He drove to the green, then a distance of about 290 yards (265 m), and when his putt was a foot (30 cm) or so from the hole he thought it would drop for an eagle 2. Alas, in the end he needed four putts.

Oakmont was tamed but not defeated in the next two US Opens held there. In 1953, Ben Hogan was at his all-time peak. He began with a 67 but Sam Snead, 5 behind at that point, began to overhaul him. Hogan's last four holes of par, par, birdie and birdie were too good for Snead, who finished 6 strokes behind. Hogan's astonishing 283 was equalled by Jack Nicklaus and Arnold Palmer in 1962. Nicklaus had been a professional only a few months and was without a victory. He tied with Palmer, who had the support of most of the crowd, and then won the 18-hole play-off by 3 strokes.

Oakmont's first 'defeat' came in 1973. In his final round, Johnny Miller came from 6 back, and his 63 set a new record. However, we have to add the qualification that rains had made the greens soft and receptive and taken the fear out of putting.

Oakmont's most recent Open, in 1983, also featured a great move from behind, this time by Larry Nelson. At halfway, his 148 left him close to missing the cut, but he responded with 65 and 67 to beat Tom Watson by 1 stroke.

Although some of Oakmont's sharpest teeth have been drawn, it remains one of the great tests of shot-making, and has two dramatic hazards. Between the 3rd and 4th fairways lies the Church Pews, a very long bunker divided up by eight strips of turf. Leading up to the 8th green is another formidable specimen, 'Sahara': this is over 120 yards (110 m) long and about 30 yards (27 m) wide.

WILLIAM C FOWNES

ROBERT TRENT JONES
born 1906

Although born in England, Jones emigrated to America when about five years old. A good golfer while still a teenager, he was from the start interested in a career as a golf course architect and even designed his own programme of studies at university to equip himself. He did his first work while still at Cornell and rapidly became a full-time architect. Since that time Jones has designed hundreds of courses all over the world. Features of his work include vast teeing areas, testing undulations on greens, extensive use of water hazards and bunkering in dramatic shapes.

For long the world's most famous architect, Jones attracted enormous publicity by his controversial changes to Oakland Hills, Birmingham, Michigan, for the 1951 US Open. Though it wasn't what Ben Hogan had in mind, he probably did Jones a favour by calling the redesign 'a monster'.

Throughout his long career Jones has shown that it is possible to create high-class golf courses on any kind of land; draining swamps, blasting through rock and cutting through jungle. He has designed, or contributed to, several of the courses in this book. The greatest work of his old age will probably prove to be the new course at Ballybunion in County Kerry, Ireland.

CECIL HUTCHISON

ROBERT TRENT JONES

BOBBY JONES
1902 - 71

Though Jones was the greatest golfer of his day, he never became highly involved in golf course design, perhaps because he would have been working during the Depression years when courses were being closed down rather than built. Nevertheless, he was involved in the development of Augusta from its beginnings to the time of his death. With Alister Mackenzie, he seems to have cooperated mainly in giving his thoughts on how the course would test the best players and also be enjoyable for the less talented.

Much later, he was involved in the design of the par-3 course at Augusta and Peachtree, with Robert Trent Jones, also in Georgia.

BOBBY JONES

C B MACDONALD
1856 - 1939

Having learned his golf at St Andrews, Macdonald had no real opportunity to play the game until it was revived in the United States at the end of the 1880s. Macdonald was soon at the forefront of developments as player, administrator and golf architect, the latter a term he coined. His first design was in Chicago which in 1893 had the first 18-hole course in the United States. Moving to New York, he had the ambition to build a great golf course. He studied British courses and noted the features which made for great golf holes and the result was the National Golf Links of America, on Long Island, New York, perhaps the most splendid (or grandiose) name ever given a golf course. Macdonald thought he had created the best golf course in the world and, at the time, perhaps he was right.

As 1895 US Amateur Champion and with the prestige of The National behind him, he was asked to produce other designs. Amongst his most famous were The Lido, which involved major re-shaping of the landscape and Mid-Ocean on Bermuda. Macdonald did not merely imitate the best features of British linksland golf but produced original design ideas of his own, especially the use of water as a hazard and 'island' greens surrounded by sand.

C B MACDONALD

JAMES BRAID

GEORGE CRUMP

WILLIE FERNIE

HERBERT FOWLER

JAMES BRAID
1870 - 1950

Though the Great Triumvirate of Braid, Vardon and Taylor should have been in great demand as golf architects, Vardon produced few courses and most of Taylor's were really the work of his partner, Fred Hawtree. It was a very different matter with Braid, Open Champion five times in the first decade of the century. After World War I, he became the most prolific designer in Britain, being equally active in both England and Scotland at a time when most architecture was being carried out by good amateur golfers rather than professionals.
Although Braid is most known today for the Gleneagles courses, where he was greatly helped by the very favourable terrain and superb surroundings, he was just as able to work with less promising ground.

GEORGE CRUMP
died 1918

Crump has but one golf course to his credit, one which was unfinished at his death. His vision was to find a stretch of land which would yield a great golf course. He did and today we have Pine Valley, New Jersey.

WILLIE FERNIE
1851 - 1924

Open Champion in 1883, having tied and lost the play-off the previous year. Fernie was professional at Troon, Scotland, for well over 30 years from 1887. He developed that championship course and, amongst a few other designs, created the original course at Turnberry, Ayrshire, Scotland.

HERBERT FOWLER
1856 - 1941

Although not taking to golf until early middle age, Fowler rapidly became good enough to reach the later stages of the British Amateur Championship. His chance in golf architecture came when he was asked to design Walton Heath, near London, early this century. This rapidly became a famous course with a highly impressive membership list. David Lloyd George and Winston Churchill were amongst those who played there; Churchill rather reluctantly as he preferred conversation. Much work came Fowler's way as a result of this golfing and social success, and Westward Ho! was one of the courses he made considerable changes to. Fowler also worked in the United States, mainly in California. Apart from Walton Heath, his most respected courses are probably Cruden Bay in Scotland and The Berkshire to the west of London.

WILLIAM C FOWNES
1878 - 1950

A good enough golfer to win the US Amateur Championship and play for the first Walker Cup team, Fownes was a one-course man and constantly concerned himself with improving Oakmont, in Pennsylvania. This meant, in one instance, creating new bunkering when he found players able to drive them from the tee and bringing a rake into use to create furrows which made long recovery shots virtually impossible from his bunkers. He was also a believer in extremely fast greens and certainly succeeded in producing them at Oakmont. He was president of the USGA during the 1920s.

CECIL HUTCHISON
1877 - 1941

Hutchison was a top amateur golfer in the years from the turn of the century up to World War I. His greatest achievement was to be runner-up in the 1909 British Amateur Championship, losing one down at Muirfield to a fellow member of the Honourable Company of Edinburgh Golfers.
Eventually turning to golf course design after army service, Hutchison worked on the course at Prince's, Kent. However, he is best known today for his work at Turnberry, Ayrshire, Scotland.

THE OLYMPIC COUNTRY CLUB, SAN FRANCISCO
CALIFORNIA
UNITED STATES

RIGHT Crowds are massed around the final green during the 1987 US Open. Although Scott Simpson won the title, many thought it was more significant that Tom Watson returned to championship form and went on to win a US tour event later the same year.

OLYMPIC LAKESIDE

Some 20 years ago, three branches were lopped from a tree at Olympic. According to legend, 150 balls fell out.

Olympic is indeed a course of trees, even though it is just 500 yards (460 m) from the Pacific Ocean. From the tees, great and handicap players alike need to consider fairway bunkers just once, on the 6th hole; trees, on the other hand, are a constant menace and make the course one of the tightest and most claustrophobic in the world. The trees do not merely line the fairways but overhang them, ready to block the aerial route.

Once they have escaped the trees they are confronted by the camber of the fairways. The Lakeside course is built on a hillside. Nearly all the holes run side by side across the line of the slope. To hold many of the fairways you need to use a left-to-right shot; hookers are nearly always in trouble unless they can succeed in hitting along exactly the right line. Shots that drift badly off-line finish in the dense trees, the only option often being to try to regain the fairway.

The rough – unlike that at, say, Augusta National – is very severe. During the 1955 US Open Ben Hogan once took three strokes just to move his ball back to the fairway with a wedge, and Arnold Palmer lost the 1966 US Open through attempting to play long irons out instead of a safer club. This severity of the rough is a product of the damp Pacific air, and it means that the Lakeside course plays much longer than its 6,700 yards (6,125 m). The ball does not fly as far, and when it pitches, according to the members, you get a couple of yards of run . . . but backwards!

The greens are among the smallest in championship golf, but they are severely bunkered only on the short par 3s – the 8th and the 15th.

The course was first laid out during World War I, reputedly by three immigrant club professionals. A few years later it was bought by the Olympic Country Club, who immediately set about converting the land from a sandy wilderness to what it is today – a course apparently carved out of a forest. Some 20,000 trees were planted, and were later joined by another 10,000. The professional at the time was Sam Whiting, who carried out the design thoughts of Willie Watson, a Scottish immigrant with whom he designed Olympic's other course, the Ocean. As Whiting did not retire until 1954, day-to-day credit should go to him.

The 16th breaks the convention that the fade is the shot that pays off; here a long draw helps to shorten the 604 yards (551 m). Although the green is not punitively guarded by its two flank bunkers, it is said that only Bobby Jones has ever been home in two: he must have been able to drive across the angle of the dogleg over trees that had yet to reach their maturity. In championship play, the 17th is shortened from a relatively undemanding par 5 of 517 yards (473 m) (although that distance is uphill) to the far more daunting prospect of a par 4 of 443 yards (405 m) with a green which is both well bunkered and designed to receive a pitched third rather than a second shot played with a long iron.

The best hole, however, is probably the 18th, a par 4 of just 330 yards (300 m) or so. The trouble appears to be on the left for the tee shot, but the fairway runs away to the right, from where overhanging trees will block out many pitched second shots.

Olympic has hosted three US Opens. The first two brought shock results. In 1955, Ben Hogan seemed to have won a record fifth US Open when the totally unknown Jack Fleck – from a municipal course at Davenport, Iowa – managed to birdie the last hole to tie Hogan's total. Even so, no one gave Fleck a chance in the 18-hole play-off, but he held a 1-stroke lead on the final tee where Hogan, who had learned to fade the ball almost infallibly, then hooked into the deepest rough on the course and took three more to regain the fairway, saying goodbye to his championship hopes en route. Eleven years later, in 1966, Arnold Palmer seemed set to break the US Open record four-round aggregate with nine holes to play. Would Jack Nicklaus or Billy Casper be second? But Palmer, who had been hitting straight or with a little fade all week, then hooked a few and lost a 7-stroke lead. Casper and Palmer tied and, in the 18-hole play-off, Palmer again lost an early lead, Casper in the end winning by 4 strokes.

In 1987, Olympic became the first Californian course to have hosted the US Open three times. Although the early lead was taken by Ben Crenshaw, the Championship was a battle between Seve Ballesteros, Tom Watson and the eventual winner, Scott Simpson.

DR LAIDLAW PURVES
1843 - 1918

A good club-level golfer, Laidlaw Purves had learned his golf in Scotland and later, while a surgeon at Guy's Hospital in London, was an influential member at Wimbledon. Dissatisfied with the golfing terrain there, he set out to survey the south coast of England to find more suitable land. In due course he climbed the tower of St Clement's church in Sandwich, Kent, and saw the promised land – a fine stretch of duneland which was to become three golf courses, Royal Cinque Ports at Deal, Royal St George's and Prince's.

There is little doubt that he played the major role in the original layout of St George's. However, though he designed a ladies' course on Wimbledon Common and also Littlestone, he made little provision for them at St George's and to this day the club remains one of the most restrictive in Britain. It was not until the 1920s that any facilities were provided. Later the famous notice was posted: 'Ladies are authorized to wear trousers for golf provided that they take them off before entering the Clubhouse'.

DR LAIDLAW PURVES

DONALD ROSS
1872 - 1948

The most prolific architect of good golf courses ever, Ross was born at Dornoch in Sutherland, Scotland, and later used much of what he had learned of 'natural' course design in his work in the United States.

Ross served an apprenticeship in clubmaking at St Andrews before emigrating to the United States toward the end of the century to work at a Boston club, from where he began to work in the winter at Pinehurst, N Carolina. His course work at this winter resort attracted many visitors and led to ever-increasing design commissions. Ross is credited with several hundred US courses.

STANLEY THOMPSON
1894 - 1952

Scottish by birth, Thompson became active in Canadian golf course architecture shortly after World War I and famous for his designs for two Canadian Railway companies. The courses were Banff Springs, Alberta, and Jasper Park, Ontario, both set in a mountain context.

The designer of many courses in Canada, Thompson also worked in the USA and South America.

DONALD ROSS

STANLEY THOMPSON

A W TILLINGHAST

A W TILLINGHAST
1874 - 1942

A good amateur golfer, 'Tillie', as he was often known, may well have picked up many of his architectural ideas while in Scotland as a young man.

The majority of his work was done during the golf boom years of the 1920s when opportunities were at a peak. By contrast, relatively few courses were built by anybody during the Depression years.

A W Tillinghast was perhaps the greatest US architect of his day and his fame revived in modern times when it was realised how many courses of championship standard he had built. Some well-known names are Baltusrol, Inverness, Quaker Ridge and Winged Foot.

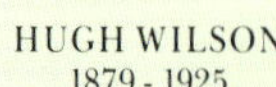

HUGH WILSON
1879 - 1925

Wilson's reputation rests on one course, the East at Merion, Ardmore, Pennsylvania. Yet this may well be considered the greatest course ever created without massive earth-moving on none too suitable ground. He also designed Merion's West course and did a little other architectural work, including the completion of Crump's course at Pine Valley, New Jersey.

HUGH WILSON

REAT HITECTS •

DR ALISTAIR MACKENZIE
1870 - 1934

Although qualified as a doctor, Mackenzie eventually gave up medicine in his late 30s to concentrate on golf course design.
Before World War I he was mainly active in England and during the war, serving in the Royal Engineers, showed brilliant use of camouflage designs. This skill was put to use in his golf course designs, where he sometimes cunningly concealed the difficulties of holes.
After the war Mackenzie increasingly worked outside Great Britain especially in Australia and the United States. Three of his courses are featured in this book – Royal Melbourne, Cypress Point and Augusta National. You would find plenty of supporters to argue that each of these is the greatest in the world. Certainly a few of the holes at Cypress Point are amongst the most photographed and, through annual exposure of the Masters on television, the last nine holes at Augusta must be the most well known stretch of golf course in the world.
Mackenzie believed that a good course must be suitable for players of every level and in this sense Augusta is possibly his greatest triumph. It tests championship level golfers to the limit while the more ordinary players quite often find they score better than at their home club.

DR ALISTAIR MACKENZIE

TOM MORRIS
1821 - 1908

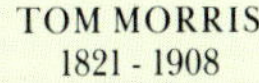

Invariably referred to as 'Old Tom' to distinguish him from his more brilliant son (as a professional golfer), Morris was the first man to be in great demand as a golf course designer. Many great links course, including Westward Ho!, Muirfield and Royal County Down are today credited to him though they have been drastically changed since he first laid them out. Even so, many of the green sites he chose remain in use to this day.

TOM MORRIS

JACK NEVILLE

JACK NEVILLE
1895 - 1978

Neville designed a few courses which were never built and later in life at least two that were. He was never a practising golf course architect, however, it was almost pure chance that he created one of the world's greatest courses at Pebble Beach. Neville was employed selling real estate for a company developing land on the Monterey Peninsula, California when he was asked to design a golf course. The result was Pebble Beach. He is said to have spent three weeks walking the land, working out the route of the course during the 1920s. Though there have been changes of detail since, Pebble Beach remains substantially as Neville made it. He said that the course was always there – he simply found the holes.
Neville was a very good amateur golfer.

JACK NICKLAUS

JACK NICKLAUS
born 1940

To be a great golfer means, in golf architecture, very little. Such a man should certainly have a grasp of what shots are the most demanding for the superior player but may fail to grasp the principles of making courses enjoyable for far humbler golfers. Nicklaus has succeeded in creating courses which are successful on both counts.
One of the very few men to set out on a professional golfing career with the aim of being the greatest player ever, Nicklaus may well also wish to be an immortal architect. With Bobby Jones as his rival as a golfer, the only one, Nicklaus's Muirfield Village could become a rival to Augusta as *the* great inland course and seems to have been inspired by his desire to create a great course in his home state, Ohio.
In Great Britain, his course near Plymouth, Devon, has created enormous interest but his main practice is in the United States, where Shoal Creek, Birmingham, Alabama, has been used for a PGA Championship. Nicklaus has earlier worked with both Desmond Muirhead and Pete Dye, both prominent figures in golf architecture today.

PEBBLE BEACH

PEBBLE BEACH
MONTEREY PENINSULA
CALIFORNIA
UNITED STATES

Among the accepted great courses of the world, Pebble Beach has to be the unanimous choice as the most spectacular. Like the classic early Scottish links courses, it is an out-and-back layout with the 11th at the far end of the course. The first three holes are inland, but the 4th and then the 6th to the 10th run along the cliffs of Carmel Bay. The 11th heads inland again and the 13th to the 16th move back toward the clubhouse. They are set among pines, eucalyptus, oaks and cypresses. Although all the inland holes are good, they lack the drama of the ones on the clifftops. The 17th returns to the shore and the 18th curves along beside the Pacific.

A real-estate salesman called Jack Neville was an amateur good enough to win the California Championship five times and to be picked for the Walker Cup team in 1923. People have always been apt to think that good golfers design good courses. This is far from always true, but property developer Sam Morse made no mistake when in 1918 he asked Neville to create a golf course for him. Neville later said: 'The golf course was there all the time. All I did was find the holes.' He spent weeks walking the land until he had decided the route and the sites for the greens. He then called in another amateur, Douglas Grant, for consultations on the subject of bunkering.

Neville certainly started with a superb piece of golfing territory. Nevertheless, it is to his credit that he produced a masterpiece. No one since has suggested anything by way of drastic alteration.

For very good golfers, Pebble Beach is a course demanding heroic shots; for the less good, however, there are usually safer routes to play the holes if you accept the loss of a stroke to par. Those heroic shots all come on the Pacific holes. The 4th is a comparatively gentle introduction, a short par 4 of just 325 yards (297 m), but even so it has the cliffs close by for any approach shot that leaks to the right. The 6th, like nearly all par 5s, is not particularly difficult, and there is the reward, as you approach the green, of one of the great golf-course views – away along the cliff-line to the 10th green. From here on, though, heroics are called for.

The 7th is only 120 yards (110 m) long and

RIGHT The 6th and 7th holes at Pebble Beach are precariously positioned on a peninsula jutting into the Pacific.

ABOVE The majestic sweep of the par-5 18th is here viewed from behind the green. From the tee the player has to decide how far he dare play out across the ocean. Even so, this hole is not a frightener, unless there is a wind towards the sea.

RIGHT Bobby Jones could have been in worse trouble on the 6th during the 1929 US Amateur Championship – he could have been in this sea!

FAR RIGHT The 8th at Pebble Beach is one of the great par 4s of world golf.

downhill, but its green is angled across the line of shot and, like all the others at Pebble Beach, very small. On a calm day, you require 'feel' for the correct length of shot. When the wind is up, judgement too is needed – the Pacific will gleefully swallow your ball should your shot be played with too strong a club. The 8th is one of the great par 4s of world golf. The tee shot is blind – not usually a recommendation in modern times – and must be weighted short of the chasm ahead . . . but not too short, for that will make the second shot more difficult by far. This shot Jack Nicklaus has called 'the finest second shot on any golf course I have seen'. If you have judged your tee shot to perfection you then have to carry a rocky inlet and some 180 yards (165 m) to the green. The 9th and 10th demand no such carries but are stern in length: both are over 430 yards (395 m), and often they must be played into the wind. The lines which shorten the holes and ease the second shots are close to the cliff edge. Alas, the slopes are in that direction too; few golfers can expect to judge the run of the ground with the requisite precision.

The 17th is much the same medicine as the 7th, but longer – much longer, in fact, at nearly 220 yards (200 m). As before, the waisted green lies across the line of shot, and it is tightly bunkered. Hitting through the back is not fatal this time, but sending anything far to the left or right

is. The hole cost Arnold Palmer, at the height of his career, a 9 during the 1964 Crosby Tournament.

The 18th is a par 5. Tournament players expect to two-putt most par 5s and score birdies. This is possible here, but for many years it used to be said that no one had ever reached the hole in two. The hole offers a classic tee shot, where golfers have to decide how good they are and how far they can hit the ball as they face either a long or a short carry – the choice is the golfer's own – over an inlet. 'Left and long' is the bold line, but it is possible to go out of bounds playing for safety to the right; even a little too far to the right may well produce the result that a tall pine blocks the second shot. If all has gone well after the tee shot, you must keep your second shot reasonably close to the cliff edge or you will find trees in your way for your approach to the green.

In 1929, Bobby Jones was the greatest golfer in the world and, although an amateur, had recently won the US Open for the third time. In the first round of the 1929 US Amateur at Pebble Beach, however, he was dismissed by the unknown Johnny Goodman. Goodman was himself eliminated from the competition the same day, but a few years later he was to be the last amateur (to date) to win the US Open.

The 8th, 9th and 10th may well be the toughest short sequence of par 4s in the world. Championships are often settled here. Nicklaus, with pars on the first two, held a 4-stroke lead in the final round of the 1972 US Open. When he landed twice on the beach at the 10th, his lead was cut to a single stroke. Was it consolation that a US Ryder Cup player had taken 19 on this hole some years before? After this alarm, a 6 at a par 4, Nicklaus made the championship his with one of the best 1-irons ever played to the 17th. Into a stiff breeze, it was on line all the way, bit, checked, ran into the flag and came to rest about 6 inches (15 cm) from the hole. Even so, his 290 is the second highest winning total in the Open during the past 50 years.

Ten years later, Nicklaus was in pursuit of a record-breaking fifth US Open Championship. Only Watson had a chance of catching him, but then apparently threw it away by sending his tee shot at the 17th into dense greenside rough where he could not hope to stop his little downhill pitch shot close to the hole. Perhaps not. Watson's solution to this little difficulty was to hole it.

PENINA

PENINA GOLF HOTEL
MONTE DE ALVOR
PENINA, PORTIMÃO
ALGARVE, PORTUGAL

ABOVE The late Sir Henry Cotton designed a golf masterpiece at Penina (RIGHT) out of former paddy fields.

Golf course designers have to practise their craft on very unlikely terrain at times. When the late Sir Henry Cotton first visited the proposed site at Penina in 1963, he was confronted by an absolutely flat rice paddy field. Not surprisingly, it was also water-logged. Yet the course he created – the first in the Algarve, opening in 1966 – will probably come to be seen as his monument.

A designer such as Robert Trent Jones might have decided to change the landscape. Cotton, however, took a different approach: he decided to plant thousands of trees, said to total more than 350,000. The purpose in this was two-fold, one reason was that they would help to absorb the excess water and the other was that they were to be the main feature of his new course. They both line the fairways and help create the doglegged holes. However, trees alone could not drain the former paddy fields and another feature that much affects play are the drainage canals. These often border fairways, swing across the front of greens or are close to hand at either side.

Cotton was determined that his course should not be made a nonsense of by the increasing carry of the modern ball. He therefore built vast tees, up to 100 yards (90 m) in length, an idea he probably took from Robert Trent Jones. The result is that although good amateurs can play Penina at under 6,900 yards (6,310 m), it can be stretched to nearly 7,500 yards (6,860 m). One of the longest courses in the world, even the ultimate power hitters are still left with distance to cover for their shots to the greens. These are usually elevated above fairway level and at their best are as good as anywhere in the world.

Cotton lived at the Penina Hotel for many years, leaving temporarily during the Portuguese 'revolution' when he was in disfavour as 'a wealthy Englishman who works too hard'. His last days were saddened when it was announced that the course would be changed by another hand. It now, however, seems that the modifications will not devastate his original design.

When Cotton died just before Christmas in 1987 his knighthood, the first awarded a golfer, had still to be announced in the New Year's Honours list, though he had learned of it some time before. Sir Henry was buried at Penina.

PINEHURST NUMBER TWO

PINEHURST HOTEL AND COUNTRY CLUB
PINEHURST
NORTH CAROLINA
UNITED STATES

Back in 1895 a Massachusetts businessman, James W. Tufts, was planning to build up a resort where northerners could escape the inclemencies of winter. He settled for the mild, dry climate of North Carolina at Pinehurst, where he bought about 5,000 acres (2,000 ha) of sandhill country at $1 an acre, a bargain if ever there was one.

Golf was not his prime objective, but before the end of the century the explosion in the game's popularity in the United States inspired him to open a nine-hole lay-out, soon expanded to 18 holes. At the end of 1900 he brought the Scotsman Donald Ross, from Dornoch in Sutherland, down from Boston as winter professional. The high quality of the golf at Pinehurst stems from that appointment. Ross went on to become one of the greatest names in golf architecture, but it was at Pinehurst that he gave his most detailed attention to golf, devoting himself almost passionately to what came to be the No. 2 course.

This was opened in 1907 but initially measured only 5,800 yards (5,300 m) or so. It did not approach anything like its present form for nearly 20 years, and it was to continue to have sand greens until the mid-1930s: it was maintained that these were so good that to sow them with Bermuda grass would actually reduce the quality of the putting surfaces. Almost as a footnote, it is worth mentioning that during summer 1987 Jack Nicklaus was hired to replace the greens' Bermuda grass with bent and to substitute a hybrid Bermuda on the fairways.

Donald Ross not only rebuilt the course he found on his arrival and created the No. 2 course, he produced two more 18-hole courses so that, shortly after the end of World War I, Pinehurst became probably the world's first golf complex to have 72 holes.

Perhaps the first great player to come to Pinehurst was Harry Vardon, who played an exhibition match during his countrywide tour in 1900. The following year, the North and South amateur event was begun; it continues to this day. Among its winners have been not one but two Nicklauses. Jack won in 1959 and was a spectator in 1985 when his son, Jack II, took the title.

BELOW The clubhouse at the Pinehurst golf complex.

Two years after the amateur event, in 1903, the professional North and South was started. For a long time it was one of the most prestigious tournaments in US professional golf, but in due course it waned, finally dying in 1951: the basic reason for its demise was that Pinehurst is not close to a major population centre, so that spectators – and hence sponsors – are hard to attract.

In that same year, 1951, however, the Ryder Cup came to Pinehurst. At the time, however, this contest attracted little interest in the United States because the result seemed too easy to predict. Beforehand, Henry Longhurst expressed the general sentiment when he forecast that Great Britain and Ireland would win one of the four foursomes and two of the eight singles. He was not far out: the actual result was United States 9½, Britain and Ireland 2½!

One of the great names playing in that match was Ben Hogan. His play on one hole has become a part of Pinehurst legend. Hogan was playing against Charlie Ward, a short hitter but a player with perhaps the best short game on the British/Irish team. After 25 holes, Ward had managed to hold Hogan to a two-hole lead. They exchanged birdies on the next two holes, but Hogan really settled the match on the 10th hole of the second round. This was listed on the card as 593 yards (542 m), but some thought that this was merely because Pinehurst did not wish to admit that its course included a truly monstrous hole of well over 600 yards (550 m) – perhaps as much as 630 yards (576 m). Even the long hitters were taking a couple of cracking woods and a mid-iron to reach the green. Ward played the hole with two woods and a long iron; Hogan hooked into the trees, wedged out, hit a wood to the front of the green and holed a monster putt for the birdie. This feat probably broke Ward's spirit.

Pinehurst No. 2 was also the scene of Hogan's first win on Tour, at the quite advanced age of 28. On Tuesday 19 March 1940 he began with birdies on three of the first four holes and was round in 66; he was 3 strokes in the lead, his eventual margin of victory after 72 holes. From that time on there was never any stopping him.

The course that Ross created – making a change here and a change there over the years – is not dramatic in the sense of a Pebble Beach or a Turnberry. No single hole, indeed, is blatantly a supreme test. The driving is to quite wide fairways, and the rough is not severe. If you wander a long way off-line you will inevitably be among the pines which offer seclusion to every hole, and the trees are often set close, so that there are no broad avenues for escape as at, for example, Augusta. There are also clumps of the lovegrass Ross planted, and you have every chance of finding that your ball is resting on an unwelcome bed of pine needles.

However, it is the shots to the greens that provide the main challenges. Most of the greens are raised and contoured, so that a long-iron which is good, but not quite good enough, will gently drift off with the run of the ground into a greenside bunker or among the humps and hollows Ross built as another type of hazard. It is this last feature which makes Pinehurst No. 2 one of the great tests of chipping in the world. If the US Open were ever to come here, there would be no need specially to ring the greens with collars of rough!

ABOVE Spring time at Pinehurst is a visual delight.

PINE VALLEY GOLF CLUB
CLEMENTON
NEW JERSEY
UNITED STATES

PINE VALLEY

The dream of a Philadelphia hotelier, George Crump, Pine Valley is a stranger to tournament golf yet is recognized as one of the very greatest courses in the world, and the most penal of all.

Crump sold his hotel in 1912 and moved out to the site. For a while, he lived in a tent, later in a bungalow. In a couple of years – by 1914 – he had 11 holes roughed out, and by 1916 14 were ready for play. George Crump was one of the great amateur architects; although he did bring H. S. Colt out from the UK for a while to help with the routing of the course, Colt gave his approval to what Crump was doing. A very great deal of work had been needed, especially in the removal of tree-stumps: it is said they stopped counting at 22,000, and there were plenty more after that! With four holes still to be made, however, Crump died early in 1918. His dream course was still a year from completion.

Once play began in 1919, it was not until 1922 that anyone managed to get round in 70. That score was not beaten until just before World War II, when the US Ryder Cup player Ed Dudley had a record 68; later in the same event he had an 85!

However, Pine Valley has been the scene of perhaps the most phenomenal feat of scoring ever. A good-class amateur, J Wood Platt, began with a birdie on the 1st hole and followed this up by eagling the 2nd. He then holed his tee shot on the 3rd and birdied the 4th. Platt was 6 under par after four holes. Alas, he had no return for the round. Perhaps overcome by the enormity of his achievement, Platt retired to the clubhouse to have a quick drink and consider his next move. He never reappeared. Although the tale takes some believing, geography favours it: golfers do indeed pass close to the clubhouse between the 4th green and the 5th tee.

Although Pine Valley is not suited to tournament play because of the lack of room for spectators, it has twice hosted the Walker Cup – in 1936 and 1985. Great Britain and Ireland were trounced by the United States on the first occasion, but the second match was closely fought out, with a win for the United States.

Pine Valley is in sandy pine-forest country. George Crump's approach was to leave the sandy wastes largely alone and to plant island fairways, so that for a great part of the time a golfer has to try to advance from one green patch to the next. If any of these 'hops' fail, the ball tends to be either lost in water or lying unkindly in an unraked wilderness. Perfect play will produce a steady flow of pars, but minor error can be – and often is – savagely punished. Club members used to bet that no visitor would break 80 on a first attempt at the course and that even competent club golfers would fail to break 100.

All great courses seem to include a superb selection of par 3s. Pine Valley's are as good as anywhere. The first of these is the 185-yard (169-m) 3rd – which, if you recall, 'Woody' Platt played in a single stroke! There are two oases of green – the tee and the putting surface – and between the two lies a sandy waste; the green itself is surrounded by more of the same. The 5th is an even sterner test of some 220 yards (200 m) from a high tee over a ravine and water to an elevated green. The 10th, at 145 yards (133 m), should be easier if only on account of its shorter length, but in fact the green is protected all around by very deep bunkers, one at the front being particularly insidious: it 'gathers' shots, and many golfers opt for playing out of it backwards. The 14th is the last of the par 3s and is played over scrub, water and bunkers to an island green; at 185 yards (169 m), it is as demanding as any of the others.

There are only two par 5s at Pine Valley, but one is perhaps the most famous hole on the course. It measures 585 yards (535 m), and has a sandy waste beginning about 280 yards (255 m) out and stretching for about 150 yards (137 m). Even the very longest hitters must aim to play short of this, while short hitters have very little chance of carrying 'Hell's Half Acre' with their second shot. It is thought that the green has never been reached in two – something that is true also of the 600-yard (550-m) 15th.

There are no weak holes among the par 4s. The 13th, at nearly 450 yards (410 m), is perhaps typical of them, with the drive being to an island in the sand. After that, the very long second to the green must carry sand all the way. The 18th is a fitting last hole. Once again, there is a wilderness to carry, and the second shot must carry over a rise liberally set with bunkers.

ABOVE George Crump built one of the world's most punishing courses, but died shortly before its completion.

RIGHT The 5th, a par 3 of over 200 yards (180 m), gives the golfer little margin for error.

PRESTWICK GOLF CLUB
PRESTWICK, AYRSHIRE
SCOTLAND

Prestwick

Prestwick is the original home of the Open Championship, although neither course nor club can claim to be one of the original homes of golf in Scotland.

There is a tradition that a monk from Crossraguel and the Lord of Culzean played a legendary challenge match in medieval times, and more regular golf was certainly in progress by the 1830s or 1840s; players paid 10 shillings a year to the Freemen of Prestwick for the privilege. The club was founded in 1851 and a couple of years later Old Tom Morris was invited to come over from his native St Andrews to be the professional. Tom Morris was to become the first really busy golf-course architect and, as one of the leading players of the time, no doubt had influence on the development of the original 12-hole lay-out. By the time Old Tom returned to St Andrews, Prestwick had become the best course in the country and his son Tommy, to go down in history as Young Tom Morris, had learned to play the game here.

The Open Championship had also begun. It was organized by Prestwick Golf Club and first played on 17 October 1860 with just eight competitors. Willie Park Sr won, Old Tom coming second. All the early championships were played at Prestwick until Young Tom caused a change. He won three years in a row during 1868–70; under the rules the trophy, a splendid belt, became his permanently. A one-year pause ensued, partly because money was being collected for the present trophy, a silver claret jug. When the championship resumed, the R & A and the Honourable Company of Edinburgh Golfers, who then played at Musselburgh, had joined the enterprise, increasing the number of courses available.

Championships continued to be played periodically at Prestwick, however, until 1925, by which time 24 Opens had been settled over the course. In that year, a Scottish-American, Macdonald Smith, went into the final round with a 5-stroke lead but collapsed with an 82, his concentration destroyed, it is said, by the wildly surging crowds.

This last Prestwick Open made it clear that the course could not accommodate large crowds packed into a small space, particularly on the last four holes. The Open will almost certainly never return.

Yet there are compensations. The course was expanded to 18 holes in 1883, but there have been relatively few changes since. Even more than at St Andrews, visitors feel they are playing traditional golf. Blind shots, for instance, are generally frowned on today, yet you will find plenty of them still at Prestwick – some of them having to be struck over high sand dunes. Another feature is that the greens are often hidden away in hollows, perhaps guarded by cross bunkers or humps which throw the ball to one side or the other.

The first famous hole is the 3rd, a par 5 of 482 yards (441 m) called the Cardinal. It takes its

RIGHT The clubhouse at Prestwick is a monument to Scottish solidity.

BELOW An example of the severe bunkering found at Prestwick. Note the sturdy timber supports typical of the course.

name from the huge timber-supported cross bunkers. These once had to be carried with, say, a brassie second; today they are hardly in play for long hitters who are firing their seconds over the angle of the dogleg directly for the green. The 5th includes the Himalayas, a range of dunes which have to be carried en route to the green of this par 3 of just over 200 yards (185 m). The conclusion of the first half lies on flatter land more away from the sea, but the 7th, 8th and 9th are all stiff par 4s of well over 400 yards (365 m). The course then heads back to the sea and dunes, much of it being set on land occupied by the original 12 holes. The 13th is a very difficult hole, at 460 yards (420 m) with a green set in typical links humps and hollows and at an angle to the line of shot.

A classic example of an 'old-fashioned' hole is still to come. This is the 17th, just under 400 yards (365 m) long. Here the second shot is blind over dunes known as the Alps, and the green beyond is then protected by a large cross bunker. In times past, one of the thrills of golf was to hit a blind shot and then, perhaps at the run, hurry to see the result; on the Alps hole, the question is will the ball be nestling close to the flag or buried in the cross bunker?

More Open Championships had been held at Prestwick than anywhere else until St Andrews caught up in 1984. Muirfield, with 13, comes next. Young Tom Morris had four victories here, and Harry Vardon three.

RIVIERA

RIVIERA COUNTRY CLUB
BEVERLY HILLS
LOS ANGELES
CALIFORNIA
UNITED STATES

Designed by George Thomas in the mid-1920s, Riviera saw some of Ben Hogan's greatest feats, so much so that the professionals and the press began to call it 'Hogan's Alley'. In 1947 and 1948 he won the Los Angeles Open here and in the latter year also the first of his four US Open titles. Jimmy Demaret broke the US Open record by three strokes with his 278, but Hogan's response was to go two better! It was his third win at Riviera in under 18 months.

Even so, a perhaps greater achievement lay ahead. Early in 1949, Hogan was grievously injured in a car crash. Not long after he had managed merely to walk a golf course once again, Hogan entered the 1950 Los Angeles Open. He wondered if he could possibly manage to play 72 holes of golf. In the event, he tied for first place, later losing the play-off to Sam Snead.

Hogan was still not done with Riviera. After his amazing comeback, Hollywood thought him a fit subject for the first (and still the only) golfing epic movie. *Follow the Sun* (1951) was largely shot at Riviera with Hogan watching every move and apparently causing both director (Sidney Lanfield) and star (Glenn Ford) some pain because of his insistence on accuracy and attention to points of detail. This has not been Riviera's only contact with the movie industry: many stars and other film people have been members. Another – totally unrelated – aspect of the glamour of the place is that the equestrian events of the 1932 Olympics were held here.

The course has two dominant features. One is a gully that comes into play on eight of the holes and the other is Kikuyu grass. This was imported to stop erosion in the gully when flash floods occurred. It did the job successfully, but it also spread all over the course. The result is unusual. Balls pitching into this erect grass in the semi-rough and even on the fairways tend to bounce upward rather than onward, so that a running approach is impossible to predict.

The course begins with the easiest hole, a par 5 downhill of about 500 yards (460 m). Birdies are not easy to come by on the 2nd, however, which is uphill and swinging to the right. It was Hogan's favourite hole. What he thought of an oddity at the short 6th is not recorded. There is a bunker actually *in* the green and club players are not allowed to chip over it, a local rule which seems hard to defend. Perhaps George Thomas, if indeed it was he who was responsible, was thinking of one of the greens at North Berwick in Scotland, which has a mini-ravine running through it!

RIGHT The crowds mass in this natural amphitheatre, which offers spectators a panoramic view of tournament play.

ABOVE Ben Hogan pictured in 1948, the year he won the US Open at Riviera.

ABOVE RIGHT George Thomas designed the course at Riviera in one of the golden ages of golf expansion – the 1920s.

RIGHT Ben Hogan (left), his wife Valerie and Glenn Ford, who played Hogan in *Follow the Sun*, the film of the golfer's epic struggle for fitness and renewed success following his devastating car accident.

ROYAL DORNOCH
GOLF CLUB
DORNOCH, SUTHERLAND
SCOTLAND

ROYAL DORNOCH

'About this town along the sea coast are the fairest and largest links or green fields of any pairt of Scotland. Fitt for archery, golfing, ryding and all other exercises, they doe surpass the fields of Montrose or St Andrews.' So wrote Sir Robert Gordon in 1630. There is an even earlier reference to golf being played near this little cathedral town. In 1616 it was noted in account books that the Earl of Sutherland had spent money on archery and golf clubs and balls while a schoolboy in the town. The only earlier references to golf links in Scotland are in connection with St Andrews and Leith, both from the preceding century. No one knows precisely when the game was first played at such famous places as St Andrews, Dornoch, Leith, Montrose, Gullane, Musselburgh and so on: all we have are the first handwritten or printed records. So it is just possible that Dornoch is the oldest golfing territory in the world.

After this early reference, Dornoch drifted out of golf history for many years, although there is no reason to doubt that golfers continued to play the links. More activity came in the mid-19th century, although it was still some time before a formal club was established, in 1877. By 1886, after two visits from St Andrews by Old Tom Morris, the club had an 18-hole course.

Famous golfers soon began to come – J H Taylor, Harry Vardon, James Braid, Horace Hutchinson and Walter Travis, for example. However, it was perhaps the spectacular achievements of the English amateur Joyce Wethered, often said to have learned the game during summer holidays here, that brought the Dornoch name to a wider public. This was in the early 1920s, when the course became very popular with summer visitors, some of whom were among the best amateur golfers of their day. Since then, the course has been very highly rated by the US golf writer Herbert Warren Wind and by Ben Crenshaw and Tom Watson, among others.

The rating of golf courses is a matter of taste, but certainly Dornoch is one of the world's great links courses. Many enthusiasts would claim it as the best in the British Isles. But, like the Royal North Devon at Westward Ho!, Dornoch is remote – 50 miles (80 km) beyond Inverness. Unfortunately this has deterred many major events from coming here, including, of course, the Open Championship.

The course has a traditional out-and-back layout, the first eight holes running between due north and northeast. These holes are on a higher level, the tee shot on the 8th having a steep fall in the fairway down to almost beach level. The 9th, 10th, 11th, 12th, 13th, 15th and 16th all play close by the shore, and the others are only a little inland.

The 1st hole is a short par 4, a gentle introduction; but the 2nd, a 180-yard (165-m) par 3, features one of the typical Dornoch plateau greens: there are steep falls to either side. The 5th is the first classic hole: at about 360 yards (330 m), not a long par 4. There is a high tee but a mound to be carried 150 yards (137 m) or so away with bunkers to the right and, to the left, the gorse-covered hillside. The plateau green is quite long but narrow and well protected.

The 6th, a par 3 of 165 yards (151 m), is easy enough – if you hit and hold the green. Otherwise, all kinds of perils lie in wait. The 8th is a very attractive hole, nearly 440 yards (400 m) long, with a steep downslope in the fairway about 200 yards (180 m) or so out which rewards a good drive. The second shot at this hole must avoid bumpy ground and bunkers to find a receptive green in a dell.

The journey home begins with a 500-yard (460-m) par 5 all along the shore to a plateau green. This is the first of only two par 5s. All told, Dornoch is not particularly long, at just under 6,600 yards (6,035 m). It is the par 4s that make it the test it is, nine of them being over 400 yards (365 m). Perhaps the most difficult is the 14th, at about 450 yards (410 m), a hole Harry Vardon greatly admired. It is the only one on the course without a bunker, but there are other problems to compensate. The second shot needs to be very good. Again there is a plateau green with a steep rise up to it. Fingers of higher ground protect the right-hand side of the green. It all makes for a very difficult target, so a long drive is necessary if you are to be able to ease the shot in.

The 15th, only some 320 yards (290 m) long, provides respite, especially if you have been battling home against the wind. The last three holes are all par 4s of over 400 yards (365 m), with the 17th being the pick. There is a downhill tee shot and then, a little less than 200 yards (180 m) out, the fairway has a step of nearly 50 feet (15 m). The hole then swings quite sharply left toward the plateau green, set well above the fairway and guarded by bunkers left and right. Unusually, this hole plays away from the club-house, going northward like the first eight holes. The final hole is over 450 yards (410 m) and very testing for second shots. There are bunkers about 30 yards (27 m) before the green, and then a grassy swale just short of it which stops many a shot from reaching the green.

At Dornoch the weather can change the course utterly. I remember two consecutive days I spent there one spring. The first was dominated by a howling snowstorm, and I saw just two lone Americans on the course – they had come a long way and they were not going to let a little thing like a blizzard deter them! I was out at dawn the following day. The sun shone and there might have been just a breath of wind.

ABOVE Dornoch is played on two levels – note the step in the fairway at the 17th hole.

LEFT Peter Alliss driving along the shoreline at dawn on a rare calm day at Dornoch.

ROYAL MELBOURNE
GOLF CLUB
SANDRINGHAM
MELBOURNE, VICTORIA
AUSTRALIA

ROYAL MELBOURNE WEST

There are two splendid courses of tournament calibre at Royal Melbourne, the East and the West. Alister Mackenzie was commissioned to design the West in 1926. He took a former Australian Open Champion, Alex Russell, into partnership for the work, and in fact it was Russell who produced the East a few years later. For major events, a composite of the two courses is used, partly to help handle large crowds and partly to avoid too many road crossings.

At the time, Alister Mackenzie was probably the most celebrated architect in the world and his work was international. In his native British Isles opportunities to work with really good golfing country had become limited: much had been used already and the Depression of the 1930s would lead to a farther decline in golf-course development. Mackenzie did most of his work in the United States, where his reputation today rests on Cypress Point and Augusta National. His Australian masterpiece is the West Course at Royal Melbourne. No other architect has such a trio of great courses to his credit. His fee for this one was 1,000 guineas (£1,050), quite a large sum for the time but hardly comparable with the hundreds of thousands of dollars a number of top architects can command today.

Although the 1st is of quite a stiff length for an opening hole, a par 4 of just under 430 yards (395 m), the fairway is almost as unmissable as on the 1st at St Andrews. The second shot, most unusually for this course, is not threatened by severe greenside and approach bunkering. However, once you are on the green, you soon become aware of one of the things that Royal Melbourne is all about: although very true, it is as fast as you will find anywhere in the world, and this means that any shot to the green that finishes far from the hole will often lead to three putts before being holed.

The 2nd, a short par 5 at only 480 yards (440 m), rewards a bold tee shot. If you carry an array of bunkers at about 200 yards (180 m), a near dogleg is straightened out and the green is reachable with a second shot by a reasonable hitter. Even so, there is a crater left of the green and other bunkers to the right. The 3rd, from the championship tees, is little more than 350 yards (320 m) in length, but the green slopes away and so the pitch must be struck with plenty of bite.

So far, the course has made no demands for long hitting, but this changes with a vengeance at the 4th, a 470-yard (430-m) par 4 for tournament players (it is a more kindly par 5 for members and visitors). For the tee shot, there is the typical Mackenzie hazard of an upslope set with bunkers. There is rough short of the green, so the second shot must carry all the way.

There follow two of the best golf holes in Australia. The first of these is a par 3 of 170 yards (155 m) or so. It is played from a high tee to an elevated green, with almost continuous bunkers to the right and more of the same to the left. The straightest of shots will not be enough unless you judge the distance just as precisely. The green slopes markedly from the rear to the front, with quite a steep slope leading up to the green. The 'safe' shot well past the flag makes three putts more than likely, and the iron shot that just reaches the green will probably drift back down the green and then the slope, so that you have to make a short pitch to get back again.

The 6th, at about 430 yards (395 m), is a dog-leg right from a high tee. This gives you the option of attempting to carry across the angle in order to shorten the second shot to the green. The shorter the better, in fact, because the bunkering on the left is very deep. The slope up to the green gives problems similar to those of the previous hole.

The next classic hole is the 10th, a par 4 of little more than 300 yards (275 m). As it is a dogleg left, a carry of about 250 yards (230 m) will find the green. However, the angle is defended by a vast, deep bunker. Long hitters must choose between the chance of a 2 if successful or a likely 5 if they fail by the merest scintilla. There are no such options on the next two holes, which are both long and tough par 4s. Then comes a lull for three holes, where not too much should go wrong, before that essential of the championship course – a stern finish. The 16th is a long par 3 of nearly 220 yards (200 m) to an island green surrounded by sand, while the 17th also requires a long second shot to the green – which can be fiendishly difficult to putt. At the

LEFT Many players have praised Alister Mackenzie's Australian masterpiece at Royal Melbourne. Note the gentle downhill approach to the green.

last hole, the shot to the green is relatively undramatic; bunkers abound, but they appear to be set to trap the poor shot rather than the one that is not quite good enough, and the green itself is of very generous size. But the tee shot is another matter entirely. Alister Mackenzie produced one of his favourite situations for the golfer, a blind tee shot over a well bunkered slope – and on this one he excelled himself. The slope is almost wholly sand, the tongues of grass that finger their way into the hazard offering menace, not relief.

Many great players have heaped praise on Royal Melbourne. Lee Trevino was particularly eloquent in the mid-1970s. He departed vowing never to return, more than a little piqued, perhaps, by a 9 on one hole. Earlier, he had thought it the best course in the world!

ROYAL GOLF
DAR-ES-SALAAM
RABAT
MOROCCO

ROYAL RABAT

At one time the present British royal family were quite enthusiastic golfers. King Edward VII started the trend: he used to play at Cannes, had a golf course laid out in the grounds of Windsor Castle and granted a number of golf clubs the right to the 'Royal' prefix. However, King Edward was hampered in developing his golf game by his enormous girth. Two of his sons, however, Edward VIII and George VI were medium-handicap players, but over the past 40 years, the interest of leading members of the House of Windsor seems to have lapsed. Two kings of Belgium, however, have been much better players of a very good amateur standard but perhaps King Hassan II of Morocco has outstripped them all, in enthusiasm if not playing skill. One result of this encouragement is the measure of popularity of golf in the country; although perhaps the first enthusiast was Haj Glaoui, Pasha of Marrakesh, where golf was certainly established by 1923.

Royal Rabat, one of Robert Trent Jones's monster designs, was opened at the beginning of the 1970s. There are now three courses but the great course is the Red, which can be stretched to about 7,500 yards (6,860 m). At this length it is almost impossible to score well as there is little run to be had on the soft, sandy soil. Royal Rabat is, in fact, shortened even for tournament play and was cut to about 7,200 yards

(6,585 m) for the 1987 Moroccan Open which began the year's European Tour. Howard Clark won with a winning score of 284, a high figure for a modern tournament. Even so, he needed a course record of 66 to help him to that total. He had no other round less than 72.

For general play, however, Royal Rabat is shortened and is a pleasure to play. The course is very well maintained with a staff said to number no fewer than 200! The greens are especially good, very fast but equally true. Long, straight tee shots are essential, for the course was basically cut through a forest of cork oak. Even if the player gets both length and direction, however, the subtly sloping fairways tend to direct many good shots into flanking bunkers.

Water, with flamingoes and duck, is often in sight, particularly at the most famous hole, the short 9th – still 199 yards (180 m) from the back tee. Here there is a lake to carry all the way to the green. A good professional once failed to make the shot six times. A lake is once again a threat on perhaps the most difficult hole on the course, the 11th, a par 4 of nearly 465 yards (425 m). Any shot wandering left will find water and then, faced with at least a long iron in, the green is tiny at only about 12 yards (11 m) from front to back. Most of the greens are far larger but you will then notice one of Jones's trade marks – severe contouring. Your approach shot needs to be quite near the hole to avoid 3-putting.

Even if the round has been a disaster from beginning to end, there are still two consolations. The setting is beautiful and the green fees low.

BELOW This walkway crosses a stretch of water to what is virtually an island green at Royal Dar es Salaam.

ROYAL ST GEORGE'S
GOLF CLUB
SANDWICH, KENT
ENGLAND

ROYAL ST GEORGE'S

Dr Laidlaw Purves was one of the most opinionated gentlemen any golf club has had to suffer among its members. His main club was Royal Wimbledon, which he joined in 1874. Within 10 years he was on the committee, but shortly afterward he resigned. Why? His daughter gave a clue when she noted that, although he had a heart of gold, he was 'the most irascible man I ever met'.

Even so, Purves was chosen captain of the club and busied himself at various times trying to unify the rules of golf (his club used a 3-inch [7.5-cm] hole in the mid-1870s while a 4¼-inch [11-cm] one was in use at St Andrews!), produced a logical handicapping system, and sent a constant stream of suggestions to the committee – all of which were ignored. The doctor is still remembered at Royal Wimbledon but his wider renown comes from his connections with Royal St George's.

Golf on Wimbledon Common was poor stuff, as on so many London courses not in the heathland belt. Purves and others were on the lookout for choicer land, perhaps mainly for weekend and holiday golf. One day in 1887 he came down to the little medieval town of Sandwich and went up the tower of the Norman church to inspect the view. What he saw excited him – a superb stretch of dunes, linksland and saltmarsh, which would many years later become not one but three courses: the Royal Cinque Ports at Deal, Prince's, and Royal St George's. Purves quickly formed the Sandwich Bay Golfing Association and we can be sure they were soon playing golf: in those times the leading lights of a club rapidly decided where the greens should be, and play began almost the next day.

Dr Purves is still credited as designer of the course, although some say that the first professional must have been closely involved. This is not necessarily so. Purves had designed a course for the ladies at Wimbledon and was later much annoyed when his plans for a new men's course were rejected by the committee. If he was in control, as at Sandwich, no one else would have been given much chance to argue a case.

The new club and course very quickly became popular with those eager to play golf away from the soggy clays of the London area. Soon it won wider recognition, the Amateur Championship coming to it just five years after the club was formed. A few years later the same championship was played here again. In between, something even more momentous happened: in 1894 the first Open Championship to be held outside Scotland was at Sandwich. (It was won by an Englishman, J H Taylor.)

There have been several other 'firsts'. In 1904 the Amateur Championship passed out of UK hands for the first time, being won by Walter Travis, an Australian-born American. More momentous events came to the area in the early 1920s. Walter Hagen turned up to play at neighbouring Deal expecting to win. He was 53rd. Two years later, at Sandwich, Hagen became the first US-born Open Champion. Of his four Open victories, the third also came at Sandwich, in 1928. Hagen's wins were part of a long string of US successes in the British Open. This was unbroken between 1924 and 1934, when probably the greatest UK golfer of all time, Henry Cotton,

ABOVE The starters' hut and 1st tee at Royal St George's with the clubhouse in the background.

won his first Open – again at Royal St George's.

The Open continued to come periodically to this corner of Kent until 1949, when attendances were very poor, so that the R & A dropped the course from the rota. There were many things against it, including notably a little toll bridge that caused traffic hold-ups any day of the week. For more than 30 years the course stayed off the rota: what chaos might ensue now that the Open Championship had become big business? Nevertheless, in 1981 the time was judged right for a return; Bill Rogers won and has scarcely been heard from since. In 1985 at Sandwich Sandy Lyle became the first UK winner since Tony Jacklin in 1969.

Despite its high rate of usage today, the 'St Andrews of the South' is less popular with professionals, US professionals especially. The main reason is the high number of blind shots. Modern professionals do not mind the occasional blind drive, but they do like to be able to see the bottom of the flag for the shots to the green. For these and other reasons, many think that Royal St George's is the most difficult of the courses

ABOVE Dr Laidlaw Purves discovered the golfing land at Sandwich.

ABOVE The US golfer Walter Travis in play during the 1904 Amateur Championship at Royal St George's.

ABOVE This Harry Rountree painting, dated c 1910, amply illustrates the wild links terrain.

used for the Open. In 1985, Jack Nicklaus missed the 36-hole cut for the first time ever, and earlier, in 1981, he had an 83 in his first round before fighting back magnificently with a 66. The winning scores likewise illustrate the difficulties of the course. In 1981 Bill Rogers was four under par at the finish; the runner-up, Bernhard Langer, equalled par, and the men in third place were three over. When Lyle won, he was two over. The course length is just over 6,800 yards (6,220 m), playing to a par of 70.

Royal St George's gives a splendid sense of space, every hole being entirely separate. (Within the course boundaries there is just about enough spare land to lay out another course!) Although the player does not return to the vicinity of the clubhouse until the 18th, this is by no means the traditional Scottish out-and-back links lay-out. There are many changes of direction, so that a wind will come at a player from every direction during the course of a round. A good score often needs to be made on the first nine, mainly because you are unlikely to pick up shots during the stern finish from the 13th onwards.

Even so, the start can be just as daunting. The 1st, over 440 yards (400 m) long, has an invitingly wide fairway, but the green is unreachable into a wind. The par-3 3rd, well over 200 yards (180 m), has an upslope to the green and often requires a wooden club shot. The 4th, at 466 yards (426 m), is one of the longest of the par 4s and a right-to-left dogleg. Bunkers on the right threaten shorter hitters, and there are more on the left at the angle of the dogleg. The 5th is another long 4, but from here on several of the holes until you reach the hard finish offer you some chance to improve the look of your scorecard.

Many think the 13th, a par 4 of length about 440 yards (400 m), the most difficult hole to par on the course, and the 14th, although not a long par 5 at just over 500 yards (460 m), is menaced by an out-of-bounds region along the right. There is the risk here that you can hit a good straight drive and then watch as your ball catches the side of a hump and bounds almost at right angles off the course. The hole takes its name,

Suez Canal, from a ditch which crosses the fairway 300 yards (275 m) or so from the tee. In fact, it should not be in play provided your drive has been a reasonable one.

At the 15th a good drive is needed to reach the fairway – but then this is true of Sandwich as a whole: it is no place for a golfer used to getting away with topping the occasional tee shot. Just short of the green on the 15th are three deep cross bunkers. The 16th is a good short par 3, certainly no monster at 165 yards (151 m), but heavily bunkered both in front and to either side. The 17th has one of the humpiest of the fairways. It is a good idea to err on the side of strength with your second shot, for the raised back of the green will very likely help the ball back on.

The last, a par 4 of nearly 460 yards (420 m), has settled a few big events. The professionals have been known to complain that they are expected to hold with a long iron a green that was originally designed to hold a more lofted shot. But there is a way to play it. The drive should be along the left; should you still need a long iron for the second, the shot should be a low runner.

In severe weather, when the rough is dense, Royal St George's is almost unplayable for moderate club golfers. Given a fine summer's day and the larks flying, it is a golfing paradise.

LEFT Sandy Lyle, the Scottish golfer, holds the famous claret jug after winning the 1985 Open over the course. He is also wearing the Championship Belt, won outright by Young Tom Morris more than a century ago. It is now owned by the Royal and Ancient Golf Club of St Andrews.

LEFT The 16th green is a heavily bunkered par 3.

THE ROYAL AND ANCIENT GOLF CLUB
ST ANDREWS
FIFE, SCOTLAND

ST ANDREWS OLD

To many golfers who have played the Old Course at St Andrews, the only thing 'great' about it is its reputation. Some of the finest players of all time have been puzzled by this reputation – some even openly contemptuous. J H Taylor, who won two Opens on the course, still never came to admire it. Sam Snead, who won the 1946 Open here, wrote later that it seemed an abandoned sort of place: he thought the land worth nothing more than planting with beet. Bobby Jones, who first played the course as a teenager in 1921 and tore up his card in disgust during his third round in the Open, at the time felt 'puzzled dislike'. Later, however, he was to declare (perhaps a couple of championship victories at St Andrews helped): 'Truly, if I had to select one course on which to play the match of my life, I should select the Old Course.' As Robert Tyre Jones Jr may well have been the most intelligent of the great golfers, his opinion cannot be lightly dismissed.

Certainly, when you first arrive at St Andrews, you wonder what all the fuss is about. Many golfers are outright puzzled when they step towards the 1st tee. The old sandstone clubhouse of the Royal and Ancient Golf Club certainly looks historic enough, a potent symbol of golf's venerability and probably more photographed than any other single feature of the course. But what is this before us? Apparently a flat field making up the 1st and 18th holes, giving both of them unbunkered fairways of very generous width indeed. Two features are visible. A swale of no great depth in front of the 18th green (the legendary Valley of Sin), from which it looks easy enough to putt, and a little stream (the Swilcan Burn) which is in play only for a very poor tee shot on the 18th but is an obvious threat just short of the 1st green. Both are manifestly holes of no more than drive-and-pitch length, unless you are playing into the wind.

If we look at our score card, more oddities immediately appear. There are only a couple of par 3s and, although they are long ones, only a couple of par 5s. There is also a surprising sequence of four par 4s between the 7th and the 12th, all of which are well under 400 yards (365 m), a couple of which are surely drivable with a tail wind. (The 10th and 12th in fact are, although you cannot have a following wind on both of them on the same day.)

And what of the feel of history? Golf has been played here for well over five and a half centuries, but there are no clear signs of this. That venerable clubhouse, built in 1854, is hardly an ancient monument. From the 1st tee you see a row of quaint shops to the left. But, further on, a few hundred yards away, is the Old Course Golf and Country Club. Some think it a hideous monstrosity, modern hotel architecture at its worst. This is to overstate things, but certainly the building does nothing to enhance the feeling that golf has been played here since the dawn of time – neither do a handful of modern houses the city fathers have allowed to be built close along the left.

Photographers know what is wanted. The sur-

LEFT A view of the town of St Andrews from the course.

BELOW LEFT The 19th-century clubhouse is the home of the R and A which, in partnership with the USGA, administers the rules of golf and independently organizes the British championships.

roundings you see in their pictures are the clubhouse, the edge of the town huddling close around the 18th green and the St Andrews skyline viewed from out on the course. There is one truly venerable feature, a little stone bridge, several hundred years old, which crosses the Swilcan Burn on the 18th. In 1810, it was 'almost impassable' and repairs were ordered to what was then known as the 'Golfer's Bridge'.

But enough of history: let us instead explore the course. At the 1st, the drive is almost too easy but, especially if the flag is to the front of the green, the second shot must be precisely weighted. It must, of course, clear the burn, but if it is only a little too strong you find yourself with a testing downhiller to the hole. The 2nd, at just over 400 yards (365 m), gives some clues as to how to play the Old Course. Almost invariably,

RIGHT A Harry Rountree painting of the Old course in 1910. It has remained virtually unchanged since that date.

the best line to ease the second shot is along the right of the fairway, as here, yet the safest line for the tee shot is usually very different – you have to drive to the left to make sure you stay clear of the worst trouble. This, of course, makes the second shot more difficult ... Because of this trait of the course Seve Ballesteros, in his plan to win the 1984 championship, adopted a simple philosophy – keep out of the bunkers. As long as he could do that from the tee, he was happy to accept more demanding shots to the green.

As early as this 2nd hole another feature of the course should become apparent. The ground in front of the greens is frequently undulating, and the humps and hollows often throw the ball off in unwelcome directions. The best shot to a green is almost always one which pitches on. This can be done in modern times, now that watering has made the greens far more holding than they used to be in dry weather. The practice started over 60 years ago, and has become increasingly used as time has gone by. Placement of the shot to the green, however, is still the main problem that prevents the stars returning lower scores than they do. Ballesteros thinks St Andrews the easiest of the British Open courses but a few statistics suggest he is wrong – or just personally lucky! To the end of 1983, for instance, there had been 22 rounds of between 63 and 65 in all of the British Opens. Only one of those was done at St Andrews; but in the 1980 championship alone, at Muirfield, there were three 64s and a 63!

The first really dramatic hole, as the course goes out over gently undulating ground, comes with the 5th, which has a steep fall down to the green. Golfers need to decide if their shots to the green at this par 5 should carry this feature or make use of it. Shortly after the 5th comes the famous 'loop', that sequence of two par 3s and four short par 4s. Most good scores for the round come from having a fair ration of 3s in this stretch. Only the 7th green, 372 yards (340 m) away with a bunker blocking the route to the flag, is not 'on' for the tee shot. However, do not take these comments to mean that you should regard these holes as easy meat. The par 3s, the 8th and 11th, can cause problems, especially the latter, a much imitated hole. The 9th, many think, is the worst on the course. It has a flat fairway and a green rather too like a tennis court. In the 1921 Open the champion, Jock Hutchison, holed the 8th in one and nearly repeated the feat on the 9th. Years later, Tony Jacklin holed his second shot to the 9th in his first round of the 1970 championship to be out in 29.

After the 12th, there are certainly no more gift holes. The 13th is one of the great par 4s of world golf. There are the Coffin bunkers, apparently in the middle of the fairway, to avoid, and the shot to the green must be well struck to hold the putting surface, which slopes away from the player. The 14th is a perilous par 5, especially if there is a wind from your left blowing towards the out-of-bounds wall. The so-called Hell bunker used to be a terror for those trying to get up in two, but it is not quite as severe today. For good players, most problems come from playing the tee shot 'safely' to the left away from the out-of-bounds and instead finding the series of bunkers called the Beardies. The hole cost Gene Sarazen the title in 1933, and six years later Bobby Locke used up 15 strokes on it in his first two rounds. The 15th and 16th are both good par 4s, and some players lose concentration, thinking of the terrors immediately ahead. The 17th, a long par 4 at 461 yards (422 m), may be the most difficult hole in world golf. The safe way to play it is to drive left, play toward the front of the green, chip up to the pin and hope for a

single putt. Bold play means going for the 4, however. This means driving blind over the outline of the former railway sheds on the right and hopefully not out of bounds. If the drive finishes just in bounds, the shot to the green then becomes more possible. A drive to the left, however, leaves the green at an angle to the line in, the famous Road bunker barring the way. A ball played with too much strength will very likely run through the green and out onto the road beyond, eventually coming to rest against a stone wall. It is unlikely that anyone has ever played this hole in level par for all four rounds of a championship. In 1984, it destroyed Tom Watson. Ironically, he had played a superb drive down the right, ideally tight by the out-of-bounds, but then he pushed his second onto the road. Seve Ballesteros, in contrast, played the hole the 'wrong way': well to the left in the rough, he played a brilliant – and lucky – second shot which held the green. Watson, close to the wall, could not get his third close, and his chance of the championship was gone. Ballesteros made doubly sure with a birdie on the last.

And so to the 18th. Here you can slice the ball right over the fence into 'the old grey town', but otherwise the tee shot should not give you too much trouble. The second, depending on flag position, will either be a high pitch or a well weighted running approach, according to taste. In 1970, Doug Sanders needed a par 4 to win the Open. His drive was good but his second was too firm, leaving him with quite a long downhill putt. He was a little too cautious, finished short of the hole, and missed the next one. The following day Jack Nicklaus won the play-off. Ironically, Sanders birdied the hole this time – but so did Nicklaus, who was already a stroke ahead.

It is often said that no one 'designed' the Old Course, as if it were some kind of spontaneous miracle. Yet human hands and minds most certainly did play their part. Those who first played over the terrain made choices about which natural features – little hollows and plateaux – made interesting sites for greens. Basically, however, these early golfers thought out a route away from their start point and then back again. Over time, 22 holes evolved, the 11th and the 22nd being played only once each while the rest were played on both outward and inward journeys. Other early homes of golf played the number of holes that suited the terrain they played over. Leith Links and Musselburgh, at one extreme, had five holes, Montrose had 25, and Prestwick, a much later arrival as a golf course, in the mid-19th century, decided that 12 was about the right number. A momentous event in the history of golf came on 4 October 1764. It was decided by the Royal and Ancient Golf Club, then in existence for just 10 years, that the first four holes were rather short and easy, and so they decided that two much longer holes would be better. They thereby invented the 18-hole course.

At much the same time, the last major changes were made at St Andrews. As it was hazardous to have golfers playing to the same greens both out and back, the course and the greens were widened, so that there would be two widely separate flag positions on each green. Today, some of these monster greens occupy virtually the whole width of the course – the only single greens are on the 1st, 9th, 17th and 18th. The last of these was made in the 1880s, and since that time very few changes at all have been made.

A few back tees have been constructed, and people say that a bunker in the middle of the joint fairways of the 1st and 18th was filled in during 1914 but apart from that the course has been left untouched.

ABOVE Bernhard Langer, the West German golfer, has never won the British Open Championship although he came close to winning the title here in 1984, finishing second.

SHINNECOCK HILLS
GOLF CLUB
SOUTHAMPTON
LONG ISLAND
NEW YORK
UNITED STATES

RIGHT The 1986 US Open was hosted by Shinnecock Hills – the first time the championship has been held there since 1896.

SHINNECOCK HILLS

This is a club whose history is filled with 'firsts', and it was also involved in a major 'second'. Three of the founders were on holiday at Biarritz and watched the Scottish professional Willie Dunn play a succession of shots over a ravine. Said one of the three, William K. Vanderbilt: 'Gentlemen, this beats rifle-shooting for distance and accuracy. It is a game I think might go in our country.'

He spoke more wisely than he knew. Golf since then has been, to understate matters, rather successful in the United States. The founders of Shinnecock Hills thought they had introduced the game to the country when they brought Dunn over to lay out 12 holes for them in 1891. Even though the 'Apple Tree Gang', with their St Andrews Golf Club, had got there a couple of years earlier, Shinnecock Hills was one of the five clubs which founded what was later to be called the United States Golf Association.

As noted, the club has enjoyed some undisputed 'firsts', however. Shinnecock Hills was the first US club to incorporate and, in only a few years, the first to have a membership waiting list. When they called in the well known architect Stanford White, he produced the United States's first proper clubhouse for them.

In 1896 the course, by then 18 holes, was the scene of both the US Amateur and Open championships. In the latter, there was trouble before the off. John Shippen and Oscar Bunn had entered; the former was part black, part American Indian, and the latter was full American Indian. Some of the emigré Scottish professionals who were competing objected, but they were thankfully overruled. Shippen might have won but for an 11 on one hole, and James Foulis became champion.

The Shinnecock Hills Club had a champion of its own, however. This was Beatrix Hoyt, who won three US Ladies' Championships in the years 1896–8 and then retired.

From this time, Shinnecock Hills, a very exclusive club, saw no more great events until 1986. Then the US Golf Association took the bold – even perhaps rash – decision to bring the US Open to the end of Long Island. The players were delighted with the course, which was stretched to just over 6,900 yards (6,310 m), but scoring was high in the cold, wind and rain of the first day – although scores tumbled later, three players coming in with 65s on the last day. Raymond Floyd's final-round 66 was enough to bring him the championship, however.

Although all traces of them are long gone, Willie Dunn's original 12 holes probably represented the first authentic golf-course design in the United States. The present course dates from 1931, when William Flynn and Dick Wilson produced a lay-out which makes good use of the prevailing wind, the long par 4s playing with it and the short ones against it. Fairways are well separated and undulating. The turf, although inland in type, is closer in texture to British links than at almost anywhere else in the United States. The rough is usually fierce, so straight driving is at a premium, and length too is needed to carry fairway crests.

The four par 3s are a strong feature at Shinnecock Hills, with the 2nd being a particularly severe test, especially so early in the round. It is some 220 yards (200 m) long and plays over a valley to a well bunkered green. Although the remaining three are far shorter, the 11th, at 160 yards (146 m), presents a small target, and the 17th is perhaps the most beautiful hole on the course; it is named the Eden, after the St Andrews hole in Scotland.

SHOAL CREEK
BIRMINGHAM, ALABAMA
UNITED STATES

SHOAL CREEK

Alabama is very much off the beaten track for tournament play. When the Professional Golfers' Association (PGA) decided to stage their championship at Shoal Creek in 1984, this was the first time that any Tour event had been held in the state since the 1960s.

The course was a relatively new one, but had risen rapidly in esteem. The reason was, to put it succinctly, Jack Nicklaus. Hall Thompson, an Augusta member, had bought some land for a golf course and a select housing development some 25 miles (40 km) south of Birmingham and, looking for a course architect, was advised to try Nicklaus, who was then at an early stage in his career as a golf architect. It took Jack, after a first visit to the site in 1974, two weeks to decide whether or not he felt he could produce a course over the rocky, forested landscape.

The result contains some of his trademarks. Many of the shots are slightly downhill. The shot to the green always allows a clear view of the flag. Another feature is that the par 5s, all over 500 yards (460 m) long – the 6th, at 554 yards (507 m), is the longest – can be reached in two by tournament players, but demand a second shot of excellence. The 11th is a good example of this. Anything short to the left, right or front will find the shallow but broad creek; then there

are bunkers that will catch most shots that are not of the highest quality. At the 17th – 539 yards (493 m) – Shoal Creek itself is in play, broadened into a lake to the left of the green. At the right front, boulders were put in. Of course, these do not come into play, but the waterfall they create makes this the most photographed hole on the course.

On the whole, the par 4s are perhaps a more severe test. Eight of these are over 400 yards (365 m) long, of which four are around 450 yards (410 m). Only one par 4 is shorter than 400 yards, the 14th: at 380 yards (347 m), even that is scarcely of drive-and-pitch length, and there is a lake confronting the tee shot. Probably the most difficult, however, is the 4th, at 458 yards (419 m). There is not a single bunker on the hole. Instead, Nicklaus used a grassy hollow in front of the green, reckoning that good players would find sand easier to play from.

Some have found the par 3s a weakness. All are between 177 and 197 yards (162–180 m) and, because of the shape of the land, may need the same club.

During the 1984 PGA, however, the most noticeable feature of all was the rough. Although it was not deep, every shot that missed the fairway seemed to settle well down. The ball simply disappeared. Perhaps that was why only one long hitter, Seve Ballesteros, finished in the top five – and he was fifth. Those ahead of him – Calvin Peete, Gary Player, Lanny Wadkins and especially the champion, Lee Trevino – are more renowned for subtlety of play than for sheer strength.

Player started badly with a 74, but after the second round it seemed very possible he could become the oldest winner ever of a major championship. He birdied all four par 3s and had six more birdies to be round in 63. That tied him with Trevino and Wadkins. They were still the leaders after the third round, and a Player miracle seemed in prospect when he holed a putt of well over 30 yards (27 m) on the 9th in the last round. However, over the last nine it proved to be a battle between Trevino and Wadkins, everyone's money being on the 34-year-old rather than on Trevino, who was by 1984, at the age of 44, a part-time competitor. In the end, however, Trevino had his way, winning by four strokes from Wadkins and Player.

Lee Trevino's victory put him in the record books as the fourth oldest golfer ever to win one of the four majors.

LEFT Lee Trevino became the US PGA Champion on this course in 1984 when he, and most others, thought his career at the top was over. He was 44.

BELOW LEFT The 11th with its shored-up green is a relatively easy hole if you are content to pitch on in 3, but presents a challenge for long hitters trying to reach it in 2.

SOUTHERN HILLS

SOUTHERN HILLS
COUNTRY CLUB
TULSA, OKLAHOMA
UNITED STATES

BELOW RIGHT Hubert Green won the 1977 US Open on this course, despite a death threat.

Hubert Green was on the 10th hole at Southern Hills in his final round of the 1977 US Open, a championship he had led throughout, when the police received an anonymous death threat: Green was going to be murdered at the 15th. He himself was not informed for quite some time, but TV cameras were put to work scanning the crowd around the 15th green. Before he played the hole, however, Green was given the option of withdrawing, carrying on or requesting a suspension of play. He decided to continue, and fortunately nothing happened.

His greatest problem, in fact, came on the 18th, not the 15th. This is a difficult par 4 of over 450 yards (410 m) which doglegs to the right, with the fairway narrowed by ponds at the angle. The tee shot is downhill, but this does not make the hole any easier, because the second shot is to an elevated green from a downhill lie. When Green came to the hole he needed a bogey 5 to win. After being bunkered and in the rough, he only just made the green with his third shot, then left his approach putt by no means dead. Unlike his similar Masters experience the next year, Green got his 3-footer – and the championship.

Only Green and the second man home, Lou

ABOVE The 4-par 12th at Southern Hills was much praised by Ben Hogan. A particularly challenging hole, the green is guarded by bunkers and a blind water hazard. (© TONY ROBERTS 1986)

Graham, were under par at the end of the championship, the main reason being the dense rough in which balls just a foot or so off the fairway settled out of sight in the Bermuda grass. Green is not a long hitter and neither is Graham, but both men are better than most at keeping the ball in play on the fairway. In a previous US Open, the 1958 champion Tommy Bolt pointed to his driver when asked what had won him the title. If only two scored below 280 in 1977, in 1958 just three managed to break 290.

In the mid-1930s, after the vast expansion of golf during the 1920s in the United States, many clubs were having to shut down as a result of the Depression. Southern Hills was one of few to be constructed during this period, the oil money of Tulsa being the benefactor. It was designed by Perry Maxwell, who had also created Prairie Dunes and been called in by Bobby Jones and Clifford Roberts to make changes to Alister Mackenzie's Augusta. At Augusta Maxwell moved the 10th green and transformed an ordinary hole into a magnificent one.

Most consider Southern Hills to be a similar triumph. The course is often rated the best in the central United States, but its name is misleading. It is very flat indeed, the only real slope being up to the clubhouse, so that the 9th and 18th have uphill second shots and the 1st and 10th play downhill. For championship play, the 13th is probably the toughest hole, shortened to a very long par 4 of 470 yards (430 m), instead of the 550-yard (500-m) par 5 the members play. This change in length is mainly because the United States Golf Association (USGA) likes the Open courses to play to a par of 70. In tournaments short hitters face a blind second shot over ponds to the left and right front of the green. Unlike the 13th, the 5th remains a par 5, a true monster at nearly 600 yards (550 m), with a tightly bunkered green at the end of the trek.

Bunkers are another main test on the course. Professionals learn and follow their trade in coarse sand. Southern Hills has very fine river sand. The professionals are not used to it – especially not to finding completely buried lies! There are also the trees which line the fairways, completing the picture of a course where it is often fatal to miss a fairway, even by inches, while perfect positioning on the fairway is also essential if you are to set up your shot into the undulating, banked greens.

Spyglass Hill

SPYGLASS HILL
GOLF CLUB
PEBBLE BEACH
CALIFORNIA
UNITED STATES

Most first holes give golfers a fairly gentle introduction to the rigours that may lie ahead, but the one at Spyglass is an exception. It is a massive par 5 of 600 yards (550 m), swinging from left to right and heading for the sea. Play used to be dominated by a lone pine in the centre of the fairway; it is said that Robert Trent Jones designed the hole with the tree as the focal point. The next four holes are as near as you get to links golf in the United States, and they are fearsome when the wind is up, even though each is a relatively short par 4 or par 3.

The remainder of the holes lie in pine parkland. There is water on several holes in this section of the course, although usually it presents a problem only if your shot is wayward. An exception is on the 11th, a par 5, where the shot to the green must carry over water.

Undoubtedly holes 2 to 5 are the ones which make the most impact, particularly on US players unused to links golf, but the 12th is as interesting as any, a par 3 of some 180 yards (165 m), modelled like so many on the Redan at North Berwick, Scotland. The green is set a little aslant the line of play, and the problems are increased by water to the left of the green. The 14th is a long double dogleg of some 550 yards (500 m), but the 16th is probably the most difficult hole, at 460 yards (420 m) or so, doglegging to the right with an elevated green.

The name of the course derives from Robert Louis Stevenson's *Treasure Island*. Stevenson spent some time living in the Del Monte Forest and is thought to have derived some of the inspiration for the book from the Pacific vistas. Names from the book were given to some of the holes – Long John Silver, Treasure Island, Jim Hawkins and so on. The course opened for play early in 1966, and Bing Crosby immediately added it to the rota for his tournament. Professionals in the first years were highly critical of its condition. Although those difficulties belong to the past, it is still considered by many to be the most difficult of the three used for the tournament, the others, of course, being Cypress Point and Pebble Beach.

When Jack Nicklaus arrived to play here for the first time, Crosby bet him '5' that he could not par the course at his first attempt. 'Five dollars or five grand?' Nicklaus asked. They settled on $500, and Nicklaus played round in a 2-under-par 70. In the tournament itself, however, his score was 2 over, 74, but he was still good enough to go on to win.

RIGHT The last 13 holes at Spyglass Hill run inland from the Monterey Peninsula through pine forest. This is the 16th which at 465 yards (425 m) is the longest par 4 of the course.

FAR RIGHT The first 4 holes are out in links territory. The shot to the 3rd green must be precise; miss and you are bound to find sand.

Sun City

THE GARY PLAYER
COUNTRY CLUB
SUN CITY, PILANSBERG
BOPHUTHATSWANA
SOUTH AFRICA

RIGHT A panoramic view of the Gary Player Country Club in its breathtaking setting at Sun City.

Set on the floor of an extinct volcano, this course – usually known as Sun City rather than by its formal name – was cut out of thorn tree and bush in little more than a matter of months during the late 1970s. At times it can be like a cauldron, and it depends very much on sophisticated watering systems.

It was created by Ronald Kirby and Gary Player, and one of their prime aims was to preserve the integrity of the land as far as possible: very few trees were cut down. The course features multiple island tees, the use of which can affect the length of some of the holes by as much as 100 yards (90 m). At full stretch, it measures over 7,650 yards (7,000 m).

Sol Kerzner, the promoter of Sun City, well knew the value of tournament play, and the first was held here in 1979, when the course was barely yet fit for play. A little later Kerzner promoted the first-ever tournament to have a prize of $1 million; it was won by Johnny Miller. The drama lay mostly in the sudden-death play-off, which was one of the longest ever. Nine holes went by before Severiano Ballesteros three-putted to give Miller his victory.

In 1987 the diminutive Welsh golfer Ian Woosnam won the $1-million cheque – his eighth important tournament victory of the year. This brought his total winnings for 1987 to over £1 million, an all-time record for a single year and approaching twice as much as anyone else had achieved. However, huge purses are becoming ever more frequent in professional tournaments and the Sun City Challenge has lost some of its appeal in recent years.

TURNBERRY AILSA

TURNBERRY HOTEL
TURNBERRY, AYRSHIRE
SCOTLAND

In 1977 Turnberry was almost at its easiest for the Open Championship. True, the course had been set up to be as tough as possible, but the hot dry summer of 1976 (the year when the UK Government appointed a Minister for Droughts!) had ensured that the rough was not punishing. Jack Nicklaus, despite driving none too well throughout, was able to card his lowest four-round total ever in a major championship, 269 – and even then he did not win. Tom Watson gave what history may well rank as his greatest performance to win a thrilling two-man encounter by a single stroke.

Mind you, the course was not as easy for the rest of the field. Only one other player, Hubert Green, beat par – and he was 10 strokes behind the leaders. One rising star found it very difficult. He was a young Australian aged 22 who already had two tournaments to his credit: in Australia he had won the 1976 Westlakes Classic and in Great Britain the 1977 Martini. His name? Yes, you probably guessed it – Greg Norman. At Turnberry in 1977 there were two cuts. Norman just scraped through the 36-hole one with rounds of 78 and 72, but he was gone after 54 holes.

It was a very different story in 1986. The R & A seemed to want to make sure that no one humiliated Turnberry. The fairways were narrowed to about 25 yards (23 m). There were only a couple of yards of semi-rough before the knee-high stuff began.

As usual, Seve Ballesteros started as favourite. He thought the champion might come home at about 5 under. That was before the weather worsened. On the first day 80s were commonplace. Anyone with a 75 or better felt he had acquitted himself well. In the very stiff wind no one finished under par, and just one player, Ian Woosnam, was round in 70 to equal it. In much better weather (cloudy and chilly!) on the second day, Greg Norman played one of the great rounds of major championship history and matched the lowest round ever shot in the British Open, a 63 by Mark Hayes in the previous Turnberry Open. Norman birdied the 2nd, 3rd and 4th and followed this up with an eagle on the 7th. He was out in a 32 which included two bogeys. On the second nine he piled up five more birdies and then – an anticlimax if ever there was one – three-putted the last for his 63. That round brought him from 4 behind to a 2-stroke lead. By the end of the championship, Norman was a commanding 5 ahead and the only man to equal par for 72 holes.

RIGHT An aerial view of the famous lighthouse, a distinctive feature of Turnberry, and of some of the sea holes. The vast hotel can be seen in the background.

But this was Turnberry in severe weather and set up to examine the best. For the visiting golfer on a reasonable day there are many more difficult courses. However, there are few that are more exhilarating.

Turnberry has a curious history. It was first laid out by a former Open Champion, Willie Fernie, early in this century as part of what is claimed to have been the first hotel-and-golf-course centre in the world. Like the very different Gleneagles, it proved very popular until World War II came. It

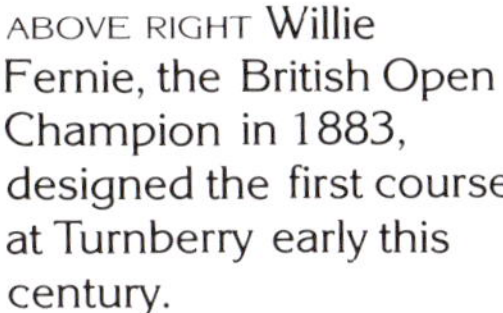

ABOVE RIGHT Willie Fernie, the British Open Champion in 1883, designed the first course at Turnberry early this century.

then became an RAF Coastal Command training airfield. Although the cause was clearly a very good one, surely no other championship course – certainly in the British Isles – has been so devastated. The characteristic sand dunes had to be levelled, bunkers were filled in, and much of the Ailsa and Arran courses was covered by concrete runways. Some of those runways still remain, although off either course, but an occasional out-of-bounds drive can bound, skip and run for hundreds of yards along what has become a parking area for spectators' cars.

After the war, it was found that detailed drawings and models had survived, and Philip Mackenzie Ross used these as a basis for recreating Turnberry Ailsa and Arran. Although the Ailsa course is much longer and is the one used for big events, the Arran is well worth playing and is perhaps a better test of straight driving.

Ailsa begins with a series of unspectacular par 4s, though the 3rd, at 475 yards (434 m) from the championship tees, can be very difficult. The stretch that most remember best, however, is that from the 4th to the 11th, running close alongside the sea. The 4th is a par 3 which looks more difficult than it really is, with a green cut into the side of a dune and much peril if you miss on the left. The 5th is a scenic hole, a fairly short par 5, played from a high tee to a valley with dunes on either side before it doglegs left. The 6th, a long par 3 of over 240 yards (220 m), again looks more difficult than it is, unless the player is in a cavernous bunker in the upslope towards the green. With the wind behind you it

ABOVE A view down the 18th towards the green photographed in a brief spell of sunshine during the 1986 Open.

can be little more than a mid-iron shot, but it is impossible for almost anyone to reach when the wind is against. The 7th is another fine hole, and can be played as a par 4 or a 5; it doglegs left to follow the shoreline. As a par 4, it is probably the toughest hole on the course, with the ground rising to the green.

The most spectacular tee shot comes at the 9th. Championship competitors retire to a tee set on a rocky promontory and require a carry of 200 yards (180 m) to reach the fairway across an inlet. However, this is nothing like the 16th at Cypress Point. Few professionals fail to make the carry, but they tend to complain when they produce a perfect tee shot only to find that their ball has kicked away into the semi-rough. During the 1986 Open, Jack Nicklaus enquired if anyone had managed to stay on the fairway here! And staying on is important at this hole because there is a long second shot to play.

As Turnberry Ailsa is an out-and-back lay-out, if the long 4s on the first nine have been almost impossible because of a wind from the north, relief comes on the inward half, which is also about 200 yards (180 m) shorter. The golf is less exhilarating, however – although still good enough for most. The 15th, at its full length of about 220 yards (200 m), is a very difficult par 3. It was very influential in helping Tom Watson win the 1977 Open when he holed a vast putt from well off the green to draw level with Nicklaus, who had played much the better tee shot but came away with a 3 to Watson's 2.

Although streams are not a major Turnberry feature, the broad one which crosses the fairway just short of the 16th green certainly is. Because the banks slope gently, there is little chance of an approach shot bounding across. To judge by

LEFT Jack Nicklaus and Tom Watson take a break during the 1977 Open. Following an epic contest between these two players, Watson finally emerged the champion – his second of five British Open victories.

RIGHT Greg Norman on his way to victory in the 1986 Open. This was to be his first major championship win.

its length, it is a potential birdie hole, but most golfers choose to play well toward the back of the green so that their shot does not spin back into the stream.

With the wind behind, the par-5 17th can be a question of a drive followed by a 6- or 7-iron shot for professionals. Club golfers who dare to give their drive everything from the high tee should be able to get home with a wood second shot.

The par-4 18th, lengthened for championship play to 430 yards (393 m), is the hole which Tom Watson played to perfection to hold onto his 1-stroke lead in 1977. He banged a 2-iron down the middle and then hit a mid-iron to about two feet (60 cm) of the hole. He needed to. Nicklaus, after sending his drive almost into the bushes along the right, holed a vast birdie putt.

WESTWARD HO!

ROYAL NORTH DEVON GOLF CLUB
WESTWARD HO!, DEVON
ENGLAND

This club is the oldest in England still playing over its original ground, in this case Northam Burrows. Golf had been played earlier elsewhere in England. Blackheath claims to have been in existence since 1608, although there is no written proof for this, and certainly goes back as far as 1766. Old Manchester was formed in 1818 and played over Kersal Moor. However, in neither of these cases do the clubs still play over their original courses.

It is likely that Scottish influence brought golf to the northwest and northeast of England before the game began to be played over Northam Burrows. There is the definite example of Old Manchester, and a club was formed at Alnmouth, Northumberland, in 1869. However, there are stories that seafarers from Holland brought a version of the game to the flat linksland by the village of Alnmouth considerably earlier, although no one knows precisely when this might have been.

The history of the Royal North Devon and golf played there even before the club's foundation in 1864 is well documented. It all began with two men, General Moncrieff and William Driscoll Gossett. They visited the Rev. I. H. Gossett at Westward Ho! and both thought that the Burrows would be suited to golf. The general went so far as to declare: 'Providence evidently intended this for a golf links.'

Casual play began in 1853, but activity was spasmodic for a few years. In 1860, however, Old Tom Morris came down from Prestwick before the first Open Championship, stayed for a month and rearranged the course. He returned in the year of the club's foundation for a week or so and very likely suggested further changes. At this time, the idea that a golf course should necessarily consist of 18 holes was still some way off. The North Devon and West of England Golf Club (its first name) gave the golfer a choice between 17 and 22 holes: if you wanted to play a 'short' round, you just missed out the 13th to the 17th.

In 1867 the club gained royal approval and its present name, and in the following year the Westward Ho! and North Devon Ladies' Club was formed, believed to be the first for women in the British Isles. There was a rule that read: 'No other club shall on any account be used on the

BELOW Spectators gather for an important match around the turn of the century. Note the boy caddies.

Ladies' Course but a wooden putter.' This was probably because it was felt unladylike to raise a club above shoulder level.

The Royal North Devon rapidly became famous. It was particularly popular with golfers from Blackheath and Wimbledon. The land they played over at home was poor stuff for golf, and Westward Ho! gave them the real thing. As Bernard Darwin later wrote: 'To go to Westward Ho! is not to make a mere visit of pleasure as to an ordinary course; it is a reverent pilgrimage.' He added: 'It is a splendid course, not only wonderfully difficult and wonderfully interesting but it has a charm given to few links. It looks more like a good golf course than almost any other in the world.' The great golf architect Herbert Fowler, who made considerable changes at Westward Ho! early this century, was referring to Prestwick, Royal St George's and Muirfield when he wrote: 'None of these courses can compare with Westward Ho! as a test of the highest form of golf and the only reason ever given why championships are not played there is that it is out of the way.' Perhaps the last word should be left with J H Taylor. He thought it simply 'the finest natural links in the world'.

Yet no Open Championships have come to Westward Ho! Perhaps the most likely time would have been, say, between the 1880s and the start of World War I. But, as Fowler noted, it *is* out of the way and so the Royal North Devon's course does not have the fame of places where the great events have been played (although both the Amateur Championship and professional tournaments have come). Travel has become far easier, but Westward Ho! is still rather far from the major population centres which are necessary if a really big event is to be staged. Maybe an act of faith is needed: the R & A acted on one when they first chose Turnberry in 1977, and again when they risked road problems when they took the Open back to Sandwich in 1981 after a gap of over 30 years.

The start is not promising. The opening and finishing holes are flat – if not as flat as they look – and the Burrows only begin with the 3rd. The 4th, at 354 yards (324 m), has a famous hazard, a vast cross bunker that must be carried from the tee. The face is timbered, and there is a local rule which allows a player within two club-lengths a free drop the same distance further back.

A much more unusual local rule concerns the 'Great Sea Rushes'. These are a unique and very sharply pointed feature of the course. If you get in them, you can declare your ball lost and drop another for a penalty of only one stroke (rather than stroke and distance) near the point of entry. These rushes are most in play on the 10th, 11th and 12th, where they have to be carried from the tee, and there are other points where they can be seen – but preferably not entered.

All the middle section of the course is played among the sand dunes of the Burrows and, as Taylor said, looks entirely natural. Fowler's work was so in keeping with the terrain that players of today tend to believe that nothing has been altered at Westward Ho! since golf began there. The arrival of the rubber core ball meant changes everywhere, however, except at the Old Course, St Andrews, which was perhaps too long for gutta percha.

Although many have thought it unfortunate, the clubhouse is not down by the sea among the dunes; its situation inland is responsible for the flatness of the first and final holes. Still, even this can help the sense of anticipation. The golfer starts off in a dull landscape, but the promised land lies ahead . . . At the flat finish, the stream which runs across short of the final green has settled many a match. Then comes the clubhouse, which contains many memories of Royal North Devon's history. A museum was opened in 1985 and rehoused in a separate building during 1987.

ABOVE In trouble in the Great Sea Rushes, this traditionalist is using hickory shafts to extricate himself from this hazard unique to Westward Ho!

WINGED FOOT WEST

WINGED FOOT GOLF CLUB
MAMARONEK
WESTCHESTER COUNTY
NEW YORK
UNITED STATES

The toughest holes in golf are those that demand long shots to the greens. These holes are not the apparently daunting par 5s – of, say, 550 yards (500 m) – but long par 3s and 4s that demand long irons and woods for the shots in. The difficulties of the West Course at Winged Foot derive from the long par 4s. When the course is set up for championship play, there are 10 over 400 yards (365 m) long – and most of them considerably longer. The members have it slightly easier, for two of these holes revert to not particularly long par 5s for normal play. Over 60 years ago, they asked their chosen architect, A W Tillinghast, for 'a man-sized course' . . . and that is what they certainly got. The East Course is almost as good.

Tillinghast was presented with heavily wooded meadowland and aimed, as always, to produce courses in which each hole would have individuality. Many of his holes are at least slightly dog-legged, being to left or right impartially. Deep bunkers hug most of the greens closely. Tillinghast considered that one of the greatest merits of a golf course was that it demanded accuracy for the shots into the greens, and Winged Foot is very testing in this respect. He gave as much attention to the green approaches as to any other features of the course, so that shots that are just not quite good enough tend to be thrown aside into the greenside bunkers. The greens themselves are subtly contoured and, at championship pitch, are both hard and bewilderingly fast. The rough can be very severe – particularly when the course is being set up for championship play – and in many places the trees pinch into the fairways.

Opened in 1923, the courses take their name from the club symbol of the New York Athletic Club. The US Open has come to Winged Foot West on four occasions, and all four championships have been memorable in one way or another.

The first, in 1929, saw Bobby Jones at both his best and his worst. He began with a flawless 69 to establish a grasp on the championship, and seemed to be cruising to an easy victory when he parred the opening holes in his final round. But this situation exemplified Jones's Achilles' heel: he tended to lose concentration when the job seemed to be done. On the 8th, he bunkered his shot to the green and then exploded out into another bunker across the green.

He repeated the performance to finish with a triple-bogey 7 on the hole. He then returned to steady golf, and with four holes to play had only to par in to win by three strokes. Easy. Jones immediately made things difficult by taking 7 on the next hole, a par 4. He then three-putted the 70th. If he could achieve two pars on the final holes, however, he could at least tie. Jones got the first with no problem but missed the green on the 18th and then pitched to 12 feet (3·5 m) or so. The putt had considerable borrow, but Jones was nevertheless able to sink it.

He was into a play-off with Al Espinosa, a man who had played the last half-dozen holes beautifully and without a care in the world – he was sure that the 8 he had just scored on the 12th had given Jones the championship. The next day, Jones went out and shot rounds of 72 and 69 to win by 23 strokes, a record 36-hole play-off margin. The wonder is how Jones managed that second round of 69 once he knew the title was already well and truly in the bag.

It was exactly 30 years before the championship returned, in 1959. This contest has not become part of golfing legend, but it is remembered, at least in part, because the champion, Billy Casper, single-putted 31 greens. In 1959, his total of only 114 putts was thought amazing. Few eyebrows would be raised today.

In 1974, the course beat the players. It could be said that no one won, but that Hale Irwin lost less than the other players! His total of 287 was 7 over par. The high scoring was the result not of difficult weather but of the severity of the course. Jack Nicklaus considered that, if players had to compete on Winged Foot most of the time, they might learn to drive and putt much better. Gary Player thought it the greatest US Open test he had ever played – but then Gary makes remarks in the superlative nearly all the time.

The selection of Winged Foot West by the USGA only 10 years later showed that the course was rated very highly. This time, two players did beat the course, Fuzzy Zoeller and Greg Norman, who were both 4 under par when

they tied for the championship. On the last hole Norman, playing just ahead of Zoeller, holed one of the great putts of championship history. The hole was set in the same spot as when Jones had won back in 1929, but Norman was some 40 feet (12 m) away with about 4 feet (1·2 m) of break on his putt. Back down the fairway, Zoeller thought Norman had birdied the hole and picked up a towel and waved it to signal surrender.

That play-off, as with Jones versus Espinosa, was one-way, with Zoeller's 8-stroke margin being a record for an 18-hole play-off in the US Open.

It is the severity of the par 4s, with 10 well over 400 yards (365 m) long for the Open, which impresses one at Winged Foot. Perhaps the best is the 17th at 444 yards (406 m), which doglegs gently right and demands a long-iron second shot of great precision between the bunkers to the long and narrow green.

The 10th is a famous par 3. Tillinghast considered the green the best he ever constructed. Although the bunkers set in the upslope to this elevated green are both large and deep, the subtle undulations on the putting surface are the hole's best defence.

ABOVE The splendid 1920s clubhouse at Winged Foot with the 9th green in the foreground.

LEFT A W Tillinghast, the creator of many top-class US golf courses, designed the two present courses at Winged Foot. They were finally opened in 1923 and the West course hosted the US Open for the first time in 1929.

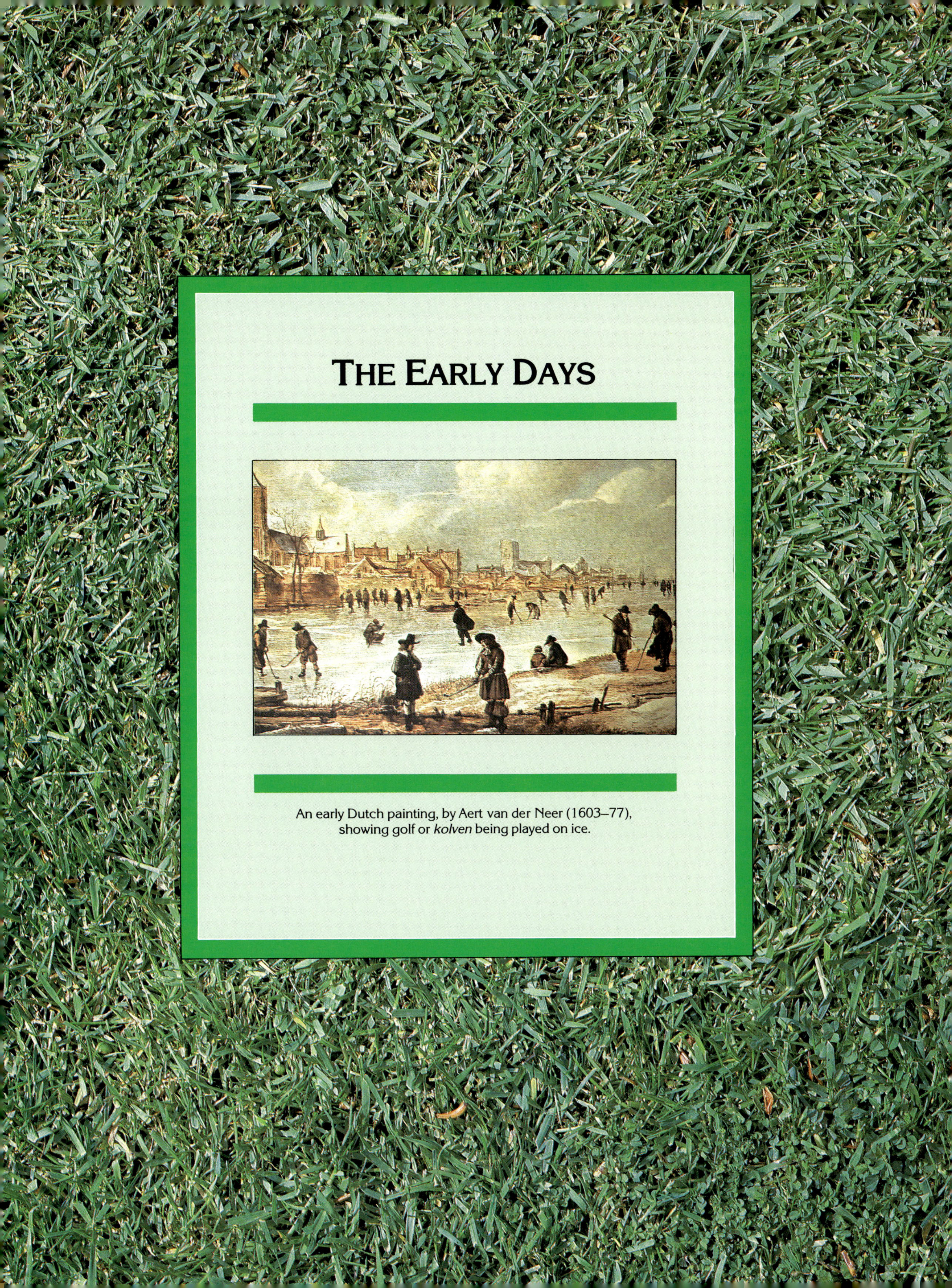

THE EARLY DAYS

An early Dutch painting, by Aert van der Neer (1603–77), showing golf or *kolven* being played on ice.

RIGHT AND BELOW RIGHT Title page and front cover of *The Art of Golf* by Sir W G Simpson, 1887.

FAR RIGHT A painting of a child playing golf by Aelbert Cuyp (1620–91).

PAGES 10 & 11 (see over) LEFT The game of *jeu de mail* (or pall mall), 1717.

RIGHT *Golfers on Ice near Haarlem, 1668,* Adriaen van de Velde (1636–72).

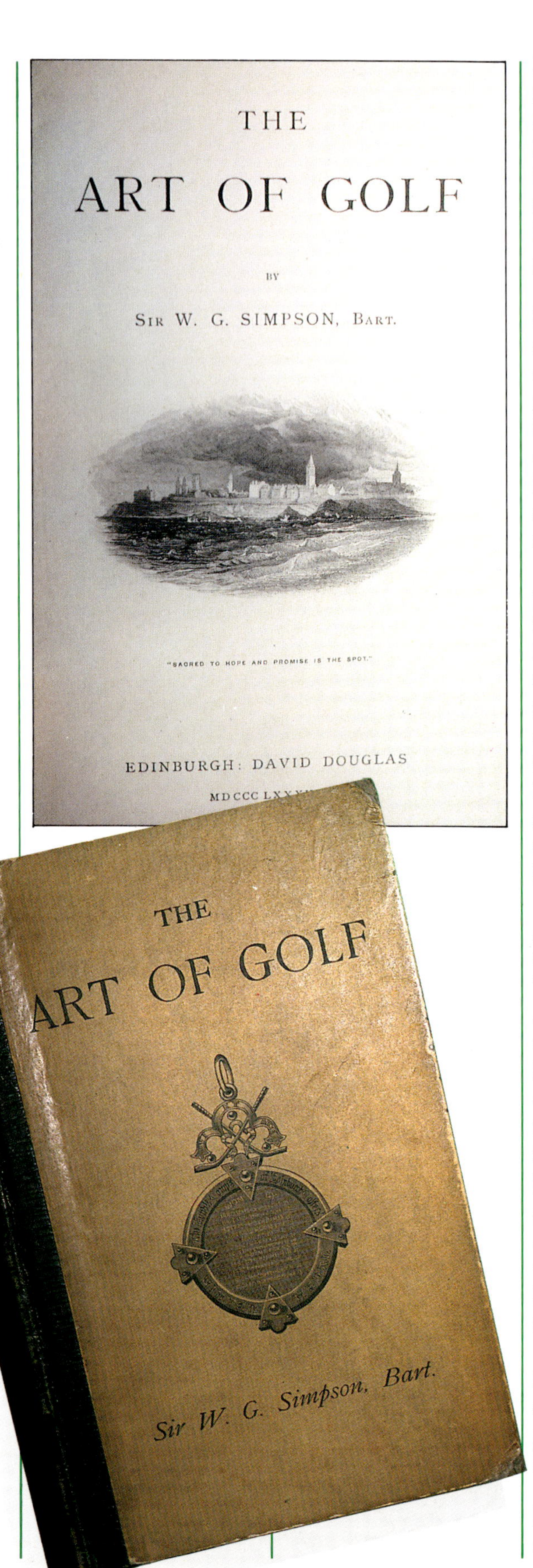

Historians agree that it was the Scots who taught the world to play golf, but who actually invented the game is open to debate. The Scots certainly have strong claims to the title, but so too have the Dutch, French and Belgians. The sad truth is that when, where and how the game of golf came into being is a complete mystery, and will probably remain so.

What can be said is that the game has existed for at least 500 years. This we know because an Act of Parliament dated 6 March, 1457 clearly states that James II of Scotland had football and golf banned because their popularity strongly interfered with archery practice, important for the defence of the realm against the English warriors. Before this there is nothing, not even the slightest of clues, to send historians back to the archives in search of fresh evidence.

The origins of golf, therefore, are a matter of pure conjecture. This has led to many plausible theories being put forward regarding the actual birth of the game. One, more fascinating than most, comes from Sir W G Simpson in his splendid book *The Art of Golf,* wherein he suggests that a shepherd tending his flock on the links of St Andrews happened by chance to knock a pebble with his crook straight into a rabbit hole. He was challenged by a companion to repeat the stroke. The first game of golf had been played!

The Dutch game of *kolven,* a club and ball game similar to golf, which was played on ice as well as land, is supported by many old paintings. The most famous of these is *Golfers on the Ice near Haarlem, 1668,* by Adriaen van de Velde, which hangs in the National Gallery, London. However, the oldest of these paintings – a watercolour by Hendrik Avercamp – was painted in the 17th century, long after the Scottish edict. It is interesting to note that *kolven* appears in what have been claimed as the oldest references to golf in the Americas. The first of these is in the *Minutes of the Court of Fort Orange and Beverwyck, 1657,* which record that three immigrant Dutchmen were charged with playing *kolven* on a day of public prayer.

References to *chole,* the Belgian game, have been traced back to the 14th century. Played across open countryside, but with both sides playing the same ball, *chole* could quite easily have been the forerunner of golf.

There are those who think that the ancient French game called *jeu de mail* bears the closest resemblance to golf. There were four

ways of playing *jeu de mail* – *Roüet, Partie, Chicane* and *Grand Coups. Roüet* meant three- or four-ball matches. *Partie*, as the word implies, required sides of equal number. *Chicane* was similar to matchplay golf between two players. It was played in open country, along the roads, paths or lanes; each player had to play his ball from wherever it happened to lie. The winner was the player reaching a predetermined point in the least number of strokes. Even the rules bear a similarity to those of golf. Among the eight rules which governed the initial stroke, there is mention of a tee being allowed. *Grand Coups* merely meant a long-driving contest between two or more players.

In a stained-glass window in the eastern end of Gloucester Cathedral is an illustration of a figure swinging what appears to be a golf club. This was erected by Sir Thomas Bradstone during the 14th century in memory of his comrades who died at the battle of Crécy. During this same period a club and ball game called *cambuca* was popular, until in 1363 an instruction was given to sheriffs to ban all games, including *cambuca*. Although the figure in the window is today referred to as the Gloucester Golfer, it is difficult to believe that the figure depicts anything other than a man playing *cambuca*.

It is known that a game with a curved bat and a leather ball stuffed with feathers was played in Britain by the Roman soldiers. Called *paganica*, there is no evidence that it was left behind by the departing Romans.

Following a peace treaty between England and Scotland in 1503, the Scots were allowed to resume their golfing activities, although it was still an offence to play on Sundays 'in tyme of sermonis'. The charge was not the playing of golf but the absence from church service. When James VI of Scotland, a keen golfer himself, succeeded to the English throne to become James I in 1603, he introduced golf to the English. It is also claimed that he was responsible for golf being started on Blackheath Common in 1608. However, the game failed to

appeal to the English and was lost until the 18th century, when the Royal Blackheath Golf Club came into existence in 1766.

In the early days of golf in Scotland, the game was played on rough common ground without any thought of class distinction, and the only class recognized was that of skill at the game. There were no greens, just crude holes cut where the surface was flattest. Golfers played together week in and week out without any thought of forming a society or club.

THE FIRST CLUB AND RULES

The distinction of forming the first club goes to the Honourable Company of Edinburgh Golfers, who in 1744 were presented with a silver club by Edinburgh Council for annual competition among 'Noblemen and Gentlemen from any part of Great Britain and Ireland'. At the same time the first Rules of Golf – 13 in all – were drawn up for the inaugural competition. In 1836 the Honourable Company moved from their home at Leith to Musselburgh, and then to their present home at Muirfield in 1892.

Ten years were to lapse before the Society of St Andrews Golfers was formed. In 1834, when King William IV became the Society's patron, the title changed to the Royal and Ancient Golf Club of St Andrews, which – along with the United States Golf Association – is still the joint governing body of the game.

The establishment of these clubs, however, failed to accelerate interest in the game or extend it beyond the east coast of Scotland, perhaps more because of the expense involved than a lack of desire to take up the game. Whatever the reason, it was not until the 19th century dawned that the game began to expand, first in Scotland and England, and later in Ireland and Wales and then, with the spread of British Empire, like a prairie fire to the rest of the world.

In 1818 the Old Manchester Club was founded on Kersal Moor and became the second oldest club outside Scotland, after Royal Blackheath. The first links (seaside) course on which golf was played outside Scotland was the links of the Royal North Devon Golf Club at Westward Ho! Founded in 1864, it now houses an impressive museum of golfing memorabilia.

For nearly 50 years Royal Blackheath and Old Manchester remained the only established clubs

ABOVE Ladies playing golf at Westward Ho!, Devon, 1873.

FAR RIGHT The Crécy window in Gloucester Cathedral. The 'Gloucester Golfer' can be seen at the base of the window to the left of the picture.

RIGHT Frank Fowler's portrait of John Reid, the Scotsman who reintroduced golf to the United States in 1888.

BELOW An engraving of the awesome Cardinal bunker at Prestwick, 1889.

in England, but in India the Calcutta Club came into being in 1829, quickly followed 13 years later by the Bombay Club. Calcutta, now Royal Calcutta, is the oldest club in the world outside Britain. The first Continental club was formed at Pau, in southern France, in 1856. Golf had earlier been introduced to this region in 1814, when officers of the Duke of Wellington's army were stationed at Pau after the battle of Orthez. Amazingly, they had their clubs with them, and laid out a temporary course on the plain of Billère. They must have enjoyed the experience, because many years later they returned to the area to take a holiday.

In 1851 the west coast of Scotland gained its first golf course when the inhabitants of Prestwick showed a lively interest in the game. The first British Open Championship was staged there in 1860.

Australia received its first taste of golf in 1871 with the opening of the Adelaide Club, while in 1885 the Cape Club, in South Africa, was formed. Both these clubs now carry the Royal prefix.

GOLF IN THE UNITED STATES

For some unexplained reason golf failed to gain a foothold in the United States when it was first tried out there in the 18th century. There is much evidence that golf courses were laid out at Charleston, South Carolina, in 1786 and at Savannah, Georgia, in 1795. But these quickly disappeared from the scene, and it was in Canada that golf took its first firm roots in North America. The oldest club is Royal Montreal, formed in the autumn of 1873, and followed two years later by the Quebec Club, and in 1876 by Toronto.

Surprisingly, when golf returned to stay in the United States, in 1888, it was from small beginnings. A Scotsman (it had to be a Scot), John Reid, from Dunfermline, hearing that a close friend, Robert Lockhart, was planning a trip to Britain, asked him to bring back some balls and clubs. Lockhart duly obliged by purchasing from the shop of Old Tom Morris in St Andrews (where else?) a set of six golf clubs and two dozen balls. Eventually a rough patch of land across Lake Avenue from Reid's home in Yonkers, New York, was eagerly converted into three holes. From that day, 22 February, 1888, golf was in full swing, literally, in the United States.

Afterwards Reid and four friends, John Upham, Harry Holbrook, Kingman Putnam and Henry O Tallnadge obtained a 30-acre site and turned it into a six-hole course. On 14 November, 1888, they formed the St Andrews Club of Yonkers, with John Reid as its first president. To mark the historic occasion they drank a toast, not to John Reid, but to Robert Lockhart, for producing the vital equipment which launched the resurrection of golf in the United States. They earned the immortal nickname The Apple Tree Gang when four years later they moved their course to a large apple orchard. Since their new course lacked a clubhouse, they made a habit of hanging jugs of liquid refreshment on a large apple tree which bordered the home hole.

In no time at all golf began to capture the hearts of Americans everywhere, and soon became a national pastime. There is an amusing tailpiece to this important piece of American sporting history. Shortly after returning from Britain with the famous clubs and balls, Mr Lockhart was arresting for hitting a golf ball about in Central Park! A little later, in 1891, the Shinnecock Hills Golf Club on Long Island was founded. It takes a prominent place in the chronicles of American golf by virtue of becoming the first incorporated club in the United States and also for having built the first clubhouse deemed necessary to cater for its 44 members.

Charles Blair Macdonald, who had expertly learned the game while a student at St Andrews University, Scotland, achieved the honour of designing and building the United States' first 18-hole course when he laid out the Chicago Golf Club course at Wheaton, Illinois, in 1893. In later life he created the National Links on Long Island, reproducing the finest holes he had played during his time in Britain. He gained further fame in 1895, when he became the United States' first National Amateur Champion by defeating Charles Sands by the wide margin of 12 and 11 at Newport, Rhode Island. The following day – also at Newport – saw the first Open Championship of the United States. It was won by a young Englishman, Horace Rawlins, who had recently arrived in the United States to take up the assistant professional post at Newport Golf Club. Willie Dunn, a Scottish professional who had earlier been hired to plan the

Shinnecock course, was the runner-up.

Both these historic tournaments took place as a direct result of the formation in December 1894 of the United States Golf Association, which remains to this day the sport's national governing body.

Never slow in doing things, the Americans, by the turn of the century, had opened over 1,000 golf clubs. Knowing a good thing when they saw it, the Scottish professionals migrated to the United States in droves to earn good money from teaching the wonderful new game. From a humble three-hole course to more clubs than the rest of the world in just 12 years is, indeed, an extraordinary happening in the history of an extraordinary pastime.

In the same year as John Reid and his friends were laying out their small course at Yonkers, the Principality of Wales gained its first recognized golf course at the seaside town of Tenby. Two others – at Pontnewydd and Borth – lay claim to having been in existence at least a decade before Tenby, but no definite record that either of these clubs precede Tenby has actually been discovered.

Golf, like a great new religion, continued to sweep the globe. Scottish officers stationed at the Curragh, Ireland, while waiting to go to the Crimean War, started what later became the Royal Curragh Golf Club, and in 1881 the Royal Belfast Club was born.

In 1889 when six British enthusiasts laid out a nine-hole links in the Portuguese fishing village of Espinho, situated some ten miles south of Oporto, they reckoned without one rather serious hazard. During the summer months of July and August – the great bull-fighting season – the bulls used in the arena were put out to grass in the area during the week prior to being driven into Oporto for the Saturday night spectacle. They made a nasty habit of tearing up the flags, and sometimes the greens. Hidden by the sand dunes, they often appeared unexpectedly. With one eye on the ball and the other on the bull, it is little wonder that golfers scored highly during this period!

Another humorous tale emerging from this course concerns the young sons of the local sardine fishermen. Frequently employed on the links as caddies, they prided themselves on knowing the name of every club in English. One was overheard telling another he had learnt to

ABOVE LEFT Early golfers at St Andrews, Yonkers, New York.

ABOVE A portrait of William Innes, Captain of Blackheath, and his caddie, by Lemuel Abbott (1760–1803).

count the strokes in English, having listened carefully to the gentleman for whom he was carrying. He then proceeded to teach the others – 'one, two, three, four, five, six, damn, eight, damn' – and then said he could not understand why the English used the same word to mean seven and nine, and why it should be used with greater emphasis than the others.

What irresistable force prompted Arthur Groom into creating Japan's first course on the summit of Mount Rokko, Kobe, in 1903 is difficult to comprehend. A merchant with a thriving business of 30-years standing in the seaport town of Kobe, he was already a very busy man and he had never played golf in his life before opening his course. What a place to choose to build a golf course: 3,000 ft (900 m) above sea level! In those days of primitive transport it took over two tortuous hours to reach the top of Mount Rokko from Kobe. Imagine the journey: half-an-hour by rickshaw to the entrance of the Cascade Valley, a 60-minute climb by foot through to the Gap before an even stiffer climb to the long stretch of flat at the top. Horse riding was possible, but extremely dangerous. Those willing to take the risk could be carried up the slopes by coolies in a *kago*, a type of basket slung on a pole. All this for a quiet game of golf. It was hardly surprising that upon arrival the golfers opted to stay the whole weekend at the clubhouse.

Mr Groom sought the advice of Messrs Adamson and Mcmurtrie, both of whom had learnt the game in their boyhood in Scotland before moving to Japan, to help him construct the original four holes. The course was finally extended to 18 holes in 1904, by which time the membership numbered over 200 – mostly British but with a sprinkling of Germans and Japanese. The first honorary secretary of the Kobe Golf Club was Arthur H Groom himself. What a remarkable man, and what a remarkable golf course.

As a result of the English merchant's enterprise other courses began to materialize inside the empire. Six holes were built on the sand flats of Yokoya, a small village 30 minutes from Kobe on the road to Osaka, and in 1906 British settlers in Yokohama formed the first links in eastern Japan, at Negishi. This was followed in 1914 by the Tokyo Club, built by the Japanese. China, Hong Kong and other countries in the Far East quickly followed suit, and golf had encircled the world.

LEFT An early photograph of Shinnecock Hills Golf Club, New York.

BELOW Charles Blair Macdonald, the first winner of the United States Amateur Championship in 1895.

The Development Of Equipment

A persimmon-headed wood club.

RIGHT Hugh Philp, a master among early 19th-century clubmakers.

In ancient times any club and ball game simply meant just that – one club and one ball – and golf was no exception. The club would have been a suitably selected branch of a tree, probably thornwood or beech, cut to an acceptable size and crudely fashioned into a curved stick. The ball would be shaped from hardwood or, as used by the Romans for *paganica*, made from leather and stuffed with feathers. If either of these primitive implements needed replacing, the job would have been done by the player himself.

THE EMERGENCE OF CLUBMAKERS

Although no evidence exists before the early part of the 17th century that clubmaking had become a profession, it is obvious that before this, as the game progressed and became popular among the gentry, craftsmen like carpenters and bowmakers would turn their skills toward producing golf clubs as a means of making a better living.

The first authentic record of a recognized clubmaker appears in 1603 when William Mayne, a maker of bows and arrows, was appointed to the court of James I of England to make, among other things, clubs for the golf-loving King and his courtiers. The only earlier reference to golf clubs being specially made dates from exactly a century before, when James IV of Scotland requested his Lord High Treasurer to purchase a supply from a bowmaker in Perth. No specimens from these periods survive, so we have no knowledge of the methods or standard of workmanship of these early craftsmen.

After Mayne, we have to go to the late 1600s before discovering two more named clubmakers – Andrew Dickson and Henry Mill of Leith and St Andrews, respectively. In addition to being a celebrated clubmaker, Dickson often acted as a caddie to James II at Leith. He is also the Dickson referred to in the immortal 1743 poem *The Goff*, by Thomas Matheson:

> Of finest ash, Castalio's shaft was made;
> Pondrous with lead and fenced with horn
> the head,
> The work of Dickson who in Letha dwells
> And in the art of making clubs excels.

An original copy of this heroic-comical poem in three cantos was sold at auction by Phillips of Chester, England, in 1985 for the staggering sum of £17,000.

The poem contains a clue as to how the clubs were made. Most of the shafts were of ash or hazel to give the club 'whip', and the back of the head had a shallow hollow which was filled with lead for extra weight and balance. On the face an insert of leather, horn or bone was often attached as a prevention against damage. The heads were fashioned from beech, holly, dogwood or blackthorn; most of the fruit-woods – plum, pear and apple – were also tried. The usual method of joining the shaft to the head was to splice the specially tapered ends together with glue, then firmly bind them with pitched twine to strengthen the join. This method became known as 'scare-headed', scare being derived from the word 'scarf' (an overlapping join). Clubs continued to be made this way until the latter part of the 19th century, when the socket-head method was invented. A scare-headed club bearing the stamp of a famous clubmaker can fetch a tidy sum at auction today.

A set of these wooden clubs, believed to have been crafted by either Dickson or Mill, was found along with two iron-headed clubs behind a false wall in an old dwelling at Hull, in northern England, during renovations in 1889. Unfortunately, the large stamp on each of the wooden clubs is illegible through wear, leaving the maker's identity a matter of conjecture. How-

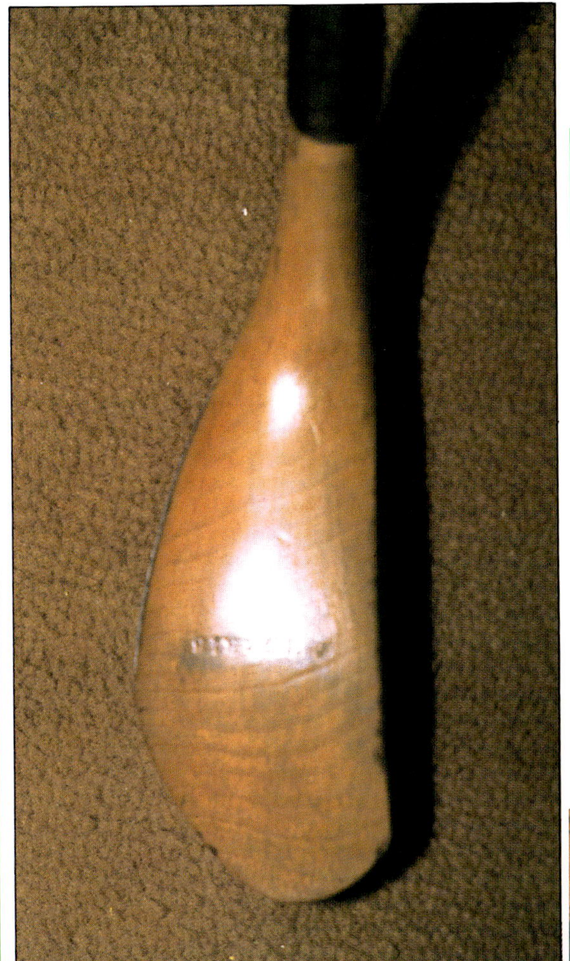

ever, among documents found with the now priceless clubs was a newspaper dated 1741 establishing them at a much earlier date than the paper. They were eventually purchased by Adam Wood, captain of the Troon Club for five years from 1893, and as the oldest extant clubs are preserved in the Big Room of the clubhouse at Troon.

No records have come to light of other clubmakers immediately following Dickson and Mill, and we have to wait until the Georgian era before finding the name of Simon Cossar of Leith, who was appointed clubmaker to the Honourable Company of Gentlemen Golfers in the middle of the 18th century. Three fine examples of his work – two wooden clubs and a putting cleek from about 1760 – can be seen in the Royal and Ancient Club of St Andrews museum.

In the wake of Cossar came notable clubmakers such as the McEwens, Philp, Wilson, Carrick and White. The last three specialized in

LEFT A scared-head driver, made by Tom Morris senior and stamped with his name.

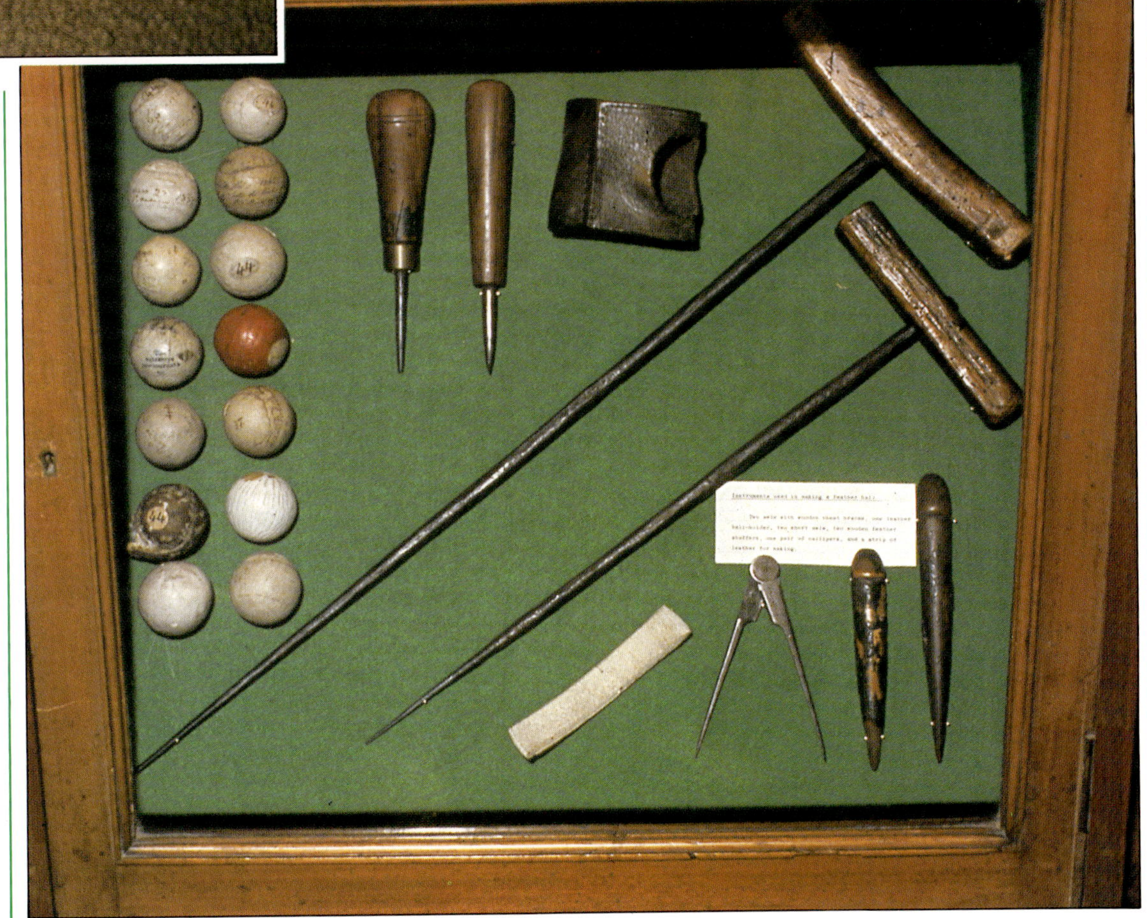

RIGHT This rare collection of feather balls and feather ball-making implements includes: two awls with chest braces, a leather ball-holder, two short awls, two wooden feather-stuffers and a set of callipers. The Royal and Ancient Trophy Room, St Andrews, Scotland.

ABOVE Horace Hutchinson, a champion golfer and a prolific sports writer, 1896.

the making of cleeks (iron-headed clubs) and the 'Carrick' cleek in particular was much in demand by virtue of its perfect balance and durability. A popular cleek at this time was the track iron, its lofted head usually made of iron although there are examples in gun-metal or bronze (used to prevent rusting). The track iron derived its name from the fact that up to about 1860 it was specially used to extricate the ball out of cart tracks, then frequently found on the Scottish links as a result of the townspeople having public right of way to cart sand, seaweed, flotsam and jetsam across the course. This club was the forerunner of the modern wedge and sand iron.

The McEwens were a famous, long-standing clubmaking family, practising their craft for well over a century. James, formerly a wheelwright, founded the business in 1770 at Leith. A son, Peter, born in 1781, followed his father into the business and later married the daughter of Douglas Gourlay of Musselburgh, a celebrated ballmaker of the period, thus linking two of the most important names in the development of golf equipment. Their son Douglas succeeded to the business and became a true master of the craft. His wooden clubs, along with those of Hugh Philp, are now much sought after by collectors of golf antiquities, who regard their works as the Chippendales of the golfing world.

Born in 1782, Hugh Philp started his working life as a carpenter but turned his attention to making golf clubs. He rapidly gained a reputation for making quality clubs that were in a special class of their own. Such was his success that in 1819 he was appointed official clubmaker to the Society of St Andrews Golfers. As often happens today with top-quality goods, many attempts were made to imitate his work. For a short time after his death in 1856, a couple of unscrupulous characters gained illegal possession of his stampmarker. However, although bearing the name of Philp, the imitations were easily recognizable as fakes by their beech heads and by their inferior quality (Philp invariably used pear, apple or thorn in his heads, and his clubs were more delicately balanced). Philp was described by many as the prince of clubmakers, and replicas of his work are being produced to this day by a number of club professionals who make a steady income from the practice. Examples of Philp's work can be seen at the Royal and Ancient Club of St Andrews, where a complete set of his woods is on display in the Trophy Room.

Most of the clubs of this period, including the putter, had wooden heads, and a set usually consisted of six or seven, with maybe a track iron added. Strange as it may seem today, a bag with which to carry the clubs was still to be invented (the first golf bag appeared about 1880). Clubs were simply carried in the crook of the arm, as if they were a bundle of garden implements. Even the medieval bowmen used a quiver to carry their arrows and the warrior a scabbard for his sword, so why the early golfer preferred not to use a container of sorts for his clubs is a mystery.

Regarding the almost total absence of iron-headed clubs in the early days, Horace

FAR LEFT A fine example of a track, or rut, iron.

LEFT An early American advertisement for golf equipment. The Boston firm of Wright & Ditson began marketing clubs *c* 1895.

BELOW Original feather balls are now valuable items, much sought after by golf collectors.

BOTTOM This collection of rare golfing memorabilia includes: old rule books, early gutty balls and a beautiful set of miniature wooden clubs, made by Willie Auchterlonie, the 1893 Open champion. Royal and Ancient Trophy Room, St Andrews.

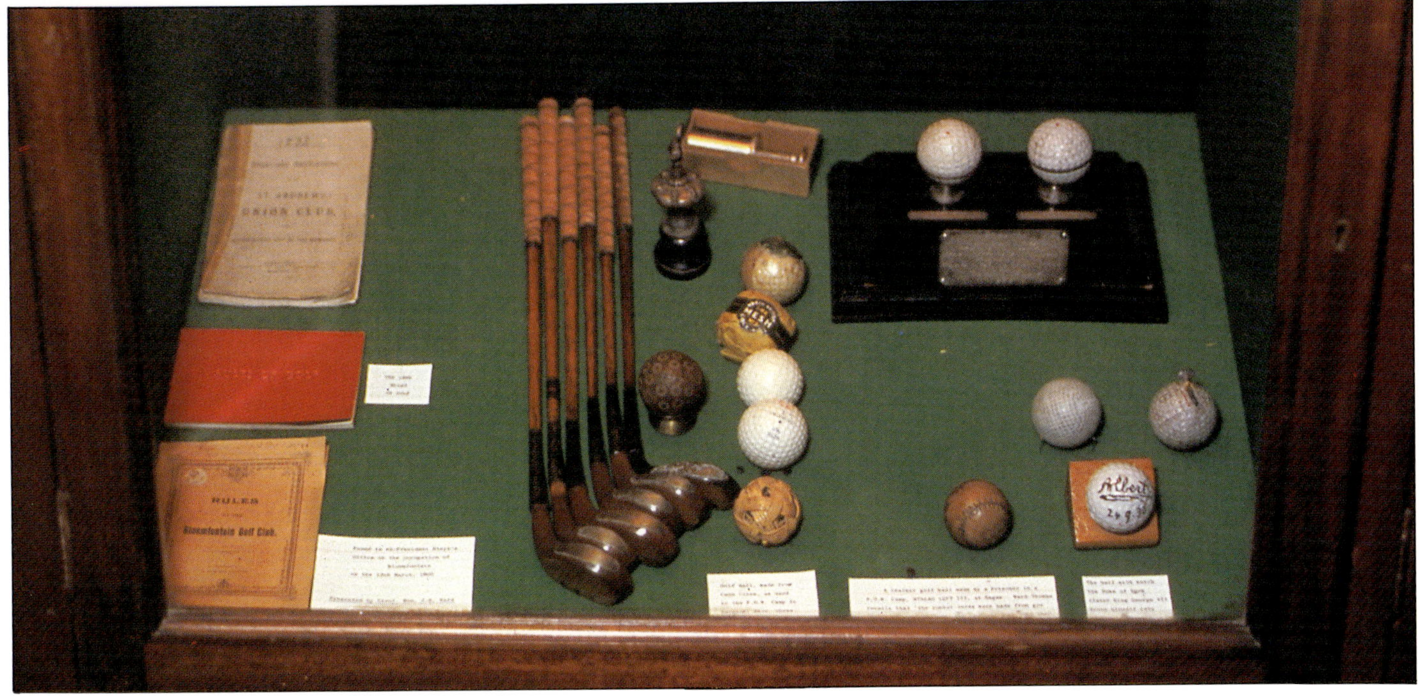

Hutchinson – a champion golfer and prolific golf writer in his day – tells a delightful story in the Lonsdale Library book, *The Game of Golf*, on how his knowledge of golf history saved a friend a considerable amount of money. Contemplating buying a golfing picture by Johann Zoffany, the friend asked Hutchinson to take a look at it. The picture showed a gentleman in the costume of the period (late 18th century) holding a club in the crook of his arm. At his feet knelt a young caddie, teeing up a ball, while a set of clubs lay on the ground, four with wooden heads and four with iron. Explaining to his friend that the use of an equal proportion of iron and wooden clubs was most unusual for Zoffany's period, Hutchinson said it loud enough to be overhead by the picture dealer. Microscopic examination by the dealer later clearly showed that the club under the gentleman's arm was originally a walking-cane – the kneeling boy, the ball and the clubs on the ground had all been added later by a faker! Collectors of golf antiques take note.

As the years rolled on and the game grew popular worldwide, the demand for clubs saw many more clubmakers appearing on the scene. Persimmon, there being a plentiful supply from the United States, replaced other wood for the making of heads, while hickory was found to be best for the shafts. With the introduction of the gutta-percha ball, iron clubs of varying loft became an important part of the golfer's armoury, giving blacksmiths a chance to show their skills.

With the dawning of the 20th century, experiments with steel-shafted clubs were being carried out but, reluctant to break with tradition, the Royal and Ancient Club banned the use of such clubs. The ban continued in Britain until 1929, five years after steel shafts had been judged legal in America by the United States Golf Association. It is believed that Thomas Horsburgh of Edinburgh first tried such clubs in the 1890s, but failed to make progress because of the eventual ban.

Today steel continues to be the primary material for shafts, but graphite and carbon-fibre shafts are gradually beginning to make their mark. Although it sounds contradictory, metal-headed woods are also becoming popular. The only wooden-shafted clubs in use today are putters – relics of the past or reproductions. Today the manufacturing of clubs, like other sports equipment, is big business and millions of clubs are mass-produced each year.

THE DEVELOPMENT OF THE BALL

We know that the Romans used a ball made from a leather bag stuffed with feathers when playing *paganica*, but whether this type of ball remained in existence until it was used by Scots golfers in the 17th century is doubtful. There is some indication that wooden balls were used by the early golfers, but the earliest modern reference to makers of the feather ball is the granting of a monopoly in 1618 by James VI of Scotland (James I of England) to James Melvill and his associate for a period of 21 years. He also decreed that the price of the ball was not to exceed a certain limit and each ball was to be marked with the maker's stamp; all balls made within the kingdom marked otherwise were to be confiscated.

The making of a 'feathery', as it became commonly known, called for much patience. The leather was of untanned bull's hide that was cut into two round pieces for the ends and a narrow strip for the middle, then softened and firmly sown together, leaving a small hole through which to stuff the feathers. To give the ball a smooth finish the leather was turned inside out so that the rough seams were hidden inside. The leather casing was then placed in a cup-shaped stand and the boiled feathers – as many as would fill a top hat – were stuffed through the hole with the aid of a metal 'pusher'. Inserting the feathers was a slow and laborious operation and the inhaling of small particles from the feathers often caused respiratory problems. A ballmaker could feel well satisfied if he produced three featheries in a full working day.

Distances achieved with the feathery depended on weather conditions. When dry it could be struck on average about 180 yards (165 m), when wet about 150 yards (135 m). It is said that a Swiss tutor at St Andrews University, one Simon Messieux, once hit a wind-assisted feathery more than 350 yards (320 m) on the Old Course. For this distance to be reached by a feathery, we must assume the strength of the wind was near gale force.

After Melvill's 21-year monopoly ended, other ballmakers began to emerge. John Dickson of Leith, who is assumed to be the son of Andrew Dickson the clubmaker mentioned earlier, was granted a licence by the town council of Aber-

LEFT A modern metal-headed wood.

BELOW LEFT A pair of Schenectady putters made in the United States at the turn of the century. This type of club, of a revolutionary centre-shafted design, was used by Walter Travis to win the 1904 British Amateur Championship. Judging it 'untraditional', the Royal and Ancient Club of St Andrews banned it a few years later.

BELOW An up-to-the-minute wood and iron, marketed by Wilson.

deen in 1642 to make balls within the borough. By the middle of the 18th century the making of the feathery had become a profitable business. About this time the family firm Gourlay of Bruntsfield and Musselburgh was founded by Douglas Gourlay of Leith. The Gourlay ball was to last for a century with a reputation that was second to none. Its fame was such that it became much praised in poetry and song by the bards of that time. Made to perfection, it commanded a high price.

In 1815 Allan Robertson was born. He was destined to become the first great professional golfer, but first he joined the family business and soon rivalled the Gourlays in the art of making feather balls. In his shop at St Andrews, in 1840, he and his assistant Tom Morris senior (also to become a famous professional) turned out 1,021 balls between them. In 1844 they produced 2,456 and, naturally, they were delighted with their progress. Little did they realize that looming on the horizon was a revolutionary new ball made from gutta-percha which was soon to make the feathery obsolete.

The Gutta-Percha Ball

During the second half of the 19th century ballmakers and golfers rejoiced when it was discovered that the reddish-brown, horn-like substance of the inspissated juice of the Malaysian gutta-percha tree made perfectly good golf balls. Ballmakers were pleased because they were freed from the daily tedious grind of turning out feather balls, and golfers because the new ball, quickly and easily made, cost but a fraction of the feathery.

The 'gutty', as it inevitably became called, was first made in 1848 by a clergyman from St Andrews, the Reverend Robert Adam Paterson, who hit upon the idea after receiving from India a marble statue of Vishna (now in St Andrews University) which was wrapped in a protective padding of gutta-percha. Knowing that gutta-percha could be softened by heat and subsequently mould-

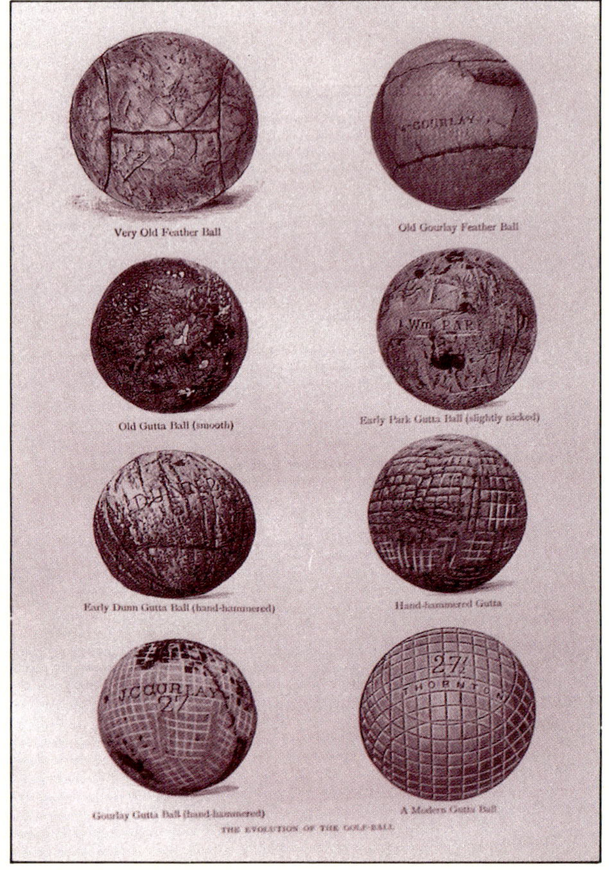

BELOW FAR LEFT One of the very first gutties, *c* 1848.

FAR LEFT A late-19th-century illustration showing the evolution of the golf ball, from a very early feather ball to a moulded gutta-percha ball dated *c* 1890.

BELOW LEFT Three types of moulds, which were used to stamp mesh or dimple markings on gutty balls.

LEFT Three early hand-hammered gutties.

ed by hand, he experimented with the substance and came up with a ball which set rock-hard when cooled. Flushed with success he patented the ball under the name 'Paterson's Patent'. The ball, however, was not an instant success. Much too smooth, it had a tendency to duck in flight. It was often remarked upon that the gutty flew better at the end of the round than it did at the beginning. It did not take long for someone to realize its performance improved after it had been cut about a bit by the cleeks. It was normal practice at the finish of a round for the ball to be soaked in hot water until soft, and the offending cuts to be erased. Used again, it behaved as before – erratic at first, becoming better as play progressed.

An experiment was carried out in which a newly moulded ball was scored all over with the sharp end of a saddler's hammer. It proved highly successful, and the demise of the feather ball was inevitable.

Some ballmakers, however, were dismayed by the advent of the gutty. They saw it as a threat to their continuing prosperity. Allan Robertson refused to have anything to do with the new ball – he would not play with it, make it or sell it in his shop. Such was his hatred of it that he bought all the old specimens that were offered him by the ball-finders who scratched a living searching for lost balls in the St Andrews rough, and set them alight without regard to the obnoxious smell the fire created. His stubbornness continuing, he

TOP Walter Travis watching the ball intently during the 1904 British Amateur Championship at Sandwich.

ABOVE Sandy Herd lining up for a shot at St Andrews, c 1899. (Notice the extra-wide stance.)

ABOVE RIGHT Lee Trevino using a four-wheeled caddie car.

RIGHT A modern professional's golf bag.

eventually lost the services of Tom Morris. Morris had promised Robertson he would never play with the gutty, but in a moment of forgetfulness he borrowed a gutty from a partner to give it a try during a friendly round over the St Andrews links. Robertson heard about this, and was furious. This resulted in Tom Morris leaving Robertson and going into business on his own in a shop overlooking the Old Course at St Andrews – the same shop Robert Lockhart was to visit 40 years later in order to purchase for his friend John Reid the balls and clubs which would resurrect golf in the United States.

As time went by Robertson grew to realize he could make as much, if not more, from selling the gutty because, being cheaper, it was being bought by people with small incomes who were now taking up the game. As they also needed to buy clubs, the arrival of the gutty eventually turned out to be a godsend for the trade. John Gourlay, who had succeeded to the head of the famous family ballmaking firm, was also reluctant to change, but upon observing that the gutty was accurate in flight, kept a good line to the hole when putted and was not prone to bursting in mid-air like the feathery, he knew that the days of the feathery were numbered, and proved more astute than Robertson by making sure that all outstanding orders for the feathery were despatched in double quick time.

Eventually, iron moulds were invented, but on leaving the mould the ball still had to be scored with a hammer. Later the moulds were improved to indent each ball automatically.

Except for a short period in the 1890s when a ball consisting of a mixture of rubber, cork and metal filings called the 'Eclipse' was introduced (without much success), the gutta-percha ball reigned supreme for almost 55 years, until it was superseded by the Haskell ball in 1903.

THE HASKELL BALL

The introduction of the Haskell rubber-cored ball brought about an even greater interest in the game, especially in the United States. The brainchild of an American dentist, Dr Coburn Haskell, of Cleveland, Ohio, the ball was composed of strips of elastic wound tightly round a liquid-filled rubber core, with a casing of gutta-percha added. Dr Haskell invented the ball in 1899 and American golfers began to take it seriously in 1901, when Walter Travis, an Australian who had made his home in America, won the United States Amateur Championship using the Haskell ball.

At first the British gave the new ball a cool reception. Even when Charles Hutchings, at the age of 53, beat Sidney Fry in the 1902 final of the British Amateur Championship at Hoylake, with both finalists using the Haskell ball, it was still looked upon with suspicion by the majority of British golfers. The British professionals, and there were quite a few of them by this time, declared openly that they would continue to play with the gutty in all their matches. But one among them was to have second thoughts. On the eve of the 1902 British Open Championship, also at Hoylake, Alex Herd used a Haskell, purely out of curiosity, during a practice round. Taking a liking to the ball he took a gamble by deciding to use the Haskell in the Championship; to everyone's amazement, he won the coveted title with a stroke to spare. As the news spread of Herd's success with the new ball, golfers everywhere wanted to play with the Haskell. The gutty was dead. Long live the Haskell!

The success of the Haskell was due largely to its behaviour when struck. It was easy to raise from the ground, it travelled much further and, even when mis-hit, usually travelled a respectable distance. People found the game much easier to play and more and more came forward to swell the ranks. Modern techniques have brought about subsequent improvements to the golf ball, which have resulted in its travelling even further than previously.

In an effort to prevent big hitters making a mockery of the shorter courses, the twin governing bodies, the R and A and the USGA, have placed a velocity restriction on the ball which at present is limited to 250 ft (76 m) per second, with a 2 percent tolerance. In addition, in the United States and all countries using USGA rules, the ball must measure at least 1.68 in (42.67 mm) in diameter and not be heavier than 1.62 oz (45.93 g). In Britain and the rest of the world, golfers playing in ordinary club competitions have the option of playing the 1.68 in (42.67 mm) ball or the smaller 1.62 in (41.15 mm) ball which must weigh the same as the larger ball, 1.62 oz (45.93 g). However, it is now compulsory to use the big ball in all professional tournaments and all important amateur events at national, state and county levels.

Most balls now have a covering of the more durable balata or surlyn in preference to gutta-percha, and the two-piece ball with its even tougher synthetic cover and solid core is becoming increasingly popular.

To say that the ball has played its part in the development of golf would be an understatement. In a little over 50 years these two ingenious men from opposite sides of the Atlantic did more to revolutionize golf than anybody else centuries before. Each of these men in turn was responsible for more people becoming golfers, thus setting in motion a chain reaction. More courses had to be constructed to accommodate them, stronger golf clubs had to be found to withstand the hardness of the balls and iron-headed clubs with varying degrees of loft became necessary. With many more clubs to carry, the golf bag finally came into being and new rules had to be introduced.

As well as the rule regarding the size and weight of the ball mentioned earlier, the twin governing bodies found it necessary to restrict to 14 the number of clubs an individual may carry in a recognized competition. Before this rule was imposed some players were carrying more than double this number, each devised by a manufacturer to make the game easier.

With the numbers of players multiplying there was, of course, a shortage of caddies. This brought about the development of the golf trolley. Manually operated when first introduced, there are now many makes of battery-operated trolleys on the market and many players, especially in Britain, use this type of trolley. Even more advanced is the four-wheeled buggy or cart or caddie-car, powered by a small petrol engine or powerful sets of batteries. These vehicles are designed to carry not only two sets of clubs but also the players to whom they belong. Although much used in the United States, elsewhere they are looked upon as more of a luxury than a necessity, except when used by disabled golfers. Another version of the golf cart or caddie-car, recently introduced, has three wheels and caters to the individual golfer.

Unlike their predecessors, golfers today wear shoes with specially moulded or metal-spiked soles, colourful casual clothing, sun visors and gloves. Wet-weather waterproof suits and large umbrellas help players stay dry. Plastic tees, hand towels, ball cleaners, distance charts, rule books, scorecards and practice aids are all very much taken for granted. How different to the golfer in those far-off days with his single club and wooden ball!

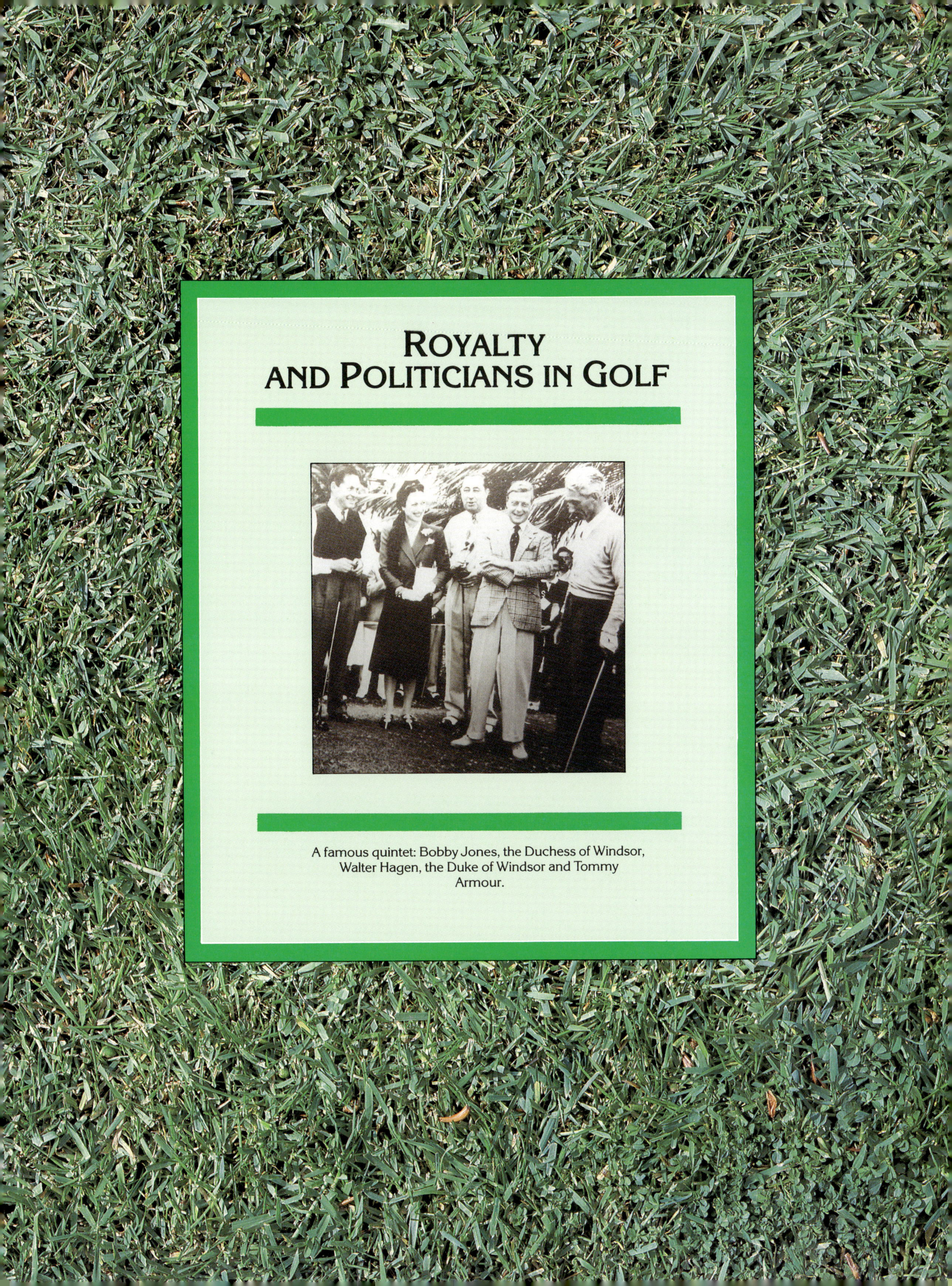

Royalty and Politicians in Golf

A famous quintet: Bobby Jones, the Duchess of Windsor, Walter Hagen, the Duke of Windsor and Tommy Armour.

harnes and weapones be the feaſte of *Midſommer* nixt to cum, quhilk ſall be the day purvaied of the ſaide harnes and weapones under the paines followand, that is to ſay, of ilk Gentle-man that defaults at the of weapon-ſchawinges, fourtie ſhillinges, and at the ſecond default, uther fourtie, and at the thrid default, firſt weapon-ſchawinges, under the paines followand, and alſmeikle als oft-times as he defaultis thereafter. And of ilk bow-man at the firſt fault ten ten pound. And alſmeikle als oft-times as he defaultis thereafter And of ilk bow-man at the firſt fault ten ſhillinges, at the ſecond ten ſhillinges, and at the thrid, fourtie ſhillinges. And ſa foorth als oft-times as he beis foundin faltiſe thereafter, fourtie ſhillinges. And after the facultie of their landes and gudes, that everie man be furniſhed & harniſhed in his bodie with quhit harnes brigantines, or gud jacks, with ſplentes and glooves of plait and weill horſed correſpondand to their lands and gudes, be the diſcretion of the Schireffe, Commiſſioner or Officiar foreſaid.

32. *Fute-ball and Golfe forbidden.*

ITEM, It is ſtatute and ordained that in na place of the Realme there be uſed fute-ball, golfe, or uther ſik unprofitable ſportes, for the commoun gude of the Realme and defenſe thereof. And that bowes and ſchutting be hanted, and bow-markes maid therefore ordained in ilk parochin, under the paine of fourtie ſhillinges to be raiſed be the Schireffe and Baillies foreſaid. And of ilk Parochin ilk zeir, quhair it beis foundin, that bow-markes beis not maid, nor ſchutting hanted, as is before ſaid.

33. *Of mettes, meaſures and wechtes.*

ITEM, It is ſtatute and ordained, for the commoun gude of the Realme, honour and profite of our Soveraine Lordis Lieges, that the auld ſtatutes and ordinances maid of befoir, baith to Burgh and to Land, alſweill of mettes and meaſures, cuſtomes and uthers, be obſerved and keiped, after the tenour and forme of the actes and ſtatutes maid thereupon, and under the paines conteined in the famin. And that the Chalmerlanes provide, that this be obſerved and keiped, and ſpecially of weichtes, alſweill of wax and ſpice, and ſextene ounce of the pound.

34. *Of convocation and gaddering in Burrowes.*

ABOVE Golf was obviously a popular pastime in 15th-century Scotland – so popular, in fact, that men of military age were found to be neglecting their compulsory archery practice. In 1491 James IV of Scotland redressed the situation by issuing an act banning golf and other 'unprofitable' sports.

In one way or another royalty has been involved with golf for over five centuries. The earliest mention we have of a monarch in connection with the game is, of course, James II of Scotland, to whom historians shall be forever grateful for providing the first written proof of the existence of golf in medieval times with his famous edict of 1457.

In 1471 James III repeated the edict and in 1491 James IV, despite his fondness for golf, saw fit to issue a similar act. Whether James IV was actually the first royal to play golf we know not. However, his is the first name recorded as having done so. Following his lifting of the ban in 1503 – repealed because his marriage to Princess Margaret, daughter of Henry VII of England, brought peace to the two countries – the Lord High Treasurer's accounts show that the King drew a sum to settle a golfing debt with the Earl of Bothwell, and to pay for the clubs and balls that had failed him.

A few years later, in 1506, two more items in the accounts tell us that more clubs and balls were purchased by the golfing monarch. But little time remained for him to pursue his favourite pastime, for he fell at the Battle of Flodden in 1515, going to war against his brother-in-law Henry VIII.

Two years before this tragic event there is evidence of Queen Catherine of Aragon, first wife of King Henry VIII, finding comfort in golf, while her husband was engaged in more worldly pursuits. In a letter to Cardinal Wolsey she regretted that she would not be hearing often from her husband, but that his subjects would be glad to hear that 'thank God she would be busy with golfe for her heart was very good to it'.

After James IV, there followed a long line of golfing Stuarts. James V played many times at Gosford, in East Lothian, on a course privately owned by the Earl of Wemyss. Mary Queen of Scots, the ill-fated daughter of James V, much enjoyed playing golf on the links of St Andrews, and is said to have played golf in fields alongside Seton House only a few days after the murder of her husband, Lord Darnley, who was found strangled at Kirk-o'-Field, outside Edinburgh, in February 1567. If Queen Elizabeth I, like Mary, had been a keen golfer maybe the two would have settled their differences over a round of golf rather than Mary having to lose her head in February 1587 at Fotheringay Castle.

James IV's great grandson, James VI, the future James I of England, acquired his golfing skills at North Inch, Perth, and when he succeeded Elizabeth to the throne of England in 1603 he took golf south into England with him and his court. Both his sons, Prince Charles and Henry, Prince of Wales, who died of a fever in 1612 before reaching manhood, were ardent golfers. Charles, who ascended the English throne as Charles I, was halfway through a round of golf at Leith when he received news of the Irish Rebellion. Following the example of Sir Francis Drake, who completed his game of bowls before dealing with the Spanish Armada, Charles did likewise and played on. Four years later, in 1645, having been captured by the Scottish army at Newcastle, Charles was permitted to play golf on the Shield field outside the walls of the castle where he was imprisoned.

Charles II also played golf, but nothing is known of his dedication to the game. However, James II of England, when Duke of York and domiciled in Scotland as Lord High Commissioner on the order of his brother Charles II in 1681, often found time to play golf on Leith links, Edinburgh. It was there that he took part in what can loosely be called the first international golf match. Two English noblemen provoked the Duke into an argument by claiming that the game was of English origin rather than Scottish. To settle the dispute the English pair suggested a foursome match be played for a large wager between themselves and the Duke with any Scotsman of his choice as his partner. The Duke wisely chose for his partner John Paterson, a shoemaker who was the local cham-

LEFT This detail of a drawing by A Forestier records the tradition that, while in St Andrews in 1563, Mary Queen of Scots enjoyed a round of golf on the local links.

tested at the annual autumn meeting. Following his death a few weeks later, his widow, Queen Adelaide, consented to become patron and presented a medal inscribed with her name, with the request that it be worn by the captain on all public occasions. Since that time successive captains have carried on the tradition of wearing the Queen Adelaide Medal.

Queen Victoria, who was to reign supreme over the British Empire for 64 years, also became patron of the Royal and Ancient Club. Her eldest son, Edward Prince of Wales, the future Edward VII, showed a deep interest in the game when he consented to be Captain of the R and A in 1863. A measure of his interest can be taken from the fact that during his reign he had a golf course laid out for himself in the Home Park at Windsor. Visitors to Windsor are able to spot part of the course, which comes up to the rear of

BELOW King Edward VII of England photographed on the links during a visit to Biarritz in 1908.

pion. The Duke and the shoemaker won handsomely with holes to spare, and the Duke, overjoyed at their victory, presented Paterson with half of the wager he had won. There being no amateur code to worry about in those days, Paterson gladly accepted the money and promptly invested it by building himself a large house in Edinburgh.

With the decline of the Stuarts, golf fell out of favour with royalty. Indeed, royal involvement lay dormant until 1833, when William IV granted permission for the Perth Golfing Society to carry the 'Royal' prefix – thus creating the first 'Royal' golf club. A year later he became patron of the St Andrews Golfing Society, and bestowed the title of The Royal and Ancient Golf Club of St Andrews on the illustrious society. Afterward, in 1837, he presented the club with the Gold Medal for a yearly competition which is still being con-

ABOVE Arthur James Balfour (far right), the first British prime minister to become addicted to golf.

Windsor Castle. In 1876 Prince Leopold, the last of Victoria's sons, followed in his brother's footsteps by also becoming Captain of the Royal and Ancient Club, and in the same year their brother Arthur, the Duke of Connaught, became Honorary President of the Musselburgh Golf Club, and marked the occasion by giving his consent for the 'Royal' prefix to be used.

George V preferred hunting and shooting to golf, but his three sons all proved competent golfers having, no doubt, learnt the game on their grandfather's course at Windsor. In their turn they all became Captains of the Royal and Ancient Club: Edward VIII in 1922 (when Prince of Wales), George VI in 1930 (when Duke of York) and the Duke of Kent in 1937.

Edward VIII, who gave up the English throne to marry Mrs Simpson, made quite a success of the game. He twice achieved a hole in one, at Santos in Brazil and at Royal Wimbledon, and won a number of medal competitions at various golf clubs. He was captain of several clubs and played in the British Army Championship as a member of the Welsh Guards team. On his tours abroad a game of golf was always included in the itinerary. With the need for security less intense in those days, he was a spectator at several major professional tournaments, and once took part in a match in which the immortal American amateur, Bobby Jones, also played.

In 1924 George VI travelled to South Wales to play in an exhibition match as part of the opening ceremony for a nine-hole course in the Rhondda Valley, built by the local miners on their weekends off. In 1948 he visited Muirfield to see Henry Cotton win his third British Open Championship title. No members of the royal family in Britain take an active part in the game today, although royal patronage does still continue.

In other parts of Europe golf has been much favoured by royalty and several clubs bear the 'Royal' prefix. Belgium, in particular, boasts a number of monarchs who have excelled at golf. King Albert was enthusiastic, and inspired the founding of the Royal Golf Club de Belgique in 1906. King Leopold created a little piece of golfing history in 1939, when he played in the Belgian Amateur Championship at Le Zoute, the only reigning monarch ever to have played in a national championship. In 1949 he played in the French Amateur Championship at St Cloud and reached the quarter-finals.

King Baudouin, Leopold's son, inherited his father's talent for the game, to such an extent that he represented his country in the Belgium-France-Holland international match in 1958. The following year, entered as Mr B de Rethy, he partnered the Welsh professional Dai Rees in the Gleneagles Hotel pro-am tournament. King

LEFT Robert Sandow, former director of golf to the Shah of Iran, playing in the Douglas Bader Foundation tournament. 'Has anyone seen my ball?'

Constantine of Greece has also played in many pro-am events since being in exile. Prince Claus of the Netherlands, partnered by Peter Oosterhuis, the English professional now living in the United States, achieved a notable royal success when he won the pro-am which preceded the 1974 Dutch Open.

The most enthusiastic of the present monarchs is, without question, King Hassan of Morocco, who likes nothing better than playing golf in the company of well-known professionals In a recent major professional tournament in his country, he put up an additional prize for the winner of the event – a jewelled dagger reputed to be worth £30,000 (*c* $45,000).

In the 1970s the Shah of Iran set in motion an extensive programme for the construction of golf complexes in Iran, when he commissioned Robert Sandow, a former English professional golfer who turned to golf architecture after gaining a BSc in both agronomy and horticulture during the 1950s, to create a championship-style course on exotic Kish Island in the Persian Gulf. The project completed, the Shah appointed Mr Sandow as his director of golf responsible for the construction of further golf projects on the mainland. Alas, the ambitions of the Shah of Iran were thwarted by the revolution, and the Kish Island course now lies overgrown and unused.

On his return to Britain, Robert Sandow designed another course on land with royal connections: the majestic Rolls of Monmouth course in South Wales, so-called because it is situated in the Home Park of the Hendre Estate, which was once the home of Charles Stewart Rolls of Rolls-Royce fame. Indeed the building which now houses the clubhouse is the actual workshop where the famous Rolls-Royce engine was developed. Fringing the arboretum and bordering the third and fourth fairways can be seen two splendid sycamores. These trees were planted in 1900 by the Duke and Duchess of York, the future King George V and Queen Mary, during a seven-day visit to The Hendre, when they were driven from London by none other than C S Rolls. The room in which the royal pair stayed during their visit was in the west wing of the magnificent Jacobean-style mansion; it now looks out over the 18th green and is called the King's Room. The two holes which are graced by the royal sycamores are named, appropriately, the Duke of York and the Duchess of York.

Prime Ministers and Presidents

Arthur James Balfour, a Scot, was the first British prime minister to be addicted to golf, and it was enthusiasm for the game which prompted many of his fellow politicians to take up the sport in and around London during the latter part of the 19th century. The word soon spread that golf was an excellent way to relax at the end of a tiring day spent in the Houses of Parliament. Two other British prime ministers, David Lloyd George and Winston Churchill, often refreshed their minds by chasing after a golf ball. Douglas Caird, a leading writer on women's golf, has many fond memories of golf in the company of David Lloyd George, and he told me the delightful story of how, as a youngster, he caddied for his father, Sir Andrew Caird, then managing director of the *Daily Mail*, in a match against the famous British prime minister. Before starting the match Douglas was warned by his father that, being fed up with losing to the prime minister, should he lose again he would deduct sixpence from the customary fee he paid Douglas for his services as a caddy. Lose he did. Come lunchtime young Caird had to do without his favourite topping of fresh cream on his apple pie dessert because of lack of funds. On being told the reason why Douglas went without his

ABOVE LEFT Vice President Richard Nixon sinking a putt while President Eisenhower looks on, 1953.

LEFT President J F Kennedy enjoying a round of golf, 1963.

ABOVE President Ford and comedian Bob Hope relaxing as they wait to play at Eldorado Country Club, Palm Springs, 1975.

cream, the prime minister guffawed loudly before whispering to the waitress to serve the young man with a double helping. Douglas remembers clearly the prime minister ribbing his father and calling him the meanest Scottish journalist he had ever set eyes on. Returning to Sunningdale alone for lunch a little later in the week, Douglas was amazed to discover that the prime minister had left instructions with the head waiter to allow Douglas to order a double helping of fresh cream whenever he wished – compliments of the prime minister!

With the exception of Arnold Palmer, President Dwight D Eisenhower probably did more to boost the game of golf in the United States in the years immediately following the conclusion of World War II than any other person. Having returned from the war a conquering hero, he swept into the White House in 1953, and immediately arranged for a practice green and bunker to be constructed on the White House lawn. Whenever the opportunity arose to slip away from the pressures of government, he often headed for Augusta National Golf Club to indulge in his favourite sport. Eisenhower's arrival on the political scene coincided with the rise of television, and viewers were constantly being shown shots of their President chipping and putting either at Camp David or on the White House lawn, and sometimes playing with friends at Augusta. The cry of 'I Like Ike' rapidly changed to 'Like Ike I Wanna Play Golf'.

Then Arnold Palmer entered the scene and won everything in sight with his swashbuckling style of golf. He and the President soon became friends and now America had two national heroes. Golf became the 'in' game and millions of Americans quickly got into the swing of the new national pastime.

Gerald Ford also turned to golf for relaxation during his term of office. In 1975 he took part in the pro-am that preceded the Jackie Gleason Classic tournament. After his defeat in the election he played in the Memphis Classic pro-am and achieved a hole in one. In 1977 he introduced his own invitational tournament, and in 1978 the US PGA made him their first honorary member. He visited Britain three times in succession from 1981 onward to play in the Bob Hope Classic charity tournament. Ronald Reagan has long been a keen golfer and is often shown on television playing a shot or two.

The Royal and Ancient game of golf is indeed a game for all people.

Great Players of the Past and Present

Old and Young Tom Morris, c 1871.

Someone once said (I believe it was Walter Hagen, but then again it could have been Ben Hogan): 'Anyone can win one major championship, but it takes a great player to win more than one.' He simply meant that one big win could be a fluke result.

In the annals of golf are the names of many golfers who found fame by winning a single major championship, and there are many more who became famous because of their failure to win when they should have. They were, of course, all endowed with a high degree of skill, otherwise they would not have been competing in such events in the first place, but one could write a book about gifted golfers who failed to achieve greatness.

This, however, is a chapter devoted to the great players – great not only because of the nerve and skill that enabled them to accumulate an impressive number of major achievements, but also for the way they modestly wore the mantle of success, thus creating the high standards and rich traditions that golfers everywhere still take care to maintain.

Allan Robertson, the first of the great players, won no major titles for he had the misfortune to be born in 1815 – 45 years before the British Open, the first of the four great championships, came into being. A product of the feather-ball age, he was known as 'Robertson the Unbeatable', because no one was able to match his remarkable skill in manoeuvring the unpredictable feathery round the windswept Scottish links. Even when he finally turned to using the gutta-percha ball, the ball he at first flatly refused to make or play with, he continued his unbeaten run in challenge matches. It has been said that he safeguarded his record by avoiding his two most dangerous challengers, Old Tom Morris ('Old' Tom to distinguish him from his brilliant son, 'Young' Tom) and Willie Park. But would Robertson's contemporary professionals have given him such an exalted title had he refused to play these two outstanding players? I think not.

Old Tom, like everyone else, held Robertson in high esteem, and described him as the most cunning player with club, cleek or putter he had ever played against. Indeed, had not an attack of jaundice ended his life in 1859, the year before the inaugural British Open Championship, Robertson's name might well have appeared among the early winners of the most coveted title in golf. A year prior to his death he astonished everyone by playing the Old Course at St Andrews in 79 strokes, the first time anyone had been under 80 there. After his death a member of St Andrews paid him a fitting tribute by saying: 'They may shut up their shops and toll their bells, for the greatest among them is gone.'

TOM MORRIS, YOUNG AND OLD

Old Tom Morris, besides being employed by Robertson as a ballmaker, often partnered the great man in foursome challenge matches and together they proved formidable opponents to anyone daring to throw out a challenge. The legendary match of the time was truly a marathon. It took place in 1849 between Robertson and Morris from St Andrews and the twin brothers, Willie and Jamie Dunn of Musselburgh. Played over three courses, Musselburgh, St Andrews and North Berwick, the St Andrews pair fought back brilliantly at North Berwick to win the match by two holes after being four holes down with only eight left to play.

Old Tom went on to learn his lessons well from Allan Robertson and quickly became a great player in his own right. In the early 1850s he left St Andrews to take up the job of professional at the newly opened Prestwick club, on the west coast of Scotland. It was there, in 1860,

that the British Open Championship was born, and Morris finished runner-up to Musselburgh's Willie Park, losing by two strokes. The following year he won the title and went on to win three more times, in 1862, 1864 and 1867, before handing over the reins of glory to his young son Tom.

Young Tom Morris was without a doubt the greatest golfer of his generation. In a brief but brilliant career he won the Open Championship four times in a row to create a record which remains unequalled to this day. He also remains the youngest man to have won the Open, being only 17 years and five months old when he gained the first of his four titles in 1868. Having completed three wins in a row he was allowed to keep the championship belt as his own property and, with no trophy to contest, the Open Championship was not played in 1871. When it was revived the following year with a brand new trophy, Young Tom, continuing to dominate, won it again. To discover how highly talented Young Tom really was, one has only to look at his winning score of 149 at Prestwick in 1870. Scored over three rounds of the then 12-hole Prestwick course, this was remarkable scoring for the gutty-ball age, and his final round score of 47, which was one shot below level fours and included an eagle three at the 500 yards (445 m) first hole, was an incredible performance. In the remaining 32 years that the gutty ball was used, not one of the great players who followed Young Tom ever equalled his brilliant winning score. Sadly, in 1875, his illustrious career came to a tragic end a few months after he received the news that his wife had died in childbirth together with his newborn son. Devoted to his young wife, to whom he had been married for only one year, he failed to recover from the shock, and on Christmas Day he died of a 'broken heart' at the

ABOVE LEFT Allan Robertson, 'The Unbeatable'.

ABOVE *On Musselburgh Links,* Charles Lees, *c* 1859.

LEFT Old Tom Morris (second from right), early in his career.

TOP RIGHT The Dyke hole at North Berwick, by John Smart, *c* 1889.

ABOVE Willie Park senior – four-times winner of the Open Championship, in 1860, 1863, 1866 and 1875.

TOP RIGHT Willie Park junior, 1889.

ABOVE RIGHT Jamie Anderson, Open Champion in 1877, 1878 and 1879, was the second of four men to win the Championship three times in a row.

age of 24. The inscription on his tombstone in St Andrews Cathedral reads: 'Deeply regretted by numerous friends and all golfers, he thrice in succession won the championship belt and held it without rivalry and yet without envy, his many amiable qualities being no less acknowledged than his golfing achievements'.

Between them the Morrises had dominated the Championship by winning eight times in 12 years – a father and son record that it is safe to say will never be broken. Willie Park won the Championship four times and his son Willie junior won twice to come closest to matching the Morrises, but there it ends.

Straying from the great champions for a while, there was among them at that time a talented amateur golfer, Gilbert Mitchell-Innes, who, it is said, could play on level terms with these great players and occasionally beat them. It was he, so Bernard Darwin, the doyen of golf writers, tells us in his book *British Golf*, who was the author of the saying that the way to beat a professional is never to let him get a hole up. It would appear that, had Mitchell-Innes not pursued other interests and pastimes but concentrated on golf, his name might well have been added to the Open Championship winners' list. Young Tom Morris once remarked of him: 'I cannot understand Mr Innes when he's playing as fine a game as any mortal man ever played, leaving golf to run after stinking beasts and then coming back, not able to hit a ball at all.' He once partnered Young Tom in a 600-hole match against Jamie Anderson and Davie Strath, two outstanding professionals,

BOB FERGUSON

Bob Ferguson came within a whisker of equalling Young Tom Morris' record of four consecutive titles when, having tied with Willie Fernie of Dumfries in the Championship at Musselburgh in 1883, he lost the play-off after going to the last hole leading by one stroke.

LEFT A Spy cartoon of John Ball. Britain's greatest amateur, he won eight amateur championships and also the 1890 Open.

and he and his partner won by eight holes. When he did give the game some serious thought he twice won the St Andrews Silver Medal, in 1864 and 1874, and the St Andrews Royal Medal, in 1870.

His grandson, Norman Mitchell-Innes, still plays with a wooden putter that Gilbert often used when playing with the Morrises.

After Young Tom Morris we go on a few years before coming to two more golfers who achieved greatness through their exploits in the Open Championship. Each of these men won three titles in a row – Jamie Anderson of St Andrews in 1877, 1878 and 1879, and Bob Ferguson of Musselburgh in the following three years.

With two Championships under his belt, Willie Park junior all but made it three when he needed a short putt to tie with Harry Vardon at Prestwick in 1898, but he missed the putt and faded away from the Championship scene. He went on to make his mark in other branches of the game and found equal success in a clubmaking business and in golf-course architecture, Sunningdale Old Course, England, being one of his famous courses.

Going back to the early 1890s we must give a mention to John Ball and Harold Hilton, the two outstanding amateurs of the time and the first Englishmen to win the Open Championship. Ball, a member of the Royal Liverpool Club, won in 1890 at Prestwick, and achieved a notable double that year by also winning the British Amateur Championship at Hoylake. Between 1888 and 1912 he won the British Amateur title a record eight times. Hilton, also from the Royal Liverpool Club, won the Open in 1892 and repeated the feat in 1897. He was equally successful in major amateur championships, winning the British Amateur in 1900, 1901 and 1911, and the United States Amateur Championship in 1911. He was the author of several books on golf and the editor of *Golf Illustrated*.

Another famous amateur of this period who did much for golf with his writings on the game was Horace Hutchinson. He twice won the British Amateur, in 1886 and 1887, and in 1890 he finished in fifth place in the Open Championship. In 1908 he was elected captain of the Royal and Ancient Club, the first Englishman to receive the honour. Playing much of his golf at the Royal North Devon Club at Westward Ho! he is credited as the man who influenced John Henry Taylor to take up the game.

ABOVE LEFT Harold Hilton, the only British amateur to win the Open twice (1892 and 1897).

LEFT Horace Hutchinson by Spy.

ABOVE The Great Triumvirate – Taylor, Braid and Vardon – by Clement Flower, 1913.

THE GREAT TRIUMVIRATE

John Henry Taylor, who often acted as Hutchinson's caddie at Westward Ho!, was the first English professional to win the British Open and, appropriately, he won it at Royal St Georges, Sandwich, in 1894, the first time the Championship moved out of Scotland and onto English soil. Taylor's name will forever be linked with those of Harry Vardon and James Braid. In a span of 21 years, beginning in 1894 and ending with World War I in 1914, they completely dominated the British golfing scene by winning the Open Championship 16 times. It is no wonder they were dubbed the Great Triumvirate. In those 21 years Taylor won the Open five times, was runner-up three times and on two other occasions was joint runner-up. If that was not enough he added the British Professional Matchplay title to the list in 1904, won the French Open twice in succession in 1908 and 1909 and the German Open in 1912. In 1900 he

HARRY VARDON

Harry Vardon won the Open for the first time in 1896 and was 44 years old when he picked up his last title in 1914, a few months before the outbreak of World War I. Three times in succession from 1900 he had to be content with second place, and was again runner-up in 1912.

ABOVE RIGHT J H Taylor, c1912.

ABOVE FAR RIGHT Francis Ouimet, the young American amateur, broke the British-born domination of the US Open in 1913.

BELOW RIGHT Harry Vardon (white boots, back to camera) and J H Taylor (touching cap) during the play-off for the 1896 Open Championship at Muirfield.

was runner-up in the United States Open to his great friend and rival Harry Vardon.

Known to his friends as 'J H', Taylor was a dignified man and a credit to the game. In 1933 he was elected non-playing captain of the British Ryder Cup team and led his team to a rare victory over the Americans at Southport and Ainsdale. In 1950, at the age of 79, he was made an honorary member of the Royal and Ancient Golf Club, and on his 90th birthday the captain and past captains of the club again honoured him by presenting him with a silver salver suitably inscribed and bearing their signatures.

In 1957 Taylor was elected President of the Royal North Devon Golf Club – the club where he once eked out a living as a caddie had paid him the highest honour they could. His book *Golf, My Life's Work*, has now become a collectors' item. In 1963, at the grand old age of 92, he died where he had been born in the village of Northam overlooking the links of Westward Ho!

The second and most celebrated member of the Great Triumvirate was Harry Vardon. Every golfer in the world who has consulted a teaching manual will be familiar with his name on account of the 'Vardon grip', which is now the standard grip of the majority who play golf. His record of six victories in the British Open still stands, but the American, Tom Watson, with his five victories, is still young and capable enough to equal if not break the record during the next few years.

In January 1900 Vardon was persuaded to spend a year touring the United States, the object of the exercise being to promote a new ball called the Vardon Flyer. The ball, made of gutta-percha, was to have a limited life because it coincided with the advent of the Haskell rubber-cored ball.

For the game itself the tour proved to be an enormous success, as thousands flocked to watch the English genius in action in the many exhibition matches he played. While there he won the United States Open Championship, beating J H Taylor by two strokes. Vardon returned to America 13 years later hoping to repeat his victory, but he reckoned without the young American amateur, Francis Ouimet. Such was the British-born domination of the US Open at the time that everyone expected the winner to be either Ted Ray, the current British Open Champion, or Harry Vardon. The American, who decided to play in the event only because it took place in his home town, shocked the whole of the golfing world by winning it after a play-off with the two great Englishmen.

Vardon returned to the United States in 1920 and to his credit finished joint runner-up in the US Open at the age of 50. Although he won only the one championship in the United States, his flowing style and accurate iron play left a lasting impression on young Americans, and it was he more than any other golfer of his time who gave American golf its initial boost. What is not generally known is that Vardon had a younger brother, Tom, who was also a top-class golfer, so much so that he finished second in the 1903 British Open behind his famous brother, was fourth in 1904, one stroke ahead of his brother, and joint third in 1907.

The last but not least of the Great Triumvirate was James Braid, a Scotsman who made golfing history by becoming the first man to win the British Open five times. Equally impressive as a matchplayer, in nine years he won four British Matchplay Championships. Legend has it that he owes his victories to finding two clubs, a driver and an aluminium-headed putter, that suited him. Before discovering these precious implements he struggled with length from the tee, and his putting was once described as so bad it was enough to make angels weep! Certainly something suddenly worked for him, for from the time he turned professional in 1893 he was to win nothing of note until 1901, when he made the breakthrough and won the first of his five British Open Championships, and with it the added satisfaction of leaving Vardon and Taylor trailing in his wake in second and third places, respectively. Braid had finally arrived, and thus was formed the famous trio who did more to popularize golf before World War I than any other players. In 1950 James Braid was elected honorary member of the Royal and Ancient Club, and in the same year he died in his London home at the age of 80.

Before leaving the period prior to World War I, a mention must be made of Willie Anderson, a talented Scottish professional who emigrated to the United States in 1895. The first man to win the US Open Championship four times (three of them in a row from 1903 to 1905), he also finished runner-up in 1897, was third once, fourth twice and fifth three times – a tremendous record that has never been equalled. Who knows what he might have achieved had he not died suddenly of arteriosclerosis at the early age of 32.

THE FLAMBOYANT WALTER HAGEN

While the British were preparing for war there emerged in the United States a character, in every sense of the word, who was to take golf by the scruff of the neck and give it a thorough shaking. Indeed, Walter Hagen did more to take the starchiness out of the game – both on and off the course – than any other man. Not for him the swing-restricting tweed jackets and breeches; when he was on the course there was no mistaking him for anyone else. Colourful casual clothing and black and white shoes were his trademark. His play and his manner were as flamboyant as his dress. Here was the first of the truly swashbuckling golfers who had the rare ability of scoring well from deep rough and other almost unplayable positions. Be it matchplay or strokeplay, golf to him was all about winning, and win he did in no uncertain fashion.

Making his breakthrough with victory in the United States Open in 1914, Hagen sat on his laurels for five years before suddenly bursting into action like a firecracker. In 1919 he again won the US Open, was US PGA Champion (it was then matchplay) in 1921, 1924, 1925, 1926 and 1927 and British Open Champion in 1922, 1924, 1928 and 1929.

ABOVE LEFT James Braid at the height of his career.

ABOVE Willie Anderson was the first man to win the US Open four times, in 1901, 1903, 1904 and 1905.

ABOVE RIGHT New York gives Bobby Jones a hero's welcome following his victory in the 1926 British Open.

When Hagen made his first trip to Britain to compete in the British Open, at Deal in 1920, he was politely informed that professionals were not allowed entry into the clubhouse. In typical Hagen fashion he hired a Rolls-Royce and a suitably dressed butler, and parked outside the main windows of the clubhouse where he lunched on smoked salmon, caviar, champagne and all the trimmings. The club members had the last laugh on this occasion because Hagen could do no better than finish in last but one place in the Championship.

Hagen quickly came to terms with the British seaside courses, and emerged triumphant in 1922 at Royal St George's Sandwich to become the first American-born player to win the British Open. Unimpressed by the prize money he received at the presentation ceremony, he promptly handed the cheque to his caddie. At Troon the following year, when he finished runner-up to Arthur Havers, Hagen took another embarrassing dig at those who looked upon professionals as second-class citizens. Being told that a concession by the committee allowed the presentation to be made inside the clubhouse and that he had been invited to attend, Hagen declined the offer, turned to the crowd and invited them to join him at a party he was throwing at a local inn. In a single sentence the golf writer Bernard Darwin described perfectly the greatness of Walter Hagen: 'The difference between Hagen and other players is that he just wins and they just don't'.

THE GREATEST OF ALL AMATEURS

The arrival of Walter Hagen marked the almost complete domination of major championship golf by American players, which was to last for no less than 20 years. Playing a major part in the American dominance was one Robert Tyre Jones Junior, from Atlanta, Georgia, an amateur who, with the exception of Jack Nicklaus, is the greatest golfer ever to set foot on a golf course. In a short but brilliant career he became the idol of the ordinary club golfer. For here was a man who, like themselves, played the game purely for the glory of winning once in a while without any thought of gaining rich rewards – a true-blue amateur in every sense of the word.

In a space of eight years from 1923 to 1930 Jones amassed an incredible total of 13 major titles. A measure of his amazing ability is the fact that he played hardly any competitive golf outside the 'big ones', much preferring to play friendly matches with his friends. He practised little, and often entered the championships with only a warm-up beforehand. In 1930 he achieved the ultimate when he won what was then regarded as the Grand Slam of golf – the Open and Amateur titles of both Britain and the United States – a feat that will probably remain unequalled.

With these four historic victories under his belt in the space of a single year Jones, feeling there was nothing worthwhile left to achieve, decided enough was enough and announced his retirement from top-class competitive golf at the tender age of 28. His outstanding achievements were recognized by the United States and Great Britain in several ways. After winning his first British Open at Royal Lytham in 1926 he arrived home to a tumultuous ticker-tape welcome in New York City. His picture also appeared on a national postage stamp, one of the few golfers to receive this honour. In 1958 he made a nostalgic return to Scotland to receive the freedom of the Burgh of St Andrews. When he had first played on the Old Course at St Andrews in 1921 he had hated it so much that he tore his card up in frustration halfway through his fourth round of the British Open. But as the years rolled by he grew to love the place and afterward declared it his favourite golf course.

During World War II Jones served with the US Army, rising to the rank of lieutenant-colonel,

WALTER HAGEN

Walter Hagen was a Ryder Cup player and captain in all five matches between 1927 and 1935 and non-playing captain in 1937, when he led the American team to a first-ever Ryder Cup victory on British soil.

GENE SARAZEN

Gene Sarazen is another great golfer from the Hagen and Jones era who dented the pride of the British golfer. Born Eugene Saraceni in Harrison, New York, the son of Italian immigrants, he changed his name because it sounded more suited to a violinist than a golfer.

RIGHT Henry Cotton became Open Champion for the third time at Muirfield in 1948.

ABOVE RIGHT Sweet-swinging Sam Snead, 1962.

BELOW FAR RIGHT A rare shot of Ben Hogan hitting out of deep rough, 1938.

but on returning home he began to suffer from a muscular disease called syringomyelia which eventually confined him to a wheelchair. He finally gave up a long and brave battle against the disease in 1971 and died in Atlanta, Georgia, at the age of 69. It was a sad end for a great champion and a great man whose record reads: US Open Champion 1923, 1926, 1929 and 1930; British Open Champion 1926, 1927 and 1930; US Amateur Champion 1924, 1925, 1927, 1928 and 1930; British Amateur Champion 1930; Walker Cup appearances 1922, 1924, 1926, 1928 and 1930. His name is immortalized not only in the record books but also in one of the world's greatest golf courses at Augusta, which he created along with what is one of the major championships of modern times, the United States Masters, staged there every April.

Gene Sarazen made his niche in golfing history by becoming the first man to win the world's four major championships – the British Open, US Open, US PGA Championship and the

United States Masters. Only three others, Ben Hogan, Jack Nicklaus and Gary Player, have equalled the feat. At the age of 71 he accepted an invitation to play at Troon, in the 1973 British Open. By coincidence, it marked the 50th anniversary of his undistinguished debut in the British Open, on the very same course, when he failed to qualify. However, this time he created a sensation when, partnered by two other past champions, Max Faulkner and Fred Daly, and in full view of the television cameras, he holed in one at Troon's famous Postage Stamp eighth hole. As recently as April 1987 millions of television viewers saw Gene Sarazen teeing off with two other American greats of the past, Sam Snead and Byron Nelson, when they started off the American Masters at Augusta National, Florida. Not bad for an 85-year-old senior citizen.

HENRY COTTON'S FAMOUS ROUND

The almost complete stranglehold that American golfers had on the British Open for 13 years was finally broken by Henry Cotton, a former London public schoolboy who made up his mind while still at school to become a professional golfer and a champion in the bargain. Such was his burning desire to succeed that he weekly hit thousands of balls in practice and in his own words: 'Chipped and putted for such a time it was easier to stay bent than to stand up'. His dedication was rewarded when he won the Open by five strokes at Royal St George's, Sandwich, in 1934. The 65 which he scored in the second round was then the lowest round ever recorded in the British Open, and led to the famous Dunlop '65' ball being made to commemorate the occasion. He won again in 1937 at Carnoustie, a win that gave him much satisfaction, for he took on and beat the mighty Americans who were there in force as part of the visiting Ryder Cup team. Had not World War II put an end to the Championship for six years who knows what records he might have created? He was then in his prime and the most talented player in Europe.

As it was, Cotton still managed one more Open victory after the war. This came at Muirfield in 1948 when, aged 41, he broke the course record by scoring 66 in the second round. He had been invalided out of the RAF when the war ended, and he did much work to help raise funds for the Red Cross. In recognition of this he was made an MBE. Like Walter Hagen before him, he also did much to further the cause of his fellow professionals. After receiving his cheque for winning the French Open in 1946, he let it be known quite clearly that it was an insult to his profession. His maxim was that if sponsors wanted the best players in the world, they should expect to pay them well.

As well as being three-times winner of the British Open, Cotton won the British Matchplay Championship three times and numerous other national championships on the Continent. He played in the Ryder Cup matches of 1929, 1937 and 1947 and was non-playing captain in 1953. For many years the Grand Old Man of British golf, Cotton sadly died on 23 December, 1987, at the age of 80, after suffering a short illness. A few days later he received a posthumous knight-

hood for his services to golf, the first golfer ever to receive such an honour.

Henry Cotton proved to be the last of the great British players, and only Tony Jacklin, when he won the British Open in 1969 and the US Open in 1970, has since caused a flutter in the hearts of the success-starved British golf fan. However, the demands put on the talented young Jacklin at the height of his success proved too much and he gradually faded out of the tournament scene. Nevertheless, he still remains very much in the limelight as the successful non-playing captain of the Great Britain and Europe Ryder Cup team.

HOGAN COMES BACK FROM INJURY

While Cotton was continuing his lone battle to put British golf back at the top, the United States was producing a new crop of great golfers in the shapes of Ben Hogan, Sam Snead and Byron Nelson. All three were born in the same year (1912), and from 1937 to 1955 they amassed among them 21 major title wins. Without a doubt Hogan was the greatest player of the three, and is regarded by many as the supreme golfer of the modern era. His impressive record tells us that he won the US Open four times; the British Open once; the US PGA twice and the Masters twice. However, what it does not tell us is that in 1949 Hogan was involved in a horrendous car smash that almost ended his life. Multiple injuries, which included a broken leg, ankle, shoulder and pelvis, convinced everyone that Hogan's golf career was over. Hogan, however, had other ideas. As soon as he was declared fit enough to leave the hospital, he went home to Fort Worth, Texas, to practise in secret. By sheer determination, guts and a lot of gruelling effort, he made an amazing comeback and went on to win the 1950 US Open after a play-off with George Fazio and Lloyd Mangrum. Indeed, six of the nine major championships he won came after his serious injuries. Despite being known as 'The Hawk' in the United States and 'The Iceman' in Britain, because of the way he shunned publicity and refused to give his autograph, the crowds loved him and flocked in the thousands to watch him play. He now lives in quiet retirement in Fort Worth.

Sam Snead first started to play 'golf' by cutting suitable branches from trees and shaping them into makeshift golf clubs to play on waste ground near his home in Hot Springs, Virginia. Progressing to 'real' golf, he learnt how to win the hard way by betting on himself to win without a dollar in his pocket to pay out should he ever have lost. It was in this tough school that he perfected the slow, sweet swing which earned him the nickname 'Swinging Sam'. It was this casual repeating action which helped him to carry on competing at the top well into his 60s. In 1974, at the age of 62, he amazingly finished in third place in the US PGA, three strokes

FAR LEFT Bing Crosby shares a joke with Byron Nelson.

BELOW FAR LEFT Bobby Locke, one of the finest putters the world of golf has ever known.

BELOW LEFT Peter Thomson remains the greatest golfer to come out of Australia, 1962.

ABOVE Arnold Palmer, the first golfing media star.

behind the winner, Lee Trevino. Three times the winner of both the Masters and the US PGA, he also won the British Open at his second attempt, in 1946. Fate decreed that he should never win the US Open, but he came close four times, finishing runner-up on each occasion. With a tournament career of almost 200 victories, he now plays for fun with a swing that looks as good as ever.

Byron Nelson achieved his first major breakthrough in 1937 with a victory in the Masters, a win he repeated again in 1942. He also won the US PGA title twice, in 1940 and 1945, and the US Open in 1939. In 1945 he recorded an incredible sequence of tournament victories, winning 11 in a row. But for the war he, like Hogan and Snead, could well have added more championships to this impressive list. He played in two Ryder Cup matches, in 1937 and 1947, and was non-playing captain in 1965. Retiring from competitive golf in the early 1950s, Nelson found success both as a teacher and television commentator on the game. In 1974 he was awarded the Bobby Jones Award in recognition of his outstanding contribution to golf.

BOBBY LOCKE AND PETER THOMSON

While the American stars concentrated mainly on their own circuit during this era, it was left to two other great overseas players, South African Bobby Locke and Peter Thomson of Australia, to dominate the British Open. Locke had already proved he was as good as the Americans by winning seven tournaments in the United States in the summer of 1947. Had he not become disillusioned with the American tournament scene, brought about as a result of his being refused the same appearance money offered to Americans, he probably would have won a number of major championships there. Turning his back on American golf he concentrated all his efforts on the British Open, which he won four times between 1949 and 1957. A slow, meticulous player, especially on the greens, he took great care over every shot. One of the greatest putters in the world, he won the Open Championships of many countries in all parts of the world, and won the South African Open Championship nine times between 1935 and 1955. A great player and a gentleman, he died in 1987 at the age of 69.

Many fine golfers have come from Australia, but Peter Thomson is still regarded as the greatest Australian golfer of them all. His early victories in the British Open are looked upon by some as not counting for much because they were achieved at a time when the American players were not appearing regularly. Nevertheless, he is the only man this century to achieve a hat-trick of victories in the Open Championship (1954, 1955 and 1956). The following year he came close to making it four in a row when he finished runner-up to Bobby Locke. In 1958 he won again to make it four wins and two seconds in the space of six years (he came second to Ben Hogan in 1953). In 1965 at Royal Birkdale he silenced his critics by winning again, this time

ABOVE Jack Nicklaus and Arnold Palmer recall old memories during the 1987 US Masters.

with all the top Americans in the field including Tony Lema, the holder, Arnold Palmer and Jack Nicklaus. With this win he joined J H Taylor and James Braid as a five-time winner of the Championship. A quiet, likeable person, Peter Thomson is now enjoying much success playing on the American Seniors' tour.

PALMER MAKES A MILLION

Arnold Palmer may not have been the greatest golfer in the world, but he was certainly the most exciting. When he played golf he was Tarzan, Errol Flynn and Superman rolled into one. To him there was just one way to hit a golf ball – an almighty swipe in the right general direction. If it landed in jungle it mattered little; a quick swashbuckling, superhuman stroke would get it flying back on course. He played a type of game (only better) that thousands played every weekend, and they loved him for it. Coming on the scene when television was in its infancy, he was the television producers' dream. Here was the guy-next-door making good, and it made for good viewing. He loved going for broke from impossible positions. In 1960, when all seemed lost, he won both the Masters and the US Open with last-round charges.

The British took him to their hearts when he went to St Andrews to play in the centenary Open of 1960. He lost by one stroke to the Australian Kel Nagle, but the fact that he was there triggered off a revival of American interest in the great event. The following year he was back and won at Royal Birkdale, and in 1962, at Troon, he successfully defended the title. He captured the imagination of people of all ages and thousands took up the game. As box-office material he rivalled the film stars. His picture appeared everywhere, on magazine covers, bill-board hoardings and television commercials – Arnie had arrived, and he quickly became a multi-millionaire. The way he played was not a gimmick, it was the only way he knew how to play the game – hit it hard and get it into the hole as quickly as possible.

Behind the aggression on the course Arnold Palmer has a quiet, gentle nature, completely unaffected by his successful rise to stardom. No one really cared if he won or not so long as he entertained them with his swashbuckling style, but for the record he was: British Open Champion 1961 and 1962; US Open Champion 1960; Masters Champion 1958, 1960, 1962 and 1964; US Amateur Champion 1954; Ryder Cup player 1961, 1963, 1965, 1967, 1971 and 1973, and non-playing captain 1975.

THE MAN IN BLACK

When Gary Player left his home in South Africa to try his luck as a professional golfer in Great Britain in 1955, no one dreamt that here was a man who was destined to become one of the all-time greats of golf. Small in stature at 5ft 7ins (1.70 m) and 154 lb (69.85 kg), he looked not to possess the physique and stamina required of a champion. But to his everlasting credit he set out to prove that fitness and strength allied to talent were more important than size. His dedication to fitness and practice bordered on the fanatical. Every spare minute was taken up with exercise – running, jumping, skipping, press-ups, weight training and practising golf shots. It was Player who invented the saying: 'The more I practise, the luckier I become'. He lived on a special diet and even took to wearing black clothing because he was told that black attracted the sun's rays, which would give him extra strength. He also trained his mind to be positive at all times. Fanatical it may have seemed, but the belief that what he was doing was the way to success certainly paid off handsomely for the diminutive South African.

Player gained his first big success in 1959 with victory in the British Open at Muirfield, a feat he repeated in 1968 and 1974, thus producing a remarkable treble of Open victories spanning three decades. In 1961 he became the first non-American to win the Masters, and also topped the money-winners' list for that year. In 1965 he became the first South African to win the US Open and with that win the first non-American to win the world's four major championships. Altogether he totalled nine major titles, the last being the Masters in 1978. He won the British Open three times, the Masters three times, the US PGA twice and the US Open once. He also won the South African Open 13 times and the Australian Open seven times. Still as fit as ever, he made the last round

BELOW Gary Player, the great South African golfer, in full swing.

BELOW RIGHT The greatest of them all, Jack Nicklaus, playing in the 1987 US Open.

in the Masters tournament at Augusta in 1987. Not bad for a 52-year-old! It is no wonder he is ranked alongside Arnold Palmer and Jack Nicklaus as one of the 'Big Three'.

THE GREATEST OF ALL

One only has to look at Jack Nicklaus' record in the major championships to realize he is the greatest golfer of all time. In the 25 years since he turned professional in 1962, he has won 18 of the world's premier championships. Add the two US Amateur titles he won in 1959 and 1961 to the total and it puts him seven ahead of Bobby Jones, who was his boyhood idol. In 1959, at the age of 19, Nicklaus became the youngest winner of the US Amateur Championship for 50 years. Also as an amateur, in 1960, he finished runner-up to Palmer in the US Open. He is the only man to win the four major titles three times, and in 1972 he came within two strokes of achieving the Grand Slam in the same year. The most successful golfer in the history of the game, he is still, at 47, trying to add to his impressive total of major titles. In 1986 he caused a sensation by winning the Masters for the sixth time – this 24 years after winning his first major tournament. In 1987 he rose to the Masters' challenge once more, but faded away in the last couple of holes.

JACK NICKLAUS

Jack Nicklaus' record, of winning the British Open three times, the US Open four times, the US PGA five times, the Masters six times and the US Amateur twice, will almost certainly never be beaten, and who knows, he may yet add a few more titles to the list before he decides to retire.

Like the other two members of the 'Big Three', Arnold Palmer and Gary Player, Jack Nicklaus is a credit to his profession both on and off the golf course.

Lee Trevino, a contemporary of Jack Nicklaus, first shot into the limelight when he finished fifth in the US Open at Baltusrol in 1967, having borrowed the money from his wife, Claudia, to enter the event. Born in Dallas, Texas, in 1939, he was the last person anyone would have predicted to become an ordinary golfer, let alone a professional and a champion. His background was such that he never knew his father, whom he was named after, and neither his Mexican mother nor his grandfather could read or write. He learnt to play golf after being offered a job at a local driving range, and like Sam Snead before him, he supplemented his earnings by becoming a hustler at the game.

In 1968 Lee Trevino surprised the golfing world by winning the US Open at Oak Hill, New York, scoring below 70 in every round – still the only man to achieve this feat. Proving that his victory was no fluke, he won the title again in 1971, beating the great Jack Nicklaus in a play-off at Merion, Ardmore. A few weeks later he joined a select band of players who have won the US Open and the British Open in the same year – Bobby Jones, Gene Sarazen and Ben Hogan being the others.

A man who loves to crack jokes and talk and laugh with the crowd in between shots, Trevino is truly the clown prince of the fairways. But inwardly he is a person of deep compassion and generosity. When he won the Hawaiian Open in 1968 he gave most of his money to the family of Ted Makalena, a colleague who was killed in a surfing accident. During the 1976 Western Open he almost lost his own life when struck by lightning. Despite surgery on his back, which forced him into semi-retirement, he bounced back in typical Trevino style to win the 1984 US PGA title and in doing so amazingly scored in the 60s in all four rounds to repeat what he had accomplished 15 years previously in the US Open.

The greatest exponent of the wedge shot the world has ever seen, Trevino has won the British Open, the US Open and the US PGA titles twice each, but sadly the Masters title has eluded him. In 1985, having seen action with six Ryder Cup teams, he was selected as non-playing captain of the American team, a fitting finale to a brilliant career.

LEFT Lee Trevino, the 'Clown Prince of Golf', is the finest exponent of the classic wedge shot.

ABOVE Tom Watson, US Open Champion in 1982, is looking to win the British Open one more time to equal Harry Vardon's record six wins.

THE MASTE

Gene Sarazen

GENE SARAZEN
Born 1902

British Open Champion: 1932
US Open Champion: 1922, 1932
US PGA Champion: 1922, 1923, 1933
US Masters Champion: 1935

HENRY COTTON
1907–1987

British Open Champion: 1934, 1937, 1948

Henry Cotton

Ben Hogan

BEN HOGAN
Born 1912

British Open Champion: 1953
US Open Champion: 1948, 1950, 1951, 1953
US PGA Champion: 1946, 1948
US Masters Champion: 1951, 1953

Sam Snead

SAM SNEAD
Born 1912

British Open Champion: 1946
US PGA Champion: 1942, 1949, 1951
US Masters Champion: 1949, 1952, 1954

BYRON NELSON
Born 1912

US Open Champion: 1939
US PGA Champion: 1940, 1945
US Masters Champion: 1937, 1942

Byron Nelson

Allan Robertson

ALLAN ROBERTSON
1815 - 1859

TOM MORRIS SENIOR
1821 - 1908

British Open Champion: 1861, 1862, 1864, 1867

TOM MORRIS JUNIOR
1851 - 1875

British Open Champion: 1868, 1869, 1870, 1872

J H TAYLOR
1871 - 1963

British Open Champion: 1894, 1895, 1900, 1909, 1913

Tom Morris Senior

Tom Morris Junior

JAMES BRAID
1870 - 1950

British Open Champion: 1901, 1905, 1906, 1908, 1910

J H Taylor

HARRY VARDON
1870 - 1937

British Open Champion: 1896, 1898, 1899, 1903, 1911, 1914
US Open Champion: 1900

WALTER HAGEN
1892 - 1969

British Open Champion: 1922, 1924, 1928, 1929
US Open Champion: 1914, 1919
US PGA Champion: 1921, 1924, 1925, 1926, 1927

Harry Vardon

James Braid

Walter Hagen

BOBBY JONES
1902 - 1971

British Open Champion: 1926, 1927, 1930
US Open Champion: 1923, 1926, 1929, 1930

Bobby Jones

Watson's Great Matches

Tom Watson and Severiano Ballesteros, two players with contrasting styles, are the last of the established modern greats still with a realistic chance of adding to their tally of major championship titles. Watson, although picking up his first title when winning the British Open at Carnoustie in 1975, will long be remembered for his epic duel in the British sun with Jack Nicklaus at Turnberry in 1977. With both players tied after three days with identical rounds of 68–70–65, the last day produced the most exciting, nail-biting, heart-pounding, man-to-man last-round encounter in the history of the Championship. And what a climax – still tied with two holes remaining, Watson broke the deadlock by rolling in a putt from off the edge of the 17th green. When all seemed lost for Nicklaus at the final hole, he looked to have forced a play-off by sinking a monster putt for a birdie. Watson, now needing to hole his putt for a birdie and the title, did so and the crowd erupted. Watson had scored a 65 to Nicklaus' 66. (Happily, a video recording has since been produced of this historic match.)

Nicklaus suffered another dramatic defeat at the hands of Watson in the 1982 US Open at Pebble Beach, when the latter chipped in from an impossible position at the 17th hole to swing the result in his favour when Nicklaus looked the certain winner. With five wins to his name in the British Open, Watson now needs but one more to equal the six achieved by Harry Vardon. He almost did it at St Andrews in 1984, foiled only by Ballesteros, who won with a par-birdie finish which Watson could not match. Two Masters titles, in 1977 and 1981, bring Watson's total of major wins to eight, and although championship wins have eluded him during the last few years he is still young enough to make a comeback.

The Swashbuckling Spaniard

Unlike the American Tom Watson, with his crisp, rhythmic swing, Severiano Ballesteros looks to have come out of the same mould that produced Arnold Palmer, especially when performing one of his famous last nine-hole charges. Ballesteros first served notice that he possessed

the exceptional talent to become a great player when, aged just 19, he entered the British Open at Royal Birkdale in 1976 and almost pulled off a sensational victory. He led for three rounds, only to fall at the last hurdle to give Johnny Miller the title. Nevertheless, finishing in a tie for second place with the great Jack Nicklaus, he had made his mark on the championship.

Born in Pedrena, Spain, in 1957, Ballesteros learnt to play by hitting stones with a makeshift golf club on the beaches near his humble home. He was drawn to the game because one of the best Spanish golfers of that time, Raymond Sota, was his mother's brother. Seve practised for countless hours on the lonely beaches, determined one day to emulate his favourite uncle. Before the start of the 1979 British Open at Royal Lytham, the experts were saying that the rough was so severe that the man who could consistently keep his ball on the fairways would be the eventual winner. Ballesteros proved them wrong by deliberately aiming for the rough from the tee rather than run the risk of putting his ball in the dangerous fairway bunkers. With amazing consistency in all four rounds he smashed his ball onto the greens from the deep rough. The effect on the rest of the field was one of demoralization as the swashbuckling Spaniard swung his way to an incredible victory. He captured not only the coveted trophy but also the hearts of the public like no other since Arnold Palmer, and with his film-star looks he quickly became the most marketable golfer ever to come out of Europe – and continues to be so to this very day. Without a doubt he has done more for European golf than any other player, and to his credit he has not entirely abandoned the European tournament circuit.

In 1980 Ballesteros went to the United States and became the first European to win the Masters title, a performance he repeated in 1983. He all but did it again in 1987, losing in a three-man play-off which was won by the young American Larry Mize. Ballesteros' victory at St Andrews in 1984 gave him his second British Open title and his fourth major title in all. As a matchplayer he is the most difficult of men to beat, as he proved when helping the Great Britain and Europe Ryder Cup team to historic victories against the Americans at The Belfry in 1985 and at Muirfield Village, Ohio, in 1987. Still winning tournaments with amazing regularity all round the world, Ballesteros continues to be the most exciting European golfer ever seen.

LEFT Seve Ballesteros in full flow.

ABOVE A triumphant Seve winning the Masters for the second time in three years, 1983.

JACK NICKLAUS
Born 1940

British Open Champion: 1966, 1970, 1978
US Open Champion: 1962, 1967, 1972, 1980
US PGA Champion: 1963, 1971, 1973, 1975, 1980
US Masters Champion: 1963, 1965, 1966, 1972, 1975, 1986

LEE TREVINO
Born 1939

British Open Champion: 1971, 1972
US Open Champion: 1968, 1971
US PGA Champion: 1974, 1984

Jack Nicklaus

Lee Trevino

Tom Watson

TOM WATSON
Born 1949

British Open Champion: 1975, 1977, 1980, 1982, 1983
US Open Champion: 1982
US Masters Champion: 1977, 1981

SEVERIANO BALLESTEROS
Born 1957

British Open Champion: 1979, 1984
US Masters Champion: 1980, 1983

Severiano Ballesteros

S OF GOLF

Bobby Locke

BOBBY LOCKE
1918-1987

British Open Champion: 1949, 1950, 1952, 1957

PETER THOMSON
Born 1929

British Open Champion: 1954, 1955, 1956, 1958, 1965

Peter Thomson

ARNOLD PALMER
Born 1929

British Open Champion: 1961, 1962
US Open Champion: 1960
US Masters Champion: 1958, 1960, 1962, 1964

GARY PLAYER
Born 1935

British Open Champion: 1959, 1968, 1974
US Open Champion: 1965
US PGA Champion: 1962, 1972
US Masters Champion: 1961, 1974, 1978

Gary Player

Arnold Palmer

THE LADIES

The first really outstanding woman golfer in the world was Cecilia Leitch, who was born at Silloth, Cumberland, in 1891. Known by all as Cecil, she first came into prominence by reaching the semi-finals of the British Women's Championship in 1908 at the age of 17. In 1914 she won the title for the first time, and when the Championship was resumed a few years after World War I, she collected the title three more times – the last being in 1926.

Cecilia Leitch also won the French Ladies' Open five times between 1912 and 1924, the Canadian Ladies' Open in 1921 and was twice the English Women's champion, in 1914 and 1921 – an impressive array of victories.

ABOVE LEFT Glenna Collet, winner of six US Women's Amateur titles between 1922 and 1935.

ABOVE Kathy Whitworth – the first woman golfer to record career earnings of $1-million.

LEFT Cecil Leitch at the age of 19.

JOYCE WETHERED

Miss Leitch's greatest rival was Joyce Wethered (now Lady Heathcote Amory) who went on to become the greatest woman golfer of her time. As a 19-year-old unknown she caused a sensation by defeating Miss Leitch in the final of the English Women's Championship at Sheringham, Norfolk, in 1920. With that win under her belt, she remained unbeaten in the event for five successive years. Bobby Jones paid her the compliment of saying she was the finest golfer of either sex he had ever seen. Born in 1901 at Witley, Surrey, her greatest triumphs were in the British Women's Amateur Championship, which she won four times, in 1922, 1924, 1925 and 1929. She also won the French Ladies' Open in 1921. On her way to winning the British title in 1925 she prevailed over the United States champion, Glenna Collett, when they met in the third round. The next time she was to play Miss Collett was in the final at St Andrews in 1929 and again she emerged triumphant over the American, winning by 3 and 1 after being five holes down at one stage.

After this victory Miss Wethered went into semi-retirement, playing only in foursomes events. She won the Worplesdon Foursomes title eight times with seven different partners. In 1935 she was persuaded to turn professional and made a tour of America. There she played in exhibition matches with Bobby Jones, Gene Sarazen and Babe Zaharias. During her stay she played in 52 matches and earned many thousands of dollars.

THE ALL-ROUND BABE

Babe Zaharias ranks as the first of the great American women golfers. Born Mildred Didrikson at Port Arthur, Texas, in 1914, she became known as 'The Babe' after winning seven track and field events in the American Athletic Championships of 1931 when just a 17-year-old. A brilliant athlete, she won gold medals at the 1932 Olympics in the javelin and 80-metre hurdles before deciding to turn seriously to golf.

In 1954 Babe Zaharias surprised everyone by winning her third US Open title after having undergone major surgery for cancer the previous year. During her professional career Zaharias won 31 tournaments in all, seven of them after her operation. Having fought bravely against the disease she finally lost the struggle and died in 1956.

During the early 1930s there appeared on the scene an English girl named Pamela Barton who looked to be destined for a brilliant career in women's golf. She was only 17 when, in 1934, she won the French Ladies' Open. Two years later she caused a stir on both sides of the Atlantic by winning both the British and American Amateur titles within the space of a month. Typical of many of the young British women of that time, she volunteered to serve in the forces when Britain declared war on Germany, and left home to join the Women's Auxiliary Air Force. In the winter of 1943, aged only 26, she was tragically killed when the plane in which she was travelling crashed in Kent.

BABE ZAHARIAS

In 1946 Zaharias won the US Women's Amateur title and the following year the British Women's title. Having achieved this notable double she joined the professional ranks and found immediate success by winning the US Women's Open at Atlantic City in 1948 and again in 1950 at Rolling Hills.

LEFT Jo-Anne Carner, born in 1939, is still a force to be reckoned with on the US women's professional circuit.

LOUISE SUGGS

Upon turning professional Louise Suggs twice won the US Open, in 1949 and 1952, and won 50 tournaments in all, including the LPGA title in 1957.

ABOVE Catherine Lacoste, the French sensation.

ABOVE RIGHT Pam Barton looked destined for a brilliant career in golf, but was tragically killed in an air crash, in 1943, during war service with the RAF.

FAR RIGHT One of the United States' all-time golfing greats, Nancy Lopez.

Two Americans who did much for the professional circuit in the early days were Patty Berg and Louise Suggs. Before joining the professional ranks, where she won 41 tournaments, Patty Berg won the US Women's Amateur Championship in 1938. Helping to form the Ladies' Professional Golf Association with eleven others, she gained the distinction of becoming its first president.

Louise Suggs, the daughter of a golf professional, made her mark in amateur golf by winning both the British and US Amateur titles. In reward for her long list of achievements she was elected president of the LPGA in 1956-57.

WRIGHT AND WHITWORTH RECORDS

Mickey Wright turned professional in 1954 and made a remarkable success of playing golf for a living. Her record 82 tournament wins included four US Opens and four LPGA titles. When she was born in 1935 in San Diego, California, she was named Mary Kathryn, but her attorney father, expecting a boy, had already chosen Michael as the name, and it is by this name she has become known. In 1961 she created a tournament record by winning 10 events – four of them in a row, including the US Open. Not surprisingly, she was leading money-winner several times during the height of her career. Ranked as one of the greatest women golfers of all time, she is a member of the LPGA Hall of Fame.

If Mickey Wright was successful, Kathy Whitworth was even more so. She entered the professional ranks as Miss Wright was ceasing to compete on a full-time basis. In a lucrative period between 1963 and 1973, she had 70 tournament victories to her name, and in 1982 she recorded her 83rd victory to beat the record of Mickey Wright. The previous year she had set up an amazing record by becoming the first woman golfer to reach total career earnings of $1-million – quite a feat for someone who won no money at all in her first six months and only picked up a mere $30 when she first got among the prizewinners. In 1975 she joined Mickey Wright as a member of the LPGA Hall of Fame.

When Jo-Anne Carner finally decided to join the professional tournament scene in 1969, when she was 30, she left behind her an impressive amateur career which included five US

Women's Amateur Championships. Born Jo-Anne Gunderson in Massachusetts in 1939, she first came into prominence in 1956 when, still at high school, she won the US Junior Girls' title. Her physique, powerful hitting and extrovert personality have resulted in her being affectionately nicknamed 'Big Momma' by her professional colleagues. In 1981 she topped $1-million in career earnings and is now fast approaching an all-time record of $2-million. She is still participating on the US professional circuit and her many victories include two US Open Championships. In 1982 she was elected to the LPGA Hall of Fame, having the previous year become only the fifth woman golfer to receive the Bobby Jones Award for her outstanding contribution to the game. Had she remained an amateur there is little doubt that she would have exceeded the total of six US Women's Amateur titles that Glenna Collett (later Mrs Edwin Vare), achieved between 1922 and 1935.

THE PRECOCIOUS FRENCHWOMAN

One who preferred to remain an amateur was the French sensation Catherine Lacoste, the daughter of Wimbledon tennis champion, René Lacoste, and Simone de la Chaume, a British Women's Amateur Champion. Miss Lacoste, having won everything of note in France, decided it was time to take on the professionals at their own game and crossed the Atlantic to compete in the US Open. The year was 1967 and the field included the top American professionals of the day. Ignored by the media and competitors alike, she created the biggest sensation the world of women's golf had ever known by becoming the youngest player, the first foreigner and the first amateur to win the coveted title. Two years later she proved she was a really great player by winning both the British and American Amateur Championships. Also that year she won the French Open again and the Spanish Open, to record a remarkable Grand Slam. At the age of only 24 she retired from competitive golf to marry.

Had Miss Lacoste entered the professional ranks, who knows what fortune she would have amassed on the lucrative American tournament circuit? Nancy Lopez was only 20 when she turned professional in 1977 and ended the year as the top money winner with earnings of $189,813 – a record. This was even more than any man had achieved in his first year at that time, and playing in tournaments in Great Britain and Japan she did more to influence women's golf throughout the world than anyone before her. Still playing, she is one of the many women dollar millionaires playing golf in the United States. Women's professional golf in Europe is beginning to take off, and with the prize money now increasing to a worthwhile figure it is likely that great golfers will emerge to challenge the American supremacy. One such could be Laura Davies. This big-hitting English girl won the 1986 British Women's Open at Royal Birkdale, and the 1987 US Women's Open at Plainfield, New Jersey – the first ever British winner of the event.

These great golfers, with their different styles and personalities, all have one thing in common – none thought themselves greater than the game itself. This is why golf still remains the finest character-building sport in the world.

THE MAJOR CHAMPIONSHIPS

Greg Norman, 'The Awesome Aussie', holding the Open Championship trophy after his win at Turnberry in 1986.

RIGHT The 13th Earl of Eglington presented the Championship Belt for the first British Open, which was contested at Prestwick in 1860. The trophy was won by Willie Park of Musselburgh.

FAR RIGHT Young Tom Morris wearing the Championship Belt which he won outright, in 1870, after three Open Championship wins in a row.

The British Open, the United States Open, the US PGA and the US Masters are the four major championships that constitute the Grand Slam of golf. Only four golfers – Gene Sarazen, Ben Hogan, Jack Nicklaus and Gary Player – have won all four titles, but no one has ever won all four in the same year. The Australian, Greg Norman, led in all four going into the last round in 1986, but managed to win only one, the British Open at Turnberry.

Of these four championships the British Open is the oldest and is therefore generally regarded as the supreme championship. Played only on links (seaside) courses, which have the tightest fairways, the most punishing rough, the slickest greens and the strongest winds, the event is also regarded by the finest golfers in the world as the toughest of championships to win – the supreme test of their outstanding talents. Being the first in the field, the Open originally needed no prefix, and by custom even now when golfers refer to the Open they mean the British Open.

THE OPEN CHAMPIONSHIP

The Open first saw the light of day at the then small and peaceful fishing town of Prestwick on the west coast of Scotland in the 19th century. At the suggestion of Major J O Fairlie, the secretary of the Prestwick Golf Club, the event first took place on 17 October, 1860, and was contested by eight professionals. The first winner of the red leather Championship Belt was Willie Park of Musselburgh, with a total of 174 for the three rounds played over what was then a 12-hole course. This is now generally accepted as the first Open Championship, but, strictly speaking, this is not quite correct. The contest of 1860 was staged for professionals only and therefore not an open competition in the true sense. However, the following year it was decided to open the Championship to 'all the world', which has been the situation ever since.

LEFT Taiwan's Liang Huan Lu, 'Mr Lu' to the crowds and everyone's favourite during the 1971 Open at Royal Birkdale, Southport, Merseyside.

ABOVE The Frenchman Arnaud Massy was the first overseas player to win the Open with his victory at Hoylake, the home of the Royal Liverpool Golf Club, in 1907.

When the Championship Belt was presented by the Earl of Eglington, it was agreed that anyone who won the title three times in succession would be allowed to keep the belt as his own property. This rule was responsible for the first of three interruptions (the others caused by World Wars I and II) that the event has suffered in its history. Young Tom Morris won three in a row from 1868 to 1870, and with no trophy to play for, the Championship was held in abeyance in 1871. The event was restarted in 1872 when the Royal and Ancient Golf Club of St Andrews and the Honourable Company of Edinburgh Golfers (then at Musselburgh) agreed to join Prestwick in subscribing to the purchase of a new trophy in the shape of a silver claret jug – a permanent trophy which the champion would retain for one year.

Nowadays, the precious trophy remains safely locked away and it is but a replica which is handed to each new champion to retain for a year. He also gets a gold medal, which is a keepsake. It was also agreed that the Championship would be staged by the three clubs in rotation.

The first man to win the new trophy was Young Tom Morris, a victory which gave him four Championships in a row – a record still unequalled. The Open continued to be played at the three clubs until 1892, when the Honourable Company moved from Musselburgh to Muirfield, where the tournament was hosted that year. In 1894 it was decided to introduce other venues into the rota, and Royal St George's, Sandwich, gained the distinction of becoming the first non-Scottish club to stage the Open Championship. Hoylake, the home of the Royal Liverpool Golf Club, became the second English club to enter the Championship rota when invited to stage the event in 1897, and there was cause for a double celebration because Harold Hilton, a member of the host club, upstaged the professionals to win the coveted title for the second time, having previously won at Muirfield in 1892. Earlier, in 1890, John Ball, also from the Royal Liverpool Club, had become the first amateur and the first Englishman to win the Open when it first took place at Prestwick.

The American Bobby Jones still remains the only other amateur to win the title (in 1926, 1927 and 1930) since the two Englishmen's victories in the last century. But the first time the Championship was won by an overseas player was at Hoylake in 1907 when Arnaud Massy, a Frenchman, held on to beat J H Taylor by two strokes. The title went across the Atlantic for the first time in 1921 when Jock Hutchison, a Scotsman who had emigrated to the United States when a youngster, won after a play-off with the amateur, Roger Wethered, the brother of the great woman golfer, Joyce Wethered.

Before that, in 1919, at the suggestion of Mr Robert Maxwell of the Honourable Company, the Royal and Ancient Club took over the complete running of the Open, a task performed by their Championship Committee ever since. With Prestwick no longer considered a suitable venue because of its lack of length and limited space to accommodate the increasing volume of traffic, the centenary Open in 1960 was held, appropriately, at St Andrews, and was won by the Australian, Kel Nagle, who beat Arnold Palmer

TOP LEFT A classic 1920s photograph of Ted Ray, who won the US Open at Inverness, Ohio, in 1920.

ABOVE LEFT Ralph Guldahl, the first man to score four sub-par rounds in the US Open, in 1937, playing a perfect sand shot.

ABOVE The famous duel between Tom Watson and Jack Nicklaus during the 1977 Open at Turnberry, Strathclyde.

TOP Willie Anderson (bow tie), four times winner of the US Open, with Alex Smith (polo neck), who won the event twice. Sitting at their feet is Horace Rawlins, the first US Open champion with his victory at Newport, Rhode Island, in 1895.

ABOVE The immortal Bobby Jones (left) with the British and United States Open and Amateur trophies, which he won in the space of one year in 1930.

by one stroke. The actual 100th Open Championship took place at Royal Birkdale, Southport, in 1971 and was won by Lee Trevino after an epic struggle with the unknown Liang Huan Lu from Taiwan – dubbed Mr Lu by the appreciative crowds who warmed to his charming smile and politeness.

The Open, with its massive tented village accommodating hundreds of exhibition stands appertaining to golf, its huge media coverage and the entry of talented international golfers, competing in famous historic arenas for the ultimate prize of instant worldwide fame and fortune, is the greatest golf show on Earth. No other Championship attracts so many visitors from overseas, all wanting to soak in the atmosphere of the ancient game.

THE US OPEN CHAMPIONSHIP

Unlike the British Open, which has been played on only 14 links courses in its entire history, the United States Open Championship has been staged on both inland and coastal venues and the number of courses used will shortly pass the 50 mark. With a far greater land mass than Great Britain to cover in order to spread the Championship to all parts of the United States, the use of more courses is, of course, an undeistandable policy. The inaugural Championship took place at Newport, Rhode Island, in 1895, a day after the first United States Amateur Championship was played on the same course, and was won by a young Englishman named Horace Rawlins, an assistant professional at the host club, who scored 45, 46, 41, 41 in his four rounds on the nine-hole course.

British players who had emigrated to the United States dominated the event for a further

15 years, and during that time Harry Vardon added to the misery of the Americans by picking up the title during a promotional tour of the United States. The first American-born player to win the US Open was John J McDermott at Chicago, Illinois, in 1911 after a play-off with Mike Brady and George Simpson. The previous year McDermott, in the last year of his teens, had tied with the Smith brothers, Alex and Macdonald, only to lose to Alex in the play-off by six strokes while finishing ahead of Macdonald by two.

In 1912 McDermott successfully defended his title with an outright win after holding off a strong challenge from another American-born player, Thomas McNamara, who scored a 69 in the last round, having previously recorded the same score in the 1909 Open to become the first man to score below 70 in the Championship. Altogether McNamara finished three times in the runner-up position (1909, 1912 and 1915), but never once was he to win the great event. As for McDermott, he was forced to give up the game in 1915 because of a mental illness, thought by many at the time to have been sparked off by his obsessive determination to personally end the domination of the English and Scottish professionals who had emigrated to his country.

The last Briton to win the US Open was Tony Jacklin at the Hazeltine National, Chaska, Minnesota in 1970, when he led from start to finish and became only the second man to score four sub-par rounds in the event – Ralph Guldahl, an American from Dallas, Texas, being the first at Oakland Hills, Michigan, in 1937. Jacklin's winning margin of seven strokes was the widest since Jim Barnes won with 11 strokes to spare in 1921. The previous British winner before Jacklin's brilliant victory was Ted Ray in 1920 – a span of exactly 50 years. How different from the early days of the US Open!

Only four men – Willie Anderson, Bobby Jones, Ben Hogan and Jack Nicklaus – have managed to win the US Open four times, and Anderson's record of three wins in a row, beginning in 1903, has never been matched. The only amateur among these four is Bobby Jones, and he belongs to a select band of only five amateurs who have won the Championship; the others being Francis Ouimet in 1913, Jerome D Travers in 1915, Charles Evans in 1916 and Johnny Goodman in 1933. Ouimet's victory in 1913 caused the biggest sensation by virtue of his play-off defeat of two-thirds of the Great Triumvirate, Harry Vardon and J H Taylor. Bobby Jones' fourth victory in the event in 1930 was also sensational, as it helped him achieve the then Grand Slam of the Open and Amateur titles of both the United States and Great Britain in the same year.

Another milestone in the tournament came at Bellerive, Mississippi, in 1965, when for the first time ever there was a play-off between two players who were born in neither Great Britain nor The United States. Gary Player of South Africa beat the Australian, Kel Nagle, and in doing so became the first overseas player outside Britain to win the US Open. The only overseas golfer, other than Jacklin, to take the trophy out of the United States since Player's historic victory is David Graham of Australia at Merion, Pennsylvania, in 1981, although Greg Norman, another Australian, came close at Winged Foot, New York, in 1984, losing only after a play-off with Fuzzy Zoeller.

Nowadays, unless one is an exempt player, attempting to qualify for one of the limited non-exempt places in the final field of 150 in the US Open is a costly and time-consuming exercise. Over 5,000 entries are now received by the USGA, and there is a long process of pre-qualifying and qualifying rounds at various venues to determine which handful of players gets into the main event. It is therefore not surprising that the US Open is now predominantly an all-American event. With only a remote chance of getting through, overseas players are not prepared to spend the time nor the money in trying.

Nevertheless, for those who make the grade, the prize money is surging toward the $1-million mark, and the winner is guaranteed much more than that from the fringe benefits which follow such a victory. The United States Open Championship has certainly come a long way since it was formed more or less as an afterthought by the United States Golf Association as an appendage to the National Amateur Championship in 1895. Although the tournament celebrates its Centenary in 1995, the two interruptions (1917-18 and 1942-45) because of the World Wars have unwittingly determined that the 100th US Open will be played in the year 2,000. To somebody will fall the historic distinction of becoming the 100th winner and the first of the 21st century.

ABOVE The 6th hole at the PGA National, Palm Beach, Florida. The home of the US PGA hosted the 1971 Championship which was won by Jack Nicklaus. This win gave Nicklaus the second of his PGA titles and made him the first man to win all four major championship titles twice.

THE PROFESSIONAL GOLFERS CHAMPIONSHIP

The Professional Golfers Championship of America, widely known as the US PGA, is the third in seniority among the four major championships. It was first held in 1916 at Siwanoy Country Club, New York, the same year that the Professional Golfers Association of America was formed. For the professional it is a most important event to win because each winner receives exemption for life from pre-qualifying for any of the PGA tournaments. This in itself is a great incentive for the players, who are naturally anxious to avoid strain and anguish of the strenuous pre-qualifying tournaments.

Jim Barnes was the first winner of the event, and because of World War I he had to wait three years before successfully defending his title. The following year (1920), Jock Hutchison, British-born like Barnes, emerged the victor. The first American-born player to record a victory in the event was Walter Hagen in 1921, a win which heralded a glorious chapter of PGA triumphs for the flamboyant American. In seven years he won the Championship five times – four of them in a row from 1924. Typical of Hagen, when his impressive run came to an end in 1928 he said he had not seen the trophy since 1925, but vaguely remembered leaving it in a taxi! However, when the time came to hand over the trophy to the new champion, Leo Diegel, it was in its proper place on the presentation stand. In those days the PGA was a matchplay event, and the cut and thrust of the knockout matches was ideally suited to Hagen's swashbuckling style of recovery play, which intimidated his opponents.

All the great players who were around when the Championship was matchplay won the event at least twice. Gene Sarazen and Sam Snead each won it three times, Byron Nelson and Ben Hogan twice. The only great name missing is that of Bobby Jones who, being an amateur, was barred from the tournament. However, with six former champions being beaten in the first two rounds of the 1953 PGA at Birmingham, Michigan, the writing was on the wall for the Championship in its matchplay format. Television viewing was on the increase and demanded from golf the need not only for the game to be still in progress at peak viewing times, but also that the stars would be in action. Matchplay golf could not guarantee this, and in 1958 the tournament finally became strokeplay, decided over 72 holes.

Since changing to strokeplay the PGA title has eluded two great golfers, Arnold Palmer and Tom Watson. Palmer came close to winning on three occasions, only to finish the runner-up each time. The 1964 Championship at Columbus, Ohio, was particularly frustrating for him. Becoming the first player ever to score below 70 in all four rounds, he still finished in a tie for second place with Jack Nicklaus. Bobby Nichols, with a brilliant opening round of 64, won by three strokes and a record total of 271.

Gary Player, from South Africa, won at Aronimink, Pennsylvania, in 1962 to become the first overseas-based member of the Association to hold the title, which he regained at Oakland Hills, Michigan, in 1972. When the Championship was held for the first time at the PGA headquarters at Palm Beach, Florida, in 1971, it was rather fitting that Jack Nicklaus, the greatest golfer of all time, should win the second of his five PGA titles, thus becoming the first man to have won all four majors twice. An even more historic moment for Nicklaus came at Canterbury, Ohio, in 1973, when his third PGA victory saw him pass Bobby Jones' tally of 13 major titles, and at Oak Hills, New York, in 1980 he equalled Walter Hagen's outstanding record of five PGA titles.

The only Australian to have held the title is David Graham, who won at Oakland Hills in 1979 after a play-off with Ben Crenshaw. Graham's fellow countryman, the luckless Greg Norman, almost emulated him at Inverness, Ohio, in 1986, only to see the title escape from his grasp at the very last moment when Bob Tway holed out from a sand trap at the finishing hole. An equally memorable occasion was Lee Trevino's win in the battle of the 'Golden Oldies' at Shoal Greek, Alabama, in 1984, when he scored below 70 in every round. Gary Player incredibly tied for second place with the help of a 63 which equalled the lowest-ever round in the Championship set by Bruce Crampton in 1975. Trevino was then a 44-year-old and Player 49!

TOP The magnificent Masters trophy.

ABOVE Roberto de Vicenzo, the popular Argentinian golfer, lost the 1968 Masters title to Bob Goalby due to a scorecard error.

RIGHT At last a major title. Ben Crenshaw (right) proudly receives the traditional Masters green jacket from Seve Ballesteros after winning the 1984 Masters.

THE MASTERS

The last, but certainly not least, of the four major championships is the United States Masters tournament. It is unique for a major in that it is always staged at the same venue, the Augusta National Club, Georgia. Other differences include the field being limited to about 75 competitors – half the size of that in the other majors – and the organizing committee reserving the right to invite whom they think fit, although most invitations are now guided by rules of qualification. Past champions have their own private locker room which no one else is allowed to enter unless invited, and each year before the tournament a past champions' dinner takes place, hosted by the reigning champion. Tradition also has it that the tournament winner becomes an honorary member of the Augusta National Club, and a ceremony is held whereby he receives the club's special green blazer into which he is helped by the immediate past champion. Amazingly, no matter the size of the new champion, the jacket is always the perfect fit. No advertising is allowed on the course and the programme is a single sheet of paper with just enough space for a map of the course, the starting times and a plea to the spectators not to applaud bad shots. Until 1987 it has been the policy not to announce the size of the prize money.

Bobby Jones founded the Masters in 1934 after having been responsible for creating the great golf course along with the golf architect, Alister Mackenzie, who had earlier designed Cypress Point, California. Previously the site had been owned by a Belgian, Baron Berckmans, and was called Fruitlands. Fittingly, Jones became the club president of Augusta National in perpetuity, and it was he who insisted on the highest standards for the tournament. When he died in 1971, Clifford Roberts, the club chairman, took over the running of the Masters, and he continued along the same traditional path as Jones. His successor, Bill Lane, who sadly died within two years of taking office, and the present incumbent, Hord Hardin, have been equally successful in maintaining the high standards set by Bobby Jones. Thankfully, the temptation to turn the Masters into a sponsors' money-making circus has been resisted and the tournament still retains its old-fashioned charm and sobriety.

Although Jones had retired from competitive golf four years prior to the staging of the first

RIGHT Jack Nicklaus being helped into his green jacket by Bernhard Langer after winning the Masters title for a record sixth time in 1986.

FAR RIGHT Germany's Bernhard Langer swinging his way to victory in the 1985 Masters at Augusta.

Masters tournament in 1934, he agreed to take part to help draw the crowds. Inviting many of the fine golfers he had competed against in the past, Jones managed to finish tied in 13th place; and the honour of winning the first Masters went to Horton Smith, with a four-round total of 284. The following year the tournament was firmly put on the golfing map after making front-page news in the national press. Gene Sarazen was the man responsible for this when he sensationally holed his four-wood second shot at the par five 15th for an unbelievable albatross (three below par) during the final round, which enabled him to tie with the leader in the clubhouse, Craig Wood.

The following day Sarazen won the 36-hole play-off, and the Masters has not looked back since. Incidentally, Wood had also been the runner-up in the inaugural Masters, but he finally won the tournament in 1941.

Byron Nelson, who had won the title in 1937, was again the champion in 1942 – this year the tournament was suspended for the duration of World War II. Jimmy Demaret's victory in 1950 gave him the distinction of becoming the first man to win the Masters three times, and four years later Sam Snead equalled the record. Although a sprinkling of amateurs is invited to play each year, no amateur has yet managed to gain immortal fame by winning the coveted title; but Frank Stranahan in 1947, Ken Venturi in 1956 and Charlie Coe in 1961 all finished in second place. The Big Three – Arnold Palmer, Jack Nicklaus and Gary Player – dominated the event for nine years from 1958. During this period Palmer won four times, Nicklaus three times and Player once. Player's triumph in 1961 saw him become the first non-American to hold the title. However, the famous trio did not feature in the winners' list again until 1972, when Palmer's record of four victories was equalled by Nicklaus. Player won again in 1974 and 1978.

Without a doubt, the saddest year in the history of the Masters was 1968. Millions of televison viewers witnessed the joy on the face of Roberto de Vicenzo, the popular Argentinian player, as he walked off the final green having forced a play-off with Bob Goalby. Vicenzo's joy, however, was short-lived when it was discovered that in his excitement he had failed to notice a four marked on his card for the 17th hole where, in fact, he had scored three. Having signed the scorecard as correct, the four had to stand under the rules. Therefore, Goalby was declared the winner and the luckless Vicenzo the runner-up. In the true spirit of the game Vicenzo graciously accepted the decision as correct and did his best to console his partner, Tommy Aaron, who had inadvertently marked the incorrect score on the Argentinian's card. For his sportsmanship Vicenzo was awarded the Bobby Jones Award in 1970.

Such are the pressures of this great tournament, that no man had ever won the Masters at his first attempt until the fun-loving, easy-going Fuzzy Zoeller won after a play-off with Tom Watson and Ed Sneed in 1979. In 1980 Severiano Ballesteros, fresh from his British Open victory in 1979, became the youngest man to win the title at the age of 23 – beating Nicklaus' record, achieved in 1963, by a couple of months. Ballesteros won again in 1983, but the title went the following year to the American most people wanted to see win – Ben Crenshaw. A great lover of the history and traditions of the game, and a keen collector of golfing relics, the likeable Texan's burning desire to win a major title looked doomed to failure after many near misses. Crenshaw had been runner-up three times in the Masters, twice in the British Open, once in the PGA and had tied for third place in the US Open. At last, with the crowd willing him home, his putter worked like a magic wand in the final round and he won with two strokes to spare over Tom Watson. A memorable moment for the proud young man known by all as Gentle Ben.

Bernhard Langer's win in 1985 made him the first German to win any major golf championship. The son of a Bavarian bricklayer, Langer has had a great influence on golf in Germany, and golf courses are springing up in all parts of West Germany as more and more people take up the sport.

In the Masters of 1986 Jack Nicklaus proved that age is no barrier to winning tournaments, providing one has the talent and stamina. At the age of 46 he won the masters for a record sixth time, notching his 18th major championship win in all. It is little wonder that Bobby Jones once remarked of Nicklaus: 'He plays a game with which I am not familiar'.

Greg Norman, the highly talented Australian, has good cause to remember that particular tournament, for had he not sent his approach shot to the final hole into the crowd, it might have been his triumph. Again, in 1987, Norman stood on the threshold of a Masters victory only to have it snatched from his grasp. Involved in a three-man sudden-death play-off with Ballesteros and Larry Mize, which had seen the Spaniard eliminated at the first extra hole, Norman looked home and dry at the very next hole. Mize, however, chipped in for an unlikely birdie three and the Awesome Aussie was deprived of yet another major title.

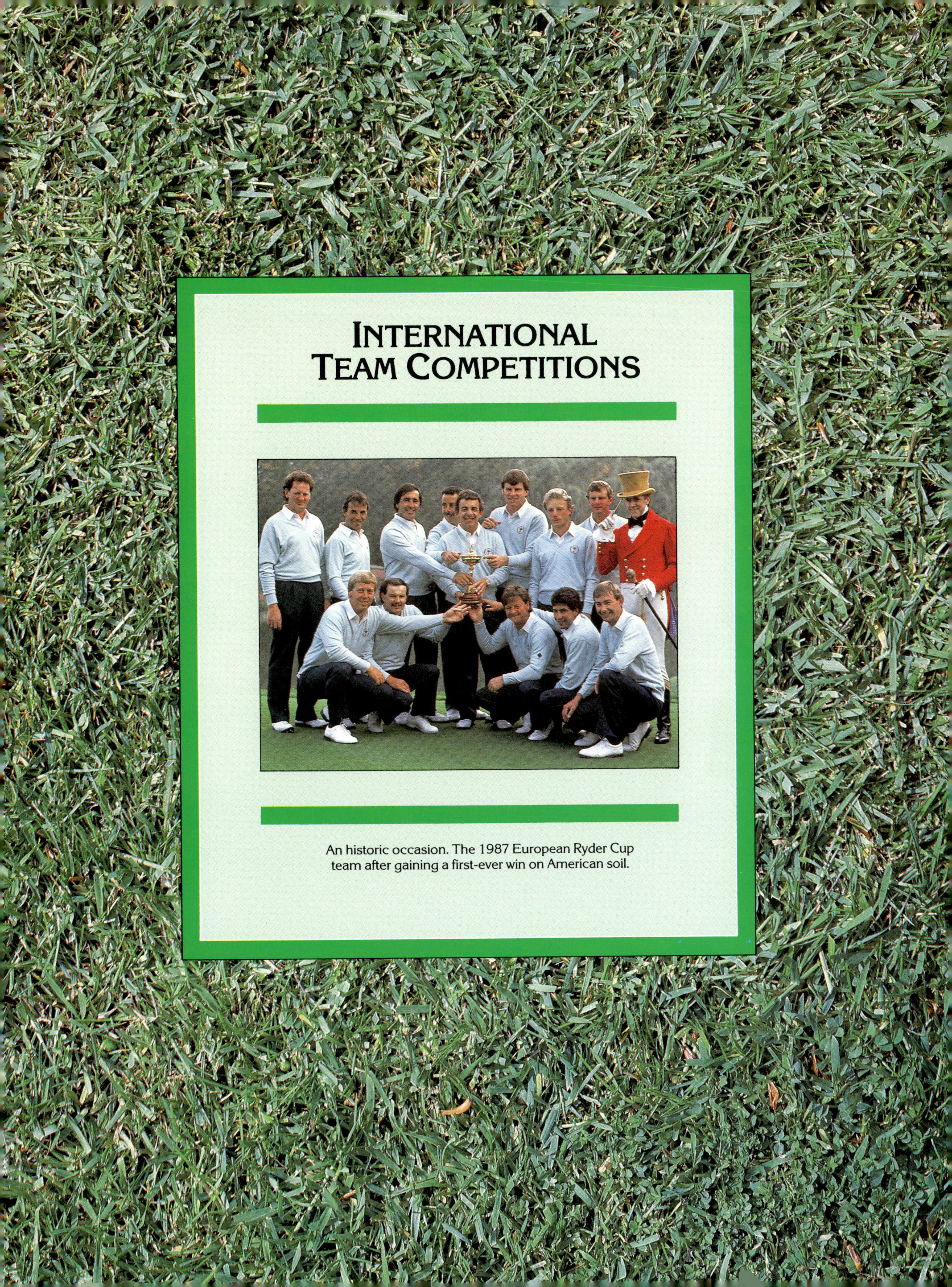

International Team Competitions

An historic occasion. The 1987 European Ryder Cup team after gaining a first-ever win on American soil.

Had not an unofficial match between members of the United States and the British Professional Golfers Associations taken place at Wentworth, Surrey, in 1926, there might never have been a Ryder Cup. The fact that the British team won so convincingly by 13½ points to 1½ made little impact on the British public, and only a handful of people thought it worthwhile to go along to watch. People in the Britain of 1926 had more important issues to occupy their minds than a mere game of golf, for this was the year of the National Strike – and life was at a standstill. But among the small crowd who witnessed the staggering victory by the British team was one Samuel Ryder, a wealthy Englishman who had made his fortune selling inexpensive packets of seeds. The match left a lasting impression on him, so much so that the following year he donated a magnificent trophy made of solid gold to be contested for biennially by the two great golfing nations.

THE RYDER CUP

Played alternately in Great Britain and the United States, the first Ryder Cup match took place at Worcester, Massachusetts, in June 1927. The Americans gained ample revenge for their unofficial defeat of 1926 by thrashing the British team 9½ points to 2½. Honours remained even after the first four encounters – each side winning the trophy when playing on home soil. The pattern, however, changed dramatically as the years went by. From the time the British team scraped to a narrow victory by 6½ points to 5½ when Syd Easterbrook sunk his vital putt at Southport and Ainsdale, Lancashire, in 1933 to defeat Densmore Shute in the last game, the Americans remained undefeated until 1957. Then a rare British victory proved but a minor setback in the American domination of the series. In 1961, at Royal Lytham and St Annes, Lancashire, an attempt was made to make the series more interesting by changing the format with matches being reduced from 36 holes to

FAR LEFT Harry Vardon, J H Taylor, Sandy Herd and James Braid flank Samuel Ryder (centre), the wealthy Englishman who donated the wonderful solid-gold trophy (below far left) in 1927.

LEFT Massed crowds surround the first hole for the 1985 Ryder Cup at the Belfry, England.

RIGHT 1987 Open Champion Nick Faldo in Ryder Cup action at Muirfield Village, Ohio.

PAGE 84 (see over) The triumphant 1987 US Walker Cup team at Sunningdale, England. The United States have been victorious in all but two of their encounters with Britain and Ireland since the inauguration of the Walker Cup in 1922.

PAGE 85 (see over) The Walker Cup trophy.

18. This only resulted in more matches, and more points at stake, and thus emphasized the superiority of the Americans, who went on to win by 14½ to 9½.

The encounter at Atlanta, Georgia, in 1963 saw a further change made in the format. Four-ball matches and an extra day were introduced for the first time, but this merely meant the British suffering humiliation on a much wider scale – crushed by 23 points to 9. Nevertheless, America's stranglehold on the series was forced to relax slightly when, at Royal Birkdale, in 1969, a British team, no doubt inspired by Tony Jacklin's Open Championship triumph earlier that year, forced a most memorable draw. With the teams level and Jacklin in the very last match needing to hole his two-foot putt on the 18th green to prevent the United States team winning yet again, Jack Nicklaus, with a heart-warming show of sportsmanship, conceded the putt by picking up Jacklin's ball, and the match was tied 16–16. This was the first drawn match in the history of the Ryder Cup and each country held the trophy for 12 months. Unknown to anyone at that time, a solely British team was never again to get nearer to beating the powerful Americans.

Defeat followed defeat, which led to a decision being made in 1979 whereby the team to

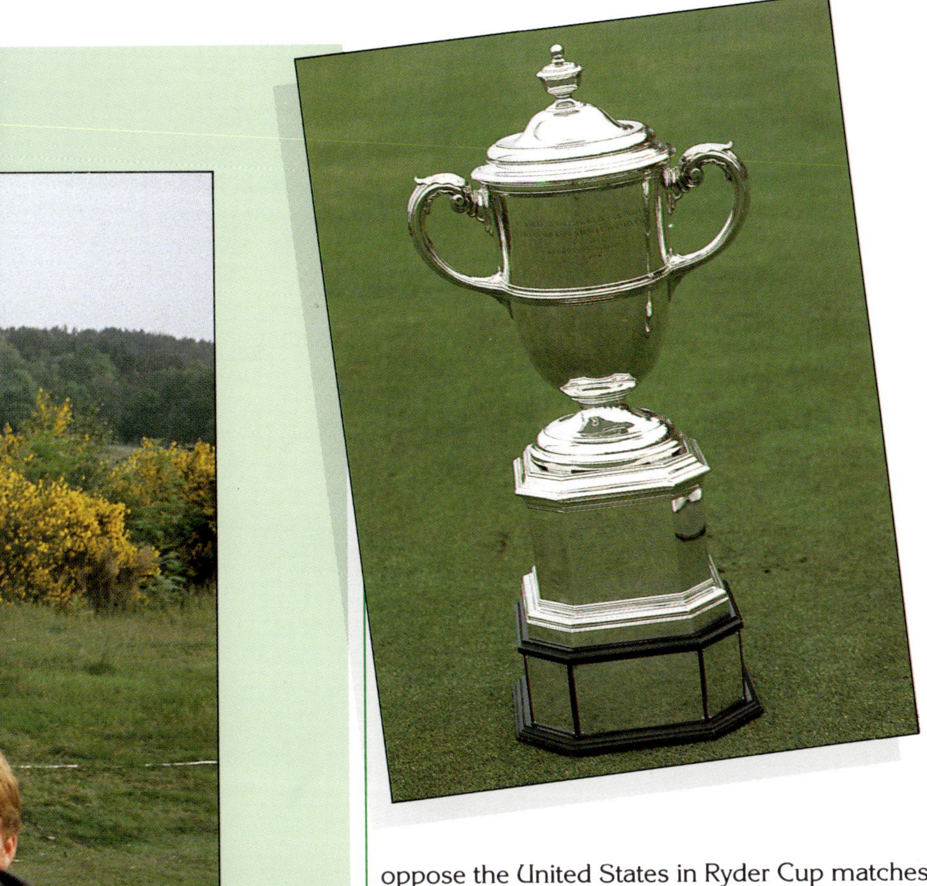

oppose the United States in Ryder Cup matches from that date should represent the European PGA circuit. This meant that other European professionals could now play alongside the British in the team. Gradually, very gradually, this brought about an improvement in stemming the United States victory march. In 1983, under the brilliant non-playing captaincy of Britain's Tony Jacklin, the European side came within a whisker of inflicting a first-ever home defeat on the Americans – losing by a mere point, 14½–13½, at the PGA National course in Florida. Not surprisingly, Jacklin was again in charge of the Great Britain and Europe side when the teams next met at The Belfry, the headquarters of the European PGA, in September 1985.

The atmosphere was electric on the final day as the European team, which included the Open champion, Sandy Lyle, the Masters champion, Bernhard Langer, and Severiano Ballesteros, the world's number one golfer at that time, ended the American domination by 16½ points to 11½ – the first American defeat for 28 years. In 1987, the European team, again captained by Tony Jacklin, retained the title with a 15–13 victory, and added a new chapter to the history of the Ryder Cup with a first-ever win on US soil.

THE WALKER CUP

Like the Ryder Cup, the Walker Cup series began as a result of an unofficial match played between teams of American and British golfers. Unlike the Ryder Cup, however, the Walker Cup is for competition between teams of amateurs. The unofficial match took place on the day before the British Amateur Championship at Royal Liverpool, Hoylake, in 1921. Earlier that same year the United States Golf Association had sent invitations to all golfing nations to send teams to compete for the Walker Cup, donated by George Herbert Walker, the president of the USGA. For various reasons they all declined the invitation, but following the 1921 match the Royal and Ancient Club sent a British team to America in 1922 to play the United States for the trophy at the National Links, Long Island, the home club of George H Walker. The Americans won that match and the next two at St Andrews and Garden City, New York, in 1923 and 1924 respectively. Since then the match has been biennial with the United States dominating the series.

Of all the notable amateurs who have played in the Walker Cup, Bobby Jones had a particularly fine record. In his four appearances between 1924 and 1930, he was unbeatable in his singles matches, winning them all by wide margins, and in the foursomes he lost only once.

Leonard Crawley, one of the great characters of British golf, literally made his mark on the Walker Cup at the Country Club, Brookline, Massachusetts, in 1932 when his approach shot to the 18th green overshot and struck the famous trophy, which was out on display awaiting the presentation ceremony, a fierce metal-denting blow.

An even more remarkable incident happened in the inaugural meeting on Long Island. The British team of eight players was not covered by reserves, and when Robert Harris, the captain, withdrew because of illness before the match, his place as captain and player was taken by Bernard Darwin, the doyen of golf writers, who was covering the match for *The Times* newspaper. Although losing in the foursomes when playing with Cyril Tolley, Darwin, an English international golfer of note, played a captain's part in the singles by beating the American captain, William Fownes.

RIGHT Belle Robertson, at 50 the oldest-ever Curtis Cup participant when selected for the 1986 British team.

FAR RIGHT The Curtis Cup and the victorious 1976 US team, captained by Barbara McIntire.

Despite the fact that the United States won 27 of the first 30 matches played, the appeal of the Walker Cup has never waned, and golfers of both countries regard being selected as the highest honour of their career. Both British victories, in 1938 and 1971, took place at St Andrews, but they would dearly like the next one to be on American soil. The nearest they have come to achieving this was in Baltimore, Maryland, in 1965 when, having led 10–4 with eight games left to play, Clive Clark was left with the daunting task of sinking his 35-foot putt on the 18th green to halve his match and save his country from yet another defeat. Clark's attempt was successful and Britain managed to escape with a 12–12 draw.

THE CURTIS CUP

Unofficial international matches between the women golfers of the United States and Great Britain were played long before their male counterparts took up the idea. Indeed, the women's matches go back as far as 1905, when an American team challenged the British to a match on the eve of the British Women's Amateur Championship at Cromer, Norfolk. Included in the American team were the sisters Margaret and Harriot Curtis, who were both destined to win the US Women's Amateur Championship twice. A number of these unofficial matches took place in later years, and the match at Sunningdale in 1930 created a great deal of interest on both sides of the Atlantic. This prompted the sisters to present a trophy for a regular biennial contest between the US and British women's teams – and thus was born the Curtis Cup.

The first match took place at Wentworth, Surrey, in 1932 and, like the Ryder Cup and the Walker Cup, the series has been dominated by the United States. With victory going to the Americans by 5½ matches to 3½ in the inaugural match, Britain had to wait until 1952 to record their first win, at Muirfield, Scotland, although they had forced a draw at Gleneagles, Scotland, in 1936. Four years later, at Prince's, Kent, they won again, and in the very next encounter they all but brought off a sensational result on American soil at Brae Burn, Massachusetts, where they tied 4½–4½. The British, however, lost the next home match in 1960 at Lindrick, Yorkshire, by 6½ points to 2½, and the Americans continued on their victory trail for the next 24 years.

The 1984 match at Muirfield gave an indication of better things to come for the British who, fighting hard for every point, lost only by 9½–8½. And so it proved at Prairie Dunes, Kansas, in 1986 when the British team, against all odds, made golfing history by becoming the first team ever, male or female, to bring about the downfall of an American team on American soil. With three of their 1984 team lost to the professional ranks, the British selectors made a bold gamble in bringing back Belle Robertson who, aged 50, became the oldest ever to take an active part in the Curtis Cup. Jill Thornhill, 44, retained her place and three young players, Patricia (Trish) Johnson, Karen Davies and Lilian Behan, were making their debut. As far as the pundits were concerned this was a team of no-hopers, but they reckoned without Diane Bailey, the determined non-playing captain whom the selectors had kept faith with after the near miss of 1984. She was in charge of a team which contained a blend of youth and experience and knew exactly the mix needed to produce a successful recipe. At the end of two unbelievable days the British achieved an astonishing result – winning by 13 points to 5.

MAJOR CHAMPIONSHIP AND INTERNATIONAL TEAM COMPETITION RESULTS

BRITISH OPEN

UNITED STATES OPEN

UNITED STATES MASTERS

UNITED STATES PROFESSIONAL GOLFERS ASSOCIATION

RYDER CUP

WALKER CUP

CURTIS CUP

BRITISH OPEN

YEAR	WINNER	VENUE	SCORE
1860	W. Park	Prestwick	174
1861	T. Morris Sen.	Prestwick	163
1862	T. Morris Sen.	Prestwick	163
1863	W. Park	Prestwick	168
1864	T. Morris Sen.	Prestwick	167
1865	A. Strath	Prestwick	162
1866	W. Park	Prestwick	169
1867	T. Morris Sen.	Prestwick	170
1868	T. Morris Jr.	Prestwick	157
1869	T. Morris Jr.	Prestwick	154
1870	T. Morris Jr.	Prestwick	149
1871	No Championship		
1872	T. Morris Jr.	Prestwick	166
1873	T. Kidd	St. Andrews	179
1874	M. Park	Musselburgh	159
1875	W. Park	Prestwick	166
1876	B. Martin	St. Andrews	176
1877	J. Anderson	Musselburgh	160
1878	J. Anderson	Prestwick	157
1879	J. Anderson	St. Andrews	169
1880	B. Ferguson	Musselburgh	162
1881	B. Ferguson	Prestwick	170
1882	B. Ferguson	St. Andrews	171
1883	W. Fernie	Musselburgh	159
1884	J. Simpson	Prestwick	160
1885	B. Martin	St. Andrews	171
1886	D. Brown	Musselburgh	157
1887	W. Park Jr.	Prestwick	161
1888	J. Burns	St. Andrews	171
1889	W. Park Jr.	Musselburgh	155
1890	J. Ball (Am)	Prestwick	164
1891	H. Kirkaldy	St. Andrews	166
1892	H. Hilton (Am)	Muirfield	305
1893	W. Auchterlonie	Prestwick	322
1894	J. H. Taylor	Sandwich	326
1895	J. H. Taylor	St. Andrews	322
1896	H. Vardon	Muirfield	316
1897	H. Hilton (Am)	Hoylake	314
1898	H. Vardon	Prestwick	307
1899	H. Vardon	Sandwich	310
1900	J. H. Taylor	St. Andrews	309
1901	J. Braid	Muirfield	318
1902	A. Herd	Hoylake	307
1903	H. Vardon	Prestwick	300
1904	J. White	Sandwich	296
1905	J. Braid	St. Andrews	318
1906	J. Braid	Muirfield	300
1907	A. Massy	Hoylake	312
1908	J. Braid	Prestwick	291
1909	J. H. Taylor	Deal	295
1910	J. Braid	St. Andrews	299
1911	H. Vardon	Sandwich	303
1912	E. Ray	Muirfield	295
1913	J. H. Taylor	Hoylake	304
1914	H. Vardon	Prestwick	306
1915–1919	No Championship		
1920	G. Duncan	Deal	303
1921	J. Hutchison	St. Andrews	296
1922	W. Hagen	Sandwich	300
1923	A. G. Havers	Troon	295
1924	W. Hagen	Hoylake	301
1925	J. Barnes	Prestwick	300
1926	R. Jones (Am)	Lytham	291
1927	R. Jones (Am)	St. Andrews	285
1928	W. Hagen	Sandwich	292
1929	W. Hagen	Muirfield	292
1930	R. Jones (Am)	Hoylake	291
1931	T. Armour	Carnoustie	296
1932	G. Sarazen	Prince's	283
1933	D. Shute	St. Andrews	292
1934	T. H. Cotton	Sandwich	283
1935	A. Perry	Muirfield	283
1936	A. H. Padgham	Hoylake	287
1937	T. H. Cotton	Carnoustie	290
1938	R. Whitecombe	Sandwich	295
1939	R. Burton	St. Andrews	290
1940–1945	No Championship		
1946	S. Snead	St. Andrews	290
1947	F. Daly	Hoylake	293
1948	T. H. Cotton	Muirfield	284
1949	A. D. Locke	Sandwich	283
1950	A. D. Locke	Troon	279
1951	M. Faulkner	Ry. Portrush	285
1952	A. D. Locke	Ry. Lytham	287
1953	B. Hogan	Carnoustie	282
1954	P. Thomson	Ry. Birkdale	283
1955	P. Thomson	St. Andrews	281
1956	P. Thomson	Hoylake	286
1957	A. D. Locke	St. Andrews	279
1958	P. Thomson	Hoylake	278
1959	G. Player	Muirfield	284
1960	K. Nagle	St. Andrews	278
1961	A. Palmer	Ry. Birkdale	284
1962	A. Palmer	Troon	276
1963	R. J. Charles	Ry. Lytham	277
1964	A. Lema	St. Andrews	279
1965	P. Thomson	Ry. Birkdale	285
1966	J. Nicklaus	Muirfield	282
1967	R. de Vicenzo	Hoylake	278
1968	G. Player	Carnoustie	289
1969	A. Jacklin	Ry. Lytham	280
1970	J. Nicklaus	St. Andews	283
1971	L. Trevino	Ry. Birkdale	278
1972	L. Trevino	Muirfield	278
1973	T. Weiskopf	Troon	276
1974	G. Player	Ry. Lytham	282
1975	T. Watson	Carnoustie	279
1976	J. Miller	Ry. Birkdale	279
1977	T. Watson	Turnberry	268
1978	J. Nicklaus	St. Andrews	281
1979	S. Ballesteros	Ry. Lytham	283
1980	T. Watson	Muirfield	271
1981	W. Rogers	Ry. St. George's	276
1982	T. Watson	Ry. Troon	271
1983	T. Watson	Ry. Birkdale	275
1984	S. Ballesteros	St. Andrews	276
1985	S. Lyle	Ry. St. George's	282
1986	G. Norman	Turnberry	280
1987	N. Faldo	Muirfield	279

U.S. MASTERS TOURNAMENT

ALWAYS PLAYED AT AUGUSTA NATIONAL

YEAR	WINNER	SCORE
1934	Horton Smith	284
1935	Gene Sarazen	282
1936	Horton Smith	285
1937	Byron Nelson	283
1938	Henry Picard	285
1939	Ralph Guldahl	279
1940	Jim Demaret	280
1941	Craig Wood	280
1942	Byron Nelson	280
1943–1945	No Tournament	
1946	Herman Keiser	282
1947	Jim Demaret	281
1948	Cld. Harmon	279
1949	Sam Snead	282
1950	Jim Demaret	283
1951	Ben Hogan	280
1952	San Snead	286
1953	Ben Hogan	274
1954	San Snead	289
1955	Cary Middlecoff	279
1956	Jack Burke Jr.	289
1957	Doug Ford	282
1958	Arnold Palmer	284
1959	Art Wall Jr.	284
1960	Arnold Palmer	282
1961	Gary Player	280
1962	Arnold Palmer	280
1963	Jack Nicklaus	286
1964	Arnold Palmer	276
1965	Jack Nicklaus	271
1966	Jack Nicklaus	288
1967	Gary Brewer Jr.	280
1968	Bob Goalby	277
1969	George Archer	281
1970	Billy Casper	279
1971	Chas Coody	279
1972	Jack Nicklaus	286
1973	Tommy Aaron	283
1974	Gary Player	278
1975	Jack Nicklaus	276
1976	Ray Floyd	271
1977	Tom Watson	276
1978	Gary Player	277
1979	Fuzzy Zoeller	280
1980	Seve Ballesteros	275
1981	Tom Watson	280
1982	Craig Stadler	284
1983	S. Ballesteros	280
1984	Ben Crenshaw	277
1985	Bern. Langer	282
1986	Jack Nicklaus	279
1987	Larry Mize	285

U.S. OPEN CHAMPIONSHIP

YEAR	WINNER	VENUE	SCORE
1895	Hor. Rawlins	Newport, RI	173
1896	James Foulls	Shinnecock Hills	152
1897	Joe Lloyd	Chicago CC	162
1898	Fred Herd	Myopia CC, Mass	328
1899	Willie Smith	Baltimore, Md	315
1900	Harry Vardon	Chicago CC	313
1901	Wm. Anderson	Myopia CC	331
1902	L. Auchterlonie	Garden City, NY	307
1903	Wm. Anderson	Baltrusol CC, NY	307
1904	Wm. Anderson	Glen View, Ill	303
1905	Wm. Anderson	Myopia CC	314
1906	Alex Smith	Onwentsia CC, Ill	295
1907	Alex Ross	Philadelphia CC	302
1908	Fred McLeod	Myopia CC	322
1909	George Sargent	Englewood, NY	290
1910	Alex Smith	Philadelphia CC	298
1911	J. McDermott	Chicago GC	307
1912	J. McDermott	Buffalo CC, NY	294
1913	Fr. Ouimet (am)	County Club	304
1914	Walter Hagen	Midlothian, Ill	290
1915	Jerome Travers	Baltrusol, NJ	297
1916	Chas Evans Jr	Minikahda, Minn	286
1917–1918 No Championship			
1919	Walter Hagen	Brae Burn, Mass	301
1920	Ted Ray	Inverness, Ohio	295
1921	James Barnes	Columbia, Md.	289
1922	Gene Sarazen	Skokie CC, Ill	288
1923	R. Jones (am)	Inwood CC, NY	296
1924	Cyril Walker	Oakland Hills, Mi	297
1925	W. MacFarlane	Worcester, Mass	291
1926	R. Jones (am)	Scioto, Ohio	293
1927	T. Armour	Oakmont CC, Pa	301
1928	J. Farrell	Olympia Flds. Ill	294
1929	R. Jones (am)	Winged Foot, NY	294
1930	R. Jones (am)	Interlachen, Min	287
1931	B. Burke	Inverness, Ohio	292
1932	G. Sarazen	Fresh Meadows	286
1933	J. Goodman	North Shore, Ill	287
1934	Olin Dutra	Merion CC, Pa	293
1935	S. Parks, Jr.	Oakmont, Pa	299
1936	T. Manero	Baltrusol, NJ	282
1937	R. Guldahl	Oakland Hills, Mi	281
1938	R. Guldahl	Cherry Hills, Col.	284
1939	B. Nelson	Philadelphia CC	284
1940	L. Little	Canterbury, Oh.	287
1941	C. Wood	Colonial, Texas	284
1942–1945 No Championship			
1946	L. Mangrum	Canterbury, Oh.	284
1948	L. Worsham	St. Louis, Mo	282
1949	C. Middlecoff	Medinah, Ill	286
1950	B.Hogan	Merion GC, Pa	287
1951	B.Hogan	Oakland Hills, Mi	287
1952	J. Boros	Northwood, Tex	281
1953	B. Hogan	Oakmont CC, Pa	283
1954	E. Furgol	Baltrusol, NJ	284
1955	J. Fleck	Olympic CC, Cal	287
1956	C. Middlecoff	Oak Hill, NY	281
1957	D. Mayer	Inverness, Ohio	282
1958	T. Bolt	Southern Hills	283
1959	B. Casper	Winged Foot, NY	282
1960	A. Palmer	Cherry Hills, Col	280
1961	G. Littler	Oakland Hills, Mi	281
1962	J. Nicklaus	Oakmont, Pa	283
1963	J. Boros	Country Club	293
1964	K. Venturi	Congressional	278
1965	G. Player	Bellerive CC, Mo	282
1966	B. Casper	Olympic CC, Cal	278
1967	J. Nicklaus	Baltrusol, NJ	275
1968	L. Trevino	Oak Hill, NY	275
1969	O. Moody	Champions, Tex	281
1970	A. Jacklin	Hazeltine, Minn	281
1971	L. Trevino	Merion GC, Pa	280
1972	J. Nicklaus	Pebble Beach	290
1973	J. Miller	Oakmont CC, Pa	279
1974	H. Irwin	Winged Foot, NY	287
1975	L. Graham	Medinah, Il	287
1976	J. Pate	Atlanta Athletic	277
1977	H. Green	Southern Hills	278
1978	A. North	Cherry Hills, Col	285
1979	H. Irwin	Inverness, Ohio	284
1980	J. Nicklaus	Baltrusol, NJ	272
1981	D. Graham	Merion, Pa	273
1982	T. Watson	Pebble Beach	282
1983	L. Nelson	Oakmont CC, Pa	280
1984	F. Zoeller	Winged Foot, NY	276
1985	A. North	Oakland Hills, Mi	279
1986	R. Floyd	Shinnecock Hills	279
1987	S. Simpson	San Francisco	277

U.S. PGA CHAMPIONSHIP

YEAR	WINNER & RUNNER-UP	VENUE	SCORE
1916	James Barnes bt. Jock Hutchison	Siwanoy CC, NY	1-hole
1917–1918 No Championship			
1919	James Barnes bt. Fred McLeod	Engineers CC, NY	6 & 5
1920	Jock Hutchison bt. J. D. Edgar	Flossmoor CC, Ill.	1-hole
1921	Walter Hagen bt. James Barnes	Inwood CC, Ny	3 & 2
1922	Gene Sarazen bt. Emmet French	Oakmont CC, Pa.	4 & 3
1923	Gene Sarazen bt. Walter Hagen	Pelham CC, Ny	38th
1924	Walter Hagen bt. James Barnes	Fench Lick CC, Ind	2-holes
1925	Walter Hagen bt. Bill Melhorn	Olympia Fields, Ill	6 & 5
1926	Walter Hagen bt. Leo Digel	Salisbury GC, NY	5 & 3
1927	Walter Hagen bt. Joe Turnesa	Cedar Crest CC, Tex	1-hole
1928	Leo Diegel bt. Al Espinosa	Five Farms CC, Md.	6 & 5
1929	Leo Diegel bt. Johnny Farrell	Hill Crest CC, Cal.	6 & 4
1930	Tommy Armour bt. Gene Sarazen	Fresh Meadow, NY	1-hole
1931	Tom Creavy bt. Denny Shute	Wannamoisett R.I.	2 & 1
1932	Olin Dutra bt. Frank Walsh	Keller CC, Minn	4 & 3
1933	Gene Sarazen bt. Willie Goggin	Blue Mound, Wisc.	5 & 4
1934	Paul Runyan bt. Craig Wood	Park CC, NY	38th
1935	John Revolta bt. Tom Armour	Twin Hills CC, Okl	5 & 4
1936	Denny Shute bt. Jimmy Thomson	Pinehurst CC, NC	3 & 2
1937	Denny Shute bt. Har. McSpaden	Pittsburgh CC, Pa	37th
1938	Paul Runyan bt. Sam Snead	Shawnee CC, Pa	8 & 7
1939	Henry Picard bt. Byron Nelson	Pomonok CC, NY	37th
1940	Byron Nelson bt. Sam Snead	Hershey CC, Pa	1-hole
1941	Vic Ghezzi bt. Byron Nelson	Cherry Hills, Colo	38th
1942	Sam Snead bt. Jim Turnesa	Seaview CC, NJ	2 & 1
1943 No Championship			
1944	Bob Hamilton bt. Byron Nelson	Manito CC, Wash.	1-hole
1945	Byron Nelson bt. Sam Byrd	Morraine CC, Ohio	4 & 3
1946	Ben Hogan bt. Ed Oliver	Portland GC, Ore	6 & 4
1947	Jim Ferrier bt. Chick Harbert	Plum Hollow, Mich.	2 & 1
1948	Ben Hogan bt. Mike Turnesa	Norwood Hills, Mo.	7 & 6
1949	Sam Snead bt. Johnny Palmer	Hermitage CC, Pa	3 & 2
1950	Chandler Harper bt. H. Williams	Scioto CC, Ohio	4 & 3
1951	San Snead bt. Walter Burkemo	Oakmont CC, Pa	7 & 6
1952	Jim Turnesa bt. Chick Harbert	Big Spring CC, Ky.	1-hole
1953	Walter Burkemo bt. Felice Torza	Birmingham, Mich	2 & 1
1954	Chick Harbert bt. Walt. Burkemo	Keller CC, Minn	4 & 3
1955	Doug Ford bt. Cary Middlecoff	Meadowbrook, Mich	4 & 3
1956	Jack Burke bt. Ted Kroll	Blue Hill CC, Mass	3 & 2
1957	Lion Hebert bt. Dow Finsterwald	Miami Valley, Ohio	2 & 1
1958	Dow Finsterwald	Llanerch, Pa	276
1959	Bob Rosburg	Minneapolis CC	277
1960	Jay Hebert	Firestone, Ohio	281
1961	Jerry Barber	Olympia Fields	277
1962	Gary Player	Aronomink, Pa	278
1963	Jack Nicklaus	Dallas AC, Tex	279
1964	Bobby Nichols	Columbus, Ohio	271
1965	Dave Marr	Laurel Valley, Pa	280
1966	Al Gelberger	Firestone, Ohio	280
1967	Don January	Columbine, Colo	281
1968	Julius Boros	Pecan Valley, Tex	281
1969	Ray Floyd	NCR CC, Ohio	276
1970	Dave Stockton	Southern Hills	279
1971	Jack Nicklaus	PGA Natl., Fla	281
1972	Gary Player	Oakland Hills, Mi	281
1973	Jack Nicklaus	Firestone, Ohio	277
1974	Lee Trevino	Tanglewood, NC	276
1975	Jack Nicklaus	Firestone, Ohio	276
1976	Dave Stockton	Congressional	281
1977	Lanny Wadkins	Pebble Beach, Ca	282
1978	John Mahaffey	Oakmont, Pa	276
1979	David Graham	Oakland Hills, Mi	272
1980	Jack Nicklaus	Oak Hill, NY	274
1981	Larry Nelson	Atlanta AC, Ga	273
1982	Ray Floyd	Southern Hills	272
1983	Hal Sutton	Riviera CC, Cal.	274
1984	Lee Trevino	Shoal Creek, Al.	273
1985	Hubert Green	Cherry Hills, Co.	278
1986	Bob Tway	Inverness, Ohio	276
1987	Larry Nelson	West Palm Beach	287

THE RYDER CUP

1927 WORCESTER, MASSACHUSETTS

CAPTAINS TED RAY AND WALTER HAGEN

FOURSOMES:	
W. Hagen & J. Golden bt. E. Ray & F. Robson	2 & 1
J. Farrell & J. Turnesa bt. G. Duncan & A. Compston	8 & 6
G. Sarazen & A. Watrous bt. A. G. Havers & H. C. Jolly	3 & 2
L. Diegel & W. Melhorn lost to A. Boomer & C. A. Whitcombe	7 & 5
SINGLES:	
Melhorn bt. Compston	1-hole
Farrell bt. Boomer	5 & 4
Golden bt. Jolly	8 & 7
Diegel bt. Ray	7 & 5
Sarazen ½–with Whitcombe	Halved
Hagen bt. Havers	2 & 1
Watrous bt. Robson	3 & 2
Turnesa lost to Duncan	1-hole

RESULT: USA, 9½. BRITAIN, 2½

1929 MOORTOWN, LEEDS

CAPTAINS: TED RAY AND WALTER HAGEN

FOURSOMES:	
J. Farrell & J. Turnesa ½–with C. A. Whitcombe & A. Compston	Halved
L. Diegel & A. Espinosa bt. A. Boomer & G. Duncan	7 & 5
G. Sarazen & E. Dudley lost to A. Mitchell & F. Robson	2 & 1
J. Golden & W. Hagen bt. E. R. Whitcombe & H. Cotton	2–holes
SINGLES:	
Farrell lost to Whitcombe	8 & 6
Hagen lost to Duncan	10 & 8
Diegel bt. Mitchell	9 & 8
Sarazen lost to Compston	6 & 4
Turnesa lost to Boomer	4 & 3
Smith bt. Robson	4 & 2
Watrous lost to Cotton	4 & 3
Espinosa ½–with Whitcombe	Halved

RESULT: BRITAIN, 7. USA, 5.

1931 SCIOTO, COLUMBUS, OHIO

CAPTAINS: C. A. WHITCOMBE AND WALTER HAGEN

FOURSOMES:	
G. Sarazen & J. Farrell bt. A. Compston & W. H. Davies	8 & 7
W. Hagen & D. Shute bt. G. Duncan & A. G. Havers	10 & 9
L. Diegel & A. Espinosa lost to A. Mitchell & F. Robson	3 & 1
W. Burke & W. Cox bt. S. Easterbrook & E. R. Whitcombe	3 & 2
SINGLES	
Burke bt. Compston	7 & 6
Sarazen bt. Robson	7 & 6
Farrell lost to Davies	4 & 3
Cox bt. Mitchell	3 & 1
Hagen bt. C. A. Whitcombe	4 & 3
Shute bt. Hodson	8 & 6
Espinosa bt. E. R. Whitcombe	2 & 1
Wood bt. Havers	4 & 3

RESULT: USA, 9. BRITAIN, 3

1933 SOUTHPORT & AINSDALE

CAPTAINS: J. H. TAYLOR AND WALTER HAGEN

FOURSOMES	
Percy Alliss & C. A. Whitcombe ½–with G. Sarazen & W. Hagen	Halved
A. Mitchell & A. G. Havers bt. O. Dutra & D. Shute	3 & 2
W. H. Davies & S. Easterbrook bt. C. Wood & P. Runyan	1–hole
A. H. Padgham & A. Perry lost to E. Dudley & W. Burke	1–hole
SINGLES	
Sarazen bt. Padgham	6 & 4
Dutra lost to Mitchell	9 & 8
Hagen bt. Lacey	2 & 1
Wood bt. Davies	4 & 3
Runyan lost to Alliss	2 & 1
Diegel lost to Havers	4 & 3
Shute lost to Easterbrook	1–hole
Smith bt. C. A. Whitcombe	2 & 1

RESULT: BRITAIN, 6½. USA, 5½

1935 RIDGEWOOD, NEW JERSEY

CAPTAINS: C. A. WHITCOMBE AND WALTER HAGEN

FOURSOMES:	
G. Sarazen & W. Hagen bt. A. Perry & J. Busson	7 & 6
H. Picard & J. Revolta bt. A. H. Padgham & Percy Alliss	6 & 5
P. Runyan & H. Smith bt. W. Cox & E. W. Jarman	9 & 8
O. Dutra & K. Laffoon lost to C. A. and E. R. Whitcombe	1–hole
SINGLES:	
Sarazen bt. Busson	3 & 2
Runyan bt. Burton	5 & 3
Revolta bt. R. A. Whitcombe	2 & 1
Dutra bt. Padgham	4 & 2
Wood lost to Alliss	1–hole
Smith ½–with Cox	Halved
Picard bt. E. R. Whitcombe	3 & 2
Parks ½–with Perry	Halved

RESULT: USA, 9. BRITAIN, 3

1937 SOUTHPORT & AINSDALE

CAPTAINS: C. A. WHITCOMBE AND WALTER HAGEN

FOURSOMES:	
E. Dudley & B. Nelson bt. A. H. Padgham & H. Cotton	4 & 2
R. Guldahl & T. Manero bt. A. Lacey & W. Cox	2 & 1
G. Sarazen & D. Shute ½–with C. A. Whitcombe & D. Rees	Halved
H. Picard & J. Revolta lost to Percy Alliss & R. Burton	2 & 1
SINGLES:	
Guldahl bt. Padgham	8 & 7
Shute ½–with King	Halved
Nelson lost to Rees	3 & 1
Manero lost to Cotton	5 & 3
Sarazen bt. Alliss	1–hole
Snead bt. Burton	5 & 4
Dudley bt. Perry	2 & 1
Picard bt. Lacey	2 & 1

RESULT: USA, 8. BRITAIN, 4

1947 PORTLAND, OREGON

CAPTAINS: HENRY COTTON AND BEN HOGAN

FOURSOMES:	
E. Oliver & L. Worsham bt. H. Cotton & A. Lees	10 & 9
S. Snead & L. Mangrum bt. F. Daly & C. Ward	6 & 5
B. Hogan & J. Demaret bt. J. Adams & M. Faulkner	2–holes
B. Nelson & H. Barron bt. D. Rees & S. King	2 & 1
SINGLES	
Harrison bt. Daly	5 & 4
Worsham bt. Adams	3 & 2
Mangrum bt. Faulkner	6 & 5
Oliver bt. Ward	4 & 3
Nelson bt. Lees	2 & 1
Snead bt. Cotton	5 & 4
Demaret bt. Rees	3 & 2
Keiser lost to King	4 & 3

RESULT: USA, 11. GB & IRE, 1

1949 GANTON

CAPTAINS: C. A. WHITCOMBE AND BEN HOGAN

FOURSOMES:	
E. J. Harrison & J. Palmer lost to M. Faulkner & J. Adams	2 & 1
R. Hamilton & S. Alexander lost to F. Daly & K. Bousfield	4 & 2
J. Demaret & C. Heafner bt. C. Ward & S. King	4 & 3
S. Snead & L. Mangrum lost to R. Burton & A. Lees	1–hole
SINGLES:	
Harrison bt. Faulkner	8 & 7
J. Palmer lost to Adams	2 & 1
Snead bt. Ward	6 & 5
Hamilton lost to Rees	6 & 4
Heafner bt. Burton	3 & 2
Harbert bt. King	4 & 3
Demaret bt. Lees	7 & 6
Mangrum bt. Daly	4 & 3

RESULT: USA, 7. GB & IRE, 5

1951 PINEHURST, NORTH CAROLINA

CAPTAINS: A. J. LACEY AND SAM SNEAD

FOURSOMES:	
C. Heafner & J. Burke bt. M. Faulkner & D. Rees	5 & 3
E. Oliver & H. Ransom lost to C. Ward & A. Lees	2 & 1
S. Snead & L. Mangrum bt. J. Adams & J. Panton	5 & 4
B. Hogan & J. Demaret bt. F. Daly & K. Bousfield	5 & 4
SINGLES:	
Burke bt. Adams	4 & 3
Demaret bt. Rees	2–holes
Heafner ½–with Daly	Halved
Mangrum bt. Weetman	6 & 5
Oliver lost to Lees	2 & 1
Hogan bt. Ward	3 & 2
Alexander bt. Panton	8 & 7
Snead bt. Faulkner	4 & 3

RESULT: USA, 9½. GB & IRE, 2½

1953 WENTWORTH

CAPTAINS: HENRY COTTON AND LLOYD MANGRUM

FOURSOMES:	
D. Douglas & E. Oliver bt. H. Weetman & P. Alliss	2 & 1
L. Mangrum & S. Snead bt. E. Brown & J. Panton	8 & 7
T. Kroll & J. Burke bt. J. Adams & B. J. Hunt	7 & 5
W. Burkemo & C. Middlecoff lost to F. Daly & H. Bradshaw	1–hole
SINGLES:	
Burke bt. Rees	2 & 1
Kroll lost to Daly	9 & 7
Mangrum lost to Brown	2–holes
Snead lost to Weetman	1–hole
Middlecoff bt. Faulkner	3 & 1
Turnesa bt. Alliss	1–hole
Douglas ½–with Hunt	Halved
Haas lost to Bradshaw	3 & 2

RESULT: USA, 6½. GB & IRE, 5½

1955 THUNDERBIRD GOLF & CC, CALIFORNIA

CAPTAINS: DAI REES AND CHICK HARBERT

FOURSOMES:	
C. Harper & J. Barber lost to J. Fallon & J. Jacobs	1–hole
D. Ford & T. Kroll bt. E. Brown & S. Scott	5 & 4
J. Burke & T. Bolt bt. A. Lees & H. Weetman	1–hole
S. Snead & C. Middlecoff bt. H. Bradshaw & D. Rees	3 & 2
SINGLES:	
Bolt bt. O'Connor	4 & 2
Harbert bt. Scott	3 & 2
Middlecoff lost to Jacobs	1–hole
Snead bt. Rees	3 & 1
Furgol lost to Lees	3 & 2
Barber lost to Brown	3 & 2
Burke bt. Bradshaw	3 & 2
Ford bt. Weetman	3 & 2

RESULT: USA, 8. GB & IRE, 4.

1957 LINDRICK, SHEFFIELD

CAPTAINS: DAI REES AND JACK BURKE

FOURSOMES:	
P. Alliss & B. J. Hunt lost to D. Ford & D. Finsterwald	2 & 1
K. Bousfield & D. Rees bt. A. Wall & F. Hawkins	3 & 2
M. Faulkner & H. Weetman lost to T. Kroll & J. Burke	4 & 3
C. O'Connor & E. Brown lost to R. Mayer & T. Bolt	7 & 5
SINGLES:	
Brown bt. Bolt	4 & 3
Mills bt. Burke	5 & 3
Alliss lost to Hawkins	2 & 1
Bousfield bt. Hebert	4 & 3
Rees bt. Furgol	7 & 6
Hunt bt. Ford	6 & 5
O'Connor bt. Finsterwald	7 & 6
Bradshaw ½–with Mayer	Halved

RESULT: GB & IRE, 7½. USA, 4½

THE RYDER CUP

1959 ELDORADO CC, CALIFORNIA

CAPTAINS: DAI REES AND SAM SNEAD

FOURSOMES:	
R. Rosburg & M. Souchak bt. B. J. Hunt & E. Brown	5 & 4
J. Boros & D. Finsterwald bt. D. Rees & K. Bousfield	2–holes
A. Wall & D. Ford lost to C. O'Connor & P. Alliss	3 & 2
S. Snead & C. Middlecoff ½–with H. Weetman & D. Thomas	Halved
SINGLES:	
Ford ½–with Drew	Halved
Souchak bt. Bousfield	3 & 2
Rosburg bt. Weetman	6 & 5
Snead bt. Thomas	6 & 5
Wall bt. O'Connor	7 & 6
Finsterwald bt. Rees	1–hole
Hebert ½–with Alliss	Halved
Middlecoff lost to Brown	4 & 3

RESULT: USA, 8½. GB & IRE, 3½

1961 ROYAL LYTHAM & ST. ANNES

CAPTAINS: DAI REES AND JERRY BARBER

FOURSOMES:	
D. Ford & G. Littler lost to C. O'Connor & P. Allis	4 & 3
A. Wall & J. Hebert bt. J. Panton & B. J. Hunt	4 & 3
W. Casper & A. Palmer bt. D. Rees & K. Bousfield	2 & 1
W. Collins & M. Souchak bt. T. Haliburton & N. Coles	1–hole
FOURSOMES (2):	
A. Wall & J. Hebert bt. C. O'Connor & P. Alliss	1–hole
W. Casper & A. Palmer bt. J. Panton & B. Hunt	5 & 4
W. Collins & M. Souchak lost to D. Rees & K. Bousfield	4 & 2
J. Barber & D. Finsterwald bt. T. Haliburton & N. Coles	1–hole
SINGLES (1):	
D. Ford bt. H. Weetman	1–hole
M. Souchak bt. R. Moffitt	5 & 4
A. Palmer ½–with P. Alliss	Halved
W. Casper bt. K. Bousfield	5 & 3
J. Hebert lost to D. Rees	2 & 1
G. Littler ½–with N. Coles	Halved
J. Barber lost to B. Hunt	5 & 4
D. Finsterwald bt. C. O'Connor	2 & 1
SINGLES (2):	
A. Wall bt. H. Weetman	1–hole
W. Collins lost to P. Alliss	3 & 2
M. Souchak bt. B. Hunt	2 & 1
A. Palmer bt. T. Haliburton	2 & 1
D. Ford lost to D. Rees	4 & 3
J. Barber lost to K. Bousfield	1–hole
D. Finsterwald lost to N. Coles	1–hole
G. Littler ½–with C. O'Connor	Halved

RESULT: USA, 14½. GB & IRE, 9½

1963 ATLANTA, GEORGIA

CAPTAINS: JOHNNY FALLON AND ARNOLD PALMER

FOURSOMES (1):	
A. Palmer & J. Pott lost to B. Huggett & G. Will	3 & 2
W. Casper & D. Ragan bt. C. O'Connor & P. Alliss	1–hole
J. Boros & A. Lema ½–with N. Coles & B. Hunt	Halved
G. Littler & D. Finsterwald ½–with D. Thomas & H. Weetman	Halved
FOURSOMES (2):	
W. Maxwell & R. Goalby bt. D. Thomas & H. Weetman	4 & 3
A. Palmer & W. Casper bt. B. Huggett & G. Will	5 & 4
G. Littler & D. Finsterwald bt. N. Coles & G. M. Hunt	2 & 1
J. Boros & A. Lema bt. T. Haliburton B. Hunt	1–hole
FOURBALLS (1):	
A. Palmer & D. Finsterwald bt. B. Huggett & D. Thomas	5 & 4
G. Littler & J. Boros ½–with P. Alliss & B. Hunt	Halved
W. Casper & W. Maxwell bt. H. Weetman & G. Will	3 & 2
R. Goalby & D. Ragan lost to N. Coles & C. O'Connor	1–hole
FOURBALLS (2):	
A. Palmer & D. Finsterwald bt. N. Coles & C. O'Connor	3 & 2
A. Lema & J. Pott bt. P. Alliss & B. Hunt	1–hole
W. Casper & W. Maxwell bt. T. Haliburton & G. M. Hunt	2 & 1
R. Goalby & D. Ragan ½–with B. Huggett & D. Thomas	Halved
SINGLES (1):	
Lema bt. Hunt	5 & 3
Pott lost to Huggett	3 & 1
Palmer lost to Alliss	1–hole
Casper ½–with Coles	Halved
Goalby bt. Thomas	3 & 2
Littler bt. O'Connor	1–hole
Boros lost to Weetman	1–hole
Finsterwald lost to B. Hunt	2–holes
SINGLES (2):	
Palmer bt. Will	3 & 2
Ragan bt. Coles	2 & 1
Lema ½–with Alliss	Halved
Littler bt. Haliburton	6 & 5
Boros bt. Weetman	2 & 1
Maxwell bt. O'Connor	2 & 1
Finsterwald bt. Thomas	4 & 3
Goalby bt. B. Hunt	2 & 1

RESULT: USA, 23. GB & IRE, 9

1965 ROYAL BIRKDALE

CAPTAINS: HARRY WEETMAN AND BYRON NELSON

FOURSOMES (1):	
J. Boros & A. Lema bt. L. Platts & P. Butler	1–hole
A. Palmer & D. Marr lost to D. Thomas & G. Will	6 & 5
W. Casper & G. Littler bt. B. Hunt & N. Coles	2 & 1
K. Venturi & D. January lost to P. Alliss & C. O'Connor	5 & 4
FOURSOMES (2):	
A. Palmer & D. Marr bt. D. Thomas & G. Will	6 & 5
W. Casper & G. Littler lost to P. Alliss & C. O'Connor	2 & 1
J. Boros & A. Lema bt. J. Martin & J. Hitchcock	5 & 4
K. Venturi & D. January lost to B. Hunt & N. Coles	3 & 2
FOURBALLS (1):	
D. January & T. Jacobs bt. D. Thomas & G. Will	1–hole
W. Casper & G. Littler ½–with L. Platts & P. Butler	Halved
A. Palmer & D. Marr bt. P. Alliss & C. O'Connor	6 & 4
J. Boros & A. Lema lost to B. Hunt & N. Coles	1–hole
FOURBALLS (2):	
A. Palmer & D. Marr lost to P. Alliss & C. O'Connor	2–holes
D. January & T. Jacobs bt. D. Thomas & G. Will	1–hole
W. Casper & G. Littler ½–with L. Platts & P. Butler	Halved
K. Venturi & A. Lema bt. B. Hunt & N. Coles	1–hole
SINGLES (1):	
Palmer bt. Hitchcock	3 & 2
Boros bt. Platts	4 & 2
Lema bt. Butler	1–hole
Marr bt. Coles	2–holes
Littler lost to B. Hunt	2–holes
T. Jacobs bt. Thomas	2 & 1
Casper lost to Alliss	1–hole
January ½–with Will	Halved
SINGLES (2):	
Lema bt. O'Connor	6 & 4
Boros bt. Hitchcock	2 & 1
Palmer bt. Butler	2–holes
Venturi lost to Alliss	3 & 1
Casper lost to Coles	3 & 2
Littler bt. Will	2 & 1
Marr bt. B. Hunt	1–hole
T. Jacobs lost to Platts	1–hole

RESULT: USA, 19½. GB & IRE, 12½

1967 HOUSTON, TEXAS

CAPTAINS: DAI REES AND BEN HOGAN

FOURSOMES (1):	
W. Casper & J. Boros ½–with B. Huggett & C. Will	Halved
A. Palmer & G. Dickinson bt. P. Alliss & C. O'Connor	2 & 1
D. Sanders & G. Brewer lost to A. Jacklin & N. Coles	4 & 3
R. Nichols & J. Pott bt. B. Hunt & N. Coles	6 & 5
FOURSOMES (2):	
W. Casper & J. Boros bt. B. Huggett & G. Will	1–hole
G. Dickinson & A. Palmer bt. M. Gregson & H. Boyle	5 & 4
G. Littler & A. Geiberger lost to A. Jacklin & D. Thomas	3 & 2
R. Nichols & J. Pott bt. P. Alliss & C. O'Connor	2 & 1
FOURBALLS (1):	
W. Casper & G. Brewer bt. P. Alliss & C. O'Connor	3 & 2
R. Nichols & J. Pott bt. B. Hunt & N. Coles	1–hole
G. Littler & A. Geiberger bt. A. Jacklin & D. Thomas	1–hole
G. Dickinson & D. Sanders bt. B. Huggett & G. Will	3 & 2
FOURBALLS (2):	
W. Casper & G. Brewer bt. B. Hunt & N. Coles	5 & 3
G. Dickinson & D. Sanders bt. P. Alliss & M. Gregson	3 & 2
A. Palmer & J. Boros bt. G. Will & H. Boyle	1–hole
G. Littler & A. Geiberger ½–with A. Jacklin & D. Thomas	Halved
SINGLES (1):	
Brewer bt. Boyle	4 & 3
Casper bt. Alliss	2 & 1
Palmer bt. Jacklin	3 & 2
Boros lost to Huggett	1–hole
Sanders lost to Coles	2 & 1
Geiberger bt. Gregson	4 & 2
Littler ½–with Thomas	Halved
Nichols ½–with B. Hunt	Halved
SINGLES (2):	
Palmer bt. Huggett	5 & 3
Brewer lost to Alliss	2 & 1
Dickinson bt. Jacklin	3 & 2
Pott bt. Will	3 & 1
Geiberger bt. Gregson	2 & 1
Boros ½–with B. Hunt	Halved
Sanders lost to Coles	2 & 1

RESULT: USA, 23½. GB & IRE, 8½

1969 ROYAL BIRKDALE

CAPTAINS: ERIC BROWN AND SAM SNEAD

FOURSOMES (1):	
N. Coles & B. Huggett bt. M. Barber & R. Floyd	3 & 2
B. Gallagher & M. Bembridge bt. L. Trevino & K. Still	2 & 1
A. Jacklin & P. Townsend bt. D. Hill & T. Aaron	3 & 1
C. O'Connor & P. Alliss ½–with W. Casper & F. Beard	Halved
FOURSOMES (2):	
N. Coles & B. Huggett lost to D. Hill & T. Aaron	1–hole
B. Gallacher & M. Bembridge lost to L. Trevino & G. Littler	1–hole
A. Jacklin & P. Townsend bt. W. Casper & F. Beard	1–hole
P. Butler & B. Hunt lost to J. Nicklaus & D. Sikes	1–hole
FOURBALLS (1):	
C. O'Connor & P. Townsend bt. D. Hill & D. Douglass	1–hole
B. Huggett & A. Caygill ½–with R. Floyd & M. Barber	Halved
B. Barnes & P. Alliss lost to L. Trevino & G. Littler	1–hole
A. Jacklin & N. Coles bt. J. Nicklaus & D. Sikes	1–hole
FOURBALLS (2):	
P. Butler & P. Townsend lost to W. Casper & F. Beard	2–holes
B. Huggett & B. Gallacher lost to D. Hill & K. Still	2 & 1
M. Bembridge & P. Hunt ½–with T. Aaron & R. Floyd	Halved
A. Jacklin & N. Coles ½–with L. Trevino & M. Barber	Halved
SINGLES (1):	
Alliss lost to Trevino	2 & 1
Townsend lost to Hill	5 & 4
Coles bt. Aaron	1–hole
Barnes lost to Casper	1–hole
O'Connor bt. Beard	5 & 4
Bembridge bt. Still	1–hole
Butler bt. Floyd	1–hole
Jacklin bt. Nicklaus	4 & 3
SINGLES (2):	
Barnes lost to Hill	4 & 2
Gallacher bt. Trevino	4 & 3
Bembridge lost to Barber	7 & 6
Butler bt. Douglass	3 & 2
Coles lost to Sikes	4 & 3
O'Connor lost to Littler	2 & 1
Huggett ½–with Casper	Halved
Jacklin ½–with Nicklaus	Halved

RESULT: GB & IRE, 16. USA, 16

THE RYDER CUP

1971 ST. LOUIS, MISSOURI

CAPTAINS: ERIC BROWN AND JAY HEBERT

FOURSOMES (1):	
W. Casper & M. Barber lost to N. Coles & C. O'Connor	2 & 1
A. Palmer & G. Dickinson bt. P. Townsend & P. Oosterhuis	2–holes
J. Nicklaus & D. Stockton lost to B. Huggett & A. Jacklin	3 & 2
C. Coody & F. Beard lost to M. Bembridge & P. Butler	1–hole
FOURSOMES (2):	
W. Casper & M. Barber lost to H. Bannerman & B. Gallacher	2 & 1
A. Palmer & G. Dickinson bt. P. Townsend & P. Oosterhuis	1–hole
L. Trevino & M. Rudolph ½–with B. Huggett & A. Jacklin	Halved
J. Nicklaus & J. C. Snead bt. M. Bembridge & P. Butler	5 & 3
FOURBALLS (1):	
L. Trevino & M. Rudolph bt. C. O'Connor & B. Barnes	2 & 1
F. Beard & J. C. Snead bt. N. Coles & J. Garner	2 & 1
A. Palmer & G. Dickinson bt. P. Oosterhuis & B. Gallacher	5 & 4
J. Nicklaus & G. Littler bt. P. Townsend & H. Bannerman	2 & 1
FOURBALLS (2):	
L. Trevino & W. Casper lost to B. Gallacher & P. Oosterhuis	1–hole
G. Littler & J. C. Snead bt. A. Jacklin & B. Huggett	2 & 1
A. Palmer & J. Nicklaus bt. P. Townsend & H. Bannerman	1–hole
C. Coody & F. Beard ½–with N. Coles & C. O'Connor	Halved
SINGLES (1):	
Trevino bt. Jacklin	1–hole
Stockton ½–with Gallacher	Halved
Rudolph lost to Barnes	1–hole
Littler lost to Oosterhuis	4 & 3
Nicklaus bt. Townsend	3 & 2
Dickinson bt. O'Connor	5 & 4
Palmer ½–with Bannerman	Halved
Beard ½–with Coles	Halved
SINGLES (2):	
Trevino bt. Huggett	7 & 6
Snead bt. Jacklin	1–hole
Barber lost to Barnes	2 & 1
Stockton bt. Townsend	1–hole
Coody lost to Gallacher	2 & 1
Nicklaus bt. Coles	5 & 3
Palmer lost to Oosterhuis	3 & 2
Dickinson lost to Bannerman	2 & 1

RESULT: USA, 18½. GB & IRE, 13½

1973 MUIRFIELD, SCOTLAND

CAPTAINS: BERNARD HUNT AND JACK BURKE

FOURSOMES (1):	
L. Trevino & B. Casper lost to B. Barnes & B. Gallacher	1–hole
T. Weiskopf & J. C. Snead lost to C. O'Connor & N. Coles	3 & 2
J. Rodriguez & L. Graham ½–with A. Jacklin & P. Oosterhuis	Halved
J. Nicklaus & A. Palmer bt. M. Bembridge & E. Polland	6 & 5
FOURBALLS (1):	
T. Aaron & G. Brewer lost to B. Barnes & B. Gallacher	5 & 4
A. Palmer & J. Nicklaus lost to M. Bembridge & B. Huggett	3 & 1
T. Weiskopf & B. Casper lost to A. Jacklin & P. Oosterhuis	3 & 1
L. Trevino & H. Blancas bt. C O'Connor & N. Coles	2 & 1
FOURSOMES (2):	
J. Nicklaus & T. Weiskopf bt. B. Barnes & P. Butler	1–hole
A. Palmer & D. Hill lost to P. Oosterhuis & A. Jacklin	2–holes
J. Rodriguez & L. Graham lost to M. Bembridge & B. Huggett	5 & 4
L. Trevino & B. Casper bt. N. Coles & C. O'Connor	2 & 1
FOURBALLS (2):	
J. C. Snead & A. Palmer bt. B. Barnes & P. Butler	2–holes
G. Brewer & B. Casper bt. A. Jacklin & P. Oosterhuis	3 & 2
J. Nicklaus & T. Weiskopf bt. C. Clark & E. Polland	3 & 2
L. Trevino & H. Blancas ½–with M. Bembridge & B. Huggett	Halved
SINGLES (1):	
Casper bt. Barnes	2 & 1
Weiskopf bt. Gallacher	3 & 1
Blancas bt. Butler	5 & 4
Aaron lost to Jacklin	3 & 1
Brewer ½–with Coles	Halved
Snead bt. O'Connor	1–hole
Nicklaus ½–with Bembridge	Halved
Trevino ½–with Oosterhuis	Halved
SINGLES (2):	
Blancas lost to Huggett	4 & 2
Snead bt. Barnes	3 & 1
Brewer bt. Gallacher	6 & 5
Casper bt. Jacklin	2 & 1
Trevino bt. Coles	6 & 5
Weiskopf ½–with O'Connor	Halved
Nicklaus bt. Bembridge	2–holes
Palmer lost to Oosterhuis	4 & 2

RESULT: USA, 19. GB & IRE, 13

1975 LAUREL VALLEY, PENNSYLVANIA

CAPTAINS: BERNARD HUNT AND ARNOLD PALMER

FOURSOMES (1):	
J. Nicklaus & T. Weiskopf bt. B. Barnes & B. Gallacher	5 & 4
G. Littler & H. Irwin bt. N. Wood & M. Bembridge	4 & 3
A. Geiberger & J. Miller bt. A. Jacklin & P. Oosterhuis	3 & 1
L. Trevino & J. C. Snead bt. T. Horton & J. O'Leary	2 & 1
FOURBALLS (1):	
B. Casper & R. Floyd lost to A. Jacklin & P. Oosterhuis	2 & 1
T. Weiskopf & L. Graham bt. E. Darcy & C. O'Connor Jnr	3 & 2
J. Nicklaus & B. Murphy ½–with B. Barnes & B. Gallacher	Halved
L. Trevino & H. Irwin bt. T. Horton & J. O'Leary	2 & 1
FOURBALLS (2):	
B. Casper & J. Miller ½–with A. Jacklin & P. Oosterhuis	Halved
J. Nicklaus & J. C. Snead bt. T. Horton & N. Wood	4 & 2
G. Littler & L. Graham bt. B. Barnes & B. Gallacher	5 & 3
A. Geiberger & R. Floyd ½–with E. Darcy & G. Hunt	Halved
FOURSOMES (2):	
L. Trevino & B. Murphy lost to A. Jacklin & B. Barnes	3 & 2
T. Weiskopf & J. Miller bt. C. O'Connor Jnr. & J. O'Leary	5 & 3
H. Irwin & B. Casper bt. P. Oosterhuis & M. Bembridge	3 & 2
A. Geiberger & L. Graham bt. E. Darcy & G. Hunt	3 & 2
SINGLES (1):	
Murphy bt. Jacklin	2 & 1
Miller lost to Oosterhuis	2–holes
Trevino ½–with Gallacher	Halved
Irwin ½–with Horton	Halved
Littler bt. Huggett	4 & 2
Casper bt. Darcy	3 & 2
Weiskopf bt. G. Hunt	5 & 3
Nicklaus lost to Barnes	4 & 2
SINGLES (2):	
Floyd bt. Jacklin	1–hole
Snead lost to Oosterhuis	3 & 2
Geiberger ½–with Gallacher	Halved
Graham lost to Horton	2 & 1
Irwin bt. O'Leary	2 & 1
Murphy bt. Bembridge	2 & 1
Trevino lost to Wood	2 & 1
Nicklaus lost to Barnes	2 & 1

RESULT: USA, 21. GB & IRE, 11

THE RYDER CUP

1977 ROYAL LYTHAM & ST. ANNES

CAPTAINS: BRIAN HUGGETT AND DOW FINSTERWALD

FOURSOMES:	
L. Wadkins & H. Irwin bt. B. Gallacher & B. Barnes	3 & 1
D. Stockton & J. McGee bt. N. Coles & P. Dawson	1–hole
R. Floyd & L. Graham lost to N. Faldo & P. Oosterhuis	2 & 1
E. Sneed & D. January ½–with E. Darcy & A. Jacklin	Halved
J. Nicklaus & T. Watson bt. T. Horton & M. James	5 & 4
FOURBALLS:	
T. Watson & H. Green bt. B. Barnes & T. Horton	5 & 4
E. Sneed & L. Wadkins bt. N. Coles & P. Dawson	5 & 3
J. Nicklaus & R. Floyd lost to N. Faldo & P. Oosterhuis	3 & 1
D. Hill & D. Stockton bt. A. Jacklin & E. Darcy	5 & 3
H. Irwin & L. Graham bt. M. James & K. Brown	1–hole
SINGLES:	
Wadkins bt. Clark	4 & 3
Graham bt. Coles	5 & 3
January lost to Dawson	5 & 4
Irwin lost to Barnes	1–hole
Hill bt. Horton	5 & 4
Nicklaus lost to Gallacher	1–hole
Green bt. Darcy	1–hole
Floyd bt. James	2 & 1
Watson lost to Faldo	1–hole
McGee lost to Oosterhuis	2–holes

RESULT: USA, 12½. GB & IRE, 7½

1979 GREENBRIER, WEST VIRGINIA

CAPTAINS: JOHN JACOBS AND BILLY CASPER

FOURBALLS (1):	
L. Wadkins & L. Nelson bt. A. Garrido & S. Ballesteros	2 & 1
F. Zoeller & L. Trevino bt. K. Brown & M. James	3 & 2
A. Bean & L. Elder bt. P. Oosterhuis & N. Faldo	2 & 1
H. Irwin & J. Mahaffey lost to B. Gallacher & B. Barnes	2 & 1
FOURSOMES (1):	
H. Irwin & T. Kite bt. K. Brown & D. Smyth	7 & 6
F. Zoeller & H. Green lost to S. Ballesteros & A. Garrido	3 & 2
L. Trevino & G. Morgan ½–with A. Lyle & A. Jacklin	Halved
L. Wadkins & L. Nelson bt. B. Gallacher & B. Barnes	4 & 3
FOURSOMES (2):	
L. Elder & J. Mahaffey lost to A. Jacklin & S. Lyle	5 & 4
A. Bean & T. Kite lost to N. Faldo & P. Oosterhuis	6 & 5
F. Zoeller & M. Hayes lost to B. Gallacher & B. Barnes	2 & 1
L. Wadkins & L. Nelson bt. S. Ballesteros & A. Garrido	3 & 2
FOURBALLS (2):	
L. Wadkins & L. Nelson bt. S. Ballesteros & A. Garrido	5 & 4
H. Irwin & T. Kite bt. A. Jacklin & S. Lyle	1–hole
L. Trevino & F. Zoeller lost to B. Gallacher & B. Barnes	3 & 2
L. Elder & M. Hayes lost to N. Faldo & P. Oosterhuis	1–hole
SINGLES:	
Wadkins lost to Gallacher	3 & 2
Nelson bt. Ballesteros	3 & 2
Kite bt. Jacklin	1–hole
Hayes bt. Garrido	1–hole
Bean bt. King	4 & 3
Mahaffey bt. Barnes	1–hole
Elder lost to Faldo	3 & 2
Irwin bt. Smyth	5 & 3
Green bt. Oosterhuis	2–holes
Zoeller lost to Brown	1–hole
Trevino bt. Lyle	2 & 1
G. Morgan halved match with M. James	

RESULT: USA, 17. EUR, 11

1981 WALTON HEATH

CAPTAINS: JOHN JACOBS AND DAVE MARR

FOURSOMES (1):	
L. Trevino & L. Nelson bt. B. Langer & M. Pinero	1–hole
B. Rogers & B. Leitzke lost to S. Lyle & M. James	2 & 1
H. Irwin & R. Floyd lost to B. Gallacher & D. Smyth	3 & 2
T. Watson & J. Nicklaus bt. P. Oosterhuis & N. Faldo	4 & 3
FOURBALLS (1):	
T. Kite & J. Miller ½–with S. Torrance & H. Clark	Halved
B. Crenshaw & J. Pate lost to S. Lyle & M. James	3 & 2
B. Rogers & B. Leitzke lost to D. Smith & J. M. Canizares	6 & 5
H. Irwin & R. Floyd bt. B. Gallacher & E. Darcy	2 & 1
FOURSOMES (2):	
L. Trevino & J. Pate bt. P. Oosterhuis & S. Torrance	2 & 1
J. Nicklaus & T. Watson bt. S. Lyle & M. James	3 & 2
B. Rogers & R. Floyd bt. B. Langer & M. Pinero	3 & 2
T. Kite & L. Nelson bt. D. Smyth & B. Gallacher	3 & 2
FOURBALLS (2):	
L. Trevino & J. Pate bt. N. Faldo & S. Torrance	7 & 5
L. Nelson & T. Kite bt. S. Lyle & M. James	1–hole
R. Floyd & H. Irwin lost to B. Langer & M. Pinero	2 & 1
J. Nicklaus & T. Watson bt. J. M. Canizares & D. Smyth	3 & 2
SINGLES:	
Trevino bt. Torrance	5 & 3
Kite bt. Lyle	3 & 2
Rogers ½–with Gallacher	Halved
Nelson bt. James	2–holes
Crenshaw bt. Smyth	6 & 4
Lietzke ½–with Langer	Halved
Pate lost to Pinero	4 & 2
Irwin bt. Canizares	1–hole
Miller lost to Faldo	2 & 1
Watson lost to Clark	4 & 3
Floyd bt. Oosterhuis	1–hole
Nicklaus bt. Darcy	5 & 3

RESULT: USA, 18½. EUR, 9½

1983 PGA NATIONAL, PALM BEACH GARDENS, FLORIDA

CAPTAINS: TONY JACKLIN AND JACK NICKLAUS

FOURSOMES (1):	
T. Watson & B. Crenshaw bt. B. Gallacher & S. Lyle	5 & 4
L. Wadkins & C. Stadler lost to N. Faldo & B. Langer	4 & 2
T. Kite & C. Peete bt. S. Ballesteros & P. Way	2 & 1
R. Floyd & R. Gilder lost to J. M. Canizares & S. Torrance	4 & 3
FOURBALLS (1):	
G. Morgan & F. Zoeller lost to B. Waites & K. Brown	2 & 1
T. Watson & J. Haas bt. N. Faldo & B. Langer	2 & 1
R. Floyd & C. Strange lost to S. Ballesteros & P. Way	1–hole
B. Crenshaw & C. Peete ½–with S. Torrance & I. Woosnam	Halved
FOURSOMES (2):	
T. Kite & R. Floyd lost to N. Faldo & B. Langer	3 & 2
J. Haas & C. Strange bt. B. Waites & K. Brown	3 & 2
G. Morgan & L. Wadkins bt. S. Torrance & J. M. Canizares	7 & 5
T. Watson & B. Gilder lost to S. Ballesteros & P. Way	2 & 1
FOURBALLS (2):	
L. Wadkins & C. Stadler bt. B. Waites & K. Brown	1–hole
B. Crenshaw & C. Peete lost to N. Faldo & B. Langer	4 & 2
G. Morgan & J. Haas ½–with S. Ballesteros & P. Way	Halved
T. Watson & B. Gilder bt. S. Torrance & I. Woosnam	5 & 4
SINGLES:	
Zoeller ½–with Ballesteros	Halved
Haas lost to Faldo	2 & 1
Morgan lost to Langer	2–holes
Gilder bt. Brand	2–holes
Crenshaw bt. Lyle	3 & 1
Peete bt. Waites	1–hole
Strange lost to Way	2 & 1
Kite ½–with Torrance	Halved
Stadler bt. Woosnam	3 & 2
Wadkins ½–with Canizares	Halved
Floyd lost to Brown	4 & 3
Watson bt. Gallacher	2 & 1

RESULT: USA, 14½. EUR, 13½

1985 THE BELFRY, SUTTON COLDFIELD

CAPTAINS: TONY JACKLIN AND LEE TREVINO

FOURSOMES (1):	
S. Ballesteros & M. Pinero bt. C. Strange & M. O'Meara	2 & 1
B. Langer & N. Faldo lost to C. Peete & T. Kite	3 & 2
S. Lyle & K. Brown lost to L. Wadkins & R. Floyd	4 & 3
H. Clark & S. Torrance lost to C. Stadler & H. Sutton	3 & 2
FOURBALLS (1):	
P. Way & I. Woosnam bt. F. Zoeller & H. Green	1–hole
S. Ballesteros & M. Pinero bt. A. North & P. Jacobsen	2 & 1
B. Langer & J. M. Canizares ½–with C. Stadler & H. Sutton	Halved
S. Torrance & H. Clark lost to R. Floyd & L. Wadkins	1–hole
FOURBALLS (2):	
S. Torrance & H. Clark bt. T. Kite & A. North	2 & 1
P. Way & I. Woosnam bt. H. Green & F. Zoeller	4 & 3
S. Ballesteros & M. Pinero lost to M. O'Meara & L. Wadkins	3 & 2
B. Langer & S. Lyle ½–with C. Stadler & C. Strange	Halved
FOURSOMES (2):	
J. M. Canizares & J. Rivero bt. T. Kite & C. Peete	7 & 5
S. Ballesteros & M. Pinero bt. C. Stadler & H. Sutton	5 & 4
P. Way & I. Woosnam lost to C. Strange & P. Jacobsen	4 & 2
B. Langer & K. Brown bt. R. Floyd & L. Wadkins	3 & 2
SINGLES:	
Pinero bt. Wadkins	3 & 1
Woosnam lost to Stadler	2 & 1
Way bt. Floyd	2–holes
Ballesteros ½–with Kite	Halved
Lyle bt. Jacobsen	3 & 2
Langer bt. Sutton	5 & 4
Torrance bt. North	1–hole
Clark bt. O'Meara	1–hole
Rivero lost to Peete	1–hole
Faldo lost to Green	3 & 1
Canizares bt. Zoeller	2–holes
Brown lost to Strange	4 & 2

RESULT: EUR, 16½. USA, 11½

1987 MUIRFIELD VILLAGE, OHIO

CAPTAINS: TONY JACKLIN AND JACK NICKLAUS

FOURSOMES (1):	
Torrance & Clark lost to Strange & Kite	4 & 2
Brown & Langer lost to Sutton & Pohl	2 & 1
Faldo & Woosnam bt. Wadkins & Mize	2–holes
Ballesteros & Olazabal bt. Nelson & Stewart	1–hole
FOURBALLS (1):	
Brand Jr. & Rivero bt. Crenshaw & Simpson	3 & 2
Lyle & Langer bt. Bean & Calcavecchia	1–hole
Faldo & Woosnam bt. Sutton & Pohl	2 & 1
Ballesteros & Olazabal bt. Strange & Kite	2 & 1
FOURSOMES (2):	
Rivero & Brand lost to Strange & Kite	3 & 1
Faldo & Woosnam ½–with Sutton & Mize	Halved
Lyle & Langer bt. Wadkins & Nelson	2 & 1
Ballesteros & Olazabal bt. Crenshaw & Stewart	1–hole
FOURBALLS (2):	
Woosnam & Faldo bt. Kite & Strange	5 & 4
Darcy & Brand lost to Bean & Stewart	3 & 2
Ballesteros & Olazabal lost to Sutton & Mize	2 & 1
Lyle & Langer bt. Wadkins & Nelson	1–hole
SINGLES:	
I. Woosnam lost to A. Bean	1–hole
H. Clark bt. D. Pohl	1–hole
S. Torrance ½–with L. Mize	Halved
N. Faldo lost to M. Calcavecchia	1–hole
J.-M. Olazabal lost to P. Stewart	2–holes
J. Rivero lost to S. Simpson	2 & 1
S. Lyle lost to T. Kite	3 & 2
E. Darcy bt. B. Crenshaw	1–hole
B. Langer ½–with L. Nelson	Halved
S. Ballesteros bt. C. Strange	2 & 1
K. Brown lost to L. Wadkins	3 & 2
G. Brand Jr. ½–with H. Sutton	Halved

RESULT: EUR, 15. USA, 13.

WALKER CUP RESULTS

1922 NATIONAL GOLF LINKS OF AMERICA, N.Y.

CAPTAINS: R. HARRIS AND W. C. FOWNES JR.

FOURSOMES:	
C. Tolley & B. Darwin lost to J. Guilford & F. Quimet	8 & 7
R. Wethered & C. Aylmer bt. C. Evans Jr. & R. Gardner	5 & 4
W. Torrance & C. Hooman lost to R. Jones Jr. & J. Sweetser	3 & 2
J. Caven & W. Mackenzie lost to M. Marston & W. Fownes Jr.	2 & 1
SINGLES:	
C. Tolley lost to J. Guilford	2 & 1
R. Wethered lost to Jones	3 & 2
Caven lost to Evans Jr.	5 & 4
Alymer lost to Ouimet	8 & 7
Torrance lost to Gardner	7 & 5
Mackenzie bt. Marston	6 & 5
Darwin bt. Fownes Jr.	6 & 5
C. Hooman bt. Sweetser	37th

RESULTS: USA, 8. GB & IRE, 4.

1923 ST. ANDREWS

CAPTAINS: CYRIL TOLLEY AND ROBERT GARDINER

FOURSOMES:	
C. Tolley & R. Wethered bt. F. Ouimet & J. Sweetser	6 & 5
R. Harris & C. Hooman lost to R. Gardiner & M. Marston	7 & 6
E. Holderness & W. Hope bt. G. Rotan & S. Herron	1–hole
J. Wilson & W. Murray bt. H. Johnston & J. Neville	4 & 3
SINGLES:	
Wethered ½–with Ouimet	Halved
Tolley bt. Sweetser	4 & 3
Harris lost to Gardner	1–hole
Mackenzie lost to Rotan	5 & 4
Hope lost to Marston	6 & 5
Wilson bt. Herron	1–hole
Murray lost to Willing	2 & 1

RESULTS: USA, 6½. GB & IRE, 5½.

1924 GARDEN CITY, N.Y.

CAPTAINS: CYRIL TOLLEY AND ROBERT GARDINER

FOURSOMES:	
E. Storey & W. Murray lost to M. Marston & R. Gardner	3 & 1
C. Tolley & C. Hezlet lost to J. Guilford & F. Ouimet	2 & 1
Hon. M. Scott & R. Scott Jr. bt. R. Jones Jr. & W. Fownes Jr.	1–hole
T. Torrance & O. Bristowe lost to J. Sweetser & H. Johnston	4 & 3
SINGLES:	
Tolley bt. Marston	1–hole
Hezlet lost to Jones Jr.	4 & 3
Murray lost to Evans Jr.	2 & 1
Storey lost to Ouimet	1–hole
Scott bt. Sweetser	7 & 6
Hope lost to Gardner	3 & 2
Torrance lost to Guilford	2 & 1
Kyle lost to Willing	3 & 2

RESULT: USA, 9. GB & IRE, 3.

1926 ST. ANDREWS

CAPTAINS: R. HARRIS AND ROBERT GARDINER

FOURSOMES:	
R. Wethered & E. Holderness bt. F. Ouimet & J. Guilford	5 & 4
C. Folley & A. Jamieson Jr. lost to R. Jones Jr. & W. Gunn	4 & 3
R. Harris & Co. Hezlet lost to G. Von Elm & J. Sweetzer	8 & 7
E. Storey & Hon. W. Brownlow lost to R. Gardner & R. MacKenzie	
SINGLES:	
Tolley lost to Jones Jr.	12 & 11
Holderness lost to Sweetser	4 & 3
Wethered bt. Ouimet	5 & 4
Hezlet ½–with Von Elm	Halved
Harris bt. Guilford	2 & 1
Brownlow lost to Gunn	9 & 8
Storey bt. MacKenzie	2 & 1
Jamieson Jr. bt. Gardner	2 & 1

RESULT: USA, 6½. GB & IRE, 5½.

1928 CHICAGO GC, ILLINOIS

CAPTAINS: WILLIAM TWEDDELL AND BOBBY JONES

FOURSOMES:	
T. Perkins & W. Tweddell lost to J. Sweetser & G. Von Elm	7 & 6
C. Hezlet & W. Hope lost to R. Jones Jr. & C. Evans Jr.	5 & 3
T. Torrance & E. Storey lost to F. Ouimet & H. Johnston	4 & 2
J. Beck & A. MacCullum lost to W. Gunn & R. MacKenzie	7 & 5
SINGLES:	
Perkins lost to Jones Jr.	13 & 12
Tweddell lost to Von Elm	3 & 2
Hezlet lost to Ouimet	8 & 7
Hope lost to Sweetzer	5 & 4
Storey lost to Johnston	4 & 2
Torrance bt. Evans Jr.	1–hole
Hardman lost to Gunn	11 & 10
Martin lost to MacKenzie	2 & 1

RESULT: USA, 11. GB & IRE, 1.

1930 ROYAL ST. GEORGE'S, SANDWICH

CAPTAINS: ROGER WETHERED AND BOBBY JONES

FOURSOMES:	
C. Tolley & R. Wethered bt. G. Von Elm & G. Voigt	2–holes
R. Hartley & T. Torrance lost to R. Jones Jr. & O. Willing	8 & 7
E. Holderness & J. Stout lost to R. MacKenzie & D. Moe	2 & 1
W. Campbell & J. Smith lost to H. Johnston & F. Ouimet	2 & 1
SINGLES:	
Tolley lost to Johnston	5 & 4
Wethered lost to Jones Jr.	9 & 8
Hartley lost to Von Elm	3 & 2
Holderness lost to Voigt	10 & 8
Smith lost to Willing	2 & 1
Torrance bt. Ouimet	7 & 6
Stout lost to Moe	1–hole
Campbell lost to MacKenzie	6 & 5

RESULT: USA, 10. GB & IRE, 2.

1932 THE COUNTRY CLUB, BROOKLINE, MASS.

CAPTAINS: T. A. TORRANCE AND FRANCIS OUIMET

FOURSOMES:	
R. Hartley & W. Harley lost to J. Sweetser & G. Voigt	7 & 6
T. Torrance & J. de Forest lost ot C. Seaver & G. Moreland	6 & 5
J. Stout & J. Burke lost to F. Ouimet & G. Dunlap Jr.	7 & 6
E. Fiddian & E. McRuvie lost to D. Moe & W. Howell	5 & 4
SINGLES:	
Torrance ½–with Ouimet	Halved
Stout ½–with Sweetser	Halved
Hartley lost to Moreland	2 & 1
Burke ½–with Westland	Halved
Crawley bt. Voigt	1–hole
Hartley lost to McCarthy Jr.	3 & 2
Fiddian lost to Seaver	7 & 6
McRuvie lost to Dunlap Jr.	10 & 9

RESULT: USA, 9½. GB & IRE, 2½.

1934 ST. ANDREWS

CAPTAINS: HON. MICHAEL SCOTT AND FRANCIS OUIMET

FOURSOMES:	
R. Wethered & C. Tolley lost to J. Goodman & L. Little Jr.	8 & 6
H. Bentley & E. Fiddian lost to G. Moreland & J. Westland	6 & 5
Hon. M. Scott & S. McKinlay lost to H. Egan & M. Marston	3 & 2
E. McRuvie & J. McLean bt. F. Ouimet & G. Dunlap Jr.	4 & 2
SINGLES:	
Scott lost to Goodman	7 & 6
Tolley lost to Little Jr.	6 & 5
Crawley lost to Ouimet	5 & 4
McLean lost to Dunlap Jr.	4 & 3
Fiddian lost to Fischer	5 & 4
McKinlay lost to Moreland	3 & 1
McRuvie ½–with Westland	Halved
Torrance bt. Marston	4 & 3

RESULT: USA, 9½. GB & IRE, 2½.

1936 PINE VALLEY GC, N.J.

CAPTAINS: WILLIAM TWEDDELL AND FRANCIS OUIMET

FOURSOMES:	
H. Thomson & H. Bentley lost to J. Goodman & A. Campbell	7 & 5
J. McLean & J. Langley lost to R. Smith & E. White	8 & 7
G. Peters & J. Dykes ½–with C. Yates & W. Emery	Halved
G. Hill & C. Ewing ½–with H. Givan & G. Voigt	Halved
SINGLES:	
Thomson lost to Goodman	3 & 2
McLean lost to Campbell	5 & 4
Ewing lost to Fischer	8 & 7
Hill lost to Smith	11 & 9
Peters lost to Emery	1–hole
Dykes lost to Yates	8 & 7
Bentley ½–with Dunlap Jr.	Halved
Langley lost to White	6 & 5

RESULT: USA, 10½. GB & IRE, 1½.

1938 ST. ANDREWS

CAPTAINS: JOHN BECK AND FRANCIS OUIMET

FOURSOMES:	
H. Bentley & J. Bruen ½–with J. Fisher & C. Kocsis	Halved
G. Peters & H. Thomson bt. J. Goodman & N. Ward	4 & 2
A. Kyle & C. Stowe lost to C. Yates & R. Billows	3 & 2
F. Pennick & L. Crawley bt. R. Smith & F. Haas Jr.	3 & 1
SINGLES:	
Bruen lost to Yates	2 & 1
Thomson bt. Goodman	6 & 4
Crawley lost to Fischer	3 & 2
Stowe bt. Kocsis	2 & 1
Penninck lost to Ward	12 & 11
Ewing bt. Billows	1–hole
Peters bt. Smith	9 & 8
Kyle bt. Haas Jr.	5 & 4

RESULT: GB & IRE, 7½. USA, 4½.

1947 ST. ANDREWS

CAPTAINS: JOHN BECK AND FRANCIS OUIMET

FOURSOMES:	
J. B. Carr & C. Ewing lost to S. Bishop & Skee Riegel	3 & 2
L. Crawley & P. Lucas bt. H. Ward & S. Quick	5 & 4
A. Kyle & J. Wilson lost to W. Turnesa & A. Kammer J.r	5 & 4
R. White & C. Stowe bt. F. Stranahan & R. Chapman	4 & 3
SINGLES:	
Crawley lost to Ward	5 & 3
Carr bt. Bishop	5 & 3
Micklem lost to Riegel	6 & 5
Ewing lost to Turnesa	6 & 5
Stowe lost to Stranahan	2 & 1
White bt. Kammer Jr.	4 & 3
Wilson lost to Quick	8 & 6
Lucas lost to Chapman	4 & 3

RESULT: USA, 8. GB & IRE, 4.

1949 WINGED FOOT GC, N.Y.

CAPTAINS: LADDIE LUCAS AND FRANCIS OUIMET

FOURSOMES:	
J. B. Carr & R. White bt. R. Billows & W. Turnesa	3 & 2
J. Bruen & S. McCready lost to C. Kocsis & F. Stranahan	2 & 1
C. Ewing & G. Micklem lost to S. Bishop & Skee Riegel	9 & 7
K. Thom & A. Perowne lost to J. Dawson & B. McCormick	8 & 7
SINGLES:	
White bt. Turnesa	4 & 3
McCready lost to Stranahan	6 & 5
Bruen lost to Riegel	5 & 4
Carr lost to Dawson	5 & 3
Ewing lost to Coe	1–hole
Thom lost to Billows	2 & 1
Perowne lost to Kocsis	4 & 2
Micklem lost to McHale Jr	5 & 4

RESULT: USA, 10. GB & IRE, 2.

WALKER CUP RESULTS

1951 ROYAL BIRKDALE

CAPTAINS: RAYMOND OPPENHEIMER AND WILLIE TURNESA

Match	Result
FOURSOMES:	
R. White & J. B. Carr ½–with F. Stranahan & W. Campbell	Halved
C. Ewing & J. Langley ½–with C. Coe & J. McHale Jr.	Halved
N. Kyle & I. Caldwell lost to R. Chapman & R. Knowles Jr.	1–hole
J. Bruen & J. Morgan lost to W. Turnesa & S. Urzetta	1–hole
SINGLES:	
McCready lost to Urzetta	4 & 3
Carr bt. Stranahan	2 & 1
White bt. Coe	2 & 1
Langley lost to McHale Jr.	2–holes
Ewing lost to Campbell	5 & 4
Kyle bt. Turnesa	2–holes
Caldwell ½–with Paddock Jr.	Halved
Morgan lost to Chapman	7 & 6

RESULT: USA, 7½. GB & IRE, 4½.

1953 KITTANSETT GC, MASS

CAPTAINS: A. A. DUNCAN AND CHARLES YATES

Match	Result
FOURSOMES:	
J. B. Carr & R. White lost to S. Urzetta & K. Venturi	6 & 4
J. Langley & A. Perowne lost to H. Ward Jr. & J. Westland	9 & 8
J. Wilson & R. MacGregor lost to J. Jackson & G. Littler	3 & 2
G. Micklem & J. Morgan bt. W. Campbell & C. Coe	4 & 3
SINGLES:	
Carr lost to Ward Jr.	4 & 3
White bt. Chapman	1–hole
Micklem lost to Littler	5 & 3
MacGregor lost to Westland	7 & 5
Drew lost to Cherry	9 & 7
Wilson lost to Venturi	9 & 8
Morgan bt. Coe	3 & 2
Langley lost to Urzetta	3 & 2

RESULT: USA, 9. GB & IRE, 3.

1955 ST. ANDREWS

CAPTAINS: G. A. HILL AND BILL CAMPBELL

Match	Result
FOURSOMES:	
J. B. Carr & R. White lost to H. Ward Jr. & D. Cherry	1–hole
G. Micklem & J. Morgan lost to W. Patton & R. Yost	2 & 1
I. Caldwell & B. Millward lost to J. Conrad & D. Morey	3 & 2
D. Blair & J. Cater lost to B. Cudd & J. Jackson	5 & 4
SINGLES:	
White lost to Ward Jr.	6 & 5
Scrutton lost to Patton	2 & 1
Caldwell bt. Morey	1–hole
Carr lost to Cherry	5 & 4
Blair bt. Conrad	1–hole
Millward lost to Cudd	2–holes
Ewing lost to Jackson	6 & 4
Morgan lost to Yost	8 & 7

RESULT: USA, 10. GB & IRE, 2.

1957 MIMIKIHADA GC, MINNESOTA

CAPTAINS: GERALD MICKLEM AND CHARLES COE

Match	Result
FOURSOMES:	
J. B. Carr & F. Deighton lost to R. Baxter Jr. & W. Patton	2 & 1
F. Bussell & P. Scrutton lost to W. Campbell & F. Taylor Jr.	4 & 3
R. Jack & D. Sewell bt. A. Blum & C. Kocsis	1·hole
A. Shepperson & G. Wolstenholme ½–with H. Robbins Jr. & M. Rudolph	Halved
SINGLES:	
Jack lost to Patton	1–hole
Carr lost to Campbell	3 & 2
Thirlwell lost to Baxter Jr.	4 & 3
Deighton lost to Hyndman III	7 & 6
Bussell bt. Campbell	2 & 1
Sewell lost to Taylor Jr.	1–hole
Scrutton lost to Rudolph	3 & 2
Wolstenholme bt. Robbins Jr.	2 & 1

RESULT: USA, 8½. GB & IRE, 3½.

1959 MUIRFIELD GC, SCOTLAND

CAPTAINS: GERALD MICKLEM AND CHARLES COE

Match	Result
FOURSOMES:	
R. Jack & D. Sewell lost to H. Ward Jr. & F. Taylor Jr.	1–hole
J. B. Carr & G. Wolstenholme lost to W. Hyndman III & T. Aaron	1–hole
M. Bonnallack & A. Perowne lost to W. Patton & C. Coe	9 & 8
M. Lunt & A. Shepperson lost to H. Wettlaufer & J. Nicklaus	2 & 1
SINGLES:	
Carr bt Coe	2 & 1
Wolstenholme lost to Ward Jr	9 & 8
Jack bt Patton	5 & 3
Sewell lost to Hyndman III	4 & 3
Shepperson bt Aaron	2 & 1
Bonallack lost to Beman	2–holes
Lunt lost to Wettlaufer	6 & 5
Smith lost to Nicklaus	5 & 4

RESULT: USA, 9. GB & IRE, 3.

1961 SEATTLE GC, WASHINGTON

CAPTAINS: C. D. LAWRIE AND JACK WESTLAND

Match	Result
FOURSOMES:	
J. Walker & G. Chapman lost to D. Beman & J. Nicklaus	6 & 5
D. Blair & M. Christmas lost to C. Coe & D. Cherry	1–hole
J. B. Carr & G. Huddy lost to W. Hyndman III & R. Gardner	4 & 3
M. Bonallack & R. Shade lost to R. Cochran & E. Andrews	4 & 3
SINGLES:	
Bonallack lost to Beman	3 & 2
Lunt lost to Coe	5 & 4
Walker lost to Taylor Jr.	3 & 2
Frame lost to Hyndman III	7 & 6
Carr lost to Nicklaus	6 & 4
Christmas bt. Smith	3 & 2
Shade lost to Gardner	1–hole
Blair lost to Cherry	5 & 4

RESULT: USA, 11. GB & IRE, 1.

1963 TURNBERRY

CAPTAINS: C. D. LAWRIE AND R. S. TUFTS

Match	Result
FOURSOMES (1):	
M. Bonallack & S. Murray bt. W. Patton & R. Sikes	4 & 3
J. B. Carr & C. Green lost to D. Gray & L. Harris	2–holes
M. Lunt & D. Sheahan lost to D. Beman & C. Coe	5 & 3
D. Madeley & R. Shade ½–with R. Gardner & E. Updegraff	Halved
SINGLES (1):	
Murray bt. Beman	3 & 1
Christmas lost to Patton	3 & 2
Carr bt. Sikes	7 & 5
Sheahan bt. Harris	1–hole
Bonallack bt. Davies	1–hole
Saddler ½–with Coe	Halved
Shade bt. Gray	4 & 3
Lunt ½–with Smith	Halved
FOURSOMES (2):	
M. Bonallack & S. Murray lost to W. Patton & R. Sikes	1–hole
M. Lunt & D. Sheahan lost to D. Gray & L. Harris	3 & 2
C. Green & S. Saddler lost to R. Gardner & E. Updegraff	3 & 1
D. Madeley & R. Shade lost to D. Beman & C. Coe	3 & 2
SINGLES (2):	
Murray lost to Patton	3 & 2
Sheahan bt. Davies	1–hole
Carr lost to Updegraff	4 & 3
Bonallack lost to Harris	3 & 2
Lunt lost to Gardner	3 & 2
Saddler ½–with Beman	Halved
Shade bt. Gray	2 & 1
Green lost to Coe	4 & 3

RESULT: USA, 14. GB & IRE, 10.

1965 BALTIMORE GC, MD.

CAPTAINS: JOE CARR AND JOHNNY FLETCHER

Match	Result
FOURSOMES (1):	
M. Lunt & G. Cosh bt. W. Campbell & D. Gray	1–hole
M. Bonallack & C. Clark ½–with D. Beman & D. Allen	Halved
R. Foster & G. Clark lost to W. Patton & E. Tutwiler	5 & 4
P. Townsend & R. Shade bt. J. Hopkins & D. Eichelberger	2 & 1
SINGLES (1):	
Bonallack lost to Campbell	6 & 5
Foster lost to Beman	2–holes
Shade bt. Gray	3 & 1
Clark bt. Hopkins	5 & 3
Townsend bt. Patton	3 & 2
Saddler bt. Morey	2 & 1
Lunt bt. Updegraff	2 & 1
FOURSOMES (2):	
A. Saddler & R. Foster lost to W. Campbell & D. Gray	4 & 3
R. Shade & P. Townsend bt. D. Beman & D. Eichelberger	2 & 1
G. Cosh & M. Lunt lost to E. Tutwiler & W. Patton	2 & 1
C. Clark & M. Bonallack bt. D. Allen & D. Morey	2 & 1
SINGLES (2):	
Foster lost to Campbell	3 & 2
Saddler lost to Beman	1–hole
Shade lost to Tutwiler	5 & 3
Cosh bt. Allen	4 & 3
Townsend lost to Gray	1–hole
Clark ½–with Hopkins	Halved
Bonallack lost to Eichelberger	5 & 3
Lunt lost to Patton	4 & 2

RESULT: GB & IRE, 13. USA, 12.

1967 ROYAL ST. GEORGE'S, SANDWICH

CAPTAINS: JOE CAR AND JESSE SWEETSER

Match	Result
FOURSOMES (1):	
R. Shade & P. Oosterhuis ½–with R. Murphy Jr. & R. Cerrudo	Halved
R. Foster & A. Saddler lost to W. Campbell & W. Lewis	1–hole
M. Bonallack & M. Attenborough lost to D. Gray & E. Tutwiler	4 & 2
J. B. Carr & T. Craddock lost to R. Dickson & J. Grant	3 & 1
SINGLES (1):	
Shade lost to Campbell	2 & 1
Foster lost to Murphy	2 & 1
Bonallack ½–with Gray	Halved
Attenborough lost to Cerrudo	4 & 3
Oosterhuis lost to Dickson	6 & 4
Craddock lost to Lewis	2 & 1
Pirie ½–with Allen	Halved
Saddler bt. Fleckman	3 & 2
FOURSOMES (2):	
M. Bonallack & T. Craddock bt. R. Murphy & R. Cerrudo	2–holes
A. Saddler & A. Pirie lost to W. Campbell & W. Lewis	1–hole
R. Shade & P. Oosterhuis bt. D. Gray & E. Tutwiler	3 & 1
R. Foster & D. Millensted bt. D. Allen & M. Fleckman	2 & 1
SINGLES (2):	
Shade lost to Campbell	3 & 2
Bonallack bt. Murphy	4 & 2
Saddler bt. Gray	3 & 2
Foster ½–with Cerrudo	Halved
Pirie lost to Grant	1–hole
Craddock bt. Lewis	5 & 4
Oosterhuis lost to Grant	1–hole
Millensted lost to Tutwiler	5 & 1

RESULT: USA, 15. GB & IRE, 9.

WALKER CUP RESULTS

1969 MILWAUKEE GC, WISCONSIN

CAPTAINS: MICHAEL BONALLACK AND BILLY JOE PATTON

FOURSOMES (1):	
M. Bonallack & T. Craddock lost to M. Giles & S. Melynk	3 & 2
P. Benka & B. Critchley ½–with B. Fleisher & A. Miller	Halved
C. Green & A. Brooks bt. L. Wadkins & R. Siderowf	3 & 2
R. Foster & G. Marks lost to W. Hyndman & J. Inman	2 & 1
SINGLES (1):	
Bonallack ½–with Fleisher	Halved
Green lost to Giles	1–hole
Critchley lost to Miller	1–hole
Tupling lost to Siderowf	6 & 5
Benka bt. Mclnyk	3 & 1
Marks bt. Wadkins	1–hole
M. King lost to J. Bohmann	2 & 1
Foster lost to E. Updegraff	6 & 5
FOURSOMES (2):	
C. Green & A. Brooks ½–with M. Giles & S. Mclnyk	Halved
P. Benka & B. Critchley bt. B. Fleisher & A. Miller	2 & 1
R. Foster & M. King lost to R. Siderowf & L. Wadkins	6 & 5
M. Bonallack & P. Tupling bt. E. Updegraff & J. Bohmann	4 & 3
SINGLES (2):	
Bonallack bt. Fleisher	5 & 4
Critchley ½–with Siderowf	Halved
King lost to Miller	1–hole
Craddock ½–with Giles	Halved
Benka lost to Inman	2 & 1
Brooks bt. Bohmann	4 & 3
Green ½–with Hyndman	Halved
Marks bt. Updegraff	3 & 2

RESULT: USA, 13. GB & IRE, 11.

1973 THE COUNTRY CLUB, BROOKLINE, MASS.

CAPTAINS: DAVID MARSH AND JOHN SWEETSER

FOURSOMES (1):	
M. King & P. Hedges ½–with M. Giles & G. Koch	
H. Stuart & J. Davies lost to R. Siderowf & M. Pfeil	5 & 4
C. Green & W. Milne lost to D. Edwards & J. Ellis	2 & 1
R. Foster & T. Homer lost to M. West & D. Ballenger	2 & 1
SINGLES (1):	
Stuart lost to Giles	5 & 4
Bonallack lost to Siderowf	4 & 2
Davies bt. Koch	1–hole
Clark bt West	2 & 1
Foster lost to Edwards	2–holes
King bt. Killian	1–hole
Green bt. Rodgers	1–hole
Milne bt. Pfeil	4 & 3
FOURSOMES (2):	
T. Homer & R. Foster lost to M. Giles & G. Koch	7 & 5
H. Clark & J. Davies ½–with R. Siderowf & M. Pfeil	Halved
P. Hedges & M. King lost to D. Edwards & J. Ellis	2 & 1
H. Stuart & W. Milne lost to W. Rodgers & M. Killian	1–hole
SINGLES (2):	
Stuart bt. Ellis	5 & 4
Davies bt. Siderowf	3 & 2
Homer lost to Edwards	2 & 1
Green ½–with Giles	Halved
King lost to West	1–hole
Milne bt. Killian	2 & 1
Hedges ½–with Koch	Halved
Clark lost to Pfeil	1–hole

RESULT: USA, 14. GB & IRE, 10.

1977 SHINNECOCK HILLS, N.Y.

CAPTAINS: SANDY SADDLER AND R. W. OEHMIT

FOURSOMES (1):	
J. Fought & V. Heafner bt. P. McEvoy & A. Lyle	4 & 3
S. Simpson & L. Miller bt. J. Davies & M. Kelley	5 & 4
R. Siderowf & G. Hallberg lost to I. Hutcheon & P. Deeble	1–hole
J. Sigel & M. Brannan bt. A. Brodie & S. Martin	1–hole
SINGLES (1):	
Miller bt. McEvoy	2–holes
Fought bt. Hutcheon	4 & 3
Simpson bt. G. Murray	7 & 6
Heafner bt. Davies	4 & 3
B. Sander lost to Brodie	4 & 3
Hallberg lost to Martin	3 & 2
F. Ridley bt. Lyle	2–holes
Sigel bt. P. McKellar	5 & 3
FOURSOMES (2):	
Fought & Heafner bt. Hutcheon & Deeble	4 & 3
Miller & Simpson bt. McEvoy & Davies	2–holes
Siderowf & Sander lost to Brodie & Martin	6 & 4
Ridley & Brannan lost to Murray & Kelley	4 & 3
SINGLES (2):	
Miller bt. Martin	1–hole
Fought bt. Davies	2 & 1
Sander lost to Brodie	2 & 1
Hallberg bt. McEvoy	4 & 3
Siderowf lost to Kelley	2 & 1
Brannan lost to Hutcheon	2–holes
Ridley bt. Lyle	5 & 3
Sigel bt. Deeble	1–hole

RESULT: USA, 16. GB & IRE, 8.

1971 ST. ANDREWS

CAPTAINS: MICHAEL BONALLACK AND J. M. WINTERS

FOURSOMES (1):	
M. Bonallack & W. Humphreys bt. L. Wadkins & J. Simons	1–hole
C. Green & R. Carr bt. S. Mclnyk & M. Giles	1–hole
D. Marsh & G. Macgregor bt. A. Miller & J. Farquhar	2 & 1
J. Macdonald & R. Foster bt. W. Campbell & T. Kite	2 & 1
SINGLES (1):	
Green lost to Wadkins	1–hole
Bonallack lost to Giles	1–hole
Marks lost to Miller	1–hole
Macdonald lost to Mclnyk	3 & 2
Carr ½–with Hyndman	Halved
Humphreys lost to Gabrielsen	1–hole
Stuart bt. Farquhar	3 & 2
Foster lost to Kite	3 & 2
FOURSOMES (2):	
G. Marks & C. Green lost to S. Mclnyk & M. Giles	1–hole
H. Stuart & R. Carr bt. W. Wadkins & J. Gabrielsen	1–hole
D. Marsh & M. Bonallack lost to A. Miller & J. Farquhar	5 & 4
J. Macdonald & R. Foster ½–with W. Campbell & T. Kite	Halved
SINGLES (2):	
Bonallack lost to Wadkins	3 & 1
Stuart bt. Giles	2 & 1
Humphreys bt. Mclnyk	2 & 1
Green bt. Miller	1–hole
Carr bt. Simons	2–holes
Macgregor bt. Gabrielsen	1–hole
Marsh bt. Hyndman	1-hole
Marks lost to Kite	3 & 2

RESULT: GB & IRE, 13. USA, 11.

1975 ST. ANDREWS

CAPTAINS: DAVID MARSH AND ED UPDEGRAFF

FOURSOMES (1):	
M. James and G. Eyles bt. J. Pate and R. Siderowf	1–hole
J. Davies and M. Poxon lost to G. Burns & C. Stadler	5 & 4
C. Green and H. Stuart lost to J. Haas and C. Strange	2 & 1
C. Macgregor and I. Hutcheon lost to M. Giles and G. Koch	5 & 4
SINGLES (1):	
James bt. Pate	2 & 1
Davies ½–with Strange	Halved
P. Mulcare bt. Siderowf	3 & 2
Stuart lost to Koch	3 & 2
Poxon lost to J. Grace	3 & 1
Hutcheon ½–with W. Campbell	Halved
Eyles lost to Haas	2 & 1
Macgregor lost to Giles	3 & 2
FOURSOMES (2):	
Mulcare & Hutcheon bt. Pate & Siderowf	1–hole
Green & Stuart lost to Burns & Stadler	1–hole
James & Eyles bt. Campbell & Grace	5 & 3
Hedges & Davies lost to Haas & Strange	3 & 2
SINGLES (2):	
Hutcheon bt. Pate	3 & 2
Mulcare lost to Strange	4 & 3
James lost to Koch	5 & 4
Davies bt. Burns	2 & 1
Green lost to Grace	2 & 1
Macgregor lost to Stadler	3 & 2
Eyles lost to Campbell	2 & 1
Hedges ½–with Giles	Halved

RESULT: USA, 15. GB & IRE, 8½.

1979 MUIRFIELD, SCOTLAND

CAPTAINS: RODNEY FOSTER AND R. L. SIDEROWF

FOURSOMES (1):	
P. McEvoy & B. Marchbank lost to S. Hock and J. Sigel	1–hole
G. Goodwin & I. Hutcheon bt. M. West & H. Sutton	2–holes
G. Brand & M. Kelley lost to D. Fischesser and J. Holtgrieve	1–hole
A. Brodie & I. Carslaw bt. G. Moody & M. Gove	2 & 1
SINGLES (1):	
McEvoy ½–with Sigel	Halved
Davies lost to Clark	8 & 7
Hutcheon lost to Holtgrieve	6 & 4
Buckley lost to Hoch	9 & 7
Marchbank bt. Peck	1–hole
Godwin bt. Moody	3 & 2
Kelley bt. Fischesser	3 & 2
Brodie lost to Gove	3 & 2
FOURSOMES (2):	
Goodwin & Brand lost to Hock and Sigel	4 & 3
McEvoy & Marchbank bt. Fischesser and Holtgrieve	2 & 1
Kelley & Hutcheon ½–with West & Sutton	Halved
Carslaw & Brodie ½–with D. Clarke and Peck	Halved
SINGLES (2):	
McEvoy lost to Hoch	3 & 1
Brand lost to Clarke	2 & 1
Godwin lost to Gove	3 & 2
Hutcheon lost to Peck	2 & 1
Brodie bt. West	3 & 2
Kelley lost to Moody	3 & 2
Marchbank lost to Sutton	3 & 1
Carslaw lost to Sigel	2 & 1

RESULT: USA, 15½. GB & IRE, 8½.

WALKER CUP RESULTS

1981 CYPRESS POINT, CALIFORNIA

CAPTAINS: RODNEY FOSTER AND J. GABRIELSON

FOURSOMES (1):	
H. Sutton & J. Sigel lost to P. Walton & R. Rafferty	4 & 2
J. Holtgrieve & F. Fuhrer bt. R. Chapman & P. McEvoy	1–hole
B. Lewis & D. von Tacky bt. P. Deeble & I. Hutcheon	2 & 1
R. Commans & C. Pavin bt. D. Evans & P. Way	5 & 4
SINGLES (1):	
Sutton bt. Rafferty	
J. Rassett bt. C. Dalgleish	1–hole
Commans lost to Walton	1–hole
Lewis lost to Chapman	2 & 1
Pavin bt. Hutcheon	3 & 4
J. Mudd bt. J. Godwin	1–hole
von Tacky lost to Way	3 & 1
Sigel bt. McEvoy	4 & 2
FOURSOMES (2):	
Sutton & Sigel lost to Chapman & Way	1–hole
Holtgrieve & Fuhrer lost to Walton & Rafferty	6 & 4
Lewis & von Tacky lost to D. Evans & Dalgleish	3 & 2
Rassett & Mudd bt. Hutcheon & Godwin	5 & 4
SINGLES (2):	
Sutton lost to Chapman	1–hole
Holtgrieve bt. Rafferty	2 & 1
Fuhrer bt. Walton	4 & 2
Sigel bt. Way	6 & 5
Mudd bt. Dalgleish	7 & 5
Commans ½–with Godwin	Halved
Rassett bt. Deeble	4 & 3
Pavin ½–with Evans	Halved

RESULT: USA, 15. GB & IRE, 9.

1983 HOYLAKE

CAPTAINS: CHARLES GREEN AND JAY SIGEL

FOURSOMES (1):	
M. Lewis & M. Thompson lost to B. Lewis & J. Holtgrieve	7 & 6
G. MacGregor & P. Walton bt. J. Sigel & R. Fehr	3 & 1
L. Mann & A. Oldcorn bt. W. Hoffer & D. Tentis	5 & 4
S. Keppler & A. Pierse lost to W. Wood & B. Faxon	3 & 1
SINGLES (1):	
P. Parkin bt. N. Crosby	6 & 4
Mann lost to Holtgrieve	6 & 5
Oldcorn bt. B. Tuten	4 & 3
Walton bt. Sigel	1–hole
Keppler lost to Fehr	1–hole
D. Carrick lost to Faxon	3 & 1
Macgregor ½–with Wood	Halved
Pierse lost to Lewis	3 & 1
FOURSOMES (2):	
Macgregor & Walton lost to Crosby & Hoffer	2–holes
Parkin & M. Thompson bt. Faxon & Wood	1–hole
Mann & Oldcorn bt. Lewis & Holtgrieve	1–hole
Keppler & Pierse ½–with Sigel & Fehr	Halved
SINGLES (2):	
Walton bt. Wood	2 & 1
Parkin lost to Faxon	3 & 2
Macgregor lost to Fehr	2 & 1
Thompson lost to Tuten	3 & 2
Mann ½–with Tentis	Halved
Keppler lost to Lewis	6 & 5
Oldcorn bt. Holtgrieve	3 & 2
Carrick lost to Sigel	3 & 1

RESULT: USA, 13½. GB & IRE, 10½.

1985 PINE VALLEY GC, N.J.

CAPTAINS: CHARLES GREEN AND JAY SIGEL

FOURSOMES (1):	
C. Montgomerie & G. Macgregor lost to S. Verplank & J. Sigel	1–hole
J. Hawksworth & G. McGimpsey bt. D. Waldorf & S. Randolph	4 & 3
P. Baker & P. McEvoy bt. R. Sonnier & J. Haas	6 & 5
C. Bloice & S. Stephen ½–with M. Podolak & D. Love	Halved
SINGLES (1):	
McGimpsey lost to Verplank	2 & 1
P. Mayo lost to Randolph	5 & 4
Hawksworth ½–with Sonnier	Halved
Montgomerie lost to Sigel	5 & 4
McEvoy bt. Lewis	2 & 1
Macgregor bt. C. Burroughs	2–holes
D. Gilford lost to Waldorf	4 & 2
Stephen bt. Haas	2 & 1
FOURSOMES (2):	
Mayo & Montgomerie ½–with Verplank & Sigel	Halved
Hawksworth & McGimpsey lost to Randolph & Haas	3 & 2
Baker & McEvoy lost to Lewis & Burroughs	2 & 1
Bloice & Stephen lost to Podolak & Love	3 & 2
SINGLES (2):	
McGimpsey ½–with Randolph	Halved
Montgomerie lost to Verplank	1–hole
Hawksworth bt. Sigel	4 & 3
McEvoy lost to Love	5 & 3
Baker bt. Sonnier	5 & 4
Macgregor bt. Burroughs	3 & 2
Bloice lost to Lewis	4 & 3
Stephen bt. Waldorf	2 & 1

RESULT: USA, 13. GB & IRE, 11.

1987 SUNNINGDALE

CAPTAINS: S. RIDLEY AND GEOFFREY MARKS

FOURSOMES (1):	
Alexander & Mayfair bt. Montgomerie & Shaw	5 & 4
Kite & Mattiace bt. Curry & Mayo	2 & 1
Lewis & Loeffler bt. Macgregor & Robinson	2 & 1
Sigel & Andrade bt. McHenry & Girvan	3 & 2
SINGLES (1):	
B. Alexander lost to D. Curry	2–holes
Sorenson lost to C. Montgomerie	3 & 2
J. Sigel bt. Eggo	3 & 2
B. Andrade bt. J. Robinson	7 & 5
Montgomery bt. J. McHenry	1–hole
B. Lewis bt. P. Girvan	3 & 2
B. Mayfair bt. D. Carrick	2–holes
C. Kite lost to G. Shaw	1–hole
FOURSOMES (2):	
Lewis & Loeffler bt. Curry & Carrick	4 & 3
Kite & Mattiace bt. Montgomerie & Shaw	1–hole
Sorenson & Montgomery bt. Mayo & Macgregor	4 & 3
Siegel & Andrade lost to McHenry & Robinson	4 & 2
SINGLES (2):	
B. Alexander bt. D. Curry	5 & 4
B. Andrade lost to C. Montgomerie	4 & 2
B. Loeffler lost to J. McHenry	3 & 2
Sorenson ½–with G. Shaw	Halved
L. Mattiace lost to J. Robinson	1–hole
B. Lewis bt. D. Carrick	3 & 2
J. Sigel bt. P. Girvan	6 & 5
B. Mayfair bt. Eggo	1–hole

RESULT: USA, 16½. GB & IRE, 7½.

CURTIS CUP

1932 WENTWORTH

CAPTAINS: JOYCE WETHERED AND MARION HOLLINS

FOURSOMES:	
J. Wethered & W. Morgan lost to G. Collett Vare & Mrs. O. S. Hill	1–hole
E. Wilson & J. B. Watson lost to V. Van Wic & H. Hicks	2 & 1
M. Gourlay & D. Park lost to M. Orcutt & Mrs. L. D. Cheney	1–hole
SINGLES:	
J. Wethered bt. G. Collett Vare	6 & 4
E. Wilson bt. H. Hicks	2 & 1
W. Morgan lost to V. Van Wic	2 & 1
D. Fishwick bt. M. Orcutt	4 & 3
M. Gourlay ½–with Mrs. O. S. Hill	Halved
E. Corlett lost to Mrs. L. D. Cheney	4 & 3

RESULT: USA, 5½. GB & IRE, 3½.

1934 CHEVY CHASE, MD.

CAPTAINS: DORIS CHAMBERS AND GLENNA COLLETT VARE

FOURSOMES:	
M. Gourlay & P. Barton ½–with V. Van Wic & C. Glutting	Halved
D. Fishwick & W. Morgan lost to M. Orcutt & Mrs. L. D. Cheney	2–holes
D. Plumpton & Mrs. J. B. Walker bt. Mrs. O. S. Hill & L. Robinson	2 & 1
SINGLES:	
D. Fishwick lost to V. Van Wic	2 & 1
M. Gourlay lost to M. Orcutt	4 & 2
P. Barton lost to Mrs. L. D. Cheney	7 & 5
W. Morgan lost to C. Glutting	3 & 2
D. Plumpton lost to Mrs. O. S. Hill	3 & 2
Mrs. J. Walker bt. Mrs. Goldthwaite	3 & 2

RESULT: USA, 6½. GB & IRE, 2½.

1936 GLENEAGLES

CAPTAINS: DORIS CHAMBERS AND GLENNA COLLETT VARE

FOURSOMES:	
W. Morgan & M. Ross Garon ½–with G. Collett Vare & P. Berg	Halved
P. Barton & Mrs. J. B. Walker lost to M. Orcutt & Mrs. L. D. Cheney	2 & 1
J. Anderson & Mrs. A. M. Holm bt. Mrs. O. S. Hill & C. Glutting	3 & 2
SINGLES:	
Morgan lost to Collett Vare	3 & 2
Holm bt. Berg	4 & 3
Barton lost to Glutting	1–hole
Walker bt. Orcutt	1–hole
Anderson bt. Cheney	1–hole
Ross Garon bt. Hill	7 & 5

RESULT: GB & IRE, 4½. USA, 4½.

1938 ESSEX COUNTRY CLUB, MASS.

CAPTAINS: MRS. WALLACE-WILLIAMS AND FRANCES E. STREBBINS

FOURSOMES:	
Mrs. M. Holm & C. Tiernan bt. Mrs. A. Page Jr. & M. Orcutt	2–holes
J. Anderson & E. Corlett bt. G. Collett Vare & P. Berg	1–hole
Mrs. J. B. Walker & P. Wade ½–with M. Miley & K. Hemphill	Halved
SINGLES:	
Holm lost to Page Jr.	6 & 5
Anderson lost to Berg	1–hole
Corlett lost to Miley	2 & 1
Walker lost to Collett Vare	2 & 1
Tiernan beat Orcutt	2 & 1
Baird lost to Glutting	1–hole

RESULT: USA, 5½. GB & IRE, 3½.

1948 ROYAL BIRKDALE

CAPTAINS: DORIS E. CHAMBERS AND GLENNA COLLETT VARE

FOURSOMES:	
J. Gordon & J. Donald bt. L. Suggs & G. Lenczyk	
P. Garvey & Z. Bolton lost to G. Collett Vare & D. Kirby	4 & 3
M. Ruttle & Mrs. V. Reddan lost to D. Kielty & Mrs. J. A. Page Jr.	5 & 4
SINGLES:	
Garvey ½–with Suggs	Halved
Donald bt. Kirby	2–holes
J. Gordon lost to Lenczyk	5 & 3
Holm lost to Page Jr.	3 & 2
Ruttle lost to Riley	3 & 2
Bolton lost to Kielty	2 & 1

RESULT: USA, 6½. GB & IRE, 2½.

CURTIS CUP

1950 COUNTRY CLUB OF BUFFALO, N.Y.

CAPTAINS: MRS. A. C. CRITCHLEY AND GLENNA COLLETT VARE

FOURSOMES:	
J. Donald & Mrs. G. Valentine lost to D. Porter & B. Hanson	3 & 2
F. Stephens & E. Price bt. Sigel & P. Kirk	1–hole
P. Garvey & J. Bisgood lost to D. Kielty & D. Kirby	6 & 5
SINGLES:	
Stephens ½–with Porter	Halved
Valentine lost to Riley	7 & 6
Donald lost to Hanson	6 & 5
Garvey lost to Kielty	3 & 1
Bisgood lost to Kirk	1–hole
Price lost to Lenczyk	5 & 4

RESULT: USA, 7½. GB & IRE, 1½.

1952 MUIRFIELD

CAPTAINS: LADY KATHERINE CAIRNS AND MRS. FRANK GOLDTHWAITE

FOURSOMES:	
J. Donald & E. Price bt. D. Kirby & G. DeMoss	
F. Stephens & Mrs. G. Valentine lost to C. Doran & M. Lindsay	6 & 4
M. Paterson & P. Garvey bt. P. Riley & P. O'Sullivan	2 & 1
SINGLES:	
Donald lost to Kirby	1–hole
Stephens bt. Lindsay	2 & 1
Paterson lost to Riley	6 & 4
Bisgood bt. Murray	6 & 5
Garvey lost to Doran	3 & 2
Price bt. DeMoss	3 & 2

RESULT: GB & IRE, 5. USA, 4.

1954 MERION GC, PA.

CAPTAINS: MRS. JOHN BECK AND MRS. HARRISON FLIPPIN

FOURSOMES:	
F. Stephens & E. Price lost to M. L. Faulk & P. Riley	6 & 4
Mrs. G. Valentine & P. Garvey lost to C. Doran & P. Lesser	6 & 5
Mrs. R. T. Peel & J. Robertson lost to D. Kirby & B. Romack	6 & 5
SINGLES:	
Stephens bt. Faulk	1–hole
Bisgood lost to Doran	4 & 3
Price lost to Riley	9 & 8
Garvey bt. Kirby	3 & 1
Valentine lost to De Moss Smith	4 & 3
Robertson bt. Ziske	3 & 1

RESULT: USA, 6. GB & IRE, 3.

1956 PRINCE'S GC, SANDWICH

CAPTAINS: MRS. SLOAN BOLTON AND MRS. H. FLIPPIN

FOURSOMES:	
Mrs. G. Valentine & P. Garvey lost to P. Lesser & M. Smith	2 & 1
Mrs. P. Smith & E. Price beat Riley & B. Romack	5 & 3
J. Robertson & V. Anstey lost to M. A. Downey & P. J. Cudone	6 & 4
SINGLES:	
Valentine bt. Lesser	6 & 4
Garvey lost to Smith	9 & 8
Smith bt. Riley	1–hole
Robertson lost to Romack	6 & 4
Ward bt. Downey	4 & 3
Price bt. Nelson	7 & 6

RESULT: GB & IRE, 5. USA, 4.

1958 BRAE BURN GC, MASS.

CAPTAINS: DAISY FERGUSON AND MRS. CHARLES DENNEHY

FOURSOMES:	
Mrs. A. Bonallack & E. Price bt. B. Romack & P. Riley	2 & 1
J. Robertson & F. Smith bt. J. A. Gunderson & A. Quast	3 & 2
B. Jackson & Mrs. G. Valentine lost to B. McIntire & A. Johnstone	6 & 5
SINGLES:	
Valentine lost to Gunderson	2–holes
Bonallack ½–with McIntire	Halved
Price lost to Quast	4 & 2
Robertson bt. Johnstone	3 & 2
Jackson lost to Romack	4 & 2
Smith bt. Riley	2–holes

RESULT: GB & IRE, 4½. USA, 4½.

1960 LINDRICK

CAPTAINS: MAUREEN GARRETT AND MRS. HENRI PRUNARET

FOURSOMES:	
A. Bonallack & E. Price bt. J. A. Gunderson & B. McIntire	1–hole
B. McCorkindale & J. Robertson lost to J. Eller & A. Quast	4 & 2
R. Porter & F. Smith lost to J. Goodwin & A. C. Johnstone	3 & 2
SINGLES:	
Price ½–with McIntire	Halved
Bonallack lost to Gunderson	2 & 1
Robertson lost to Quast	2–holes
Garvey lost to Eller	4 & 3
McCorkindale lost to Bell	8 & 7
Porter bt. Goodwin	1–hole

RESULT: USA, 6½. GB & IRE. 2½.

1962 BROADMOOR, COLORADO

CAPTAINS: FRANCIS SMITH AND POLLY RILEY

FOURSOMES:	
A. Bonallack & Mrs. M. Spearman lost to A. Decker & B. McIntire	7 & 5
A. Irvin & S. Vaughan lost to C. A. Creed & J. A. Gunderson	4 & 3
Mrs. A. Frearson & R. Porter beat J. Ashley & A. Johnstone	8 & 7
SINGLES:	
Spearman lost to Decker	5 & 4
Bonallack lost to Gunderson	2 & 1
Frearson bt. Bell	8 & 7
Roberts lost to Preuss	1–hole
Bonallack lost to Creed	6 & 5
Vaughan lost to McIntire	5 & 4

RESULT: USA, 8. GB & IRE, 1.

1964 ROYAL PORTCAWL

CAPTAINS: ELSIE CORLETT AND MRS. T. W. HAWES

FOURSOMES (1):	
Mrs. M. Spearman & A. Bonallack bt. B. McIntire & P. Preuss	2 & 1
B. Jackson & S. Armitage lost to C. Sorenson & B. White	8 & 6
S. Vaughan & R. Porter bt. J. A. Gunderson & N. Roth	3 & 2
SINGLES (1):	
Spearman ½–with McIntire	Halved
Bonallack lost to Gunderson	6 & 5
Lawrence lost to Conley	1–hole
Greenhalgh lost to White	3 & 2
Jackson bt. Sorenson	4 & 2
Porter bt. Roth	1–hole
FOURSOMES (2):	
Mrs. M. Spearman & A. Bonallack bt. B. McIntire & P. Preuss	6 & 5
S. Armitage & B. Jackson lost to J. A. Gunderson & N. Roth	2–holes
R. Porter & S. Vaughan ½–with C. Sorenson & B. F. White	Halved
SINGLES (2):	
Spearman ½–with Gunderson	Halved
Lawrence lost to McIntire	4 & 2
Greenhalgh bt. Preuss	5 & 2
Jackson lost to Conley	1–hole
Bonallack lost to White	3 & 2
Porter lost to Sorenson	3 9 2

RESULT: USA, 10½. GB & IRE, 7½.

1966 CASCADES GC, HOT SPRINGS, VA.

CAPTAINS: MRS. S. M. BOLTON AND DOROTHY G. PORTER

FOURSOMES (1):	
A. Bonallack & S. Armitage lost to J. Ashley & P. Preuss	1–hole
Mrs. I. C. Robertson & J. Hastings ½–with A. Q. Welts & B. McIntire	Halved
E. Chadwick & P. Tredinnick lost to B. Boddie & C. Sorenson Flenniken	1–hole
SINGLES (1):	
Robertson lost to Ashley	1–hole
Armitage ½–with Welts	Halved
Bonallack lost to Boddie	3 & 2
Chadwick lost to Roth Syms	2–holes
Burke bt. Sigel Wilson	3 & 1
Fowler lost to Sorenson Flenniken	3 & 2
FOURSOMES (2):	
A. Bonallack & S. Armitage lost to J. Ashley & P. Preuss	3 & 1
E. Chadwick & L. Burke bt. A. Q. Welts & B. McIntire	1–hole
Mrs. I. C. Robertson & J. Hastings lost to B. Boddie & C. Sorenson Flenniken	2 & 1
SINGLES (2):	
Bonallack bt. Ashley	2 & 1
Robertson ½–with Welts	Halved
Armitage lost to Boddie	3 & 2
Tredinnick ½–with Roth Syms	Halved
Chadwick lost to Preuss	3 & 2
Burke lost to Sorenson Flenniken	2 & 1

RESULT: USA, 13. GB & IRE, 5.

1966 ROYAL CO. DOWN GC, IRELAND

CAPTAINS: MRS. S. M. BOLTON AND MRS. ROBERT MONSTED

FOURSOMES (1):	
Mrs. I. C. Robertson & A. Irvin bt. S. Hamlin & A. Q. Welts	6 & 5
M. Pickard & V. Saunders bt. M. L. Dill & P. Conley	3 & 2
A. Howard & P. Tredinnick lost to P. Preuss & J. Ashley	1–hole
SINGLES (1):	
Irvin bt. Welts	3 & 2
Saunders lost to Hamlin	1–hole
Robertson lost to Albers	1–hole
Jackson ½–with Conley	Halved
Oxley ½–with Preuss	Halved
Pickard bt. Ashley	2–holes
FOURSOMES (2):	
Mrs. I. C. Roberts & A. Irvin ½–with M. L. Dill & P. Conley	
M. Pickard & V. Saunders lost to S. Hamlin & A. Q. Welts	2 & 1
D. Oxley & P. Tredinnick lost to P. Preuss & J. Ashley	5 & 4
SINGLES (2):	
Irvin bt. Hamlin	3 & 2
Robertson ½–with Welts	Halved
Saunders ½–with Albers	Halved
Pickard lost to Conley	1–hole
Howard lost to Dill	4 & 2
Jackson lost to Preuss	2 & 1

RESULT: USA, 10½. GB & IRE, 7½.

CURTIS CUP

1970 BRAE BURN GC, MASS.

CAPTAINS: JEANNE BISGOOD AND MRS. PHILIP CUDONE

Match	Result
FOURSOMES (1):	
D. Oxley & M. McKenna bt. S. Hamlin & J. Bastanchury	4 & 3
Mrs. I. C. Robertson & A. Irvin lost to P. Preuss & M. Wilkinson	4 & 3
M. Everard & J. Greenhalgh bt. C. Hill & J. Fassinger	5 & 3
SINGLES (1):	
Oxley lost to Bastanchury	5 & 3
Irvin lost to Wilkinson	1–hole
Robertson ½–with Hamlin	Halved
McKenna bt. Preuss	4 & 2
Pickard lost to Hager	5 & 4
Greenhalgh lost to Dye Jr.	1–hole
FOURSOMES (2):	
D. Oxley & M. McKenna lost to P. Preuss & M. Wilkinson	6 & 4
Mrs. I. C. Robertson & A. Irwin lost to S. Hamlin & J. Bastanchury	1–hole
M. Everard & J. Greenhalgh ½–with C. Hill & Mrs. P. Dye Jr.	Halved
SINGLES (2):	
Oxley ½–with Hamlin	Halved
Irvin lost to Bastanchury	4 & 3
Robertson lost to Preuss	1–hole
Greenhalgh bt. Wilkinson	6 & 4
Everard bt. Hager	4 & 3
McKenna lost to Hill	2 & 1

RESULT: USA, 11½. GB & IRE, 6½.

1972 WESTERN GALLES

CAPTAINS: MRS. F. SMITH & MRS. J. CRAWFORD

Match	Result
FOURSOMES (1):	
M. Everard & B. Huke lost to L. Baugh & Mrs. M. Kirouac	2 & 1
Mrs. I. C. Robertson & Mrs. D. Frearson bt. J. Booth & B. McIntire	2 & 1
M. Walker & M. McKenna bt. B. Barry & H. Stacy	1–hole
SINGLES (1):	
Walker ½–with Baugh	Halved
Robertson lost to Booth	3 & 1
Everard lost to Kirouac	4 & 3
Oxley lost to McIntire	4 & 3
Phillips bt. Smith	2–holes
McKenna lost to Barry	2 & 1
FOURSOMES (2):	
M. Walker & M. McKenna bt. L. Baugh & Mrs. M. Kirouac	3 & 2
M. Everard & B. Huke lost to J. Booth & B. McIntire	5 & 4
Mrs. I. C. Robertson & Mrs. D. Frearson ½–with B. Barry & H. Stacey	Halved
SINGLES (2):	
Robertson lost to Baugh	6 & 5
Everard bt. McIntire	6 & 5
Walker bt. Booth	1–hole
McKenna bt. Kirouac	3 & 1
Frearson lost to Smith	3 & 1
Phillips lost to Barry	3 & 1

RESULT: USA, 10. GB & IRE, 8.

1974 SAN FRANCISCO GC, CALIFORNIA

CAPTAINS: MRS. BELLE ROBERTSON AND MRS. ALLISON CHOATE

Match	Result
FOURSOMES (1):	
M. McKenna & J. Greenhalgh ½–with C. Semple & C. Hill	Halved
J. Lee-Smith & C. Le Feuvre lost to A. Sander & J. Booth	6 & 5
M. Walker & M. Everard bt. Budke & Lauer	5 & 4
SINGLES (1):	
Walker bt. Semple	2 & 1
McKenna lost to Booth	5 & 3
Everard lost to Massey	1–hole
Lee–Smith lost to Lauer	6 & 4
Greenhalgh lost to Barry	1–hole
Perkins ½–with Hill	Halved
FOURSOMES (2):	
M. McKenna & M. Walker lost to A. Sander & J. Booth	5 & 4
M. Everard & C. Le Feuvre lost to M. Budke & B. Lauer	5 & 3
J. Greenhalgh & T. Perkins bt. C. Semple & C. Hill	3 & 2
SINGLES (2):	
Everard lost to Sander	4 & 3
Greenhalgh lost to Booth	7 & 5
Le Feuvre lost to Massey	6 & 5
Walker lost to Semple	2 & 1
Perkins lost to Budke	5 & 4
McKenna bt. Lauer	2 & 1

RESULT: USA, 13. GB & IRE, 5.

1976 ROYAL LYTHAM & ST. ANNE'S

CAPTAINS: BELLE ROBERTSON AND BARBARA MCINTIRE

Match	Result
FOURSOMES (1):	
M. McKenna and J. Greenhalgh lost to B. Daniel and C. Hill	3 & 2
Mrs. D. Henson and S. Cadden lost to D. Massey and D. Horton	6 & 5
A. Irvin and T. Perkins lost to Mrs. N. Syms and C. Semple	3 & 2
SINGLES (1):	
Irvin lost to Daniel	4 & 3
Henson bt. Hill	1–hole
Cadden lost to Lopez	3 & 1
McKenna lost to Syms	1–hole
Perkins lost to Massey	1–hole
Greenhalgh ½–with Barrow	Halved
FOURSOMES (2):	
A. Irvin and S. Cadden lost to B. Daniel and C. Hill	4 & 3
Mrs. D. Henson and T. Perkins bt. C. Semple and Mrs. N. Syms	2 & 1
M. McKenna and Mrs. A. Stant lost to N. Lopez and B. Barrow	4 & 2
SINGLES (2):	
Henson lost to Daniel	3 & 2
Greenhalgh bt. Syms	2 & 1
Cadden lost to Horton	6 & 5
Lee-Smith lost to Massey	3 & 2
Perkins bt. Hill	1–hole
McKenna bt. Semple	1–hole

RESULT: USA, 11½. GB & IRE, 6½.

1978 APAWAMIS GC, N.Y.

CAPTAINS: CAROL COMBOY AND HELEN SIGEL WILSON

Match	Result
FOURSOMES (1):	
J. Greenhalgh and V. Marvin bt. B. Daniel and B. Goldsmith	3 & 2
M. Everard and M. Thompson bt. C. Hill and L. Smith	2 & 1
T. Perkins & M. McKenna ½–with P. Cornett & Carolyn Hill	Halved
SINGLES (1):	
Marvin lost to Daniel	5 & 4
Everard bt. Uihlein	7 & 6
Uzielli lost to Smith	4 & 3
Greenhalgh lost to Hill	2 & 1
Caldwell ½–with Carolyn Hill	Halved
Perkins lost to Oliver	2 & 1
FOURSOMES (2):	
M. Everard and M. Thomson lost to Cynthia Hill and L. Smith	1–hole
T. Perkins and M. McKenna lost to B. Goldsmith and B. Daniel	1–hole
J. Greenhalgh & V. Marvin lost to Mrs. N. Uihlein & Mrs. J. Oliver	4 & 3
SINGLES (2):	
McKenna lost to Daniel	2 & 1
Caldwell lost to Cornett	3 & 2
Thomson bt. Cynthia Hill	2 & 1
Perkins lost to Smith	2–holes
Greenhalgh ½–with Oliver	Halved
Everard ½–with Uihlein	Halved

RESULT: USA, 12. GB & IRE, 6.

1980 ST. PIERRE GC, CHEPSTOW

CAPTAINS: CAROL COMBOY AND NANCY ROTH SYMS

Match	Result
FOURSOMES (1):	
M. McKenna & C. Nesbitt ½–with L. Smith & T. Moody	Halved
Mrs. T. Thomas & G. Steward lost to P. Sheehan & L. Castillo	5 & 3
M. Madill & Mrs. C. Caldwell ½–with Mrs. J. Oliver & C. Semple	Halved
SINGLES (1):	
McKenna lost to Sheehan	3 & 2
Nesbitt ½–with Smith	Halved
Connachan lost to Goldsmith	2–holes
Madill lost to Semple	4 & 3
Moore ½–with Hafeman	Halved
Caldwell lost to Oliver	1–hole
FOURSOMES (2):	
Mrs. C. Caldwell & M. Madill lost to P. Sheehan & L. Castillo	3 & 2
C. Nesbitt & M. McKenna lost to L. Smith & T. Moody	6 & 5
Mrs. T. Thomas & L. Moore lost to Mrs. J. Oliver & C. Semple	1–hole
SINGLES (2):	
Madill lost to Sheehan	5 & 4
McKenna bt. Castillo	5 & 4
Connachan lost to Hafeman	6 & 5
Stewart bt. Smith	5 & 4
Moore bt. Goldsmith	1–hole
Thomas lost to Semple	4 & 3

RESULT: USA, 13. GB & IRE, 5.

1982 DENVER, COLORADO

CAPTAINS: MAIRE O'DONNELL AND BETTY PROBASCO

Match	Result
FOURSOMES (1):	
Mrs. Robertson & M. McKenna lost to J. Inkster & C. Semple	5 & 4
K. Douglas & J. Soulsby ½–with K. Baker & L. Smith	Halved
G. Stewart & J. Connachan lost to A. Benz & C. Hanlon	2 & 1
SINGLES (1):	
McKenna lost to Benz	2 & 1
Connachan lost to Hanlon	5 & 4
Aitken lost to McDougall	2–holes
Robertson lost to Baker	7 & 6
Soulsby bt. Oliver	2–holes
Douglas lost to Inkster	7 & 6
FOURSOMES (2):	
J. Connachan & W. Aitken lost to J. Inkster & C. Semple	3 & 2
K. Douglas & J. Soulsby lost to K. Baker & L. Smith	1–hole
M. McKenna & Mrs. Robertson bt. A. Benz and C. Hanlon	1–hole
SINGLES (2):	
Douglas lost to Inkster	7 & 6
Stewart lost to Baker	4 & 3
Thomas lost to Oliver	5 & 4
Soulsby lost to McDougall	2 & 1
McKenna lost to Semple	1–hole
Robertson bt. Smith	5 & 3

RESULT: USA, 14½. GB & IRE, 3½.

1984 MUIRFIELD, SCOTLAND

CAPTAINS: DIANE BAILEY AND PHYLLIS PREUSS

Match	Result
FOURSOMES (1):	
C. Waite & B. New bt. J. Pacillo & A. Sander	2–holes
J. Thornhill & P. Grice ½–with L. Smith & J. Rosenthal	Halved
M. McKenna & L. Davies lost to M. Widman & H. Farr	1–hole
SINGLES (1):	
Thornhill ½–with Pacillo	Halved
Waite lost to Hammel	4 & 2
Hourihane lost to Rosenthal	3 & 1
Thomas bt. Howe	2 & 1
Grice bt. Sander	2–holes
New lost to Widman	4 & 3
FOURSOMES (2):	
C. Waite & B. New lost to L. Smith & J. Rosenthal	3 & 1
J. Thornhill & P. Grice bt. M. Widman & H. Farr	2 & 1
V. Thomas & C. Hourihane ½–with D. Howe & P. Hammel	Halved
Singles (2):	
Thornhill lost to Pacillo	3 & 2
Davies bt. Sander	1–hole
Waite bt. Smith	5 & 4
Grice lost to Howe	2–holes
New lost to Farr	6 & 5
Hourihane bt. Hammel	2 & 1

RESULT: USA, 9½. GB & IRE, 8½.

1986 PRAIRIE DUNES, KANSAS

CAPTAINS: DIANE BAILEY AND JUDY BELL

Match	Result
FOURSOMES (1):	
P. Johnson & K. Davies bt. D. Mochrie & D. Ammaccapane	2 & 1
L. Behan & J. Thornhill bt. K. Kessler & C. Shreyer	7 & 6
B. Robertson & M. McKenna bt. K. Gardner & K. McCarthy	1–hole
SINGLES (1):	
Johnson bt. Shannon	1–hole
Thornhill bt. Williams	4 & 3
Behan bt. Ammaccapane	4 & 3
Thomas lost to Kessler	3 & 2
Hourihane lost to Schreyer	2 & 1
Davies ½–with Mochrie	Halved
FOURSOMES (2):	
P. Johnson & P. Davies bt. D. Mochrie & D. Ammaccapane	1–hole
L. Behan & J. Thornhill bt. L. Shannon & K. Williams	5 & 3
B. Robertson & M. McKenna ½–with K. Gardner & K. McCarthy	Halved
SINGLES (2):	
Thornhill ½–with Shannon	Halved
Johnson bt. McCarthy	5 & 3
Behan lost to Gardner	1–hole
Thomas bt. Williams	4 & 3
Davies ½–with Kessler	Halved
Hourihane bt. Schreyer	5 & 3

RESULT: GB & IRE, 13. USA, 5.

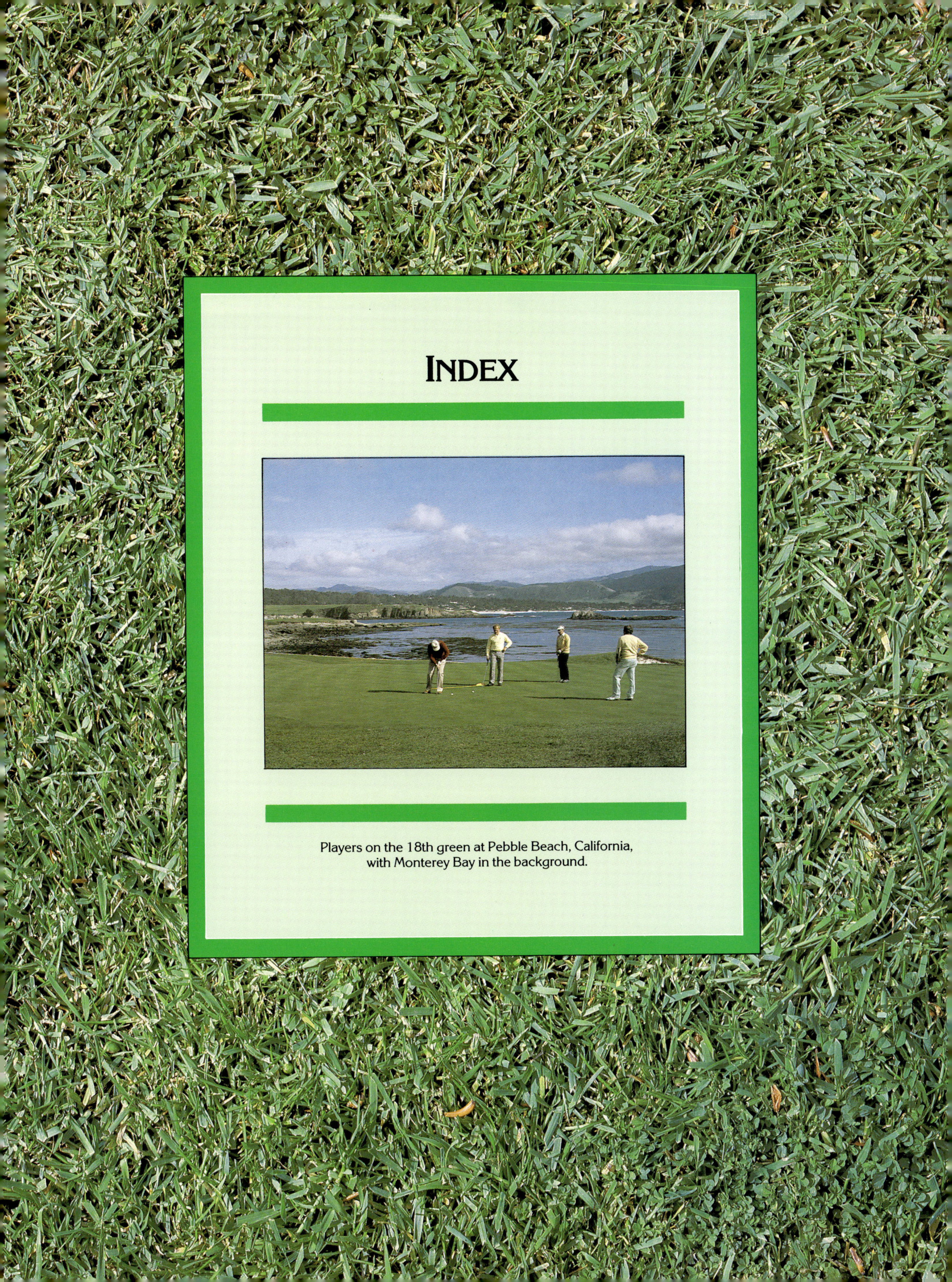

INDEX

Players on the 18th green at Pebble Beach, California, with Monterey Bay in the background.

Page numbers in *italics* refer to captions and illustrations.

A

B

C

D

E

F

G

H

I

J

K

L

M

N

O

P

T

U

V

W

Y

Z

• ACKNOWLEDGEMENTS •

The contributors and publishers would like to thank: H A (Bud) Bottomley, president of Llandrindod Wells Golf Club; Douglas Caird, *Golf World Magazine;* N (Mandy) Mitchell-Innes, Rolls of Monmouth Golf Club; *Badminton Magazine of Sports and Pastimes* for extracts from 'Golf in Portugal' by Ethel M Skeffington (1897) and for information on golf in Japan from an article by H E Daunt (1906). The contributors would also like to acknowledge their debt to numerous books on the Royal and Ancient game without which research for this book would have been impossible.

• PICTURE CREDITS •

Key: *t* = top; *b* = bottom; *l* = left; *r* = right; *c* = centre.

The contributors and publishers had made every effort to identify the copyright owners of the pictures used in this publication; they apologize for any omissions and would like to thank the following:

All-sport (UK) Ltd: 110 *b*, 111, 114/115, 115 *b*, 130/131, 131 *b*, 138, 138–140, 144–149, 150, 159, 163, 169 *r*, 172, 183 *t*, 187–189, 191, 194, 201 *b* (photos David Cannon); 112/113, (photo Adrian Murrell); 152/153, 201 *t*, 205 *t*, 219 *b*, 221 *b*, 248/249, 250 *b*, 251/252, 253, 255, 264 *r*, 265 *l*, 266 *tl*, 267 (photos David Cannon) 269 (photo Simon Bruty) 271 *l*, 276 *b* (photo Don Morley), 277/279 (photo David Cannon) 281, 282 *b*, 282/283, 283, 284, 285, 286 (photo David Cannon); **Bridgeman Art Library:** 209, 210, 211 (courtesy of National Gallery, London); **Course Guide Publications Ltd:** 113 *t*; **Peter Dazeley:** 108, 109, 109, 110 *t*, 122/123, 123, 141 *b*, 164/165, 170/171, 177, 178/179, 184/185, 190/191, 195, 254, 256, 258, 262 *bl*, *br*, 273 *r*, 275, 276 *b*, 287, 289, 292/293, 295, 298 *t*; **Courtesy The Gleneagles Hotel:** 126; **Michael Hobbs Collection:** 113 *b*, 115 *t*, 116 *l*, 117 *b*, 121 *b*, 125 *r*, 127, 136/137, 141 *t*, 142/143, 147 *b*, 149 *b*, 151, 153, 155–158, 162 *b*, 164, 169 *l*, 173, 175, 181 *tb*, 182, 186/187, 192, 199, 202/3, 205 *b*, 207, 208, 210 *l*, 212 *tb*, 212/213, 214 *r*, 218, 219 *t*, 220, 221 *tl*, *tr*, *c*, 222, 224–225, 227 *t*, 229, 230, 232, 237–247, 248, 249 *b*, 250 *b*, 259, 260, *tl*, *tr*, *cr*, *br*, 261, *tr*, 264 *tl*, *bl*, 265 *r*, 266 *r*, 270, 271 *tr*, 272, 273 *tl*, *bl;* **Illustrated London News:** 231 *t*, *b;* **Courtesy Inverness Club:** 131 *b* (Photo J. Brunt); **Courtesy Jagorawi Golf and Country Club:** 132/133; **Leonard Kamsler:** 120, 121 *t*, 146/147, 147 *t*; **Courtesy Pebble Beach Company:** 160/161, 162 *t*; **John Pinner:** 233; © **Tony Roberts:** 116 *r*, 117 *t*, 118/119, 134/135, 148/149, 149 *t*, 150/151, 152, 193; **Courtesy Royal St George's Golf Club:** 180/181, 183 *b*; © **Satour:** 124, 125; **Courtesy Sea Pines Resorts:** 107, 128/129; © **Patrick Squire: 123, *tb*; Courtesy Sun International (Bophuthatswana) Ltd:** 196, 197; **United States Golf Association:** 212 *c*, 214 *l*, 215 *tb*; **UPI/ Bettman:** 234/235; **Courtesy Venice Simplon Orient-Express Hotels:** 198/199, 200/201; **Wilson Sporting Goods Co:** 223, 227 *b*.